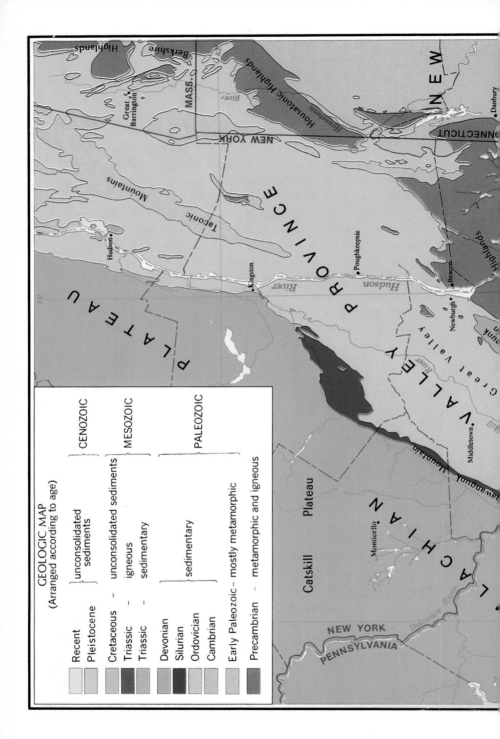

GEOLOGIC MAP
(Arranged according to age)

	Recent	CENOZOIC
	Pleistocene	unconsolidated sediments
	Cretaceous – unconsolidated sediments	
	Triassic – igneous	MESOZOIC
	Triassic – sedimentary	
	Devonian	
	Silurian	PALEOZOIC
	Ordovician	sedimentary
	Cambrian	
	Early Paleozoic – mostly metamorphic	
	Precambrian – metamorphic and igneous	

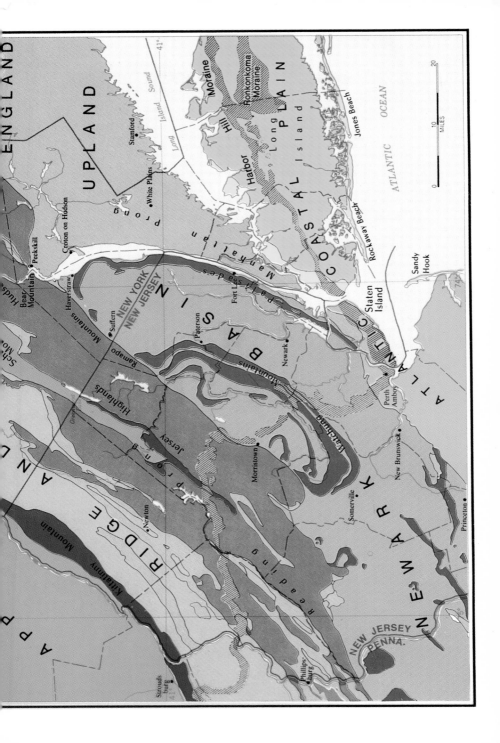

NEW YORK WALK BOOK

SIXTH EDITION

NEW YORK
WALK BOOK

A COMPANION TO THE NEW JERSEY WALK BOOK

NEW YORK–NEW JERSEY TRAIL CONFERENCE
1998

PUBLISHED BY
NEW YORK-NEW JERSEY TRAIL CONFERENCE
G.P.O. BOX 2250
NEW YORK, NEW YORK 10116

First edition published in 1923.

Library of Congress Cataloging-in-Publication Data
New York walk book. — 6th ed.
         p.   cm.
      "A companion to the New Jersey walk book."
      Includes bibliographical references (p.   ) and index.
      ISBN 1-880775-11-5
      1. Hiking—New York Metropolitan Area—Guidebooks   2. Trails—New
York Metropolitan Area—Guidebooks.   3. New York Metropolitan Area—
Guide-books.   I. New York-New Jersey Trail conference.
GV199.42N652N486   1998
917.47'10443—dc21   97-35069
                                                CIP

Illustrations by Robert L. Dickinson, Richard Edes Harrison, Jack Fagan, James E.
     Dyekman
Cover & text design by Pollard Design
Book design, layout, and typesetting by Nora Porter

Although the authors and publisher have tried to make the information as accurate as possible, they accept no responsibility for any loss, injury or inconvenience sustained by any person using this book.

CONTENTS

MAPS

GEOLOGY OF THE LOWER HUDSON VALLEY/ *(frontis)*

TRAIL MAPS

(b a c k   o f   b o o k)

PREFACE

New York—particularly, New York City—is not usually associated with outdoor activities. But to the millions of people who call the metropolitan area "home," New York offers something unique: access to more than 2,000 miles of hiking trails. The trails in the New York area offer trampers of all levels a vast variety of experiences, from a level stroll along a paved converted railbed, to a hike beside a mountain stream, to a scramble over rocks that ends in a spectacular view. Some of the trails in the region, such as the Jessup Trail on Schunemunk and the Long Island Pine Barrens Trail lead hikers through an area of special ecological interest. Others, like the 1779 Trail and the Old Croton Aqueduct Trail are steeped in history. Still others, like the Howell Trail and the Shawangunk Ridge Trail, which were built in the early 1990s, exemplify the work of today's volunteer trail builders.

In 1934, the editors of the *New York Walk Book* lamented the fact that hiking areas for trampers were declining. Yet by 1997, our trail lands have expanded so greatly that it was necessary to publish companion volumes—the *New York Walk Book* and the *New Jersey Walk Book*.

As the number of hiking trails has increased, the *New York Walk Book* has been right there to describe them. First published in 1923, the *Walk Book* quickly became a favorite book with hikers. It was revised and greatly expanded in 1934 and then revised again in 1951. I first learned about the *Walk Book* in 1968, when I started hiking, but by then it was out of print. Along with thousands of other hikers, I eagerly read the long-awaited fourth edition when it came out in 1971. In 1984, the fifth edition received similar attention.

Over the years, the *New York Walk Book*'s special aura has not changed. Both inexperienced and experienced hikers continue to rely on it. To the beginner, it is a rich source of information. To the experienced hiker, it is a reference book, a reminder of what has changed, and a guide to new areas to explore.

The companion volumes build upon the previous editions of the *New York Walk Book*, yet at the same time they reflect the changes that the world has seen in the intervening years. Thanks to the advent of personal computers and desktop publishing, the Trail Conference can self-publish the volumes, which gives greater control over both the content and the timing of future editions.

Users of older editions of the *New York Walk Book* will notice other major modifications. Chapters covering areas for which the Trail Conference has a separate, comprehensive publication have been trimmed back, and references are made to that other book. As a result of the space gained, more of the smaller parks, particularly those at the county level, are included. These areas are likely to be of special interest to the beginning hiker, to senior citizens who still want to hike and are looking for new places to go. These smaller trail systems are also great for quick fitness walks. Long-distance trails are in a chapter of their own, a return to the way the Appalachian Trail was presented in the 1934 edition. Rail-trails are included for the first time, as are bridges as places to walk. Rail-trails are frequently accessible to the handicapped.

In keeping with the spirit of the older editions, much of the original artwork by Robert L. Dickinson has been used. To update the book, new drawings have been added.

The world has changed since the first edition of the *New York Walk Book* was published in 1923. What seems to remain the same is the interest in trails and the need to hike—whether to enjoy nature, to stay in shape, to socialize or to savor views. Within these pages are many hours of reading and even more hours of exploration. Whatever your reason for hiking, somewhere there is a trail that you can enjoy by yourself or with others.

Jane Daniels
Editor
New York Walk Book, 6th edition

ACKNOWLEDGMENTS

The sixth edition of the *New York Walk Book* would not be possible without those members, friends, and partners of the New York-New Jersey Trail Conference who contributed to this edition. Many people, including those who contributed to earlier editions and are now deceased, wrote the words in this edition. Alice Tufel, the text editor, managed to take their words and skillfully modify sentences, delete phrases, and rearrange paragraphs to somehow make the book appear to be written by one author. The result is that the good ideas belong to everyone.

The Trail Conference's traditional partners—park managers, superintendents, and regional administrators—helped review material, sometimes on short notice. Contacts with county parks personnel were made, some for the first time.

John and Karen Magerlein coordinated the East Hudson chapters. Dale Timpe coordinated all the changes to the maps and interacted with the cartographers. Daniel Chazin supplied general advice on publishing and made helpful suggestions and corrections. Jack Fagan donated his sketches of the Shawangunks and vegetation. Auralie Logan, a professional indexer, prepared the index for the book.

Walt Daniels helped in immeasurable ways. He not only wrote Suggestions for Hikers, but compiled the Long Distance chapter, provided technical assistance with computers, made corrections, formatted text, and made sure the text was consistent. Without his help, the project would have taken much longer.

The following people donated their time to walk the trails, gather information, check facts, measure trails, write chapters, and recheck material. Their enthusiasm for the project on short notice is commendable. They are:

Fr. Fred Alvarez
Ann Marie Autieri
Ben Barrett
Karl Beard

Lenny Bernstein
Edmund Blair Bolles
Ellen Butowsky
Tom Casey

Christian Lenz Cesar
Daniel Chazin
Ed Clarke
Hal Cohen
Walt Daniels
David Day
JoAnn and Paul Dolan
Albert Field
Robert A. Flavin
B. Harrison Frankel
Victor Gabay
John J. Gallagher
Jim Gardineer
Susan Gerhardt
Alfred Goldstrom
Brian Goodman
Stella Green
Gary Haugland
Jack Hennessey
Cheryl Heyman
Roger Hoover
Joan James
H. F. Kaplan
Paul Leikin
Anne Lutkenhouse
David Lutz
John and Karen Magerlein
Robert Marshall
Seth McKee
Bill Miller
Don Morgan
Jim Morgan
Richard Morris
Robert Moss
William Myles
G. Gail Neffinger
Peter Osborne, III

George Perten
Bill and Mary Ann Pruehsner
Dick Redfield
Peter Rigotti
Ronald Rosen
Ruth Rosenthal
Weiland Ross
Glenn Scherer
William Schuster
Peter Senterman
Ike Siskind
Bettye and Steve Soffer
Ellen Stern
Dave Sutter
Sallie Sypher
Kate Whitney-Bukofzer
Kenneth Zadeck

I'end your road is clear before you when the old
Spring-fret comes o'er you
And the Red Gods call for you

Kipling: Feet of the Young Men

THE LOOK-OFF

(from the first edition, 1923)

oil that was ever *Indian* seems to never lose all of that impress. On the Island of Islands, borne down at one end by the world's biggest burden of steel and stone and pressure of haste and material gain, the primitive sweep of its further free tip, with the forest trees on the stately ledges, still holds the red man's cave, the beached canoe, the air of the Great Spirit. The magic of the moccasin still makes good medicine. Fortunate we are that in civilization lurks the antidote to civilization— that strain in the blood of us, all of us, of cave man and tree man, nomad and seaman, chopper and digger, fisher and trailer, crying out to this call of the earth, to this tug of free foot, up-and-over, to this clamor for out-and-beyond. Happy are we, in our day, harking back to this call, to be part of an ozone revival that fits the growth of our desire, to see the beginning of a break-away into everybody's out-of-doors, and the happy find of a wide, fair wilderness.

The order and fashion of the revival were somewhat in this wise. Our seniors remember the days of swift expansion, when the sole concern was the building site. "Blast the scenery," said the seventies and proceeded to do it. Railroads and roads and money returns from quarries and lumber had full right of way. Into our towns one came through ugly suburbs into uglier urbs. And then, when hope was least, a messenger of the new-old freedom appeared. The bicycle swung us, a generation now gray-haired, round a wide radius of country roads and gave back to us the calves and the leg gear of our patroon saint, Father Knickerbocker, and with the legs two eyes for environs. When the time came for supplanting tandem tires by a rubber quartette, and a touch of the toe leapt past all two legs could do, the motor radius that swept a circle almost infinitely wide gave a new concept of the country. Still attention was focussed on the roadway, and the new driver saw even less over wheel than over handlebar. Next golf arose, and the well-to-do strolled upon greenswards, ever watching a ball. Then scout training arrived to set the young generation on its feet and to teach it to see what it saw and to care for itself in the open. With it came nature study to fill the woods and fields with life and growth. (Our Old-World citizens brought their outing habits with them.) Last of all the war gave us brief glimpses of the happiness of simple living and to marching multitudes of indoor men the sense of hardy well-being. And now the fashion for walking is upon us—walking, with its leisure to observe the detail of beauty; walking, organized and planned, imparting impetus to safeguard and preserve the best of the countryside; walking, the single simple exercise, at once democratic, open-air, wide-eyed, year-round.

It is amusing to watch New York, which is hardly in other ways hesitant, waken by degrees to the idea that as a center for exercise on foot she may claim variety and advantage and adventure surpassed by few cities. You shall choose your walk along the sweep of the beaches of the Atlantic, or the deep hill bays of Long Island, or the rocky coves of Connecticut; over ridges showing fair silhouettes of the citadels and cathedral of commerce—or where beavers build; on the looped, mile-long bridges that span an estuary—or across a canal lock; above precipices overhanging a mighty river and through noble community forests between lonely peaks and little lakes—or just in lovely common country, rolling and wooded, meadowed and elm-dotted, interlaced with chuckling brooks. To and from these multitudinous footways and campsites transportation is provided with an expedition and diversity possible only to a large city. And last of all the chance at all this will be under the variegated stimulus of our particular climate and around the only great capital that is within easy reach of the second color wonder of the world—Indian summer in steep-hill country.

Truly with the "Englysche Bybels" that antedate King James', we may say:
Blessed of the LORDE is *this* land,
for the sweetnesse of heven, and of the scee vnderliende;
for the sprynges;
for the precious thinges off the Sonne;
for the sweetnesse of the toppes of the oold mounteynes,
and for the daynties of the hillis that last foreuer.

ONE

TRAILS AND TRAIL DEVELOPMENT

rails were the first paths in America. The routes of the early Native Americans[1] led from villages and camp-sites to hunting and fishing grounds, often following streams and crossing mountain ranges through the notches and divides of the rugged terrain. The white settlers adopted these routes for hunting, trading, and military expeditions. But unlike the footpaths of Europe, these American paths were marked by ax blazes on trees. Because these early paths often followed the easiest grades, they were natural routes for the highways and railroads to come.

Early Trails and the Search for Open Space

By the early part of the twentieth century, few of the original Native Americans' paths remained. With the advent of railroads, rural areas became more accessible for the city dweller, and people with leisure time sought out the woods and streams for recreation. However, farmers found these fun-seekers to be a nuisance, and so they often posted their property against trespassing. In response, "clubs" of wealthy businessmen from the cities purchased lakes, ponds, and natural areas, and then closed them off to public use.

Barred from access to open space, those who sought exercise and a chance to enjoy nature followed rural roads. Up to about 1900, these roads provided pleasant walking, to be shared with only an occasional, slow-moving

[1]The term "Native American" is used throughout this book when a specific nation is not known.

3

horse-drawn vehicle. In the first decade of the twentieth century, with the invasion of the automobile, highway surfaces were improved to meet the demands of auto traffic. Secondary routes were asphalted to extend state and county road systems.

Walkers began searching for safer, more pleasurable routes. With the state park system making publicly owned land more available, walkers retreated to long-abandoned paths and eighteenth century woods roads, which offered delightful strolls through second-growth forest. However, because these routes were originally meant to take people someplace, they often missed the scenic areas. So hiking clubs and individuals began to build their own trails over routes that the Native Americans and settlers would never have thought of using. These routes were selected because they offered a vista, a stroll through a stand of silver beech, or access to a place that had previously been inaccessible or unknown. Deer paths often proved useful because they followed natural terrain and were frequently the easiest routes up a mountain or across a valley.

The New York-New Jersey Trail Conference

As trails began to spread throughout the Hudson Highlands and the Wyanokies, it became evident that planned trail systems would be necessary if hiking areas were to be properly utilized and protected. In 1920, Major William A. Welch,

general manager of the Palisades Interstate Park, called together representatives of hiking organizations in New York. Their goal was to plan a network of marked trails that would make the Bear Mountain-Harriman State Parks more accessible to the public. The meeting resulted in an informal federation known as the Palisades Interstate Park Trail Conference. Raymond Torrey, Will Monroe, Meade Dobson, Frank Place, J. Ashton Allis and their friends planned, cut, and marked what are now the major park trails. The first one to be completed was the 20-mile Ramapo-Dunderberg Trail from Jones Point on the Hudson River to Tuxedo. In 1923, the first section of the Appalachian Trail to be finished was constructed in Bear Mountain Park. That same year, the organization changed its name to the New York-New Jersey Trail Conference, uniting under one banner a number of hiking organizations throughout the metropolitan area.

From its founding, the Trail Conference has been an organization of volunteers. In 1996, this not-for-profit federation of over 85 hiking and outdoors clubs and nearly 9,500 individuals maintained a network of over 1,300 miles of marked trails from the Connecticut border to the Delaware Water Gap. With few exceptions, the trails are for foot traffic only. The Trail Conference's veritable corps of trained volunteers has been both repairing eroded and overused trails and building new trails to standards designed to prevent deteriorating conditions. In 1994, 800 volunteers and 65 clubs devoted over 18,000 hours to trail maintenance. But in spite of the Conference's massive efforts, it is estimated that only 2 to 3 percent of the hiking public knows who takes care of the trails.

The Trail Conference also serves as a unified voice for trail concerns and land protection in New York and New Jersey. While not always recognized as an environmental organization, the Trail Conference has, in fact, over many years, been involved in saving open space. When an issue affects trails, the volunteers and staff of the Trail Conference bring their concerns to the attention of organizations that are geared financially and legally to pursue the task. In other instances, the Trail Conference forms a coalition with its affiliated hiking clubs, governmental and law enforcement agencies, other nonprofit groups, and interested citizens to resolve an issue. Partners on various projects have included the Catskill Center, Highlands Coalition, Mohonk Preserve, National Parks Service (NPS), New Jersey Department of Environmental Protection (Division of Parks and Forestry), New York-New Jersey Highlands Regional Study, New York Office of Parks, Recreation and Historic Preservation (Taconic Region), New York Department of Environmental Conservation, Open Space Institute, Palisades Interstate Park Commission, Scenic Hudson, United States Forest Service (USFS), and the Sterling Forest Coalition. The Trail Conference's advocacy work also includes generating position papers, conducting public education activities, and raising funds for direct financial support.

Since its founding, Trail Conference volunteers and its member clubs have worked to extend hiking opportunities to the public and to build trails opening new areas. Although much of the land upon which they have built trails is publicly owned, about 25 percent is not. Hikers have enjoyed some areas only through the kindness of landowners on whose property the trails traversed. Unfortunately, the acquisition of public land progressed slowly. As the population grew, public access to some trails was limited when commercial developers and landowners closed trails due to occasional abuses.

Open Space Preservation

In the 1960s, federal, state, and county governments began acquiring land for public use. About the same time, but on a much smaller scale, The Nature Conservancy, the Audubon Society, and numerous local land trusts and conservancies also preserved open space. These acquisitions increased opportunities for outdoor recreation.

New York

Preservation of open space in New York is a result of Environmental Quality Bond Acts, budget line items, and private donations. The 1960 and 1972 bond acts added Highland Lakes, Goose Pond Mountain, the Old Croton Aqueduct, the Rockefeller Preserve, Storm King, and Hook Mountain to the state park system and purchased additional acres for Bear Mountain, Rockland Lakes, Fahnestock, and Taconic parks. The 1986 bond act set aside $250 million to acquire, protect, and improve state forest preserves, environmentally sensitive areas, municipal and urban cultural parks, and historic sites. Additions to the Catskill Forest Preserve were a result of both the 1972 and 1986 bond acts. Unfortunately, voters in 1990 defeated a $1.975 billion bond act that would have authorized $800 million for open space preservation.

In 1992, the state adopted the Statewide Comprehensive Plan, which set up a prioritized list for open space acquisitions. The following year the Environmental Protection Act was passed. It included the Environmental Protection Fund, a dedicated revenue stream for environmental programs which included a land acquisition fund.

New Jersey

Started in 1961, New Jersey's Green Acres program has funded the purchase of 340,000 acres of open space and the development of hundreds of recreational facilities throughout the state through eight bond issues totaling $1.1 billion. Federal grants from the Land and Water Conservation Fund supplemented state monies on a fifty/fifty basis, allowing both the state and counties to acquire acreage. The 1976 Natural Areas System Act has protected some 24,500 acres in the state, including sections of Allamuchy, High Point, Ramapo Mountain, Wawayanda, and Worthington state parks and forests.

Minnewaska

Just before the stunning Storm King victory over Con Edison in 1980 (see

chapter 15, "Storm King"), the Trail Conference helped organize yet another massive grass-roots effort, this time to preserve Shawangunk Ridge. The fight to save Minnewaska, as it became known, was to prevent the Marriott Corporation from constructing a hotel, condominium complex, and championship golf course. In the process, many miles of trails would be destroyed and Lake Minnewaska would be polluted (See chapter 13, "The Shawangunks").

In 1980, the Marriott Corporation submitted a draft of its Environment Impact Statement. Testimony at public hearings pointed out the recreational value of the area and questioned the adequacy of the proposed water supply. New York State Department of Environmental Conservation gave conditional approval to the environmental impact statement. However, DEC was taken to court, with the case eventually reaching the New York Court of Appeals. By 1985 the Marriott Corporation, exhausted by seven lawsuits, and having spent over a million dollars without ever having broken ground, gave up their plan. Environmental groups pushed for permanent protection and the property was absorbed into Minnewaska State Park Preserve.

Sterling Forest

The fight to save Minnewaska was barely over when the next threat reared its ugly head—the planned development of Sterling Forest by its owner, Sterling Forest Corporation. This 20,000-acre corridor connects New York's Harriman Park with the New Jersey Highlands. All previous land preservation efforts pale in comparison with the fight to prevent Sterling Forest from becoming a city of 35,000 people and 8 million square feet of commercial space. As early as 1930, Raymond Torrey recognized the importance of preserving Sterling Forest, with its spectacular views and its accessibility for urban residents in search of nature and open space. His vision was not to be fulfilled in his lifetime. When the Harriman family offered the land to New York State as a park, the state declined the acquisition. At that time state officials believed that the land had too many wetlands, that there were insufficient funds for management, and that New York had sufficient parklands for the future. Instead, in 1947, City Investing Company purchased the property, and immediately announced plans for development. Fortunately, the several small communities that sprang up in the valley did not impinge on the forests, which stayed intact.

By 1980 Sterling Forest had become the largest undeveloped forested private land remaining in the New York metropolitan area and had been sold several times. A consortium of European investors began actively pursuing development, which would devastate the valley, destroy the Appalachian Trail viewshed in the area, and threaten the water quality of two million New Jersey residents. In 1988, the Trail Conference and the Appalachian Mountain Club founded the Sterling Forest Coalition to press for Sterling Forest preservation. By 1996, 28 hiking and local grass-roots groups were members. In addition, a Public-Private Partnership to Save Sterling Forest was formed by the Palisades Interstate Park Commission, New York-New Jersey Trail Conference, Passaic River Coalition, Environmental Defense Fund, Regional Plan Association, Scenic Hudson, The Nature Conservancy, Sierra Club, and other regional/national organizations. In 1990 Green Acres and Passaic County took the first bold step and condemned 2,100-acres—the New Jersey section of Sterling Forest. Since the New York section of 17,500 acres included watershed land which would affect New Jersey drinking water and since the Appalachian Trail was threatened, the effort to acquire lands with federal funding toward acquisition resulted in the fight eventually reaching Congress in 1992.

New Jersey Governor Christine Todd Whitman, in 1994, signed a bill authorizing $10 million to purchase land in New York, but only if New York also funded the purchase. Subsequently, New York Governor George Pataki matched New Jersey's support and the Lila Acheson and DeWitt Wallace Fund for the Hudson Highlands pledged $5 million. Efforts in Congress were bipartisan in 1995 and 1996, but pitted representatives from the eastern states against the western ones. Conservationists presented a united stand and were prepared to sacrifice Sterling Forest if its purchase were contingent on the sale of federal lands in the mid-west or west.

During the Congressional haggling in the spring of 1996, negotiations with Sterling Forest Corporation resulted in their agreeing to sell 15,280 acres for $55 million. The land included in the sale would protect the Appalachian Trail corridor, much of the New Jersey watershed, and the habitat most critical to wildlife. The orchestration of funding sources to complete this sale was extraordinary. Congress finally appropriated $17.5 million, Governor Pataki authorized an additional $6 million, and the Victoria Foundation gave $1 million. Smaller donations from the private sector, including gifts from school children, totaled $500,000. Finally the sale was assured when, in December 1997, the Doris Duke Charitable Foundation donated the remaining $5 million. Sterling Forest Corporation claimed an interest in developing the remaining 2,220 acres and efforts continue to protect the remaining 2,200 acres.

Trail Development

Interest in trail development is more than a local issue. A nationwide project, Trails for All Americans, seeks to have trail opportunities within 15 minutes of most Americans' homes or places of work. In 1988, the President's Commission on Americans Outdoors called for the creation of a vast network of hiking and jogging trails, bikeways, and bridle paths. The commission envisioned a nationwide system of trails that would tie this country together with threads of green, linking communities and providing access to the natural world.

The New York metropolitan area already has an extensive hiking trail system in place. A perusal of the tables of contents of earlier editions of the *New York Walk Book* attests to the long-term availability of trails in this area. What was not always evident was the need for linkages between areas, although two major linkages have existed for years. The Long Path begins on the New

Jersey Palisades and extends 300 miles northward past the Catskills toward the Adirondacks, linking Harriman with smaller parks and the Catskills. On its way from Georgia to Maine, the Appalachian Trail links the Kittatinnies, the Jersey Highlands, Harriman-Bear Mountain, Hudson Highlands, Fahnestock, and the South Taconics.

Many counties, cities, and towns are connecting their parks with greenways. Existing linkages include the Patriot's Path in New Jersey and the Paumanok Path on Long Island. More linkages are possible as the Highlands Trail wends its way between the Delaware and Hudson Rivers.

Assistance in Developing Trails

The expertise gained in the 1980s when the Appalachian Trail was moved onto protected woodlands helped fuel interest in other trail projects. Although Trail Conference volunteers work with park officials to build new trails, trails connecting protected open space need another type of assistance. The National Park Service Rivers and Trails Assistance Program (later renamed the NPS Rivers, Trails and Conservation Assistance Program) funded portions of the project to extend the Long Path north to the Adirondacks. The Trail Conference's volunteer corps grew to meet the challenge of building 100 miles of trail and the Trail Conference began building relationships with local residents, municipalities, and private landowners. The 30-mile Shawangunk Ridge Trail also forged similar relationships on a smaller scale.

Another multi-partner trail project—the Highlands Trail—highlights the natural beauty of the New Jersey and the New York Highlands region. Begun in 1992 and funded through grants from the NPS Rivers, Trails and Conservation Assistance Program, this trail will run 150 miles along the Highlands Ridge from the Delaware River to the Hudson River. When complete, the Highlands Trail will be a greenway in New York and New Jersey linking the publicly owned open spaces. The threat of development in some areas along the route has spurred the project forward. By the end of 1996, 95 miles of trail were built and open to the public.

Threats to Trails and Trail Lands

Even with increased interest in protecting open space and providing more trails, threats that were never before envisioned now endanger both trails and trail lands. Interaction with other special interest or non-traditional user groups has become critical to solving problems.

Fiscal Threats

By the end of the 1980s, increased demands for reduced taxes resulted in massive cuts in state budgets. Monies were no longer available for land purchases, and funds for park management or maintenance were severely curtailed. As a result, not-for-profit organizations have formed partnerships with the state to ensure open space protection and management. For example, since its origin in 1920, the Trail Conference has supplied volunteer trail maintainers. With the budget cuts, state partners have come to rely on these maintainers even more. In New York, Scenic Hudson Land Trust and Open Space Institute own land, that by agreement, the state will manage until it has funds to purchase it. Fishkill Ridge Conservation Area and Hubbard-Perkins Conservation Area are two examples of land managed in this way. These close relationships allow each partner to specialize in what its staff and volunteers do best and to stretch ever-shrinking budgets.

Children's summer camps have also suffered from the recession. They require open space, but the cost of upkeep is sometimes too great for a not-for-profit organization to justify holding on to the property. In 1994, Open Space Institute succeeded in protecting Clear Lake, a Boy Scout property adjacent to Fahnestock State Park. A portion of the property is open to the public for hiking.

Physical Threats

Without proper education, well-meaning outdoor enthusiasts can love a particular trail or scenic place to death. For example, on a holiday weekend in 1994, a nature sanctuary was overrun with visitors because a newspaper article recommended the place. Even when an area can tolerate many visitors, it cannot accommodate the six-pack of beer and the bonfire that some folks consider a necessary part of their outdoor experience.

Non-hiking user groups instinctively use the vast trail network that exists in the New York-New Jersey region, often not realizing that hikers maintain the trails for other hikers. Bicycles, horses, and motorized vehicles cause damage because the soil and trail design are not suited for anything other than foot traffic. Education and signage are important to ensure that correct users are on the trail and to prevent user conflicts.

The illegal use of motorized and other vehicles on park lands destroys trails that volunteers have labored hard to build. Users of all-terrain vehicles (ATVs) often run through sensitive areas, destroying vegetation and damaging the trails by causing siltation, creating pot-holes, and widening the narrow path that has been built to respect and fit into the natural environment. Their noise further degrades the outdoor experience by destroying the natural tranquility that hikers seek.

Public Education

As part of its effort to promote public interest in hiking and to educate people about available resources and the safe, proper use of the trail system, the Trail Conference publishes maps and guidebooks. The maps cover trails in the Catskills, Bear Mountain-Harriman State Parks, North Jersey, West Hudson, East Hudson, Shawangunks, South Taconics, High Mountain, Hudson Palisades, Pyramid Mountain, and the Kittatinnies. Besides the *New York Walk Book*, the Trail Conference's publications include the *Guide to the Long Path, Health Hints for Hikers, Hiking Guide to the Delaware Water Gap National Recreation Area, Hiking the Catskills, Harriman Trails: A Guide and History, Iron Mine Trails*, and others. These books complement the *Walk Book*, providing more detailed information.

To join the New York-New Jersey Trail Conference, order publications, or receive more information, contact New York-New Jersey Trail Conference, G.P.O. Box 2250, New York, NY 10116; (212) 685-9699; look at the Conference's web site, http://www.nynjtc.org/~trails; or send e-mail to nynjtc@aol.com.

SUGGESTIONS FOR HIKERS

f you can walk, you can hike; age is no obstacle. Sometimes, you don't even have to be able to walk to enjoy a trail, as a few trails are now accessible to the handicapped. Whatever your goals, the suggestions presented here should provide enough information to help you start hiking.

A good way to become familiar with hiking trails is to meet and learn from experienced hikers, something easily accomplished by hiking with a club, an organized group, or friends who hike regularly. Hiking clubs abound in the New York area. For a list of them, send your request, with a self-addressed, stamped envelope, to the New York-New Jersey Trail Conference, P.O. Box 2250, New York, NY 10116.

Whether you hike with a formal club or with a group of friends, you will need a knowledge of the area in which you plan to hike if you want to have a safe and enjoyable outing. Maps, guidebooks, park offices, and experienced hikers can give you valuable information. Good trail maps show a trail's location, distance, topographic features, and contour lines. The guidebooks listed under "Further Reading" provide written descriptions of particular trails. Guidebooks and trail maps, including larger versions of the maps in this book, are available for purchase from the New York-New Jersey Trail Conference. Most camping and outdoors stores, as well as many bookstores, carry trail maps and guides. Trail maps for state, county, and local parks are sometimes available at park entrances, but often lack important details.

Planning Your Hike

Planning a hike is easy if you hike with a club. Most hiking clubs publish a regular schedule that lists and describes their planned hikes. Read the description in the club literature or talk to a member, and pick a hike that suits your abilities and interests. Hikes vary by level of difficulty and type, so choose accordingly.

If you cannot or prefer not to hike with a club, and you are a beginning hiker, go with at least two friends. Choose your route from the trails described in this book or in the books listed in "Further Reading," and bring a trail map along.

Level of Hiking Difficulty

Be realistic about your physical condition and any medical limitations you might have; neither you nor your fellow hikers will enjoy the outing if you are frequently stopping to catch your breath along the trail. Once on the trail, pace yourself. If you haven't been physically active for some time, start slowly. If you are in doubt, consult with your doctor before going on a hike.

On smooth, level ground, your pace may be three to four miles an hour. It takes longer to pick your way over a rocky path. As soon as you are going uphill, the speed of walking slows down. To calculate the amount of time needed, allow 20 minutes per mile, not including rest stops. Measure all the ascents and add one minute for every 20 feet of elevation. Downgrades take about the same time as a level trail, unless very rough and steep.

Types of Hikes

The simplest type of hike is *out and back*, which starts at a trailhead, follows the trail (or a network of trails), and returns by the same route. Often, more than one trail begins at a trailhead, so it is possible to go out on one trail and return on another trail, forming a *loop hike*. Hikers can take a *partial loop hike* by retracing their original route for only a portion of the trip. A *shuttle hike* requires planning and, depending upon the number of people hiking, two or more cars. On a shuttle hike, hikers meet at one trailhead in at least two cars. Everyone carpools (or "shuttles") to the other end of the hike—the trailhead where the hike will begin. At least one car is left at the first trailhead, which is the spot where you and your party will finish hiking. Public transportation, if available, may be used to shuttle hikers to the beginning of the hike.

Leading a Hike

Even when experienced hikers are going out with a few friends, one person should assume the role of hike leader, and the other members of the party should understand and respect that role. Like the captain of a ship, a hike leader makes the final decisions but should consider the opinions of the crew.

Every captain needs a first mate. On a hike, that role is fulfilled by the *sweep*, who should be a known strong hiker, who brings up the rear and remains at the back of the group at all times, to make sure that no one is left behind. The leader might assign a different person to be the sweep as various junctions are reached.

If you are leading a hike, consult the appropriate maps and guidebooks before leaving home to determine a place and route consistent with the time available and the interests and strength of the group. Leaders should scout the hike—that is, go on the hike themselves—before leading a group, in order to gain an accurate estimate of driving time to the trailhead, availability of park-ing, and actual hiking time. It is very important to consider the available hours of daylight so that the group will be off the trail before sundown. When estimating hiking time, leaders should consider the hike distance, level of difficulty, and time needed for rest stops (including a lunch break), and perhaps for photography and nature study, and then should allow some additional time (at least an hour) in the event of an unforeseen problem on the trail. A good hike leader plans alternate routes before starting, noting routes that may be used to shorten the hike in case of storm, illness, accident, or an overambitious hike plan.

The size of a hiking group should not exceed 25 people for day hikes. It is difficult for one leader to manage more people than that, and travel is considerably slower with a larger group. If the group has more than 25 people, it is a good idea to find another leader and split into two groups. This second group can hike the route in the opposite direction or start an hour later. In environmentally sensitive areas, such as mountain tops or wet areas, the second group should take an entirely different route.

Before starting the hike, the leader should explain the *rules of the road* (regarding pace, staying with the group, rest stops, smoking, littering, and the like), where the hike is going, and the approximate time of arrival at various junctions. Leaders should also check that the hikers are prepared with enough food and water, rain gear, proper footwear, etc. While on the hike, leaders need to stop frequently enough so that no one lags too far behind. Hike leaders have the responsibility of making sure that the group respects the trail and remains safe. If you plan to lead a hike, take your responsibility seriously!

Safety and Comfort

While the hike leader should look out for the group, individual safety and comfort are primarily the responsibilities of the individual hiker. You can do many things to make sure that your hike proceeds without incident. Begin by making sure that your maps, guidebooks, and equipment are up to date and in good condition.

Hiking Alone

Hiking alone is generally discouraged, especially for those who have not had any trail experience. Even an experienced hiker can have problems such as an accident. A group of at least three hikers is advisable, because in case of injury, one person can stay with the injured hiker while the third person goes for help.

Whether you are hiking alone or with someone else, always let someone know where you will be hiking and when you plan to return. Remember to check in upon your return. If there is a register book at the trailhead where you begin, make sure to sign your name and starting time. Even experienced hikers have gotten lost on trails that are heavily traveled.

First Aid

For a one-day hike, carry Band-Aids®, an antiseptic for cuts and scratches, moleskin for blisters, and tweezers to remove splinters and ticks. Put the moleskin on irritated spots before a blister forms. Other useful items are an Ace® bandage with clips, gauze pads, an eye cup, antibiotic ointment, adhesive tape, safety pins, aspirin, and coins for emergency phone calls upon leaving the trail. Carry these items, plus a pencil and paper, in a lightweight metal box or waterproof case, in your pack.

Learn to recognize the symptoms of hypothermia and heat stroke. These serious problems sneak up on their victims and can be fatal. Hypothermia occurs when the body loses more heat than it can generate, and the body temperature drops. The symptoms of hypothermia include shivering, difficulty using hands, stumbling, odd behavior, losing articles of clothing, speech deficiency, blurred thinking, and amnesia. In the late stages, the shivering is replaced by muscle rigidity, stupor, and drowsiness. In heat stroke, also known as sun stroke, the body temperature rises to over 105 degrees Fahrenheit, and the pulse rate can soar to over 160, possibly followed by convulsions and vomiting. For more details on hypothermia, heat stroke, and other medical emergencies on the trail, refer to books listed in "Further Reading." Even better, take a first aid course. Contact your local Red Cross chapter for information on courses given locally.

Waste Disposal and Sanitation
Carry toilet paper in a plastic bag. Use permanent toilet facilities if they exist in the vicinity where you are hiking. Otherwise, bury waste 6 inches deep, at least 200 feet away from any stream or lake, and at least 50 feet from the trail. Pack out the used toilet paper.

Hunting Season
Since many area parks have hunting season in the late fall, inquire about the dates of the season for any area in which you plan to hike. Park offices can give you hunting schedules, and the *Trail Walker*, published by the New York-New Jersey Trail Conference, prints a hunting schedule in its September/October issue. If you want to hike during hunting season, hike in areas where hunting is prohibited. Wearing blaze orange in areas where hunting is permitted is helpful, but cannot guarantee safety.

Inclement Weather
Inclement weather can be any weather from severe cold to excessive heat, with or without rain or snow, and with or without a thunderstorm—which is dangerous primarily because of lightning. If you are on an exposed ledge or on a mountain peak during a thunderstorm, go to lower, covered ground quickly. If you are on the trail, avoid taking shelter under a lone tree, which will attract lightning.

Wet weather is dangerous to hikers because it can cause hypothermia in the event of exposure. At high altitudes, even during the summer, hikers have lost their lives because they were under-prepared and overexposed. The best way to avoid hypothermia is by carrying the proper clothing in your pack: waterproof rain gear (including a jacket or parka with a hood and rain pants), a wool or pile sweater or shirt, and a polypropylene undergarment for warmth; see the section on "Clothing" (under "Equipment," below).

Winter Hiking
Hiking in winter poses special problems and requires special equipment and clothing, such as crampons or snowshoes. Before you attempt winter hiking,

consult some of the books listed under "Further Reading." The first time you try a winter hike, make sure you are properly equipped, and go with an experienced hiker or, better yet, with an experienced group.

Wild Fruits and Mushrooms
Do not eat any wild plants without positively identifying them. Learn to recognize the common edible berries by hiking with someone who has experience, and by reading some of the publications listed under "Further Reading."

Poison Ivy and Poison Sumac
Poison ivy grows aggressively in all kinds of conditions. On sandy beaches, it is a small shrub, about a foot high. Along stone walls and fences it is a spreading vine, while in the woods it either acts as a ground cover or becomes a climbing vine. It is identified by a group of three green, asymmetrical leaves, which include a short-stemmed middle leaf; often one edge of a poison ivy leaf is smooth and curved, while the other edge might have one or more serrations. It may bear white or green berries. Avoid contact with all parts of the plant including the bare vines.

Contact with poison ivy causes a rash which appears from 12 to 48 hours after exposure. The rash is accompanied by intense itching. Secondary infection from contaminated clothing, tools, or animals produces the same reaction. The rash may break out over several days, and contrary to popular opinion, it does not spread, but is the result of the original insult to the skin. Neither your own nor some else's rash can transmit poison ivy's toxic oil, only exposure to the oil itself will. Over-the-counter medications help control the itching.

If you suspect you have come in contact with poison ivy, wash the affected areas as soon as possible with strong soap, such as laundry detergent or Teknu®.

Poison sumac is a similarly dangerous shrub, found mostly in swampy areas. It has thirteen pointed leaflets, six or more inches in length. It is a rare plant in the east and you will probably not encounter it, especially if you stay on the trail.

Insects
Insect repellent, long sleeves, long pants tucked into your socks, and a hat are the best guards against insects. While DEET (*diethyl M toulamide*) is an effective insect repellent, it can be toxic, especially to infants and children, so it should be used sparingly (30 percent DEET maximum) and only when absolutely necessary.

Ticks are a problem in the New York area, especially deer ticks, which carry Lyme disease or erlichiosis—serious illnesses. Deer ticks are no bigger than a pin-head, making it difficult to spot them. Wear long sleeves, tuck in long pants into socks, and check for ticks after hiking, so that ticks should not deter you from hiking. As soon as you return home, examine your body thoroughly for ticks, especially in the groin area and armpits. (Ticks gravitate to warm, dark, moist places.) If you are bitten by a tick, take care to remove it slowly with tweezers, so that its mouth part does not remain embedded in the skin. If any part remains in the skin, treat it as a splinter.

If you suspect that you have either Lyme disease or erlichiosis, contact your doctor. Lyme disease symptoms include flu-like symptoms, joint and muscle pain, fatigue, or a bulls-eye rash. Symptoms of erlichiosis include sudden onset of flu-like symptoms, chills, sore throat, high fever, joint and muscle pain, headaches and low white cell and platelet counts. Both illnesses can be treated with antibiotics, but it is best to catch it as early as possible. Untreated Lyme disease can become a disabling chronic condition. Pamphlets on this disease are available from your doctor or county health department.

Some people are strongly allergic to bee or wasp stings. If you have had a strong reaction in the past, ask your doctor for instructions.

Snakes

Small snakes, such as the garter snake and ribbon snake, are common in the New York region. The region's two poisonous snakes, the Eastern Timber rattlesnake and the copperhead, are rarely encountered and are not found on Long Island.

A rattlesnake is recognized by the rattle on its tail. Its markings are not uniform, varying in coloration from yellow or tan to nearly black. When suddenly disturbed, a rattlesnake will rattle and attempt to escape rather than attack.

The copperhead is pale brown with reddish blotches on its body and a coppery tinge on its head. It is not a vicious snake, preferring to escape rather than to attack. But it is slow-moving and quiet, which increases the chance of an unexpected encounter.

When hiking during the snake season (May to October), be alert, particularly when climbing rock ledges and over logs. Look before placing your hand on an overhead ledge for support. If you are bitten, do not panic; note the size and distinguishing marks of the snake. Wrap the bite tightly with a bandage, but not so tight that you cut off circulation; take aspirin; and proceed at a moderate pace to seek prompt medical attention.

Rabies
In the New York metro area since 1990, rabies has been endemic to wild animals particularly skunks and raccoons. Do not attempt to feed any wild animal. Stay well clear of any animal acting strangely or a nocturnal animal that is out prowling around in broad daylight. Do not touch any dead animals, as you can contract rabies from a dead animal. Rabies is fatal if not treated promptly. If bitten by any animal, leave the trail and see a doctor immediately.

Bears
While brown bears (Grizzlies), are not found in New York's hiking areas, their smaller relative—black bears—are becoming more common in many parts of the region. They are more dangerous to your food than to you, and hence are more of a problem for backpackers than for day-hikers. Do not make any attempt to feed them. If you are lucky enough to see one, do not approach the bear. Instead, make lots of noise and move slowly but deliberately in the opposite direction.

Equipment

If you are a new hiker, try using the gear and equipment that you already own, as much as possible until you see what other hikers use, have heard their opinion, and have decided what will suit you best. Appropriate footwear is vital (see below). You might also wish to rent or borrow equipment to help you better determine what you should buy.

The principal hiking equipment are adequate footwear, clothing, a hat, rain gear, safety (first-aid) equipment, insect repellent (in season), food or at least a snack, and at least one quart of water—preferably two—for a day hike. Some hikers like to take a camera, binoculars, or flora/fauna identification books. Still others find that a hiking stick gives them added stability. It is also a good idea to carry cash, a check, or a credit card, in case you need them for an emergency upon leaving the trail. For most hikes that are more than one or two miles long, you will need a pack to carry your gear comfortably. You want to travel light, but not at the cost of being hungry, thirsty, or uncomfortable. Remember, you are supposed to be enjoying yourself.

Equipment
Form personal checklists of equipment that you normally take on various types of hikes. For example, you may have different lists for different weather, different lengths, or different levels of difficulty. Before leaving on a hike, make sure

you have all the items on the list. You will soon determine which pieces of gear you use and which are dead weight. However, do not eliminate safety and first-aid equipment just because you were lucky enough not to need it. Experienced hikers know that it is well worth the effort to carry such equipment all the time, even if you use it only one time out of a hundred, rather than fail to have it with you when you really need it.

Footwear

A good pair of boots is important for hiking. At a minimum, hiking boots should provide water resistance, ankle support, and a non-slip sole. For protection against blisters, wear heavy padded socks (such as wool) over light liner socks that can wick away moisture. Make sure your boots fit properly; your feet should have enough room, but they should neither slide forward in the boot, which can bruise the toes, nor should they have too much heel lift. When purchasing boots, try on several different brands; some will fit your feet noticeably better than others. Remember that if boots are uncomfortable in the store, they will be uncomfortable on the trail.

While many lightweight hiking boots are adequate, you will need insulated leather boots for long, rugged hikes and winter hiking. If you purchase leather boots, make sure to break them in before wearing them for a full day of hiking. Wear them for short intervals at home and then on a few short hikes, making sure they are completely comfortable before you wear them on a longer hike.

Clothing

What you wear depends, of course, on the weather and the time of year. In summer, you can wear a tee-shirt and shorts, or you may want lightweight pants and a long shirt to protect yourself against insects, sun, or scratches from vegetation. A hat with a brim provides protection from the sun. A bandanna is also useful to have in warm weather, to absorb perspiration around the head and neck. For all but the shortest hikes in warm weather, you will also need a warm layer to put on when you stop or as evening approaches; even in the summer, the weather can become severe at high altitudes.

Be prepared for wet weather, whatever the season. Wool and some synthetics such as polypropylene provide warmth when wet. Cotton is a poor choice because it retains moisture and takes hours to dry once it becomes wet. Down is also a poor choice in wet weather as it also loses its ability to insulate when wet. If there is any chance of rain or very strong winds, you will want a highly water-resistant, wind-resistant parka or perhaps a poncho.

In cold weather, layering is especially important. Wear your hiking clothes in several thin (rather than fewer heavy) layers. Begin with a light garment next to your skin, such as polypropylene, that will wick away moisture and keep you dry. Add a warm (wool or pile) shirt and/or sweater, depending on the conditions in which you will be hiking. Colder weather may warrant wool pants or long underwear and a long-sleeved wool or synthetic shirt. Do not wear turtlenecks, as they restrict air circulation and increase dampness. Your outer garment should be a waterproof and windproof parka. A hat is essential in cold weather, since you lose most of your body heat through your head. A hat also protects you from the sun (which can be just as dangerous in winter as it is in summer). Other clothing to take in cold weather are wool or synthetic gloves or mittens (mittens retain heat better) and spare dry socks in a water-proof plastic bag.

Do not let your underwear become wet from perspiration. As soon as you feel yourself beginning to perspire, remove a layer (or layers, if needed) of clothing. Put the layer(s) back on when you stop to rest.

Safety Gear
When hiking with a group, share the weight as not everyone needs everything. Everyone should have a first-aid kit, flashlight, map, and compass. For a compass to be of any use, you must know how to use it. Several books listed under "Further Reading" cover map and compass use. Additional safety items include cigarette lighter, jackknife, personal medications, safety pins, duct tape (wrapped around your water bottle), and a space blanket—an emergency blanket made from aluminized Mylar film, available in camping and outdoors stores.

Food
Take compact, nonperishable, lightweight foods on a hike. A brown-bag lunch includes one or two sandwiches, chips or pretzels, an apple or orange, and a candy bar. Many people fare better snacking continually through the day, rather than having one large meal. Fresh and dried fruit, raw vegetables, trail mix, granola bars, nuts, chocolate, and hard candy are all good snacks. Small children, in particular, run out of energy easily and need frequent refueling.

Water
The importance of taking sufficient water on a hike cannot be overemphasized. Most people need one or two quarts of water, more in hot weather or on a very long hike. Do not wait until you are thirsty to drink. Make sure you take

frequent sips of water as you hike, to prevent dehydration.

For day hikes, bring your own water in a plastic bottle, such as bottled water purchased from a store. Fill a Nalgene® bottle (available from camping supply stores) with tap water from home. Water filters eliminate the need to carry a lot of water, but the good ones are fairly expensive. Do not drink directly from springs, streams, or ponds, as they may be polluted with *Giardia* or coliform bacteria. Do not depend upon finding a reliable water supply at shelters or along the trails.

Pack (Knapsack)

A pack should be large enough to carry your extra garments, lunch, water bottle(s), safety gear, and insect repellent comfortably. A pack that is jammed tight will not be comfortable to carry, and will feel heavier than it actually is.

On the Trail

Hiking is just like walking—you put one foot in front of the other. Most hikers develop a steady rhythm that they can comfortably keep up for the entire hike. Of course, rough terrain can defeat that rhythm. Your speed will vary as the terrain varies and as you change the length of your stride—shorter going uphill or on a rough surface, longer going downhill or on a smooth surface. In rocky areas, be careful about your foot placement and do not trust a rock or a log to remain still when you put your weight on it, particularly going downhill. A log can easily roll, and lichen or moss on rocks can be deceptively slippery.

Hiking downhill is harder on your knees because of the additional weight dropped on the joint. Do not slam your foot down on the ground; take each step gently and deliberately, with a bent knee, to lessen the pounding on the joint.

Stop and rest periodically—about 5 to 10 minutes each hour. At lunchtime, take off your boots and air out your feet if it is not too cold. Stop at trail junctions if you are traveling in a group and let everyone catch up before proceeding.

Blazes and Cairns

Members of the New York-New Jersey Trail Conference volunteer to be responsible for marking and maintaining over 1,300 miles of trails in the metropolitan area. The trails are marked with either painted blazes or plastic or metal tags.

These blazes communicate various messages. Two blazes, with one painted higher than the other, indicate a change in direction; the top blaze indicates the direction of the turn. Three blazes painted as the three points of a triangle indicate a trail's end or beginning. Each trail is blazed in its own individual color or shape to distinguish it from other trails that it crosses. The trail descriptions in this book indicate the color or shape of each trail's blaze. Where a paint blaze is not practical (for example, above treeline), watch instead for a pile of stones—called a *cairn*—purposely placed to lead you to the next step on the trail.

When you are hiking, you should always be able to see the next blaze in front of you, unless you are on a trail with little chance of making an error.

Lost—You or the Trail?
If you can't find a blaze in front of you, turn around and see if you can spot one going the other way. If you can, use its placement and direction to try and find the next blaze in front of you. If you can't, you should stop, look around, then go back to the last blaze or cairn that you saw. If no blaze or cairn is in sight, look at the ground for a trace of the path. Perhaps you missed a turn in the trail. If no trail is visible, stop and relax. Think about where you have been. Look at your map. Do not wander—you will most likely go in a circle. Three of anything—a shout, whistle, or flash of light—is a call for help. If you are with a group or have recently seen other hikers, signal every few minutes while you wait for your absence to be noted, and for someone to come to your aid.

While waiting for help, begin planning what you will do next. With your map, choose the most direct route out to the nearest road or known trail, based on your best estimation of where you are. Note where north is on the map and correct your bearing for magnetic declination—generally about 12 degrees west of true north in the New York region. Use your compass to follow the route that you select. In most places, following any stream downhill is a good route. If darkness falls, stay put and keep warm with those extra garments in your pack and possibly with a fire, *but note the following precautions:* build the fire in front of a rock, because its heat will be increased by reflection, having first made sure that you have cleared the ground down to mineral soil. Be careful not to let the fire spread.

Taking Care of the Trails and Woodlands
When you are on the trail, complying with the following hiking practices will be a courtesy to your fellow hikers and lessen your impact on the environment.

Hiker Etiquette
Do not pick flowers or collect rocks or artifacts—leave them there for other

hikers to enjoy. Hike quietly! Loud noises disturb the wild animals living near the trails, as well as your fellow hikers, many of whom are on the trail to observe the wildlife and enjoy the tranquility of the woods. Use existing trails, staying in the middle of the path, not on the edge. The trails are frequently placed to protect nearby sensitive or rare vegetation. Shortcutting on switchbacks causes erosion to the area. Not everyone likes dogs, so if you hike with them, keep them under control on a leash. If your dog defecates on or near the trail, bury the waste farther away or pack it out. When hiking with a group, walk single-file except on wide woods roads. Let muddy trails dry out before you use them. If you encounter a wet or muddy spot, walk through it, getting your feet wet rather than widening the trail at the edges.

Litter
The conscientious hiker's motto is "Leave nothing but footprints." Whatever you carry into the woods, you can carry it out. Do not attempt to burn or bury refuse. Leave the trail, lunch stop, and campsite as if no one had been there. Bring an extra plastic bag along for carrying out your refuse. Help keep the trails the way you would like to find them by picking up litter left by inconsiderate trail users.

Smoking
Leave your cigarettes home when you go hiking, but if you must smoke, do it only when you stop for a break—never when you are moving along the trail. Carry a plastic bag or small metal container to carry out used matches and cigarette butts, and always make sure they are completely out.

Shared-Use Trails
Some trails mentioned in this book are shared-use trails, which means they may be shared with other users such as cyclists, horseback riders, in-line skaters, and, in season, cross-country skiers or snowshoers. People in wheelchairs, even motorized ones, are considered to be on foot. No other type of motorized vehicle, however, should be on a trail. If you encounter an ATV on the trail, take down the license number and report it to the park police.

On trails used by horseback riders, cyclists, and pedestrians, the common practice is for bicycles to yield to pedestrians, and both bicycles and pedestrians to yield to horses. On ski trails, hikers should stay out of the ski track, particularly in areas where there is a machine-set track. The footprint left in the snow by a hiker is dangerous to the skier.

Fires

On day hikes, you should have no need for a fire at all. Backpackers should cook on a backpacker's stove. The only plausible reason for building a fire is for warmth in the event you become lost, and cold and are dealing with emergency bivouac conditions.

Trail Problems

Report trail problems, such as permanent wet spots, missing blazes, and trees blocking the trail, to the New York-New Jersey Trail Conference. Their volunteers maintain most of the trails in the area, and the Trail Conference knows who maintains the remainder of the trails. If you hike often, obtain a supply of trail report cards from the Trail Conference, which you can use to keep a record of trail problems. The sooner you report problems, the sooner they will be fixed.

Do not be a phantom maintainer—that is, do not do the maintainer's work of clearing and blazing the trail. The assigned maintainer will not mind if you pick up small amounts of litter or throw an occasional small branch off the trail, but for more serious problems, make sure to contact the Trail Conference. If you want to maintain a trail, become a Trail Conference member, and let them know of your interest in trail work. A volunteer will assign you to maintain a trail or have a trail crew contact you. Trail crews are Trail Conference members who go out regularly to repair trails in a specific area. By maintaining trails with other hikers, you will learn the correct trail maintenance skills.

Private Property

Hiking trails are not always on public land. They sometimes cross private land, with the owner's permission. When hiking on private property, stay on the trail, leave no litter, and build no fires so that the landowner will continue to allow the public access.

Park Closings

When the woods are dangerously dry from lack of rain, parks and public areas may be closed to hikers. The New York-New Jersey Trail Conference urges complete cooperation with the public authorities who make these decisions. When the park lands are closed, stay out of the woods, and request others likewise.

Overnight Backpacking Trips

Some parks permit overnight backpacking. However, before you go, check with the park concerning their regulations. Adhere to the group size restrictions.

Many areas restrict group sizes to ten or fewer, a good rule even if there is no official restriction. If your group is larger, consider staying at two or more distinct campsites in order to lessen the impact on the environment.

THREE

MOUNTAIN ECOLOGY *

nly a few substantive natural history publications cover the mountains in the greater New York region where much of the hiking is done. Vegetation and fauna are shaped by hard rock and shallow soils on hills, ledges, and mountains. In most of the *New York Walk Book* region, these crest environments are widespread at elevations of about 800 to more than 2,000 feet. Elevation *per se* is not responsible for distinctive crest vegetation. Due to the sun's heat, some exposed rocky crest habitats are warmer, at least seasonally, than *coves* (sheltered lower areas). Crest vegetation also occurs at low elevations, even at sea level along the Hudson River, where rocky knobs and bluffs have thin soil exposed to the weather.

Vegetation is part of the scenery, stabilizes the soil against erosion, provides habitat, and makes up the base of the food chain. Crest vegetation is influenced by various factors. Shallow soils and bare rock exposed to extremes of weather have little space for roots, hold little water, and are prone to drought. As a result, they generally have low nutrient levels, and may be unstable. Rapid changes in temperature and moisture, high winds that desiccate and physically stress plants, and wind-driven ice crystals in winter that abrade plants all add to the harsh growing conditions. Soil drought and exposure to lightning strikes make crests fire-prone. Charred wood is rarely far away in these mountains. People are attracted to picturesque, rocky overlook areas, where untended fires

*This chapter was written by Erik Kiviat, Executive Director of Hudsonia, Annandale, New York.

and discarded cigarettes add to the fire risk. Hikers who trample vegetation by wandering off trails, and browsing deer attracted to sunny, south-facing slopes in cold weather, add to the difficult conditions. Trees, if present at all, grow slowly, do not reach large size, and are often damaged. Crest vegetation may include old-growth forests that lack large trees. Lower-growing plants may be less affected by harsh weather and poor soil, and are able to root successfully in crevices or soil pockets.

Crests of the Hudson Highlands, Shawangunks, Taconics, Stissing Mountain, Westchester Hills, Palisades, and many other areas commonly have stunted forests or savannas characterized by red oak and chestnut oak. Co-occurring trees may include red maple, pignut hickory, white oak, gray birch, pin cherry, black cherry, shadbush, red cedar, white pine, pitch pine, and—if enough moisture is available—hemlock. Sprouts and occasionally larger trees of American chestnut are generally scattered in the forest but may be absent from the rockiest habitats. The size and, in places, the density of trees generally increases on deeper soils, in areas sheltered from the weather, and at lower elevations. Also, other trees become common, such as black birch, hop-hornbeam, or sugar maple.

Pitch pine dominates large areas of the environmentally extreme crests of the Shawangunks. There, tree size decreases toward the summit of Ice Caves Mountain, where vast areas of dwarf pitch pine "plains" appear as dense thickets only 3–6 feet high. Elsewhere in the Shawangunks, tupelo and sassafras may be prominent on level crest areas that apparently collect moisture.

Between the well-spaced trees, or in bald patches where there are few or no trees, many other plants may thrive. Among the shrubs are scrub oak, mountain laurel, low blueberries, huckleberry, chokeberry, bush-honeysuckle, and occasionally bearberry. In addition, mostly in the more southern areas, there may be downy arrowwood, black-haw, and New Jersey tea. Little bluestem and a few other grasses are often present, and they may form picturesque meadows. Prickly-pear cactus thrives here and there on warm, dry rocks. Among the many typical herbaceous plants are goat's-rue, orange-grass, pink corydalis, sand-rush, and stiff-leaf aster. The most extremely exposed areas may have three-toothed cinquefoil, Greenland sandwort, or other species rare in this region. Level ledges occasionally are deeply carpeted with reindeer lichens, and vertical rock faces frequently have large rock tripe lichens. Lush growths of lichens indicate that the local air quality is relatively good and that hikers and climbers have not been trampling on the fragile ground off the trail.

Most of the more rugged hiking areas have schist, gneiss, granite, quartz conglomerate bedrock, or quartzite that has given rise to acidic soils. The common crest plants are tolerant of this acidity. Large areas of the Shawangunks and Schunemunk Mountain, and the quartzite ledges occurring locally at Stissing, are good examples of very hard rock and acidic soils. Yet, other areas have plants indicative of neutral or even alkaline soils, including many spots in the Hudson Highlands, portions of the Shawangunks, and pockets in the Taconics. It is not clear what factors have mollified acidity of the soil, but some plausible suggestions are local glacial deposits containing limestone or other limy rocks from nearby valleys, calcium-bearing bedrock such as amphibolite or calc-silicate, or ash from vegetation fires. Calcareous (limy) shales are responsible in parts of the Shawangunks. Whatever the reasons, the typical flora of acidic crests may be punctuated by species associated with limy soils such as basswood, bladdernut, round-leaf dogwood, and harebell.

Talus slopes, comprising piles of more-or-less loose rock below cliffs and ledges, are extensive in the Palisades, Shawangunks, portions of the Hudson Highlands, and at Stissing, but are more localized elsewhere. The sunnier, drier areas of talus support many of the plants found on dry, sunny crests. Moister, shadier habitats may have hemlock and a variety of other plants. The cool, moist crevices beneath talus blocks are secure refuge for many animals. Talus slopes are often unstable, and the individual blocks are subject to movement and thus may be dangerous to climb. Undercliff Road (a carriage-road hiking trail) at Mohonk Preserve in the Shawangunks crosses extensive talus; a trail guide by Daniel Smiley and Frank Egler, *The Natural History of Undercliff Road*, is superb.

The Catskills are a special case. Their near-level strata of softer sandstones and shales create flat summits that above about 3,500 feet may have moist, organic soils and red spruce-balsam fir forests. Some of the spruce-fir stands are old growth. Plant communities resembling the crest vegetation described

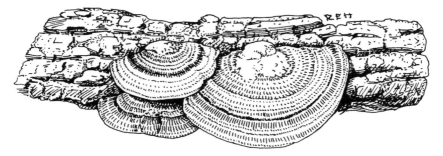

above are most noticeable on ledges or around the exposed edges of the summits. In places, one can see conifers flagged into a one-sided growth pattern by high winds, and *krummholz* (dwarf woods) spreading out at the base where deep snow shields the low branches from ice crystal abrasion.

Some areas have been disturbed historically by hard rock mining (in the early 1900s, for example). Notable examples are on the east face of Hook Mountain in the New York Palisades, Little Stissing Mountain, and at the southwest end of Breakneck Ridge (Hudson Highlands). Along with the typical crest plants, introduced and native weedy species flourish, among them tree-of-heaven, black locust, empress-tree, wineberry, Morrow or Tartarian honeysuckle, garlic-mustard, and common ragweed. The same invasions have occurred at some locations of serious trail erosion or off-road vehicle damage.

Extensive wetlands are rare at higher elevations. Yet depressions on level bedrock, pockets between ledges, or wet stream margins often support small wet meadows, bogs, or intermittent pools. These wet areas may have highbush blueberry, sweet pepperbush, red maple, sphagnum moss, and other plants tolerant of acidic, wet soils. Dwarf ginseng and other interesting wildflowers may occur in these habitats.

Wildlife may be sparse on crests, but some interesting species are associated with these habitats. Hawks, eagles, and vultures migrate along the Appalachian ridges in late summer and fall, and under some weather conditions fly close to the ridgetops. Migration is pronounced along the Shawangunks, and ledges just south of Route 44-55 provide an excellent vantage point. Breakneck Ridge and the Storm King complex are also good places to watch hawks. The peregrine falcon formerly nested on ledges along the Hudson River and in the Shawangunks. Following many years of absence due to DDT poisoning and human disturbance, reintroduction efforts have resulted in a few pairs nesting on bridges or skyscrapers. The breeding population of the common raven is slowly increasing in our region; their low-pitched, croaking calls may be heard in many mountainous areas. Eastern bluebirds commonly nest in cavities in dead or damaged trees in the balder crest habitats.

Two species of lizards occur in the mountains. The eastern fence lizard has a restricted distribution on sunny crests near the river, but the five-lined skink is widely distributed in the region and more common in the Ramapos and the Hudson Highlands west of the river. Crests and their often-associated talus slopes are frequently inhabited by snakes. The remaining winter denning and spring basking locales of the threatened timber rattlesnake are often associated with ledge-and-talus habitats that have a warm, sunny exposure. Northern copperhead dens are commonly in talus as well, as are other species, such as the black racer and black rat snake. Eastern box turtles also use crest habitats in the southwestern portions of the region. The slimy salamander may be found in pockets of moist soil among rocks. Woodland pools, where not too acidic (for example, on Breakneck Ridge, Stissing, and shale terrains in the northern Shawangunks), may support breeding congregations of spotted salamander, wood frog, and sometimes marbled salamander.

Pitch Pine

Porcupines are fond of crevices in talus and beneath ledges. The long-tailed shrew occurs in talus in the Shawangunks, and the northern water shrew may be seen along mountain streams in the Catskills. The eastern woodrat, nearly gone from the region, builds stick nests in rock crevices. Following reintroduction, the fisher occurs in the Catskills and the Northern Shawangunks. It is not unusual to find tracks or scat of bobcat in the Catskills and the Taconic Mountains.

There has been little study of invertebrates in the mountains. A rare butterfly, the falcate orange-tip, frequents ledges west of the Hudson River, where there are abundant rock cresses, food for the caterpillars. Another rare butterfly, the pipevine swallowtail, has been rediscovered on the New Jersey Palisades.

Dry rocky habitats may bear a surprising resemblance to dry sandy habitats such as those that hikers see at the New Jersey Pine Barrens, the Jersey Shore, and the Long Island shores. Pitch pine, scrub oak, blueberries, little bluestem, bluebird, box turtle, and other species that have adapted to dry soil are prominent in both rocky and sandy landscapes. Inland sand barrens are quite acidic, whereas seaside habitats may be salty. Sandy areas support many burrowing animals not found in rocky terrains.

Some rare animals and plants occur mostly or only in rugged environments that have harsh conditions and are difficult for human beings to reach. For those species that can tolerate the harsh weather, poor soil, sparse vegetation, and relatively frequent fires, these mountainous landscapes can provide refuges from biological competition, predation, and human disturbance. This appears true for animals that den in rock crevices or nest on remote ledges, as well as for those plants that can survive on nearly bare, weatherbeaten rocks but not in the shade of forests or tall shrubs. Many human populations have taken refuge in mountainous regions elsewhere in the world.

The biological refuge function of mountains, as well as the sensitivity of mountain soils to trampling and erosion, forces us to consider the carrying capacity of mountain landscapes for recreational use. Hikers in fragile areas can lessen the human impact on nature by staying on the trails and be careful not to trample vegetation and soils unnecessarily. They should avoid disturbing wildlife, especially bird nests, and resist the temptation to collect plants or animals. Hikers can cultivate interest in nature, using field guides and regional books. Rare or unusual observations may be reported to Hudsonia (Bard College Field Station, Annandale, NY 12504).

GEOLOGY

ithin a hundred-mile radius of Manhattan, there is as diverse a landscape as can be found anywhere in this country. North from the Battery, staying east of the Hudson through Westchester and on to Connecticut, are the southern reaches of rocky New England terrain. West of the Palisades is the expanse of the Newark Basin. Beyond it lie long, sinuous ridges and valleys running northeast into New York State. Still farther west stretches the Appalachian Plateau, taking in the Poconos and their more steeply eroded cousins to the north, the Catskills. Sandy coastal plains traverse the shores of Long Island and New Jersey. Each of these five distinct physiographic provinces offers its own rewards for hikers.

Distinct though they are, the provinces share a common heritage in the inexorable processes that continue to change the surface of the earth. At the root of all these forces is plate tectonics, which depicts the earth as a hot, somewhat plastic ball with a brittle skin. The interior behaves something like a pot of boiling water, convecting in a rolling motion, and the less dense skin— the continental plates—tends to follow along, floating on the mantle beneath. Where all of this material rises, it breaks up; where it falls, it is compressed or pushed down into the mantle. The junctions of colliding plates are often marked by the formation of mountain ridges, island chains, or deep trenches. These movements take place over virtually incomprehensible eons.

The current general shape of the North American continent dates from the early Cenozoic Era. Most of the locally familiar land forms predate that. The New York region has been subjected to the breakup, collision, and again the breakup of plates, coupled with the unending forces of erosion that make the surface of the earth smoother, in proportion to its size, than an eggshell. The region has also seen volcanism, *orogeny* (mountain building), deposition of sediments, *metamorphism* (heating and compression), and occasional submergence beneath advancing seas. On the surface, immense sheets of ice have periodically bulldozed, scarred, and generally rearranged the land.

Geologists measure time in eras, periods and epochs. The absolute times, in years, changes as more is learned about fossil and radioactivity dating. Table 1 indicates how many million of years have elapsed since the beginning of each era, period, or epoch as of 1995. For example, earlier editions of the *New York Walk Book* had the Cambrian beginning 600 million years ago versus the 1995 estimate of 570 million years ago.

TABLE 1

Era, Period, or Epoch	Million Years Ago (to 1995)	Era, Period, or Epoch	Million Years Ago (to 1995)
Cenozoic Era		Paleozoic Era	
Pleistocene	1.6	Permian	286
Pliocene	5.3	Pennsylvanian	320
Miocene	23.7	Mississippian	360
Oligocene	36.6	Devonian	408
Eocene	57.8	Silurian	438
Paleocene	66.4	Ordovician	505
		Cambrian	570
Mesozoic Era			
Cretaceous	144	Precambrian Era	4,500
Jurassic	208		
Triassic	245		

The New England Uplands offer hikers rich visual evidence of the forces that have shaped the earth. Two spurs of this complicated, broken terrain extend into the New York area. The Manhattan Prong underlies Westchester, the Bronx, and Manhattan before ending in the northern tip of Staten Island, while the Reading Prong gives the Hudson and New Jersey Highlands their character as it courses southwest into Pennsylvania. Both prongs present evidence of

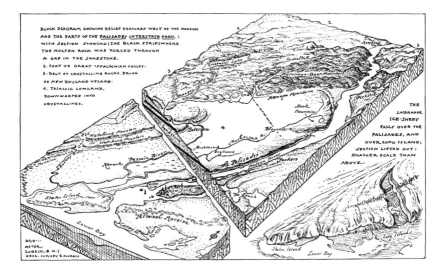

how glaciers, which receded a "mere" ten thousand years ago, left their traces on the oldest rocks visible in the region.

The Highlands are the roots of mountains formed in the middle Proterozoic Epoch of the Precambrian Era, largely from sediments deposited by ancient seas. As they accumulated to a thickness of several miles, they compressed and heated until they metamorphosed into gneiss, marble, and mica-rich schist. These rocks, along with diorite that intruded as magma, are the oldest in the area. Associated with this Highlands Complex is a medium-grained, gray granite, which may be, unlike most, metamorphic in origin. This "Canada Hill granite phase" shows clearly on Anthony's Nose, just east of the Bear Mountain Bridge. Another granite, the igneous rock of Storm King, is highly resistant to erosion and caps the crests of prominent ridges in the Highlands such as Bear Mountain, Dunderberg, and West Mountain.

Even as the mountains rose, during the Grenville Orogeny in the Precambrian Era, erosion gnawed at their flanks, limiting their height to about 15,000 feet and leaving enormous deposits of sediments to the west. By the Cambrian Period, little was left but a flat land of resistant rock. In the late Ordovician Period, the Taconic Orogeny, interpreted as the result of a collision of continental plates, another episode of uplifting and folding began, leaving the Highlands and Taconics in their present position. What was once an eastern

37

Oscawana Lake : Goose Rocks, glacial boulders wrenched from the surrounding mountains

version of the Rocky Mountains had now become a tortuously folded region with summits no higher than 1,300 feet.

The views from the top of one of these rises is a landscape of rounded knobs and ridges—the result of simple weathering, age upon age of wind and water, freeze and thaw, which reduces the mightiest peaks. Still more of this rounding is the work of waves of Pleistocene glaciers, whose handiwork is visible everywhere in the Highlands. Moving sheets of ice thousands of feet thick scraped their way across the area as they advanced south-southeast. In the process, they abraded north slopes with debris transported from the north, and pried and plucked rocks from south slopes. Called *roches moutonnées* (sheepbacks), these smooth outcrops with rugged south sides are common in the Highlands.

The glaciers also transported large boulders, called *erratics* because they are often of a different composition from the ground upon which they now rest. Sandstone erratics brought 35 miles from Schunemunk Mountain are common in the Highlands. Likewise, chunks of the Highlands appear on the Palisades, and blocks of the Palisades surface in Brooklyn. Finer debris from all these places and points north color the sands of Coney Island. In Harriman Park, erratics dot Hogencamp Mountain, among others. Occasionally, erratics, such as Hippo Rock on Stockbridge Mountain, were propped at odd angles or balanced on smaller rocks and have become popular landmarks for hikers.

Frequently, accumulations of glacial debris, or *drift*, rode to the valley bottoms on torrents of meltwater and piled up in irregular hillocks, or *kames*. The same water settled into shallow glacial lakes throughout the region. Lakes by nature are fleeting phenomena; flowing water tends to down cut their outlets and drain them, turning them into swamps. Patches of valley floor covered in willow are likely the sites of former lakes. Occasionally, the old outlets have been dammed and the lakes re-created, as in the Seven Lakes area of Harriman Park in the 1920s and 1930s.

Subtle footprints of the glaciers exist in the striations and gouges that marked many of the region's exposed rocks as drift ground into them. More pronounced pits and furrows, however, are usually the work of weathering forces. One common feature of the Highlands that is partly glacial in origin is exfoliation, the leaf-like flaking of rock as it uplifts. Much of this uplift has its roots in mountain-building forces, but some is the result of the off-loading of the great ice sheet. Bear Mountain's summit is a good place to see this rounding process at work.

As the majestic Hudson River slices through the Highlands, it illustrates yet another effect of the Pleistocene Era. Ice speeding up as it cut through the narrow Hudson Gorge cut the river channel well below sea level. Thus, the river here is a fjord, the only one on the east coast south of Maine.

The Manhattan Prong of the New England Uplands is a generally younger and less hilly terrain than the Highlands. The oldest rock in the prong, the tough, crystalline Fordham gneiss, dates anywhere from Cambrian to the middle Proterozoic Epoch of the Precambrian Era. Overlying this layer is the glittery mica schist familiar to anyone who has visited Central Park, and the softer Inwood marble. Both date from about the Cambrian–Ordovician boundary. Contact between the two is visible on the Manhattan shore of Spuyten Duyvil. In Westchester and Putnam counties, all three types are complexly folded together.

The Manhattan skyline in the midtown and Wall Street areas reflects in striking profile where the skyscrapers rest on this solid bedrock. In the area in between, which includes Chinatown and Greenwich Village, the bedrock dips too low to anchor the foundations. The tip of the prong continues on to include Clove Lakes Park, LaTourette Park, and other sections traversed by the Staten Island Greenbelt Trail. Prominent here is the greenish serpentinite, visible in Clove Lakes Park and on Forest Avenue. Along with the salt-and-pepper

Harrison diorite of the Bronx and the more northerly Hartland schist, they are the product of the collision of continental plates at the time of the Taconic Orogeny. At that time, an island arc of volcanic origin, analogous to the modern Aleutians, slammed into the East Coast, burying the region that is now the Manhattan Prong, creating igneous intrusions, and metamorphosing some formations. Thus, a portion of the prong is younger rock welded to older types by tectonic forces. Near the tip of the prong, the serpentinite is buried under the terminal Harbor Hill Moraine, the limit of the last advance of the great Wisconsin Ice Sheet. This glacial dumping ground reaches 410 feet above sea level at Todt Hill on Staten Island.

The Ridge and Valley Province constitutes the great Appalachian cordillera (a system of mountain ranges, often with a number of loosely parallel chains) that runs northeast to Newfoundland and southwest to Alabama. In this area, its two prominent features are the Great Valley, extending from the Hudson and Wallkill watersheds to the Shenandoah Valley, and a long, narrow ridge the Lenni Lenape called "Endless Mountain." The latter is now called Shawangunk Mountain in New York, Kittatinny in New Jersey, and Blue and Tuscarora mountains in Pennsylvania.

The Great Valley contains, from the bottom up, layers of sandstone, limestone and dolomite, siltstone, and claystone, all deposited over many millions of years in the Cambrian–Ordovician Period by intruding seas. The bottom layer slightly metamorphosed into quartzite; alongside Kittatinny Mountain, the top layer changed into the largest deposit of gray slate in the country, the Martinsburg formation. Low, steep-sided kames dot the valley.

The rocks of Kittatinny and Shawangunk were deposited atop the valley claystone around the time of the Taconic Orogeny. Their strikingly white quartzite originally consisted of sandstones and conglomerates, which were partially marine sediments and partially the erosional waste of the ancestral Taconics. Called the Queenston Delta, the rubble sloped to the west much in the way the Great Plains now slope to the east from the Rockies, and gradually filled in a shallow western sea that had left limestone deposits. As the mountains wore down, the rivers that ate at them flowed at a shallower angle, and so were able to carry only finer muds and silts, which formed the darker top layer of the deposits. Orogenic forces during the Acadian Orogeny, in the late Devonian Epoch, folded and faulted the Ridge and Valley Province even as the sediments accumulated. Differential erosion between soft limestones and shales and the more resistant layers created the parallel ridges that mark the region.

One of the best places to observe the features of the province is the Delaware Water Gap, one of the narrowest segments of this mountain system. The gap itself demonstrates the power of the Delaware River as it cut through the gradually uplifting terrain. The cleft was made long before the last ice sheets receded through here about seventeen thousand years ago. Large talus blocks of sandstone and conglomerate on Kittatinny's southeast side overlie Martinsburg slate, which is visible in outcrops along US 46 to the south. East of the gap on I-80, a scenic overlook offers a view of the broad valley and the "endless" mountain.

Two peculiarities of the Ridge and Valley Province are Schunemunk and Bellvale mountains, whose resistant caps of sandstone and conglomerate are more related to the Catskills, at least 20 miles distant, than they are to the surrounding ridges. Though their origin is uncertain, they seem likely to be extensions of the plateau country that lies north and west; whether the plateau once reached even beyond these points is a matter of conjecture.

The Appalachian Plateau itself presents a somewhat less complicated geological history. It was formed from a combination of sediments eroded out of mountains to the east and others deposited by seas to the west in Devonian time. Although at first glance they may seem to be different, the Poconos, Catskills, and much of Central New York are products of the same deposition. The plateau was gently westward-sloping terrain that rose to as much as 4,000 feet above sea level without being radically folded during the ancient mountain-building episodes. Thus, the Poconos and Catskills are not mountains in a strict geological sense. What gave the province the relief it now exhibits was the relentless power of streams carving deep, V-shaped valleys into the plateau.

The Poconos, in particular, retain the aspect of plateau country. From north-bound I-380 or any high overlook, the evenness of the highest elevations becomes apparent. Interspersed with these "mountains" are relatively narrow streambeds. In the Catskills, on the other hand, streams ran their courses through greater thicknesses of sediment; their valleys widened with age and eroded toward the water's source, leaving fractions of the plateau isolated as high peaks. Slide, Thomas Cole, Blackhead, and all the other summits here are what is left of the plateau. A topographical map of the Catskills gives an "aerial view" that makes it easier to understand the extent and direction of these forces.

Glaciation and weathering have helped shape the Catskills into the fabled land of Rip Van Winkle. There is evidence of this in the rounded summits, the talus slopes, the telltale grooves and gouges. Almost any wooded hillside will tell you that subtle changes still occur. Curved tree trunks bending skyward show that in their lifetime the soil has crept downhill, seeking the valley bottom. In ages to come, the plateau will be level again.

After all the orogenic and depositional forces ended, a rifting process—begun when the African continent began to split away from North America, to which it had been welded for over 100 million years—formed the Newark Basin in the Jurassic Period. The floor of the basin is a large block of undeformed sandstones and shales that faulted at its eastern and western edges and tilted slightly downward to the west. Similar fault-block basins are found near Gettysburg, Pennsylvania, and Southbury, Connecticut, and in the Connecticut River Valley. Its northwestern boundary runs roughly from Haverstraw southwest through Suffern and Morristown, and on into Pennsylvania. Called the Ramapo-Canopus Fault, the western side formed a scarp a few thousand feet higher than the eastern expanse; as it eroded, the higher block filled the regions below it with sediments.

As the basin widened, molten rock intruded through cracks in the floor parallel to the Ramapo Fault. The Watchungs and Hook Mountain were formed of fine-grained black basalt that poured out upon the surface. The Palisades—the best known geologic feature in the metropolitan area—intruded in thicknesses up to 1,000 feet, in a line extending from Haverstraw to Staten Island. Unlike the Watchungs, magma never reached the surface while the Palisades were forming. Instead, a subterranean sill cooled and crystallized more slowly into coarser diabase, the columnar rock so prominent in the cliffs along the Hudson. Uplift and weathering then exposed the sill. The freezing and expansion of water seeping into the cliffs has broken the diabase into large blocks that litter the foot of the Palisades. These slopes resemble giant stairs. Deriving its name from *trappa* (Swedish for stairs), traprock has long been quarried in the Palisades, and crushed for industrial uses. The diabase was used extensively in the late nineteenth century as "Belgian bluestone" to pave much of lower Manhattan. The creation of the Palisades Interstate Park Commission helped end quarrying operations that could have left the cliffs extensively scarred. Another basin resource, red sandstone, is still visible in the old brownstone houses of Manhattan and Brooklyn.

Hikers will notice frequent erratics and glacial scarring atop the Palisades. In this province, the Wisconsin Ice Sheet reached as far south as Metuchen and left an arc of terminal moraine that stretched north beyond Morristown before swinging west under what is now I-80. As it receded, the melting ice created Glacial Lake Hackensack, which covered the northern part of the basin west of the Palisades. Today the Meadowlands are its slowly drying vestige.

The Atlantic Coastal Plain, extending from Long Island to Florida, is the youngest of the provinces, having formed out of the unconsolidated sediments of flood plains and river deltas since the late Cretaceous. Abundant plant fossils indicate these nonmarine origins, while sharks' teeth and fragments of marine reptiles suggest periodic invasions of shallow seas. The plain was greatly reduced in width when the sea level rose at the end of the last glacial period. The prepleistocene sediments remain clearly definable throughout the flat expanse of southern New Jersey, where elevations rarely approach 300 feet. Commercial sand and gravel operations, common on the plain, attest to its deltaic origin, and clay deposits figured in a once-thriving pottery industry in New Jersey.

On Long Island, however, much of the original deposition from rivers in New England is buried under two terminal moraines—the Ronkonkoma and the younger Harbor Hill—and the outwash plain created when glacial streams carried sands and silts toward the sea. The island's backbone and eastern forks are all morainal, ending spectacularly in the bluffs of Montauk Point, where rising seas inundated the outwash and brought the surf to the base of the glacial rubble. The same seas invaded a shallow depression that is now Long Island Sound. Many erratics sprinkle the moraine, from huge Shelter Rock in Nassau County to small boulders nestled unobtrusively in quiet corners of the Pine Barrens. Isolated ice blocks left water-filled depressions or kettles such as Lake Ronkonkoma; smaller, dried-out kettles are much less apparent to the eye but are easy to spot on a topographical map of Suffolk County, which will also reveal subtle traces of channels that once bore the ice's runoff seaward.

The coast's numerous barrier beaches and sandspits are the ever-shifting manifestations of littoral drift, the transportation of sand on prevailing ocean currents. So swift is this action that colonial maps of the Jersey Shore and Long Island bear little resemblance to modern ones. Fire Island and Sandy Hook, for instance, have been reshaped considerably by tugging currents and buffeting storms. Indeed, some strands have grown at a rate approaching a mile every quarter century, by geological standards an incredibly swift pace.

The rapid changes wrought in the fragile dunes contrast markedly with the seeming stability of Highlands bedrock. Change governs the landscape. The phrase "to move at a glacial pace" is used to describe a slow procession of events; but in the unfathomable expanses of time involved in shaping the earth, the glaciers were here but yesterday. Their icy breath still chills the hollows and dells they departed ten thousand years ago. The wind atop a Highlands ridge, the surf along the shore, a rushing brook in spring, and the icy talus of the Palisades illustrate the great forces still at work. We can contemplate with awe the hundreds of millions of years of history beneath our feet as we walk in solitude in this, our speck of time in an ever-old, ever-new world.

FIVE

NEW YORK CITY

olitude and open space are in short supply within the New York City limits, but a number of places in the city still offer a respite from the bustle of the metropolis. Most of these walks are rewarding for their biological, geological, or historical significance as well as for the tranquility they offer to the city dweller. Walkers can visit valuable wetlands, parks of Staten Island, or sites of Revolutionary War skirmishes.

More than 26,000 acres of city parkland—13 percent of New York's land area—lie in the city's five boroughs. The city is in the process of connecting many of its parks with urban greenways that eventually will total some 350 miles of "walker-friendly" trails along the coasts, overland on reclaimed transit rights-of-way, and on long-forgotten paths that have been restored.

For more information on New York City parks, contact the City of New York, Parks and Recreation, at (212) 360-8111.

THE BRONX

Named for Jonas Bronck, the Bronx is a borough of contrasts. It is densely populated yet boasts the first and third largest city parks—Pelham Bay and Van Cortlandt. The prosperous section of Riverdale is a striking contrast to burned-out buildings and high-rise housing projects. Highways crisscross the borough, making it easy for a traveler to pass through, yet there are many places to stop and visit. Choices range from Van Cortlandt's urban forests to Orchard Beach Promenade. Walkers can find solitude if they know where to look.

Bronx Park

Bronx Park is really three parks in one—the New York Botanical Gardens, the Bronx Zoo International Wildlife Conservation Park, and Bronx Park East. The first two charge admission, but they offer lots of walking opportunities,

The Hemlock Gorge and Dam, Bronx Park 1922

with flora and fauna to see. Bronx Park East runs parallel to the Bronx River Parkway on the east side. It has a paved path, is accessible from numerous side streets, and is free.

To reach the New York Botanical Gardens, take the number 4, C, or D train to the Bedford Park Station and walk east to Southern Boulevard. The Gardens are also accessible via Metro-North Harlem Division (Botanical Gardens stop) and the Bx9, Bx12, Bx19, and Bx22 buses.

To reach the Bronx Zoo, take the number 2 train to the Pelham Parkway Station, walk two blocks west to Boston Road, turn left on Boston Road, and then turn right into the park; or take the Liberty Lines Express BxM11 bus.

For more information, contact the New York Botanical Gardens at (718) 817-8700 or the Bronx Zoo at (718) 367-1010.

Pelham Bay Park

Encompassing 2,764 acres, Pelham Bay Park, the largest of New York City's parks, is a natural mosaic of forest, meadows, and salt marsh. Hunter Island, Twin Islands, Orchard Beach, Thomas Pell Wildlife Sanctuary, numerous unmarked trails and four short marked hiking trails are of interest to hikers. Its recreational facilities include Orchard Beach, two golf courses, ball fields, and a running track. Orchard Beach and its parking lot are man-made facilities, created when Pelham Bay was filled in to connect Hunter Island to the Bronx.

Hunter Island is the area north of Orchard Beach. It is of interest for its great trees and jutting rocks, as well as its tide pools, salt marshes, and glacial boulders. A Native Americans' conference rock, "Mishow," located near a cove at the northern end of the Orchard Beach boardwalk, is now almost buried with fill. "Gray Mare," an unusually formed erratic, lies off the northwestern tip of the former island. In addition to waterfowl, the park harbors great horned, long-eared, and barred owls.

The Thomas Pell Wildlife Sanctuary encompasses the natural areas along the Hutchinson River and south of the park's golf courses. The tract includes woodland, salt marsh, and a tidal estuary.

Pelham Bay is accessible by car from Pelham Parkway, which can be reached via the Hutchinson River Parkway or the New England Thruway. Take Pelham Parkway east past the Pelham Bridge and make a right at the light, following the signs toward Orchard Beach. Or head straight through the light and follow the signs for Shore Road and the free parking lot for the golf course, about a quarter mile beyond the circle on the left in front of the club house.

To reach Pelham Bay Park using public transportation, take the number 6 train to the last stop, which is 2 miles southwest of the Hunter Island section of the park. Or, take the City Island bus, Bx29, to City Island Avenue, just past the Pelham Bridge. A 0.3-mile feeder trail to the Siwanoy Trail, which offers three different hiking destinations, begins directly across from the bus stop. In the summer, take the Bx5 and Bx12 buses going to Orchard Beach. The park is also accessible via an equestrian path and a shared-use pedestrian and bike path that start at the intersection of Boston Post Road and Bronx Park East and run along Pelham Parkway.

For more information, contact Van Cortlandt & Pelham Bay Parks Administrator's Office, 1 Bronx River Parkway, Bronx, NY 10462; (718) 430-1890.

Kazimiroff Nature Trail *Length: 1.3 miles, 1.0 mile Blazes: blue, red*
This trail is named in memory of Dr. Theodore Kazimiroff, a dentist, noted amateur naturalist and archeologist, and friend of Pelham Bay Park. He and other Bronx environmentalists prevented the I-95 construction from the obliterating Split Rock, a glacial erratic, but were unable to stop the Pelham Bay landfill in the center of the park.

The trail circles Hunter Island on two partially overlapping red- and blue-blazed loops, with the blue trail the longer loop. The trail is reached from the north end of Orchard Beach parking lot. A brochure describing the various

numbered posts is available from the park office. Well-trodden side trails take hikers to "Gray Mare" and Twin Islands.

Siwanoy Trail (Central Woodland)   *Length: 1.6 miles Blaze: yellow*
This hike begins from the golf course parking lot, from which hikers cross the Shore Road at the southern entrance to reach the trail. To the right is the Siwanoy Trail. In about 0.3 mile the feeder trail from the City Island bus stop joins from the right. The Siwanoy route stays to the left, passing a golf driving range on the right and a short side trail to Glovers Rock—along the route of the Battle of Pells Point (1776), in which Colonel Glover and 750 men held off the British under Lord Howe long enough for General Washington to lead his troops north to White Plains. The trail soon crosses the road to Orchard Beach, curves around a large meadow on the left, and eventually reaches Orchard Beach.

Siwanoy Trail (Bartow-Pell Mansion)   *Length: 1.0 mile Blaze: yellow*
Beginning from the golf course parking lot, hikers cross Shore Road at the southern entrance to reach the trail. Going left at the trail, hikers travel along the shore of a lagoon, used for rowing. Much of the trail here is in a phragmites swamp, so it can be muddy in the spring or after a rain. In 0.3 mile the trail splits again; hikers should stay to the right. (The two branches eventually re-join; the return hike is via the other fork.) A pond, once a lagoon, formed when its outlet was blocked by fill, is passed on the left, where a variety of birds can be found. The trail ends at a rocky high point with a view over the lagoon. The return trip stays right, using the other branch of the trail, which leads past the Bartow-Pell Mansion Museum and Pell Family Burial Plot. Built in the Federal style in 1836, the mansion was the home of the Pell family. The carriage house

has been restored. Both buildings have limited hours and an admission fee. For more information, phone the mansion at (718) 885-1461.

Siwanoy Trail (Hutchinson Marsh)   *Length: 1.5 miles Blaze: yellow*
This route is reached by exiting the golf course parking lot at the southwest corner and following the bridle path, until the trail splits off to the right. It meanders through the woods to emerge on the Orchard Beach access road, which it follows west before splitting right to the Split Rock Trail or left through the marsh and under the bridge, eventually circling back. Shortly after the bridge, a short stub trail to the left leads through a phragmites marsh to a small island, with more views over the river.

Split Rock Trail   *Length: 1.7 miles Blaze: yellow*
The Split Rock Trail parallels the marshes along the Hutchinson River to the west of the golf course parking lot. Split Rock is at the end of the trail at the southeast intersection of the New England Thruway and the Hutchinson River Parkway. Unfortunately, the parkway is between the trail and the park's westernmost marshes.

Van Cortlandt Park

The first known inhabitants of the land that now makes up Van Cortlandt Park were the Weckquaesgeek band of the Lenapes. One of their settlements stood on what is today called the Parade Ground. In 1639, they sold much of what is now the park to the Dutch West India Company. The Van Cortlandts owned the property from 1699 until 1888, when the City of New York purchased it. Today, three parkways cut across the park, making access from section to section difficult. An ecology center, historic house, and recreation areas are in the southern part of the park. Of most interest to hikers are the three large tracts of woodlands in the northern end.

The park's Northwest Forest is between Broadway and the Henry Hudson Parkway. Three interconnecting trails have loops and informal paths to provide park users with a variety of hiking choices. The 1.4-mile Cass Gallagher Nature Trail is part of a shared-use paved trail system. Along the western part of the Northwest Forest, a bridle path follows the Getty Square spur of the Putnam Division of the New York Central Railroad. Between 1888 and 1943, this short commuter route ran from High Bridge to Getty Square. The 1.3-mile Cross Country Loop is part of two cross-country running courses, of 3 and 6 miles

CROTON AQUEDUCT: VAN CORTLANDT PARK

respectively, that extend into other portions of the park. Hikers can reach the trails from Mosholu Avenue near the stables and from the Parade Ground via Vault Hill.

A second tract of woodlands in the park's northern end, known as Croton Woods, is wedged between the Henry Hudson Parkway, Mosholu Parkway, and Major Deegan Expressway. Two trails—Old Putnam and Old Croton Aqueduct— run the length of the Croton Woods. The former is an abandoned rail line—the Putnam Division of the New York Central running between High Bridge in the Bronx and Brewster, New York, where travelers could make a connection to Boston. The railroad ceased passenger operations along this line in 1958, but carried occasional freight until 1981. The 1.5-mile portion in the park serves as a wildlife corridor as it passes through wetlands and divides the Van Cortlandt Golf Course. Portions of the 1.0-mile John Kieran Nature Trail, which begins and ends near the Van Cortlandt Golf House, follow the Old Putnam Trail. The 1.1-mile Old Croton Aqueduct Trail runs through the center of Croton Woods. This central segment is part of the aqueduct—which stretched more than 40 miles into Westchester—that brought water from the Croton Dam to New York City during the 1800s. Built in the 1830s as the city's first extensive water supply, it was used until 1897, when the New Croton Aqueduct replaced it. An informal path connects the Aqueduct Trail and the Old Putnam Trail at the north end of the golf course. Access to the trails is from the Van Cortlandt Golf House and Yonkers.

Finally, the Northeast Forest is between the Major Deegan Expressway and Van Cortlandt Park East. Two major unnamed trails cross the area. One parallels the Major Deegan Expressway and the other runs east–west toward the Croton Woods. The informal trails which crisscross the forest, are hard to follow as they are often overgrown. Access to the area is through the service road from Van Cortlandt Park East, from Yonkers, and via the trails from Croton Woods.

For more information, contact the Van Cortlandt Park Administrator's Office, 1 Bronx River Parkway, Bronx, NY 10462; (718) 430-1890.

Buses along the west side, the Bx9, Westchester Beeline 1, 2, 3, and the Manhattan Express Bus BxM3 provide access to the Northwest Forest. The Bx16, Bx34, Westchester Beeline 4, 20, and 21, and the Manhattan Express Bus BxM4B provide service to the east side and the Northeast Woods. The number 1 and 9 trains provide access to the south and west, while the number 4 provides access to the east side.

BROOKLYN

First settled in 1636, Bruekelen, as it was then known, was a stronghold of religious freedom. As a result it welcomed diverse groups, reflected now as a melting pot of contrasting customs in its multi-ethnic neighborhoods. Brooklyn is also a borough of churches and synagogues, with every block boasting another one. Walkers can develop routes reflecting various themes. A walk over the Brooklyn Bridge to Manhattan can be a daily commuter route or a recreational stroll. Esplanades in Brooklyn include the Brooklyn Heights and Shore Road promenades, the Coney Island Boardwalk, and the Manhattan Beach Esplanade. A portion of the Brooklyn-Queens Greenway is described in the Queens section.

Prospect Park

Frederick Law Olmstead and Calvert Vaux designed Prospect Park in the late 1860s. Its 526 acres are divided into Long Meadow, a woodland section, and a lake. The 100-acre forested area lies across a *terminal moraine* (an accumulation of earth and stones carried and finally deposited by a glacier). Its southern sector is dominated by tulip trees. To the north, a steep valley and stream with a series of glacial knobs and kettles have oak, sycamore, and Norway maples. The roads inside the park are closed to vehicular traffic on weekends. Unmarked trails meander around the grounds.

To reach the park, take the number 2 or 3 train to Grand Army Plaza or Prospect Park.

MANHATTAN

This ultimate urban area offers something different to walkers—"theme hikes" by which routes can be charted according to architecture, churches and synagogues, or the city's many and varied neighborhoods. The pedestrian walkways on the George Washington, Brooklyn, and Henry Hudson bridges offer unique views, while Battery Park and the East River Esplanade bring the walker close to a river. Urban parks, while they do not offer the same solitude as their rural counterparts, nevertheless provide a respite from the hustle of city life. It is possible, with surprisingly little road walking, to circumnavigate Manhattan on foot, always near the water, or to walk on auto-free paths from Greenwich Village to South Street Seaport.

Riverside Park

At 7 miles, Riverside Park is the longest urban waterfront park in the United States. Frederick Law Olmstead and Calvert Vaux—the great architects of Central Park and close to eighty other parks—designed the park from West 72nd Street to approximately 125th Street, but it is not the Riverside Park of today. At that time, the waterfront was too valuable to be included in the park land and was best used for a railroad and shipping docks. Robert Moses, in the late 1930s, created the present park on landfill from the Eighth Avenue subway extending to Fort Washington Park under the George Washington Bridge. At its northern terminus, Riverside Park provides access to paths leading to Inwood Park and Fort Tryon.

The park's trail system comprises three north–south walkways: one along the river, the sidewalk along Riverside Drive, and the third winding between the first two, with frequent connections. Each path is at a different elevation in this terraced park and thus offers its own unique perspective on the nature of the park. The paved riverfront path is not continuous, although dirt paths fill the gaps between 82nd Street and 91st Street and again above 105th Street.

Highlights of a walk though Riverside Park include the 79th Street boat basin and arcaded rotunda; the Soldiers and Sailors Monument, a classically designed Civil War memorial at the Riverside Drive level at 89th Street; the community gardens at the intermediate level at 90th Street; and Riverside Church and President Grant's Tomb at about 120th Street.

Above 123rd Street, it is necessary to walk a short distance alongside a highway en-trance. The re-ward is a look at the iron arched understructure of the Riverside Drive viaduct that links the original River-side Park with its newer segment above 135th Street. At 137th Street and again at 144th Street, walkers can enter

The Drive above the steep slopes of RIVERSIDE PARK overlooking the Hudson

Grant's Tomb

Riverbank State Park, built on the roof of a sewage treatment plant.

The park is accessible via foot from Riverside Drive and via public transportation. The M5 bus travels along Riverside Drive from 72nd to 135th Street; the M11 runs from there to Riverbank State Park and connects with the Bx19 bus. The Bx6 bus provides access from 155th to 161st streets. Access from the number 1 and 9 trains is by walking west from the subway stations.

Fort Tryon and Inwood Hill Parks

At any time of year the broad views of the Hudson River are a reasonable substitute for open spaces. Several paths run through Fort Tryon Park to The Cloisters, a branch of the Metropolitan Museum of Art, with its magnificent collection of medieval art. Other paths descend to the river and run south to-ward the George Washington Bridge. The little red lighthouse beneath the bridge marks the spot where sunken ships and chained logs were anchored during the Revolution in an attempt to prevent the passage of British ships.

Inwood Hill Park occupies the northwest corner of Manhattan Island, from Dyckman Street up to Spuyten Duyvil. For the early Native Americans, the area offered shelter from the icy winds that made Manhattan's rocky ridge

SHORAKAPKOK
INWOOD.

inhospitable, a good fresh-water spring, and level planting fields. Fish, especially shad, were in ample supply, and the surrounding forests provided bear, deer, and beaver.

To reach the Indian Rock Shelters from the top of Inwood Hill, hikers should follow the ravine down the east side of the ridge, past the great glacial potholes in the exposed rock, and through the grove of spicebush. Quantities of oyster shells found here were the most obvious evidence of Native American habitation. The village was called Shorakapkok, "as far as the Sitting-Down Place." Artifacts found here are archived at the National Museum of the American Indian, 1 Bowling Green, New York (212) 668-6624.

The bedrock visible in the heights of Fort Tryon and Inwood Hill is primarily Ordovician-age Manhattan schist. On the Bronx side of Spuyten Duyvil, Inwood marble appears in the cliff faces.

From the trail along the river, one can branch inland and uphill to the footpath over the Henry Hudson Bridge. The bridge has views of the Harlem River, the New Jersey Palisades, and a serene scene of rail and river directly below.

To reach the parks, take the number 1 train to Dyckman Street or the A train to 190th Street and walk west toward the Hudson.

QUEENS

The largest in land area of the five boroughs, Queens is mostly a residential area of erstwhile small towns. Residents, when asked where they live, will reply with a local neighborhood name, such as Whitestone or Bayside. The rolling

kettle-moraine topography that existed in the 1920s has long since given way
to development. The kettle hole ponds are wholly or partially filled in. Yet,
walkers can find places to go in the network of parks and many cemeteries.

Alley Pond Park

Located in eastern Queens amid some of the busiest highways in New York,
Alley Pond Park contains fresh and salt water marshes, oak uplands, and *glacial kettles* (ponds). One kettle, Oakland Lake, is stocked with black bass. Among
the species that survive in the park are muskrat, flying squirrel, opossum, and
raccoon. Migratory waterfowl frequent the wetlands. North of Northern Boulevard, a paved pedestrian path along the Cross Island Parkway provides a
pleasant walk of 3 miles along Little Neck Bay to Fort Totten. About halfway,
an overpass leads to Crocheron Park, with a small pond just off the parkway.

Near the Winchester Boulevard parking lot at the south end of the park is
a pedestrian path that is a remnant of the original Vanderbilt Motor Parkway.
Located just east of the Cross Island Parkway intersection, the Alley Pond Environmental Center maintains trails and conducts educational programs.

Alley Pond Park is accessible by car from Northern Boulevard and via the
Q12, Q30, and Q75 buses. For more information, including a guide to trails,
contact the Alley Pond Environmental Center, 228-06 Northern Boulevard,
Douglaston, NY 11363; (718) 229-4000.

The Brooklyn/Queens Greenbelt

An unmarked greenway, the Brooklyn/Queens Greenbelt, connects Flushing
Meadow Park, Kissena Corridor Park West, Kissena Park, Kissena Corridor
Park East, Cunningham Park, and Alley Pond Park. A walk of approximately
10 miles begins at the Willets Point Station of the Flushing Line (number 7
train). Local residents use this unmarked route to go from park to park.

Beginning on the Flushing Meadow Park road, the route bears left at the
end of the World's Fair Boardwalk and continues past the pitch-and-putt golf
course. It then proceeds over the Flushing River, turns left under the Van Wyck
Expressway at the first crossroad, and crosses the pedestrian bridge to the Queens
Botanical Garden. The walk continues on the path straight ahead, which leads
to Main Street, crosses it, and then goes to the corner of 56th Avenue and Main
Street, where there is a break in the fence opening to an unpaved path. The
unpaved path heads east, past a playground. At the end of the playground, the
path turns sharply north. After about 50 feet a side path goes sharply east

again, behind a row of houses to another paved path just before the stands for a soccer field. The walking route goes to the left and around the soccer field to Kissena Boulevard, via Rose Avenue.

The route crosses Rose Avenue and enters Kissena Park, where an un-paved path angles off to the right through a corridor of trees and parallels the paved path directly ahead. The route continues along this unpaved path which follows a former railroad grade through the park until a paved path is reached, with Kissena Lake on the left. The walk proceeds along the paved path over the knoll, heading east to 164th Street, crossing Underhill Avenue, and continuing east on the grassy area along the fence by Kissena Park Golf Course and Corridor Park. The route reaches and crosses a pedestrian bridge over the Long Island Expressway and then follows the path outside the playground to an open grassy area, where a row of trees parallels 199th Street (Peck Avenue). This is the western end of the Vanderbilt Motor Parkway, a private limited-access road used from 1903 to 1938. The route follows the former parkway to an open grassy area and crosses the footbridge over Francis Lewis Boulevard into the woods. Continuing on a vague path, it heads northeast to the ball fields and the tunnel under the Clearview Expressway, which emerges on Hollis Hills Terrace. It then turns south and re-enters the woods on a former entrance road of the Vanderbilt Motor Parkway, about 100 feet before the old bridge. Joining the main road about 250 feet up from Hollis Hills Terrace, the walk follows the road for almost 2 miles—the longest unbroken stretch of the old highway that still exists—and goes under the Grand Central Parkway and into Alley Pond Park. The road ends on what was to be the ramp to a proposed bridge over Winchester Boulevard. Hikers can exit here and take the Q46 bus back to the Kew Gardens station for the E or F trains or continue walking north through the ball fields.

Those who want to continue can head north under the Grand Central Parkway and turn left on the road leading to the Alley Pond Park, which leads to the Alley Pond Park Environmental Center, located at the far end of a large open field. Well to the right of the Environmental Center, a dirt path enters the woods. The route takes the walker along the dirt path, continuing on it to the school yard, where it bears right and makes a left, paralleling 233rd Street, to the Long Island Expressway. The walker follows a bridge over the Long Island Expressway, and then makes an immediate right into the woods, following the path along the Cross Island Parkway. At the playground, the route bears right until the path goes downhill to Oakland Lake, which is one block south of

Northern Boulevard. At Northern Boulevard the walk continues for 0.25 mile east, to the Alley Pond Environmental Center, with rest rooms, phones, parking, and a nearby number Q12 bus stop.

Jamaica Bay Wildlife Refuge

Part of the Gateway National Recreation Area, created in 1972, the Jamaica Bay Wildlife Refuge dates to 1953, when the New York City Parks Department set aside 9,170 of the bay's 14,000 acres and impounded ponds on either side of Crossbay Boulevard. The west pond has walks around it and is adjacent to the Gateway Visitor Center, where walkers must obtain a free permit. The trail is a 1.75-mile loop. Near the beginning, a short (0.25 mile) side trail, Terrapin Trail, branches off and winds along the coastline, offering panoramic views of Manhattan's skyline. At the other end, the West Pond Trail merges with the Upland Trail, where markers describe the early stages of a mixed deciduous forest that includes stands of hollies, pines, and willows.

The larger east pond, directly across from the Visitor Center, has no path but is more popular with the birds. In the summer, when the pond is lower, it is possible to walk around the perimeter. Waterproof boots and insect repellent are essential.

Hundreds of thousands of birds are attracted to the sanctuary, partly because of its location at the junction of the Hudson River and Atlantic Coast flyways and partly because the management's skillful clearing and planting make food and cover available. Visitors marvel at the chance to spot some of the more than three hundred species that have been seen here, within the shadow of J. F. Kennedy International Airport. The breeding water birds include great egret, snowy egret, glossy ibis, and colonies of terns and skimmers.

By car, the Visitor Center may be reached by driving south 3 miles from the Belt Parkway, Exit 17, on Cross Bay Boulevard. Via public transportation, hikers can take the A or C train to the Broad Channel station, walk west to Cross Bay Boulevard, and walk north half a mile. By bicycle, access is via the Shore Parkway Bicycle Path from Brooklyn. For more information, contact Jamaica Bay Wildlife Refuge at (718) 474-0613.

STATEN ISLAND

Long the forgotten borough of New York City, Staten Island (Richmond County) developed rapidly after the Verrazano-Narrows Bridge opened in 1964. Nevertheless, its woods, wetlands, and hilly terrain retain rewarding walking territory.

SKYLINE FROM STATEN ISLAND

The Richmondtown Restoration provides information on the early history of Staten Island, discovered in 1524 by Giovanni de Verrazano. Henry Hudson visited it in 1609 and named it *Staaten Eylandt* in honor of the States General of the Netherlands. Hackensacks lived on the north shore, Raritans on the south, and Tappans on the east. The nearby Fresh Kills—the only river to begin and end within the city limits—was used extensively as a canoe route to link these tribes with others living in Long Island, Manhattan, and New Jersey.

Staten Island Greenbelt

Frederick Law Olmstead was never able to develop a park in the hills near his Staten Island farm. But in 1984, 2,500 acres along the spine of the island were designated the Staten Island Greenbelt under the New York City Department of Parks, including Willowbrook Park, LaTourette Golf Course, and High Rock Park Conservation Center. Together with the Great Kills section of Gateway National Recreation Area on the outwash plain below, nearly 3,000 acres are linked in the Greenbelt trail network.

Efforts to preserve the Greenbelt ran afoul of the New York State Department of Transportation's plan to push the Richmond and Willowbrook parkways through the area and destroy the heart of the Greenbelt—along with its unique refuge from urban stress. Several hard-working citizens' groups were finally able to block the plan. Between 1971 and 1979 the City Parks Department worked with Conservation and the Outdoors, founded by Tom Yoannou, to establish 28 miles of trails on four footways. As of 1997, one of those trails, the White Trail, was essentially impassable due to development. The Staten Island Greenbelt Office is planning extensive relocations and so the trail is not described here. Staten Island hikers often refer to their trails by the color of the blaze, despite the fact that only the White Trail is so officially named.

Staten Island is accessible from the other boroughs via the Staten Island Ferry that leaves from the South Ferry Terminal at the tip of Manhattan. Because parking is often limited, all trails begin and end at New York City Transit Authority bus stops. Buses depart from, and return to, the St. George ferry terminal on Staten Island. The ferry terminal on Manhattan is at South Ferry and Whitehall Street subway stations, accessible from the number 1, 4, 5, 9 and R trains and the M1, M6, and M15 buses. The Staten Island Railway accepts tokens, coins, or Metrocards at the ferry terminal. Bus transfers, if needed, are available once a fare is paid. All Staten Island buses accept Metrocards. Additional information, maps, and updates for the trails are available from Staten Island Greenbelt, 200 Nevada Avenue, Staten Island, NY 10306; (718) 667-2165.

Greenbelt Circular Trail

Length 13.4 miles Blaze: blue

Contrary to its name, the Greenbelt Circular Trail (also known as the blue trail) has two termini, one at Brielle Avenue and the other on Forest Avenue on the north side of Clove Lakes Park. This trail covers scenic and mostly hilly terrain, primarily on park land.

The S48 bus goes from the ferry terminal along Forest Avenue to Clove Road. Fifty yards past the corner, the path begins on the left, just past a stream. It runs about a mile through Clove Lakes Park, in an old glacial valley that was dammed to create four lakes and several waterfalls. After an uphill stretch on paved paths, the trail enters an oak-beech climax forest until it exits the park at Victory Boulevard. Walkers who want to skip Clove Lakes Park may take bus S62 or S66 from the ferry terminal up Victory Boulevard to Slossen Avenue and walk back one block to Little Clove Road to pick up the trail. To get to the other side of the Staten Island Expressway, walkers must descend Little Clove Road to the underpass, turn right through the underpass, and then turn right again onto the road that parallels the Staten Island Expressway. At the end of the pavement, a dirt road leads into the blue-blazed footway, which climbs Todt Hill (410 feet) from the northwest. The greenish Precambrian serpentine bedrock outcrops here, as it does in the first 9 miles of the trail. The trail offers the hiker a climb through a forest of birch, beech, oak, and sweetgum; patches of catbrier denote areas that have been burned.

The trail bears west and then south, descending a steep bank into a never-dry kettle, one of a dozen or so such ponds in the area left behind by the retreating Wisconsin glacier. It then travels along the wooded property line briefly on a paved road before turning into the woods behind a former seminary, which, it is hoped, will become part of the Greenbelt's preserved lands. It passes the Kaufman Campground and the Richmond County Country Club (RCCC) Golf Course. The golf course, purchased by New York State with Environmental Quality Bond Act funds, is on a long-term lease to the RCCC. On the side of the trail, at the high point of the golf course, is a sitting area with clear views out toward Raritan Bay, the Atlantic Highlands, and Sandy Hook. Several ponds in different stages of *eutrophication* (the gradual replacement of open water with plants, then bushes, and finally trees) appear in this section, up to and including High Rock Park. Hikers here spend a half-mile on the glacial Richmond Escarpment, with views east to the Atlantic Ocean.

Beyond the golf links lie Moravian Cemetery and the private Vanderbilt family cemetery—the burial place of Commodore Cornelius Vanderbilt and family. At the cemetery office, hikers can obtain a map of the cemetery. A visit to the Moravian Cemetery requires leaving the trail and using the main entrance on Richmond Road. The trail next enters the High Rock Park Conservation Center, which is frequented by migrating birds. Many rare and unusual plants have been introduced there; it also offers short nature trails, a visitor center, and restrooms.

When the trail reaches its midpoint, it crosses Rockland Avenue, where there are two options for concluding the hike: two blocks to the left, a bus stop across Richmond Road offers either the S57 to the New Dorp station of the Staten Island Railway, or the S74 bus, which goes back to the ferry terminal.

Across Rockland Avenue, the Greenbelt Circular joins the White Trail for 0.25 mile in the woods and then continues for a mile along the tree-shaded streets of a rather quiet residential area. The street turns left at an overgrown field, and in a few yards the trail enters the field on the right and briefly joins the red trail, which soon turns left on its way to the Richmondtown Restoration (see the description under the Richmondtown Circular, below) and the S74 bus stop at St. Patrick's Place.

Next, the trail passes the brick St. Andrew's Parish House and the mill-pond, with its waterfowl, before crossing Richmond Hill Road (hikers should be cautious) to skirt the wall of the Church of St. Andrew. Chartered by Queen Anne in 1708, the church was the scene of skirmishes between American and British troops during the Revolution. The trail then immediately enters the woods and parallels Old Mill Road, a major cart route a century ago. It passes Hessian Spring, which has provided water since colonial days, and crosses Burial Hill. On weekends, the sound of radio-controlled model airplanes can be heard to the left. The trail turns back to the LaTourette golf course at the fourth tee.

The Greenbelt Circular meets the yellow trail at this point and makes a hairpin turn to the right down the golf-cart path, following along the creek and ascending parallel to Richmond Hill Road, which the trail crosses at Forest Hill Road. The trail continues jointly with the yellow trail between Forest Hill Road and the golf links (passing the bus stop at Travis Avenue, where S61 and S91 go to the ferry terminal). The Greenbelt Circular enters the woods and departs from the yellow trail to cross Heyerdahl Hill, and is briefly joint with the White Trail, until it meets the red trail, turns left, and crosses Rockland Avenue, where a break in the concrete divider was put in just for hikers.

The trail crosses a burned-out area, descends through a stand of sweetgum, crosses Manor Creek, and ascends parallel to a deep ravine known locally as Bloodroot Valley for the white-petaled flower found there. The ravine also contains maidenhair fern, sweet cicely, and other plants common farther south but rare here. The trail then follows the fence of the Seaview Hospital much of the way to the trailhead on Brielle Avenue and the S54 bus stop. (Hikers should get a transfer for the S62 bus at Victory Boulevard, which goes to the ferry terminal.)

LaTourette Trail   *Length: 7.5 miles Blaze: yellow*
The LaTourette Trail is the oldest trail on Staten Island, dating from 1930, but only 3 miles of the original route remain, the rest having been rerouted around encroaching developments. From the ferry terminal, take bus S74 or S76 to the Spring Street stop on Richmond Road. Buses back to the ferry also stop at Doctors' Hospital on Targee Street, a block away from and parallel to Rich-

mond Road, where the trail began. The trail ascends Spring Street and proceeds for nearly a half-mile along quiet residential streets. It then enters deep woods, passing Reed Basket Willow Swamp, originally a glacial pond, 200 yards to the right on an unmarked trail. The woodlands harbor many species of trees, shrubs, vines, and ferns.

Past the swamp, the trail begins to climb Todt Hill. After a short steep climb and two blocks along Merrick Avenue, it crosses Todt Hill Road and follows the pipeline right-of-way briefly. It turns left at the end of the right-of-way and goes along the backs of several houses, eventually turning left into the woods behind the former seminary. In sight of shelters of the Kaufman Campground, it goes left and then right along the Richmond Escarpment, passing Hourglass and other ponds and the Moravian Cemetery.

Entering High Rock Park Conservation Center, the trail descends to a pond that is undergoing eutrophication and is girded with a trail and boardwalk. It then turns left and, just before reaching the road up to the Visitor Center at the High Rock Park Conservation Center, turns downhill and proceeds along one of the branches of Richmond Creek. The 1994 relocation introduced a very sharp hairpin turn to the right at this point. After crossing several short wooden bridges to Manor Road, the trail continues straight opposite a pile of rock removed from the excavation of the Staten Island Expressway. Referred to locally as "Moses Mountain," the rock was placed here in the expectation that Richmond Parkway would need a complex interchange with Rockland Avenue, which, as of 1997, has not happened.

The route crosses Rockland Avenue from bus stop to bus stop, using Meisner Avenue for 100 yards before entering the woods of the LaTourette section of the Greenbelt. After 0.2 mile on the White Trail, then another 0.2 mile to the left on the red trail, the LaTourette Trail traverses a wet section and ascends to the edge of Forest Hill Road, joining the blue trail. At Travis Street, as the route leads onto the golf course, buses S61 and S91 go back to the ferry.

The combined yellow and blue trails parallel Forest Hill Road at the edge of the course and cross Richmond Hill Road together. The route proceeds along the yellow trail, which continues along Forest Hill Road and down a faint, old dirt road to a junction with the blue trail at the third tee. The route then turns right into the open woods, skirts a swampy area, and leaves the woods on a disconnected section of Forest Hill Road behind the Transit Authority's bus garage. Ahead, along Yukon Avenue and on the opposite side of Richmond Avenue, is bus S44; it is the only one that goes directly to the ferry without transfers.

FROM STATEN ISLAND: LOWER NEW YORK EAST RIVER BRIDGES: GOVERNORS ISLAND: BROOKLYN STAPLETON

Richmondtown Circular   *Length: 4.2 miles Blaze: red with white border*
Richmondtown was once called Cocklestown because of the mounds of shells
left by the original inhabitants. It became the county seat in 1730 and remained
so for two centuries until it was eclipsed by the development of St. George on
the northeast corner of Staten Island (where the ferry terminal is located), and
lapsed into obscurity. In the 1960s the Staten Island Historical Society under-
took its restoration. Visitors can see many restored and sometimes transplanted
houses reflecting three hundred years of American history.

Inaugurated in 1970, the Richmondtown Circular starts and ends at St.
Patrick's Place on Richmond Road. Bus S74 from the ferry terminal goes to the
trailhead. The trail climbs a small hill and then the bluff overlooking Fresh
Kills to the parking area of the LaTourette House and LaTourette Golf Course.
Skirting the parked cars to the right and crossing Edinboro Road, in a few yards up
the slope it enters the woods and follows the blazes around the end of the golf
course. It then descends into Buck's Hollow, a beech and oak woodland with areas
of birch and sumac, and joins the yellow trail, turning right. It then continues for
0.2 mile until meeting the White Trail; both trails go to the right. The red trail
crosses their treadway and soon turns left to parallel Rockland Avenue.

Upon reaching the blue trail, the route for this circular makes a 90-degree left turn and gradually ascends Heyerdahl Hill (238 feet), briefly sharing the footway of the White Trail. In a thicket it joins the yellow trail and descends with it to the left. After a half-mile, the Richmondtown Circular turns right across a brook and continues to the edge of the golf course, paralleling it in the woods to the right until it reaches the end of the dense growth. In an open area of large trees, the route uses the paved golf cart path to ascend toward the LaTourette House, passing it on the right and crossing the road into a parking lot. The circular then turns left and proceeds to the top of the trail's tail, which descends to the St. Patrick's Place bus stop on Richmond Road (S74 to the ferry). There are restrooms and a restaurant in the LaTourette House, which is open seasonally from about March to December. In good weather it is pleasant to rest on the terrace overlooking the links.

Great Kills Park

Located on Raritan Bay and part of Gateway National Recreation Area, Great Kills Park offers fishing, boating, sports, swimming (in summer), and walks led by park rangers. Nature trails lead out to Crooke's Point and its ocean dunes, grasslands, marshes, and a swamp oak forest.

In 1860, John J. Crooke purchased the peninsula now known as Crooke's Point and built a cabin there. The United States purchased the land in 1919 for an Army post. In 1929, New York City purchased the Point, and Great Kills Park opened to the public in 1949 as a New York City park. In 1974, the city deeded Great Kills Park, along with Miller Field and two off-shore islands, to the U.S. Department of the Interior, National Park Service, for inclusion in the Gateway National Recreation Area.

The climate at Crooke's Point is desert-like, with little fresh water. Beach grasses grow in the dunes away from the salt spray. The plants are fragile, and the Park Service limits access to the dunes to preserve the natural balance, requesting that hikers stay on marked trails. Plants in the area include goldenrod, bayberry, beach grass, prickly pear, milkweed, reed grass, and mullein. Along the seashore are clam and mussel shells, horseshoe crabs, blue-green crabs, and lady crabs. Great Kills Park is a stopping place for Monarch butterflies on their annual migration to and from Mexico. The peak time to see the butterflies is mid-September. During the day they cluster near goldenrod, Joe pyeweed, or boneset, while at night they are on the lee side of the pine trees.

For access to the park take the S78 bus from St. George ferry terminal along Hylan Boulevard, or the S79 bus from the 86th Street subway station in

Brooklyn's Bay Ridge. Get off at the Buffalo Street stop on either bus route and walk along the paved path to a large parking lot at the water's edge. Proceed across the lot and continue past the marina to a smaller parking lot at the end of the peninsula. Trails enter the forest to the right of the road. For more information, contact the National Park Service at (718) 351-6970.

Clay Pit Ponds State Park Preserve

Undeveloped ponds, bogs, sandy barrens, nature woodlands, and spring-fed streams make up the 250-acre Clay Pit Ponds State Park Preserve. The moraine deposited by the retreating Wisconsin glacier stabilized the geological deposit of cretaceous sands and clay. These deposits are still visible in the park in a wide range of colors and thicknesses. It is likely that the Native Americans used these clays for their cookware. In the nineteenth and early twentieth centuries, extensive commercial clay mining was undertaken for brickworks and architectural terra cotta. As a result, the soil was depleted and the small pockets and larger pits filled in with water to form ponds. The result is a soft underfooting of colorful sands with an occasional outcrop of smooth white kaolin.

The park has hiking and equestrian trails; however, the equestrian trails are closed to hikers.

To reach the preserve from the St. George ferry terminal, take the S74 bus to Sharrotts Road. Cross Arthur Kill Road and walk on Sharrotts Road for 0.25 mile, to Carlin Street. Turn left on Carlin to Nielson Avenue and the park's administration building. Guided and self-guided tours are available. For more information, contact the park at (718) 967-1976.

SIX

LONG ISLAND

uch development and in-
creasing traffic have choked Long Island during the second half of the twentieth century and yet, paradoxically, it is a far more exciting place to hike today
than it was in earlier times. Visitors can walk the barrier beaches of Fire Island
National Seashore, make north–south traverses on two National Recreation
Trails, and enjoy a number of individual preserves dotting what Walt Whitman
called "fish-shape Paumanok." However, as of 1996, the best is still a-building:
the passage in 1993 of the Pine Barrens Protection Act aided in the preservation of a core of 52,000 acres in the Pine Barrens of Suffolk County, second
only to New Jersey's in size, and the Pine Barrens Greenbelt Trail traverses the
core on a nearly 50-mile route. Ambitious plans call for extending the trail another
50 miles to Montauk Point. As of 1997, parts of this route are already in place.

Lacking high peaks and unbroken wilderness, Long Island yields its treasures more subtly to the observant walker. There is delight in finding deer or
fox just minutes from a suburban tract, or in walking some of the same paths
once used by Native Americans and colonial settlers. Birders, botanists, and
biologists can revel in the richness of the island's species. Photographers can
work in the same pure, unique daylight that has attracted generations of artists
to Long Island's East End. Geologists can marvel at the abundant evidence of
the last Ice Age.

The most obvious features of the island's topography are the glacial moraines deposited in the Pleistocene Epoch by the Wisconsin Glaciation. The
glacier reached as far south as the middle of Long Island, where, like a giant

conveyor belt, it dumped debris plucked from New England as it advanced southward, forming the Ronkonkoma Moraine. This band of low hills runs from Lake Success, on the Queens-Nassau border, to Montauk Point. At Montauk, the moraine juts like the prow of a ship into the prevailing ocean currents, which have gradually scoured the bluffs and carried them westward, grain by grain, to the barrier beaches along the Atlantic shore. Eventually the glacier retreated and advanced again, at a slightly different angle and not quite as far in the eastern areas, to form the Harbor Hill Moraine, which stretches from beyond Staten Island to Orient Point and crosses the older formation near Roslyn. The ice's handiwork manifests itself today in kettlehole depressions left by stranded ice blocks after they melted, erratic boulders carried great distances by the glacier, and rows of morainal hills resembling ripples in a pond. South of the moraines lies a flat outwash plain, deposits of sand and silt left by ancient glacial streams. The major features of the plains are the wetlands and beaches for which Long Island is justly famed, and which offer much pleasure for the walker.

The great bird migrations in spring and fall make the wetlands a feast for the eye. In May the spring flowers brighten morainal woodlands; in June orchids brighten the bogs; in late summer the cranberries, blueberries, and bayberries ripen; in October the deciduous forests present their colorful valedictory to warm, lazy days. Leaf-fall may linger into mid-November, and then begin perhaps the most satisfying times for hikers. Salmon-hued sunsets glow behind traceries of bare branches, the moorlands of the South Fork offer rugged solitude, and snow dusts the woods. Most winter days on Long Island are temperate enough for the average hiker, who can cap a day of reddened cheeks and sharpened appetite with a visit to any of the many restaurants convenient to parks and trails. There one can reflect on the essence of hiking Long Island: enjoying the contrast of finding exquisite, undeveloped places nestled amid populous suburbs.

Knowing when to walk on Long Island is as important as knowing where. Hikers will enjoy best the months resort operators call the "off-season." From late May to mid-September, it is wise to walk early in the morning and finish by noon, especially in the warm interior. Because of the presence of deer ticks, hikers should avoid bushwhacking and check themselves periodically.

Most of the long-distance trails on Long Island have been built and are maintained by the Long Island Greenbelt Trail Conference. Detailed trail maps are available for a modest fee. For a map or membership information, send a self-addressed, stamped envelope to the Long Island Greenbelt Trail Conference, 23 Deer Path Road, Central Islip, NY 11722; (516) 360-0753.

LONG ISLAND GREENBELT TRAIL

The Long Island Greenbelt Trail, the oldest in a system developed by the Long Island Greenbelt Trail Conference, was officially established in 1978 through the cooperative efforts of the Long Island Greenbelt Trail Conference, the New York State Office of Parks, Recreation, and Historic Preservation, Suffolk County, and the towns of Islip and Smithtown. In 1982, the U.S. Department of the Interior granted National Recreation Trail status to the Long Island Greenbelt. Stretching almost 35 miles from Heckscher State Park on Great South Bay to Sunken Meadow State Park on Long Island Sound, the path encompasses the drainages of the Connetquot and Nissequogue rivers, which virtually bisect the island. Along the way, one finds bay beaches, pine barrens, deciduous forests, and tidal marshes. Parts of the trail follow old Native American paths and farm-to-market roads. The trail shelters populations of deer, fox, raccoon, opossum, egret, kingfisher, and many other species.

Hiking the Long Island Greenbelt Trail is like walking in an hourglass. Large tracts of relatively undeveloped land are linked by narrow corridors within sight of suburbia; as of mid-1997, short sections of roadwalking remain, though most may eventually be eliminated. Though hikers seeking stretches of rugged wilderness may not find this generally flat trail to their liking, it does offer intriguing beauty and variety. Much in the fashion of Japanese gardens set in bustling urban areas, the Greenbelt's sharp contrast with its surroundings makes it memorable.

Long Island Greenbelt Trail   *Length: 31.8 miles Blaze: white*
Beginning at the east end of Parking Field 8 in Heckscher State Park, with views of Great South Bay and Fire Island, the trail follows the shoreline east and north. At 1.0 mile, it turns inland into an area noteworthy for its transition from marshland to oak and pine woods. At 1.4 miles, a blue-blazed side trail diverges right 0.3 mile to an alternative parking place at the West Marina at Timber Point County Park. At 1.8 miles, the main trail passes through a state-operated campground, open in the summer season only. Deer, fox, osprey, and pheasant inhabit Heckscher's 1,657 acres, whose picnic facilities and beaches

make it a good place to end a summer hike. The trail continues north through a wooded corridor along the Heckscher Spur of the Southern State Parkway to Montauk Highway. Here hikers can detour a few hundred yards east to the entrance of Bayard Cutting Arboretum, a 690-acre preserve notable for its conifers, spring flowers, and paths along the Connetquot River. The arboretum, closed on Mondays, contains several miles of well-marked nature walks. The Greenbelt itself continues north, crosses Union Boulevard at 3.9 miles, and enters woods east of Connetquot Avenue. The Great River station of the Long Island Rail Road, 0.1 mile north of Union on Connetquot, provides free parking and handy trail access.

The trail crosses the tracks on a highway bridge and immediately passes through a small meadow on state-owned land that was once the Lorillard Estate, complete with two race tracks and a large circular barn, and later Westbrook Farms, a dairy. No trace remains of either. West Brook, dammed into an ice pond in the late 1800s, harbors migratory waterfowl and is a popular spot for local fishing enthusiasts. The trail crosses the dam at the south end and follows the east side of the pond to a pedestrian underpass of Sunrise Highway (NY 27) at 5.2 miles.

At this point the trail enters Connetquot River State Park Preserve, one of the crown jewels of the Greenbelt system. Hikers can obtain a free annual permit for this preserve by writing to Connetquot State Park, Box 505, Oakdale, NY 11769, or calling (516) 581-1005. The preserve is closed on Mondays. Formerly the Southside Sportsmen's Club of Long Island, a haunt of the wealthy and powerful, this lightly used area of 3,473 acres is a classic pine barrens system, featuring a light canopy of pitch pine and several varieties of oak and an understory of blueberry, huckleberry, sweet fern, and other plants adapted to the desert-like, sandy outwash soil. The Connetquot River flows gently through the center of the park, affording opportunities to observe ospreys, herons, egrets, kingfishers, and a host of other species.

Near the entrance is a grist mill from the early 1700s and the large Sportsmen's Club, parts of which were built in the early 1800s; a mile north, a trout hatchery built before the turn of the century is still in operation. The entire section between Sunrise and Veterans Memorial highways offers a sense of solitude, in stark contrast with the busy suburbs beyond. Fire roads and the park's own trail network make possible a variety of loop walks that take in both sides of the river and last the better part of a day.

Crossing Veterans Memorial Highway (NY 454) at 9.1 miles, the trail follows a short fire road, reenters woods, and descends to a low-lying area known locally as Dismal Swamp. At 11.5 miles, an underpass of the Long Island Rail Road signals the boundary between Connetquot Park and Lakeland County Park to the north, where Honeysuckle Pond marks the source of the Connetquot River. A network of handicapped-accessible boardwalks allows hikers a close view of the fresh-water wetlands north of the pond.

The trail exits Lakeland Park at Johnson Avenue, turns right, and crosses the road into a wooded corridor leading to the south service road of the Long Island Expressway (I-495). It then continues east on the service road for 0.25 mile, to an underpass at Terry Road. A short distance north of the Long Island Expressway, at 11.3 miles, the trail turns west along a Long Island Lighting Company power-line right-of-way, then diverges north through bracken, fern-carpeted woodland to begin an ascent of the Ronkonkoma Terminal Moraine. The sandy soil of the flat south shore yields to coarser gravels, and north of the Long Island Motor Parkway the trail reaches an elevation of 180 feet, with a view to Long Island's North Shore. Here oaks, maples, and hickories begin to predominate.

The trail descends the moraine through Hidden Pond Park, clinging for a time to a golf course fence, entering a grove of mixed hardwoods, then re-emerging along the fence before crossing Town Line Road, which dates from 1789, when the towns of Islip and Smithtown solved a discrepancy in competing surveys by building a road along the disputed 16-foot strip. North of Town Line at 14.9 miles lies McKinley Marsh, the red maple–lined source of the Nissequogue. A visit to this area in mid-October is worthwhile for the foliage show. The trail then skirts a condominium complex, reaching NY 347 at 15.8 miles; at busy times of day, hikers can cross at a light 0.2 mile to the left, where a large farm stand is a refreshing summer stop. The route continues north through dense woods and wetlands to NY 111 at 17.6 miles. A shopping center to the north just below NY 25 provides a handy parking place.

Across NY 111, the trail swings south and west around Miller Pond, another historic ice pond, and then emerges onto Maple Avenue. Here, hikers cross and turn west for 0.7 mile of quiet roadwalking on Wildwood Lane and Juniper Avenue to Brooksite Town Park. Undeveloped land on the south side of the road marks the course of the Nissequogue River through dense wetlands.

At 19.1 miles, the trail crosses Brooksite Drive and enters Blydenburgh County Park. With its 120-acre, L-shaped Stump Pond, early-1700s gristmill, miller's house, and quiet woods, this former estate provides a quiet refuge amid one of Suffolk County's busiest areas. From this entrance, the 3.9-mile, blue-blazed Stump Pond Trail to the left reaches a primitive campsite intended for Greenbelt users at 0.8 mile, then continues around Stump Pond. The Stump Pond Trail stays within Blydenburgh Park except for 0.3 mile of quiet roadwalking on the west side before rejoining the Long Island Greenbelt Trail; using both paths, hikers can circumnavigate the pond on a loop of 5.3 miles. The side trail affords many views of the pond with its diverse waterfowl and small Atlantic white cedar swamp near the south end. The Long Island Greenbelt Trail hugs the north side of Stump Pond, ascending at 20.5 miles to a viewpoint at the 1821 Blydenburgh-Weld House, the headquarters of the Long Island Greenbelt Trail Conference. The house is open to visitors on Saturdays.

A staircase brings the trail back to the pond at the mill complex. Beyond the dam, the blue blazes of the loop trail appear straight ahead; the main trail makes a right turn to a locked gate leading to adjacent Caleb Smith State Park. Like Connetquot, this limited-access preserve is closed on Mondays and requires a free annual permit. Write to Caleb Smith State Park, Smithtown, NY 11787, or call (516) 265-1054. When using the trail, phone ahead for the combination lock numbers for two gates here and one farther north at Sweetbriar Farm.

The trail moves away from the river into rolling wooded uplands formed by the Harbor Hill Moraine. A short, steep descent leads to a lovely stream crossing where hundreds of marsh marigolds bloom in late April. The trail ascends to a second locked gate at 21.1 miles and a crossing of busy NY 25, which bisects the Caleb Smith Park. A short roadwalk east leads to a pedestrian entrance; the hike then continues through forested terrain to Willow Pond, an arm of the river, and the park headquarters building, which houses a small nature museum. Inside this former rod-and-gun club is an impressive carving of Wyandanch, a Native American *sachem* (chief).

The trail undulates through morainal woods and crosses Peacepunk Creek as it heads northeast toward Smithtown. From a pedestrian entrance on Meadow Road, the route turns right and proceeds one-half block to a railroad underpass. On the other side, at 23.4 miles, stands a statue of a bull, commemorating Richard Smith's purchase from the Native Americans of as much land as he could encircle with his bull in one day—a ride apparently based more in legend than fact. The path crosses NY 25A and enters gently rolling woodland laced with several small streams. Parts of this area may be swampy in springtime, but boardwalks make them easy to negotiate. Here the hiker will find tulip trees, an occasional remnant chestnut, skunk cabbage, and marsh marigolds. The

trail leaves the woods on an easement between two houses; just to the right at
24.5 miles is a cul-de-sac on Summerset Drive, an excellent spot for parking
and car-shuttling.

The last of the three locked gates is at the end of the cul-de-sac; beyond it
lies the Environmental Center of Smithtown-Setauket, also known as Sweetbriar
Farm, an outdoor educational facility and wildlife rehabilitation center. Beyond, the trail is forced onto Landing Avenue and Landing Meadow Road for
1.8 miles of roadwalking, much of which may be eliminated by pending easements. The trail then follows a park road through Smithtown Landing Country Club down to the banks of the Nissequogue River. From here, the trail
follows the Nissequogue north through undeveloped Arthur Kunz County Park
to Riviera Drive, which parallels the shore. It is possible to avoid virtually all
of the roadwalk on Riviera and spend considerable time exploring the water's
edge. The views here are always a pleasure, though the spring and fall during
the waterfowl migrations may be the most spectacular times.

The trail turns right onto St. Johnland Road for 100 yards, long enough to
pass pretty Harrison Pond Park, and just south of the circa-1700 Obadiah
Smith House (open on Sundays), before turning back to the shore. The blazes
lead through the grounds of Kings Park Psychiatric Center, emerging upon an
elevated view of the river at 29.4 miles. The trail then descends to the shore and
Old Dock Road Park before reaching the final hilly section in Sunken Meadow
State Park. Hikers should stay on the trail to avoid eroding the tall bluffs,

which offer views across Long Island Sound to Connecticut. At low tide, it is possible to follow the shore below the bluffs for an easier route or as part of a loop from Sunken Meadow. The popular state park has ample parking and picnic areas. Its beaches and breezy bluffs along the Sound are a refreshing place to end a summer hike, but for hiking it shines in the off-season.

The Long Island Greenbelt Trail is better suited for day hikes than for backpacking. However, ambitious walkers may wish to attempt a two-day traverse of the trail by making use of the campsite on the Stump Pond Trail in Blydenburgh Park.

City residents who want to leave their cars at home can take the Long Island Rail Road to either end of the trail at the Smithtown station, 0.5 mile east of the trail, or to the Great River station, one block west of the trail. The S40, S45, S54, and S60 buses all cross the route.

Nassau-Suffolk Greenbelt Trail   *Length: 19.5 miles Blaze: white*
Previous editions of the *New York Walk Book* contained descriptions of walks in eastern Nassau County, now a densely populated area. Surprisingly, a narrow belt of open land still exists from Cold Spring Harbor south to Massapequa, and it is possible to walk most of this route today without resorting to roads. It includes picturesque ponds, morainal ridges, open fields, and a long watershed. The Nassau-Suffolk Greenbelt Trail, completed in 1986 and granted National Recreational Trail status in 1992, preserves this corridor. While this trail does not offer anything remotely resembling a wilderness experience, its incredibly diverse flora and fauna make up for the lack of isolation. Also, its northern end provides a surprising challenge to hikers expecting an easy stroll on flat Long Island.

From south to north, the trail first passes through the Massapequa Preserve, which straddles Massapequa Creek and contains a tiny remnant of the western reaches of the Long Island pine barrens. Over 175 species of birds have been spotted in this stop along the Atlantic Flyway. From Ocean Avenue and Merrick Road in Massapequa, blazes appear along the shore of Caroon's Lake. A footbridge leads away from the lake and into mixed woods, including the remnant pines. The trail reaches Sunrise Highway (NY 27) at 1.0 mile. The route proceeds east half a block to a traffic light crossing, then under the Long Island Rail Road overpass to a view of Massapequa Reservoir. The blazes continue along the west side, then head north through low-lying red maple and oak woodlands past two smaller ponds. At 3.3 miles, the path reaches a short, east–west fire road; to the east is a convenient parking access at the end of Walker Street; to the west, the trail quickly turns north again to crossings of Linden Street and the Southern State Parkway.

The Nassau-Suffolk Greenbelt Trail follows a narrow corridor along Bethpage State Parkway. Despite the presence of the road on one side and a paved bike path on the other, this section offers pleasant walking through diverse woods. Hikers should be careful, however, to avoid the thick poison ivy on the sides of the trail! At 4.9 miles, Boundary Avenue crosses above the route. At 6.6 miles, the route goes three-quarters of the way around the Bethpage Park traffic circle, then into the woods adjacent to the park's five golf courses before emerging into a relatively open area on the west side of the park. From here, a five-block walk west on Powell Avenue leads to the Bethpage Long Island Rail Road station.

At 7.5 miles, the trail veers left into rolling woodland, where lady's slippers appear in May. From here north, take care to avoid speeding mountain bikes, which use parallel and crossing paths. In order to avoid conflicts and limit trail erosion, the Greenbelt Trail Conference has been working with cycling groups to construct parallel paths between Bethpage State Park and Stillwell Woods to the north. At 8.7 miles, the trail crosses Hay Path Road.

North of Bethpage State Park, the Nassau-Suffolk Trail follows the right-of-way of a never-built northern extension of the Bethpage Parkway. The Plainview section of the trail traverses a narrow corridor, which includes an active farm plot and large tracts of overgrown fields, recalling a time when the treeless Hempstead Plains stretched from here to Queens Village, and a more recent era when Nassau was the breadbasket of New York City.

North of Washington Avenue at 10.8 miles, expressway service road construction has forced a 600-foot roadwalk under the Long Island Expressway and then a left turn to resume the trek northward through white pines, hemlocks, and oaks on the first slopes of the Ronkonkoma Terminal Moraine. From Washington Avenue, a blue-blazed side trail, the Parkway-Tower Loop, meanders 2.4 miles through rolling Manetto Hills Park to the east before rejoining the Nassau-Suffolk Trail below Northern State Parkway. Yet another side trail, blazed with red dots, extends eastward from the Parkway-Tower Loop to form a connection with the Walt Whitman Trail, described below.

At 12.3 miles the Nassau-Suffolk Trail rises to Sunnyside Boulevard to cross the parkway. On a clear day, look westward from here for a surprising view of the Empire State Building and World Trade Center. The woods north of here reach elevations of 300 feet before descending to a crossing of Woodbury Road and a level walk to Jericho Turnpike at 13.8 miles, where a trailside parking area is a popular spot from which to start or end a walk.

North of Jericho Turnpike the trail is marked by signs of former inhabitants: an occasional rotting fencepost, a stand of spruces probably planted near a long-disappeared farmhouse, and broken china occasionally yielded up by frost-heaved soil. A quaint, one-lane underpass of the Long Island Rail Road at 15.1 miles brings hikers into Stillwell Woods, a Nassau County Preserve characterized by early successional woodland and flat, open fields at the south end and peaceful morainal hills to the north. Red-tailed hawks often catch thermals here in warm weather. Some of the paths here are badly eroded, ironically opening habitat for the uncommon trailing arbutus.

At 16.7 miles the trail crosses Stillwell Lane and descends gradually on an old railroad bed built in the 1840s, the remnant of the never-completed Hicksville and Cold Spring Branch Railroad. Large black birches, rare in this area, appear along this delightful section. A right turn leads to a footbridge and bench, a pleasant rest stop just west of NY 108.

The final 2.2 miles of the trail offer hikers the most strenuous workout available on Long Island. Elevations vary from sea level to over 200 feet in a rapid series of steep morainal hills. Large tulip poplars, white pines, white oaks, and hickories create a beautiful canopy, while thick stands of mountain laurel light up the in late May and early June. At 18.2 miles a yellow side trail ascends 0.2 mile to Uplands Farm, headquarters of the Long Island Chapter of The Nature Conservancy, which allows hikers to park in its lot. North of Lawrence Hill Road, the main trail ascends Long Island's largest clay lens on a series of switchbacks, passes through more mountain laurel, and descends to the trailhead at NY 25A. Across the road is the free-flowing spring for which the historic whaling village of Cold Spring Harbor is named. Across the harbor lies world-renowned Cold Spring Harbor Laboratories. The trail ends two blocks from the shops, restaurants, and galleries of the village.

Walt Whitman Trail   *Length: 5.5 miles Blaze: red dot on white*
Walt Whitman himself doubtlessly walked some of the paths that now bear his name. The Whitman Trail begins at the poet's birthplace in West Hills, an historic site that draws visitors from around the world, and ends at the Parkway-Tower Loop of the Nassau-Suffolk Greenbelt Trail. Thus, the Walt Whitman Trail gives hikers access to a system of nearly 40 miles of trails.

From the birthplace, on Old Walt Whitman Road just west of NY 110, the trail is reached by walking up West Hills and Reservoir roads 0.6 mile to West Hills Park. A red-dot double blaze indicates a turn to the right to enter the woods. The loop ascends a steep, slippery hill, descends more gradually to a kettlehole, then winds around to the top of Jayne's Hill at 1.5 miles, the highest spot on Long Island at 400 feet above sea level. There is a view to the southwest, followed by a descent through rolling woodlands to a picnic area and parking lot at Sweet Hollow Road. Continuing south, the trail skirts the lot and recreational fields and leads to the junction of Sweet Hollow and Gwynne roads. It heads west on Gwynne, which quickly becomes unpaved, and continues in the woods along Northern State Parkway to Round Swamp Road at 4.8 miles. A brief roadwalk south on Round Swamp leads to a right turn, which leads the trail through a very narrow corridor to the Parkway-Tower Loop and the many options afforded by the Nassau-Suffolk Greenbelt Trail.

Walt Whitman Loop   *Length: 4.2 miles Blazes: red dot or cross on white*
The Whitman Loop, one of the most popular Greenbelt Trail walks, remains within the boundaries of West Hills County Park and includes a view all the way to the Atlantic Ocean from the top of Jayne's Hill. The walk features hills covered in oaks, maples, and hickories mixed with groves of beech and dotted with mountain laurel and trailing arbutus.

The best way to experience this trail is to park at the West Hills Picnic Area lot on Sweet Hollow Road, a short distance west of NY 110. Immediately behind the lot, red-cross blazes head counterclockwise. The trail makes a twisting ascent roughly eastward, then turns north on a section also used by horses. When the foliage is down, there are several views to the east across Broad Hollow to the Half Hollow Hills. At 1.6 miles, the trail crosses Reservoir Road. At this point the red-dot blazes of the Walt Whitman Trail supplant the red crosses. Continue on the Whitman Trail as described above to complete the loop at Sweet Hollow Road.

Other West Hills County Park Trails

A number of marked and unmarked trails crisscross this relatively unspoiled area, making a variety of loops possible. For instance, at the junction of Sweet Hollow and Gwynne roads, hikers can follow white blazes south under Northern State Parkway and immediately turn right into lovely woods with varying terrain. At 0.8 mile, the trail ascends to a junction of a white-blazed trail and a trail blazed with a red-cross-on-white. The white blazes lead hikers along the south side of a loop, with several viewpoints, and ultimately to a trailhead at Mt. Misery Road. The red-cross trail yields a gentler walk, which, in another 0.6 mile, reaches a yellow-blazed trail. The latter extends 1.0 mile to Round Swamp Road, joining the Walt Whitman Trail as it heads west. The red-cross trail turns south, west, and south again to rejoin the white in another 0.3 mile.

THE PINE BARRENS

From the towns of Smithtown and Islip east to Hampton Bays, a distance of nearly 50 miles, lies the region of the pitch pine. Once encompassing over a quarter of a million acres, the pine barrens were decimated by development in the last half of the twentieth century. The 1993 Pine Barrens Preservation Act will protect a core of 50,000 acres and allow compatible growth in another 48,000. Beneath the sandy soil of the region (the glacial outwash of the Ronkonkoma Moraine) lies a huge aquifer of pure water, rising to the surface occasionally in isolated bogs. From what remains of these barrens are born the Carmans and Peconic rivers, the latter in a chain of pristine coastal-plain ponds. In the more remote sections, the gnarled pines stretch unbroken for miles. When Walt Whitman described this area in *Specimen Days:* "wide central tracts of pine and scrub-oak . . . monotonous and sterile. But many a good day or half day did I have, wandering through those solitary cross-roads, inhaling the peculiar and wild aroma." The aroma comes from the pitch pines and an understory of scrub oak, blueberry, huckleberry, bearberry, wintergreen, and sweet fern—all rich in resins that promote burning. In this fire-adapted ecosystem, much of the biomass of the native plants resides underground, allowing brush fires to sweep the area and drive out competing species. This process has never been more apparent in modern times than in the brush fires that charred almost 9,000 acres in Rocky Point and Westhampton in the summer of 1995. Yet, even those vast

Pitch Pine

blazes pale when compared to the 1838 fire that swept from Saint James to the Shinnecock Canal.

Deer, foxes, flying squirrels, grouse, and pheasants frequent the area. Rare lichens, insectivorous plants, and such endangered creatures as the tiger salamander greet the observant walker. Modern-day hikers who sample the barrens will find them neither monotonous nor sterile, and they still have a chance at finding solitude. Caution should be observed, however, as brush fires may alter trail routes or result in the creation of additional fire roads, which may confuse travelers in the region.

Pine Barrens Trail   *Length: approximately 50 miles Blaze: white*

Officially opened by the Long Island Greenbelt Trail Conference in June 1994, the Pine Barrens Trail bisects the core area of the Barrens, giving hikers the opportunity to explore the largest tracts of undeveloped land left on Long Island. The route is completely blazed from Rocky Point to the Shinnecock Canal, but likely land acquisitions and already-planned reroutes make the exact mileage subject to change. Hikers planning to traverse the three tracts managed by the DEC (Rocky Point, Navy Co-op, and Sarnoff) should obtain a free permit, good for three years, from the DEC, Building 40, State University of New York (SUNY) at Stony Brook, Stony Brook, NY 11790.

The trail begins in Rocky Point at the entrance to the DEC's Rocky Point Preserve, on the south side of NY 25A, west of Rocky Point Road. Used as a base for transatlantic broadcasting towers for decades, this 5,100-acre tract was acquired from RCA by New York State in 1978. The initial section of trail bears blue DEC markers as well as white Pine Barrens Trail blazes. The trail passes through a morainal section of hardwoods and bisects a glacial kettlehole before leveling off and swinging southeast through classic dry, upland pine barrens. A network of paths, jeep trails, and firebreaks traverses the area. Among the ground-cover plants are yellow cinquefoil, violet, hay-scented fern, and bearberry.

The trail crosses Rocky Point Road (County 21) at 3.5 miles; a yellow-blazed side trail a short distance before the road leads south 0.2 mile to a convenient parking area. On the east side of the road, hikers will notice concrete pads and blocks, anchor points for the towers of RCA's "Radio Central," scattered in the woods. At 5.2 miles, the blue DEC blazes cease; red blazes head north to complete a loop of 9.9 miles back to the entrance on NY 25A. The white blazes of the Pine Barrens Trail turn south, reaching Whiskey Road and another parking area at 5.4 miles. In the vicinity of this crossing, hikers will see evidence of the 1995 fires.

Within half a mile, the Pine Barrens Trail leaves Rocky Point Preserve and enters Suffolk County's Pine Trail Preserve, a narrow corridor once slated for an extension of County 111. Here the wooded character of the trail remains, but the sense of isolation diminishes somewhat; houses occasionally are visible through the trees, and the path crosses four local roads before reaching William Floyd Parkway at 7.7 miles and a parking area on NY 25 at 8.6 miles. The Pine Trail section continues south and east before opening up into Robert Cushman Murphy County Park, home of the headwaters of the Peconic River.

At 10.1 miles, the Pine Barrens Trail reaches an intersection with the Brookhaven Spur Trail (yellow), which extends north 5.8 miles through Robert Cushman Murphy County and Brookhaven State parks to a trailhead behind the parking lot of Shoreham-Wading River High School on NY 25A, in Shoreham. Similar in character to the RCA tract, Brookhaven Park was originally the northern section of the U.S. Army's Camp Upton, and more recently of the Brookhaven National Laboratory. Its 2,590 acres include several small ponds but generally retain the characteristics of dry upland pine barrens.

Eastward, the land dries out briefly in an area once burned by a hot crown fire. In midsummer, the rising trill of the prairie warbler accompanies hikers. The Pine Barrens Trail crosses a footbridge between Sandy and Grassy ponds at 10.6 miles. These and the others in the chain of headwaters ponds offer viewpoints and are rich in plant and animal life. Insectivorous pitcher plants, sundew, and bladderworts line the ponds; also present are cranberries, orchids, and swamp azalea. Snapping and painted turtles abound, as do a great variety of birds. Stay away from the immediate shoreline of the ponds to prevent damage to the rare and delicate plants.

The trail crosses Schultz Road at 11.9 miles and emerges from a wetland section just south of the junction of Wading River Manor and River roads at 13.3 miles. From here eastward, hikers can expect to find reroutes in the central sections of the trail as the state and county acquire more land in the area. Currently, the trail crosses the Long Island Rail Road tracks at Mill Road, then uses the woods and nearly deserted roads to reach an overpass of the Long Island Expressway at Halsey Manor Road. South of the overpass, the trail enters the Manorville Hills and heads eastward, parallel to and near the Long Island Expressway. Nearly completed acquisitions here will make possible a more desirable route through spectacular morainal hills with several viewpoints. The east end of this 9–10-mile tract is owned by the U.S. Navy and managed by the DEC. Crisscrossed with old boundary and fire roads, the Manorville Hills nevertheless offer a sense of remoteness unexpected on modern Long Island.

After crossing County 51 and reaching Speonk-Riverhead Road, the trail lies just north of Suffolk County Community College's Riverhead Campus, where parking is available. It then traverses a hilly, winding, relatively unspoiled 7.5-mile section of pine barrens under the jurisdiction of the county and, in the David Sarnoff Preserve, the DEC. Numerous viewpoints grace the trail, including one of Wildwood Lake and another all the way to Flanders Bay and the North Fork. The path is generally narrow, with dense stands of scrub oak and pitch pine everywhere. Side trails and fire roads make possible all-day explorations. At County 104 the trail makes a 1.7-mile swing north, east, and south, then returns to 104 for a mile of roadwalking to Pleasure Drive. As there is much acquisition activity in this area, a reroute to eliminate the roadwalk is likely.

From the south end of Pleasure Drive, the trail follows a well-established route through gently rolling, quiet barrens for 7.5 miles to Sears-Bellows County Park. It follows a power line briefly before swinging northeast to Maple Swamp, a delightful stop in summer and a colorful one in autumn. About 3.3 miles from Pleasure Drive, the trail reaches a yellow-blazed side path that extends north 0.25 mile to NY 24 at Birch Creek, a good parking area. The Pine Barrens Trail descends to Owl Pond, another good place to view wildlife or to cool off tired feet. The path winds eastward, first through the driest part of the section, then past a series of pine barrens ponds, hugging the south side of the largest, Sears Pond. Near Division Pond, the trail branches, with a spur heading east to the main entrance of Sears-Bellows Park; the main trail turns north, proceeding another 0.3 mile to a crossing of NY 24.

The trail continues north to the fringes of the vast Hubbard Marshes, where the pine barrens touch tidelands, then meanders eastward past Penny Pond and through the Town of Southampton's Red Creek Park. Parts of this section are double-blazed, the yellow marks representing circular (loop) trails of the Southampton Trails Preservation Society in Red Creek. The last off-road section of the Pine Barrens Trail ends at Red Creek Road. As of mid-1995, the last 2.5 miles to the Shinnecock Canal were on pleasant roads, but reroutes along Peconic Bay are possible. For information on trail reroutes and conditions, contact the Long Island Greenbelt Trail Conference, 23 Deer Path Road, Central Islip, NY 11722; (516) 360-0753.

Dwarf Pine Plains

The Dwarf Pine Plains is a globally rare area of fully grown pines standing from 3 to 6 feet tall, products of infertile soil and frequent brush fires. It plays host to the rare buck moth, which emerges from the parched earth to mate in great numbers in mid-October. A 2.4-mile representative walk is flat and easily accessible. From Sunrise Highway (NY 27), Exit 63, a wide dirt parking area is located just south of the interchange on County 31. An unmarked trail runs south, parallel to the highway, until it reaches a commercial building in 0.25 mile and turns back to the northwest. The trail runs almost to Sunrise Highway (NY 27) and crosses a wide, sandy spot colonized by *hudsonia* and pine barrens heather. On the far side, a trail heads west and then south to an east–west road paved years ago with coal slag, traces of which remain. This area was used as a practice bombing range during World War II. To the south and west, evidence of the extremely hot crown fire that blackened the Dwarf Pines in 1995 is easily visible. The route continues east back to County 31, then north along the road and the original parallel trail back to the parking area.

Quogue Wildlife Refuge

The Quogue Wildlife Refuge, operated by the DEC, is on the north side of South Old Country Road, 1.4 miles east of an intersection with Montauk Highway. A nature exhibit, including live animals, greets visitors at the entrance. Just beyond lie Old Ice Pond and North Pond, good sites for birding. The sanctuary is rarely crowded, and few visitors venture into the quiet pine woods north of the ponds. A walk to the north end and back covers about 3 miles, depending on the exact route, and takes the visitor from wetlands through pine barrens to dwarf pines. Trails are unblazed, but a map board at the entrance and several sign posts make them easy to follow. With vacant land on one side and little-used Suffolk County Airport on the other, the narrow preserve seems much larger than it actually is. For more information, contact Quogue Wildlife Refuge, Quoque, NY 11959; (516) 653-4771.

PAUMANOK PATH

The most ambitious trails project ever undertaken on Long Island is the Paumanok Path, an umbrella term for a trail linking existing and future trails that bear discrete names. The Paumanok Path is a collaborative effort of the Long Island Greenbelt Trail Conference, Southampton Trails Preservation Society, East Hampton Trails Preservation Society, and the Group for the South Fork. When it is completed, the "Appalachian Trail of Long Island" will extend from Rocky Point eastward to Montauk Point, a distance of almost 100 miles.

The Pine Barrens Trail, described above, makes up the western half of the path. East of the Shinnecock Canal, much work remains to be done in the Town of Southampton, where the path will likely follow power-line or railroad rights-of-way until it passes the heavily developed sections of Southampton. It will then swing northeast into woods above Bridgehampton and connect with the Long Pond Greenbelt, a preserved corridor running from Bridgehampton to Sag Harbor. Beyond the town line in East Hampton, the picture is more complete, as existing county and state holdings such as Hither Hills State Park, the Lee Koppelman County Preserve, and state and county parks at Montauk make a route more feasible. The goal of the cooperating groups is to have the entire trail open by the turn of the century. Some representative hikes in the Town of East Hampton are described below.

Northwest Path   *Length 6.5 miles Blaze: yellow triangles*
The woods behind the Village of East Hampton feature glacial erratics, stands of native white pine, kettleholes, and rolling terrain. This section runs from NY 114 and unpaved Edwards Hole Road northeast to 608-acre Cedar Point County Park, and ends at a landing on Northwest Harbor at Alewive Brook Road, where hikers will find a view of Cedar Point Light.

George Sid Miller Trail   *Length: 2.0 miles Blaze: white or horse's head on white*
A key link in the Paumanok Path, this short stretch includes rolling uplands with small, steep hills near salt-water Fresh Pond. From Fresh Pond Road, 0.1 mile east of Cross Highway, it extends to Springs-Amagansett Road, also known as the Old Stone Highway.

Stephen Talkhouse Path   *Length: 4.0 miles Blaze: white*
Named for a fabled ruler of the Montaukett, this section takes in the wonderful dune lands of 1,800-acre Hither Hills State Park, one of the most spectacular places on Long Island. It will, when completed, connect directly to the Koppelman Preserve to the east and to Montauk beyond. Blazes appear about 0.2 mile north of NY 27 on Napeague Harbor Road, which intersects the state highway just west of the state park.

To the east lies an amazing world of shifting sands, the so-called Walking Dunes. Here the oak forest is slowly being buried; the tops of 50-foot trees rise from the sand like young saplings. The trail runs eastward through dunes, ancient hollies, and heather. When finished, the Stephen Talkhouse Path will encompass over 8 miles, ending near the Town of East Hampton Recycling Center. In addition to the white blazes of the Paumanok Path, this section will feature orange T markings.

Napeague State Park

A vital link of the Paumanok Path will be Napeague State Park. Once the site of the Gilbert P. Smith fish-rendering factory at Promised Land, this 1,362-acre tract of several separate parcels was transferred to the Park Commission in 1978 by The Nature Conservancy. An undeveloped park, it is largely a level area, a fragile one of salt marsh, cranberry bogs, low dunes, pitch pine woods, and a few ponds (the largest of which is called the Pond of Pines, or Napeague Pond). It includes most of the peninsula west of Napeague Harbor and runs from the tip of Hicks Island to the ocean, fronting the sea with nearly 3 miles of undeveloped beach. On that side, little more than a mile of motels and other buildings separates it from Hither Hills State Park. The northern section is composed primarily of dunes, pines, and salt marsh; the central of salt marsh and cranberry bogs; the southern of extensive primary dunes and beach vegetation, including *hudsonia*, reindeer moss, and varieties of mushrooms and orchids.

The Paumanok Path will skirt the marshes by clinging to the bay beaches north of the Long Island Rail Road tracks. To the east, it will connect with the Stephen Talkhouse Path as it ascends the Ronkonkoma Moraine. For more information about Napeague State Park, contact Montauk State Park at (516) 668-2461.

Montauk Point

With the state park of 724 acres contiguous to a county park of 1,059 acres, much of the land east of Lake Montauk is protected. It is a country of lonely, rolling moors, some forested, reaching elevations of 100 feet or more. Cattle once grazed this range, but now it is renowned for its bird life. Sea ducks and many offshore species such as gannets, kittiwakes, dovekies, and razor-billed auks are found at Long Island's easternmost point. Harbor seal visit in winter, and deer and fox are abundant.

Atop the cliff of Turtle Hill stands the octagonal sandstone tower of the Montauk Point Light Station, commissioned by George Washington in 1795. At that time, the edge of the bluff lay some 300 feet to the east; the unrelenting

*Montauk Light
and the two forms
of cliff*

sea has eroded the cliff to within a few feet of the Light.

Head west on foot from the lighthouse. Two miles along the shore of Block Island Sound lies the beautiful, land-locked Oyster Pond, its east bank lined with a thick holly forest. To the northwest stands Shagwong Point, with a view of the entire Montauk headland. From here a dirt road leads 0.4 mile southwest to Big Reed Pond, the easternmost body of fresh water on Long Island, designated a National Natural Landmark.

ATLANTIC BARRIER BEACHES

The barrier islands along the South Shore of Long Island are justly famed as some of the finest bathing beaches in the world. Consequently, they are often filled to overflowing on hot summer days. In the off-season, however, they become excellent territory for walks of almost unlimited length and surpassing beauty. Any walk along the ocean in the nearly 100-mile stretch from Atlantic Beach to Montauk will be a rewarding experience; the walks noted below may offer the best combinations of accessibility and attractiveness. The beaches are administered by a variety of federal, state, county or town governmental entities.

Until 1931, Great South Beach stretched from Fire Island Inlet eastward for more than 55 miles without a break to Southampton. A storm in March of that year breached the dunes opposite Center Moriches and carved Moriches Inlet, through which the ocean now pours swiftly and dangerously. Similarly, the great hurricane of 1938 opened the inlet to Shinnecock Bay.

When Congress passed the National Seashore legislation in 1964, the boundaries of the national seashore ran from the community of Kismet for 26 miles to Moriches Inlet. The Fire Island Lighthouse Station was added later. Seventeen beach communities occupy parts of the island, but several magnificent sections of untouched beach remain.

Access by car is limited to Robert Moses State Park on the western end and Smith Point County Park on the eastern end. Both are toll facilities during the summer season. Ferries operate from May to November from Bay Shore, Sayville (to Sailors Haven Visitor Center), and Patchogue (to Watch Hill Visitor Center). Everywhere along the barrier islands, the primary dunes offer the only coastal protection against violent storms. They have taken years to form, are extremely fragile, and can be destroyed by careless tramping—so hikers should not climb the dunes or cross them except at designated spots.

Short Beach

At the west end of 2,400-acre Jones Beach State Park, there is a winter walk 0.5 mile from the West End parking field to the jetty at Short Beach. A 2-mile boardwalk parallels the waterfront. Snowy owls, short-eared owls, and snow buntings frequent the dunes, and large flocks of brant geese come to the inlet. To reach the park, take Meadowbrook State Parkway to Jones Beach State

The South Shore of Long Island : dunes, beech grass · arbor · dories · drift-wood fire
wave markings · beech pools · wreck · coal barges · sunshine.

Park, and drive to the West End parking field. For more information, contact Jones Beach State Park, Wantagh, NY 11793; (516) 785-1600.

John F. Kennedy Memorial Bird Sanctuary

In 1959 this former hunting preserve became the first area in the state to be under the protection of the Long Island Wetlands Act. Managed jointly by the Town of Oyster Bay and the New York State Department of Environmental Conservation, its 500 acres contain several miles of trails through one of the finest sanctuaries on the Atlantic coast. Walkers can see a large, brackish pond, maritime forest, salt marsh, and dunes. The Sanctuary is accessible from Ocean State Parkway. Parking is available in the small field just east of the wooden lookout tower. A free permit can be obtained from the Town of Oyster Bay Department of Parks and Recreation, 800 South Oyster Bay Road, Hicksville, NY 11801; (516) 433-8020.

Cedar Beach

Operated by the Town of Babylon, this 1.2-mile beach is open to all in the off-season, and affords beach-walking toward Gilgo Beach or Captree State Park. It is accessible from the eastern end of the Ocean State Parkway.

Robert Moses State Park

Serving as the western gateway to Fire Island, this park offers visual proof of the power of the littoral drift—the inexorable scouring of the barrier beaches by ocean currents that carry the sand westward. To the east of Robert Moses Causeway lies the Fire Island Lighthouse Station, part of the Fire Island National Seashore. The lighthouse was built in 1858 on what was then the tip of the island; since that time, the island has grown almost 5 miles westward to Democrat Point. The lighthouse is a good destination for an out-and-back walk of 2.5 miles from Field 2. Access to it is via the Robert Moses Causeway, which has a toll during the summer and on weekends and holidays during the off-season. For more information, contact Robert Moses State Park at (516) 669-0470.

Fire Island Lighthouse

Accessible from Robert Moses State Park Field 5, this 200-acre area contains a freshwater pond, pine forests, and diverse plant communities. The 167-foot high lighthouse is open for tours on a limited basis. A short distance west on the boardwalk nature trail, the crumbling base of the original 1825 lighthouse is visible. For more information or to sign up for a tower tour, call (516) 661-4876.

Sailors Haven Visitors Center
A ferry from Sayville provides access to Sailors Haven Visitor Center. A boardwalk loop trail leads west to Sunken Forest, so called because of its location down behind the dunes. Holly, sassafras, tupelo, and shadbush envelop the walker in a cool, dark environment. For more information contact Fire Island National Seashore, 120 Laurel Street, Patchogue, NY 11772; (516) 289-4810.

Watch Hill to Smith Point
Accessible via the ferry from Patchogue, Watch Hill features a boardwalk nature trail looping through several ecosystems, including an expansive salt marsh and a small maritime forest on secondary dunes.

In 1980, the 7 miles from Watch Hill to Smith Point earned designation as a wilderness area, the only federal one in New York State. It is accessible either by taking the ferry from Patchogue to Watch Hill and walking east, or by driving to Smith Point and walking west. It attains a primitive, wild beauty that will leave an indelible impression on any visitor. Here lie thick groves of pitch pine, with deer, fox, and rabbit everywhere, though hikers are more likely to hear the animals in the dense undergrowth than to see them. The shifting dunes rise hauntingly to an elevation of 40 feet or more. In the swale behind the primary dunes, the abundant plant life includes salt spray rose, bayberry, beach plum, and poison ivy.

The area, including the wilderness area are administered by the Fire Island National Seashore. For more information, contact the park at (516) 289-4810.

Smith Point to Moriches Inlet
West of the Smith Point Ranger Station is a mile-long handicapped-accessible boardwalk trail. This self-guided route is a good introduction to Fire Island's cross section of ecosystems. Smith Point features an expanse of swale or desertlike area behind the primary dunes.

Near Old Inlet, about 2 miles west of Smith Point, the first transatlantic steamship, *S. S. Savannah*, sank on November 5, 1821. The Life Saving Service built Halfway Huts in this area, which served as shelters for shipwreck victims, and contained oil lamps and stores of dried beans. For modern hikers, the only overnight refuge is a limited primitive camping area near Old Inlet. For more information, contact the Fire Island National Seashore at (516) 289-4810.

Smith Point County Park

Heading east from the Smith Point Ranger Station, walkers can trek 4.2 miles along lonely, undeveloped beaches to the raging maw of Moriches Inlet. Harbor seal frequent the area in winter. In cold weather, a brisk walk east along any of these beaches can turn into a chilling experience when it comes time to turn back to the west in the face of the prevailing winds, so dress accordingly.

Elizabeth Morton National Wildlife Refuge

This long sandspit on Jessup Neck, west of Sag Harbor on Peconic Bay, remains relatively undiscovered despite its beauty and variety. Due east from the parking area off Noyack Road, hidden in the woods, is a wood duck pond. The trail itself goes north through cedar woods, then drops to a pristine beach facing westward. Side trails on the east side lead through the undergrowth to rich marshlands complete with short boardwalks over some of the wetter areas. Farther north lies a forested bluff, which eventually drops down to a sand bar jutting into the currents of Noyack and Little Peconic bays. There is no main trail. Once past the initial short section of woods, visitors can opt for walking either beach or bluff, or take one way out and the other back. This peninsula is very narrow, and the route becomes apparent upon reaching the beach. Total distance from the parking area to the tip is 2.0 miles; side trips can—and should—stretch a visit into an all-day affair. For more information, contact the refuge at (516) 725-2270.

OTHER PARKS AND PRESERVES

Long Island is rich in individual parklands varying greatly in size and character, ranging from converted private estates or narrow strip parks along streams to larger wooded preserves. Some are crowded, some are quiet; all offer worthwhile day walks.

Belmont Lake State Park

Easily accessible from Southern State Parkway, Exit 38, this 459-acre state park has paths on both sides of the lake, extending north to a feeder brook. In the other direction, a pedestrian underpass of the parkway leads to a 2.5-mile trail paralleling the narrow Carlls River, a good example of a Long Island stream system. For more information, contact Belmont Lake State Park at (516) 667-5055.

Caumsett State Park

The former Marshall Field estate at Lloyd Neck in the Town of Huntington is located on a beautiful peninsula. It contains 1,500 acres of woodland, meadows, rocky shoreline, salt marsh, and former farm and garden areas. A number of permanent buildings on the property are used for environmental education programs and other activities. There are paved and unpaved roads as well as some narrow foot trails. A freshwater pond 1.5 miles from the gatehouse can be viewed from a hill in the northeastern section of the park, with the expanse of Long Island Sound in the background. The northwestern section projects 2 miles into a marshy, sandy, open site from which a boardwalk directs the visitor to the tip, known as Lloyd Point.

From Main Street in Huntington, West Neck Road (four blocks west of NY 110) heads north to the park entrance. There is an entrance fee for cars from Memorial Day through Labor Day. Maps are available at the gate. For more information, contact Caumsett State Park at (516) 423-1770.

Charles T. Church Nature Sanctuary

A private preserve operated by North Shore Wildlife Sanctuary, this lovely parcel in Mill Neck is a combination of wetlands and a forest of oak, maple, and beech. A parking lot, complete with map and information board, is located on Frost Mill Road, just south of the Mill Neck Long Island Rail Road station. Hikers can wander around in the sanctuary and the woods to the south of Shu Swamp Road. The North Shore Wildlife Sanctuary also maintains two other close by mature upland forests— Coffin Woods and Pennoyer Woods. For more information, contact North Shore Wildlife Sanctuary, P.O. Box 214, Mill Neck, NY 11765.

Gardiner County Park

Originally owned by the Gardiner family, Suffolk County's first non-Native American landowners, and later part of Sagtikos Manor estate, it contains a transition zone between inland woods and bayside salt marshes within its 231 acres. The entrance is on Montauk Highway (NY 27A) in West Bay Shore, a half-mile east of Robert Moses Causeway. For more information, contact Gardiner County Park at (516) 854-0935.

Garvies Point Preserve

This preserve consists of 62 acres of glacial moraine covered by forests, thickets, and meadows and about 5 miles of trails. Small animals and over 140

species of birds have been spotted here. High cliffs along the shore of Hempstead Harbor exhibit such erosional features as alluvial fans, talus slopes, and slumping caused by ancient clays oozing from the beach. Signs from the Glen Cove Bypass direct visitors to the preserve. For more information, contact Garvies Point Preserve, Barry Drive, Glen Cove, NY 11542; (516) 671-0300.

Muttontown Preserve

With a Visitor Center and 10 miles of trails, this 50-acre tract of uplands is one of the more beautiful open areas left in populous Nassau County. The entrance is at the south end of Muttontown Lane, one block west of the intersection of NY 106 and NY 25A. For more information, contact Muttontown Preserve, Muttontown Lane, East Norwich, NY 11732; (516) 922-3123.

Orient Beach Parks

Almost at the tip of the North Fork lies 363-acre Orient Beach State Park. A 4.6-mile loop walk begins at the parking lot and heads west to Long Beach Point and back. At all times of the year, the Orient area is an outstanding birding area and a favorite place for beachcombers. In spring, the prickly-pear

cactus and beach plum bloom; in summer, there are roseate terns and por-
poises; in fall tremendous numbers of migrating monarch butterflies hang from
the cedars; in winter, there are sea birds and snowy owls.

For a shorter but equally enjoyable walk, hikers can park near the end of
NY 25 in the small lot for Orient Point County Park. Additional parking is
available at the New London ferry ramp across the road. Unmarked but clear
trails lead north through open meadows to Long Island Sound, and then head
east along the beach to the Point, which offers a view of Plum Island and Plum
Gut Light. The round trip is approximately 1.7 miles.

For more information, contact Orient Beach State Park at (516) 323-2440.

Southhaven County Park

The first and one of the largest parks opened by Suffolk County, Southhaven
protects the Carmans River. Hikers wandering north from the picnic areas and
other developed facilities will find rewarding, wild country along a major Long
Island stream. It is possible to walk for miles in the area between Sunrise Highway (NY 27) and the Long Island Expressway (I-495) far to the north. The
park entrance is on the north side of Sunrise Highway, between the Yaphank
Avenue and William Floyd Parkway exits. Farther south along the east bank of
the Carmans River, west of William Floyd Parkway, is the Wertheim National
Wildlife Refuge, a large area of pines and marshland at the end of Great South
Bay. To the east in Mastic Beach is the William Floyd Homestead, with still
more woodland and marsh, as well as peat bogs, fronting Moriches Bay. For
more information, contact Southhaven County Park at (516) 854-1414.

Tackapausha Preserve

Operated by Nassau County, this extremely narrow preserve in Seaford protects
the Seaford Creek watershed. Though walkers are rarely out of sight of neighboring houses, the preserve is worthwhile for its wet-woods walks and spring wildflowers. A nature museum is at the south end of the property, on Washington
Avenue at Merrick Road. For more information, contact Tackapausha Preserve,
Washington Avenue, Seaford, NY 11783; (516) 785-2802.

Wildwood State Park

For walkers, this park offers access to the North Shore beaches, with spectacular high bluffs overlooking Long Island Sound. These beaches are much differ-

ent in character from those along the Atlantic. Since wave action is much less intense, the beaches are not as well developed. Pebbles and boulders from many of the rock formations—sedimentary, igneous, and metamorphic—as far north as the Berkshires of Massachusetts and the Green Mountains of Vermont were carried hundreds of miles in the continental glacier and deposited on this shore. From Wildwood to Orient Point, the beach is the resting place of large boulders from the gneisses, granites, and schists of eastern Connecticut and central Massachusetts. For more information, contact Wildwood State Park at (516) 929-4314.

SEVEN

WESTCHESTER COUNTY

ewly established parkways in Westchester were praised in the 1934 edition of the *Walk Book* for setting "a new standard in highway construction" and providing "adequate highways in beautiful surroundings with paths for the walker, as well as seats, gardens, and occasional camping spots with fireplaces." This concept of leisurely auto routes wedded to idyllic walkways has long since succumbed to the pace of modern traffic and the sprawl of residential and corporate complexes. Yet the hiker will find that today's wider and straighter parkways still lead to as extensive a collection of parks and preserves as can be found anywhere this close to New York City. From smaller parks in the urbanized southern part of the county to more rugged ridges in the less populous highlands to the north, there remain quiet, open spaces rich in geological and historical interest.

The hiker has many opportunities to explore the varied history of the region. The Croton Aqueduct, for example, passes near estates that mark major periods of the county's history. The restored manor houses of Frederick Philipse, who traded with the Native Americans at Tarrytown, and the Van Cortlandts of Croton-on-Hudson recall the age of the Dutch patroons. Sunnyside, Washington Irving's cozy retreat at Irvington, overlooks the Hudson, as does Jay Gould's Lyndhurst. A large portion of the John D. Rockefeller estate just north of Tarrytown has been opened to the public as a park preserve.

Westchester County has an extensive park system that includes many of the hiking areas described in this chapter as well as numerous smaller parks. Information on Westchester County parks, preserves, and historical sites may be obtained by calling (914) 242-PARK. County residents may purchase a park pass, which is

Typical Westchester: rolling country: Nyack & Hook Mountain

required for admission to a few parks (as noted in the descriptions below) and which provides discounts on some user and parking fees. Other hiking opportunities are found in New York State parks and in preserves owned by conservation and educational institutions.

BLUE MOUNTAIN RESERVATION

The 1,538-acre Blue Mountain Reservation south of Peekskill includes some 15 miles of trails. A half-day circuit over the two principal summits, Blue Mountain and Spitzenberg, offers panoramas of the Tappan Zee and mountains to the north and west. Mountain biking is a popular activity at the reservation, and bicycles are permitted on the trails. An unusual feature of the reservation is the Blue Mountain Trail Lodge, which provides dormitory accommodations and a kitchen and dining area for groups of up to thirty people. Reservations must be made in advance by calling (914) 593-2634.

The Welcher Avenue exit from US 9 in Peekskill leads east about half a mile directly to the reservation entrance. During the summer, a parking fee is collected from day visitors. A long parking lot is located beyond the entrance booth, to the left and past the lodge. A detailed trail map is available at the park.

A hike of about 5 miles going over both of the summits in the reservation can be done by following sections of several trails. An up-to-date trail map is essential, since the dense trail network here can be confusing and the blaze colors are being changed in 1997. From the parking lot, the route begins along the access road and, once opposite the lodge, proceeds on a trail heading east along a stream. At the second trail junction, the route turns left to cross the stream on a wide wooden bridge. The trail to the right continues up the valley and after several trail junctions turns sharply right (south) to climb the northern slopes of Blue Mountain. Near the top, a trail to the left goes to a viewpoint. Just before this trail junction, a faint unmarked trail on the right leads to the flat wooded summit (665 feet). From the viewpoint, the hike can be continued to the south by doubling back to the junction.

At Montrose Station Road, the Briarcliff-Peekskill Trailway (green) merges in from the right. Signs warn of the presence of lead in the area because of the Sportsmen's Center located nearby. Continuing south toward Mt. Spitzenberg, the route stays with the green-blazed trail. Before it begins to descend in earnest, a sign marks a right turn onto an unblazed but clearly visible path to the rocky summit of Mt. Spitzenberg. This is the best viewpoint in the reservation, with the Hudson River clearly visible to the southwest and the western skyline defined by the hills of Harriman Park.

From the viewpoint, hikers can double back to the previous trail junction and turn left (west) to return along the trail followed earlier. A right turn on another trail leads north and crosses Montrose Station Road. The trail descends to a pond, skirts the southern shore, crosses the outlet, and is joined by a narrow trail coming from the northern shore. The trail rises to join the green trail and descends north toward the parking lot, where the hike ends.

BRIARCLIFF-PEEKSKILL TRAILWAY

Obtained in the 1920s for a proposed parkway extending what is now NY 9A from Briarcliff to Peekskill, this land became a trailway in the 1970s and is blazed with leaf-green diamonds. The trail is owned and maintained by the Westchester County Department of Parks, Recreation and Conservation. Most trailheads are marked with brown Westchester County Park signs. Parking is minimal except at Teatown Lake Reservation, Croton Gorge, and Blue Mountain Reservation parks, through which the trail runs. The trail offers generally level, easy walking, although occasional blowdowns and wet areas may be encountered. Attractions include the massive Croton Dam, and Hudson River views in Blue Mountain Reservation, as the trail weaves its 13-mile path through Westchester County. Trail maps are available from the Westchester County Parks Department; call (914) 242-PARK.

The southern trailhead is on Ryder Road in Ossining just east of the NY 9A overpass. The trail crosses Grace Lane, NY 134, and then Spring Valley Road at 2.9 miles. It continues along the west side of Teatown Lake, crosses Blinn Road at 5.1 miles, and follows Croton Dam Road for half a mile. Just before reaching the dam, the blazed trail turns left onto a gravel road, from which it soon turns right. The northern trailhead of the Old Croton Aqueduct Trail is about 100 yards farther along the gravel road. The Briarcliff-Peekskill Trailway descends to cross through Croton Gorge Park, crosses the Croton River below the dam, and ascends to regain Croton Dam Road on the other side of the dam.

The trail is less used and harder to follow north of Croton Gorge Park. It goes north to the intersection of Mount Airy Road East and NY 129 at 6.6 miles. Continuing along, with several short sections on paved roads, the trail crosses Furnace Dock Road at 8.7 miles. Parts of the trail between this point and Watch Hill Road at 10.0 miles were often under water, but the Parks Department built a wooden walkway to alleviate the problem. The northern trailhead of the Briarcliff-Peekskill Trailway is at Lounsbury Pond in the Blue Mountain Reservation at 12.9 miles.

BRONX RIVER RESERVATION

A bicycle and walking trail follows the Bronx River and the Bronx River Parkway in two sections from Bronxville to Scarsdale and from Hartsdale to the Kensico Dam in Valhalla. It is paved asphalt with a few short sections of packed dirt. It is accessible from several stations along the Metro-North Harlem Line. Parking is available at the Kensico Dam and, for a fee, at railroad stations. Trail maps are available from the Westchester County Department of Parks, Recreation and Conservation; call (914) 242-PARK.

Hikers should be aware that this is a popular bicycle route. On summer

Sundays from 10 A.M. to 2 P.M., the Bronx River Parkway from Scarsdale Road to the County Center is closed to automobile traffic and opened to bicycles, diverting some bicycle traffic off of the trail.

The southern section of the trail begins at the intersection of Palmer Avenue and Paxton Avenue just west of the Bronxville railroad station. The trail goes north, passing the Crestwood railroad station at 2.1 miles and continuing to Harney Road in Scarsdale at 3.6 miles. Here the southern section ends. The northern section is reached by going east on Harney Road and north on Scarsdale Avenue for 0.7 mile, then east on Crane Road and north on Fox Meadow Road for 2 miles.

The northern section starts behind Hitchcock Presbyterian Church on Greenacres Avenue just west of Walworth Avenue in Hartsdale. After reaching the White Plains railroad station at 2.0 miles, the trail follows Bronx Street north for several blocks. The trail reaches the North White Plains railroad station at 3.3 miles, where it crosses the river on the Fisher Lane bridge at the north end of the parking lot. The trail continues north and ends at the Kensico Dam at 4.7 miles.

BUTLER MEMORIAL SANCTUARY

The Arthur W. Butler Memorial Sanctuary is probably better known by birders than hikers, though a number of trails crisscross its forested lands. Mrs. Arthur W. Butler donated 225 acres of the 356-acre tract to The Nature Conservancy in 1954, in memory of her husband.

Open year-round, the sanctuary is located southeast of Mount Kisco and can be reached from NY 172. About 0.3 mile west of the interchange with I-684, Chestnut Ridge Road goes south from NY 172. In 1.2 miles, a side road to the right leads to a bridge that crosses over I-684. This unnamed side road quickly dead-ends; cars can be parked along the west side of the road. From the south, visitors can reach the sanctuary by taking Exit 4 of I-684 and following the above directions. For more information, contact The Nature Conservancy, 41 South Moger Ave., Mt. Kisco, NY 10549; (914) 244-3271.

A short distance along the main trail (red) from the parking area is a kiosk with a large wooden map. It explains the types of forest that make up the sanctuary. Trail maps are sometimes available near a register box. The hike described below is about 3.5 miles and covers most of the sanctuary. It is easy walking, with elevations varying from about 500 to 750 feet.

Starting from the kiosk, the route follows the red-blazed trail to the west. This trail soon intersects a blue-blazed trail. From here, hikers may either stay on the red trail ahead or follow the blue trail to the right. Together these trails make a figure-8 toward the north. The red trail climbs more gently as it contours two hills, while the blue trail immediately climbs the first of the two hills and stays close to the steep eastern slopes. A brief descent brings the blue trail to a valley where it intersects the red trail. After a white-blazed trail begins on the left, the blue trail climbs the second hill. Soon after passing between rock cliffs, the blue trail terminates where it meets the red trail to close the figure-8.

Hikers who want to explore the north end of the sanctuary can turn left and continue on the red trail. After passing a white-blazed trail, the route begins a gentle descent to the west into a valley that feeds into Howlands Lake (which is not accessible through the sanctuary) to the north. At the valley floor, a yellow-blazed trail begins on the left just before the red trail ends at the sanctuary boundary.

The north-end route turns left (south) to follow the yellow trail, which passes under rock cliffs, after which an alternate trail blazed orange branches to the right. The two trails rejoin in 0.2 mile. The trail then climbs more steeply and descends into a narrow valley, where to the left, a white-blazed trail goes by a tussock sedge meadow, a wetlands and rejoins the yellow trail.

The yellow trail descends steeply to the floor of a secluded valley and climbs the other side through a few short switchbacks. It intersects the blue trail, which can be followed left (north) to rejoin the red trail. More interesting, however, is to continue on the yellow trail as it climbs one of the higher hills of the sanctuary to a viewpoint called the Robert J. Hammerschlag Hawk Watch. At the height of land, for the benefit of birders, wooden bleachers have been built facing east. From the only unobstructed viewpoint in the sanctuary, birders can observe, in autumn, northern harriers, ospreys, turkey vultures, bald and golden eagles, various kinds of hawks, American kestrels, merlins, and peregrine falcons. Notwithstanding the annoying rumble of I-684, the bleachers are a place to sit and relax.

From Hawk Watch, the most direct route back to the kiosk is along an orange-blazed trail that follows the cliff edge north along a protective wire fence. The dead-end road that gives access to the sanctuary is soon visible ahead.

CRANBERRY LAKE PRESERVE

Cranberry Lake Preserve, bordered by the Kensico watershed and private property, lies across NY 22 from Kensico Dam, which was constructed from stone quarried east of the lake. The principal geographic feature of the 135-acre preserve is a 10-acre lake surrounded by bogs and wetlands. The land also rises to rocky outcroppings and wooded hillsides, furnishing a woodland trail, a lake trail, and a self-guided nature trail. There are 7 miles of trails in all. A trail map is available at the nature center, which also has rest rooms and exhibits. Picnicking is allowed near the nature center only. The nature center is open Wednesday through Sunday; for more information call (914) 428-1005.

The park is reached by following NY 22 north past Kensico Dam, turning right on Old Orchard Street, and then turning right into the preserve. Visitors wishing to travel by train should take the Metro-North Harlem Line to Valhalla, walk across Kensico Dam or across the plaza area to NY 22, and go 0.8 mile north to the preserve; alternatively, visitors can take the train to North White Plains, follow the bicycle path through the Bronx River Reservation to the dam, and continue to the preserve.

KITCHAWAN PRESERVE

Kitchawan Preserve is a Westchester County park that surrounds the main building and 12 acres of the research station of the Brooklyn Botanic Garden, the former owner. The park consists of approximately 200 acres of semi-wild land and 6 miles of trails. Access to the park is from NY 134, approximately one mile west of NY 100 or one mile east of the Taconic State Parkway. There is parking for five to ten cars and no entrance fee. No services are provided. Hiking in this area is generally easy though sometimes muddy, and trails may be poorly blazed and difficult to follow.

The terrain includes a mature hemlock forest, fields and meadows where the old demonstration gardens used to be, and a hardwood forest that borders on the North County Trailway and the Croton Reservoir. The Little Brook Nature Trail and its connecting Red Oak Trail are easy for families with younger children. These are reached by turning left down a small dirt road from the parking area.

EUGENE AND AGNES MEYER NATURE PRESERVE

From the rocky west shore of Byram Lake, 3 miles north of Armonk, rise the steep, wooded hills of the Eugene and Agnes Meyer Nature Preserve. Once the home of Eugene Meyer, editor and publisher of *The Washington Post* in the 1940s and 1950s, this woodland and open-fields tract of 247 acres has been owned and managed by The Nature Conservancy since 1973.

There are two trailheads for the preserve. The Sarles Street entrance is reached by taking Exit 4 off I-684 and going west on NY 172 toward Mt. Kisco. A left (south) turn onto Sarles Street leads in 2.7 miles to its intersection with Bretton Ridge Road; the trailhead, with parking for two cars, is directly across from this intersection. In addition to a woodland trail, unmarked but mowed trails wind just over a mile through open fields and through trees along stone walls. A walk on a hot, muggy July day is a feast of sight and sound. Among the grasses and wildflowers, move butterflies, dragonflies, and grasshoppers, their constant humming enhanced with the birds' songs.

To reach the Oregon Road entrance, take Exit 3 off I-684, follow NY 22 north for half a mile, turn left onto Cox Avenue for 0.2 mile, then fork right onto Byram Lake Road. Half a mile from the intersection, turn left on Oregon

Road and go 0.2 mile to the preserve. There is room here for one or two cars. A short distance from the road is a shelter containing trail maps. Hikers have a choice here of three parallel trails tending north through the preserve: the Cliff Trail (blue) that overlooks Byram Lake, the Ridge Trail (red), and the Ravine Trail (orange). All three emerge from the woods in approximately 1.2 miles at the private drive past Seven Springs Center, formerly the Meyer home.

For more information, contact The Nature Conservancy, 41 South Moger Ave., Mt. Kisco, NY 10549; (914) 244-3271.

MIANUS RIVER GORGE

Maintained since 1953 as a nature preserve by the Mianus Gorge Preserve, the 621-acre Mianus River Gorge Wildlife Refuge and Botanical Preserve extends approximately 2.5 miles along the gorge of the Mianus River in the Westchester County towns of Bedford, North Castle, and Pound Ridge. This preserve was the first one established by The Nature Conservancy, which manages preserves throughout the United States and in other parts of the world. A foot trail with several side loops runs south along the west bank of the gorge from the visitors' entrance to the upper end of a reservoir.

After about a mile, the hiker reaches the heart of the preserve, the Hemlock Cathedral—20 acres of hillside covered with virgin eastern hemlocks, some of which are giants dating back to the 1680s. The V-shaped gorge is rugged and spectacular, dropping sharply 200 feet below the trail. Along the path, the roar of water can be heard. Much of the path is carpeted by needles from the giant hemlocks. Mineral outcrops occur, and over five hundred species of flora and fauna have been catalogued. A round trip on the main trail requires two hours, but additional time can and should be devoted to the exploration of the various side trails, such as the one that leads to an abandoned mica and quartz mine. Detailed trail maps are available at the entrance.

From Exit 34 of the Merritt Parkway, go north 7.7 miles on Long Ridge Road (Conn. 104) to Millers Mill Road. Turn left here for 0.1 mile over the bridge to Mianus River Road and then left again for 0.7 mile to the entrance. From the Bedford area, take Pound Ridge Road and Stamford Road (Long Ridge Road) to Millers Mill Road on the right. Cross the river and turn down Mianus River Road 0.1 mile to the entrance.

The preserve has limited hours and is closed in the winter. The rules prohibiting picnicking, dogs, and mountain bikes are strictly enforced. For more information, contact the preserve at (914) 234-3455.

NORTH COUNTY TRAILWAY

The Putnam Division of the New York Central Railroad ran for 56 miles from the Bronx to Brewster between 1881 and 1958, when it ceased passenger operations. It carried occasional freight until 1981. During the 1990s, the Putnam Division railbed from Eastview to Baldwin Place is being paved to become a bicycle and walking path called the North County Trailway. Several sections have been completed, while in other areas the railbed has been cleared, but bridges remain in dangerous condition. Trail maps are available from the Westchester County Department of Parks, Recreation and Conservation at (914) 242-PARK. The Trailway is primarily a bicycle route, so hikers should be alert for passing cyclists.

In Tarrytown (in what was Tarrytown Heights), from the intersection of Neperan Road and Sunnyside Avenue, the trail runs behind the Tarrytown Reservoir reaching the Eastview exit of the Saw Mill River Parkway at 1.1 miles. Parking is available at both ends of this segment. Crossing Old Saw Mill River Road, the path continues north on a section of the railroad constructed in the 1930s to bypass the estate of John D. Rockefeller. At 4.0 miles the trail is interrupted for 0.6 mile, but begins again at NY 117 where there is parking and a tunnel for the trailway under NY 117. For the missing segment, use the narrow road shoulder of NY 9A carefully.

The trail continues north to the Briarcliff Manor station (now a public library) at 6.5 miles. The Tudor-revival style station was built in about 1915 by home furnishings magnate Walter Law. The old station was loaded on a railroad car and deposited in Millwood to be used as its station, where it still stands. The trail follows NY 100 (on the road shoulder for 1.4 miles), passes the Millwood station at 9.9 miles, where there is parking, and crosses NY 120. The trail continues to the site of the Kitchawan preserve 0.2 mile north of NY 134 and just west of NY 100, where the paved trail ends at 12.0 miles. There is parking on the road shoulder at the NY 134 crossing.

As of 1997, the 2.8-mile trail segment from the end of the pavement to Yorktown Heights has not been reconstructed. The railbed can be followed through the Kitchawan Preserve to the bridge over the Croton Reservoir. North of the reservoir, the railbed can be located on Birdsall Drive 0.1 mile north of NY 118, from which point it roughly parallels NY 118. It crosses Underhill Avenue at the south side of Railroad Park in Yorktown Heights, where parking is available. The paved trail begins again just south of the firehouse at the intersection of Hanover and Commerce streets. It continues north, crossing US 202 near Quaker Church Road after 1.0 mile and Granite Springs Road at 2.6 miles. After crossing Mahopac Avenue, the trail ends at 5.4 miles at the Westchester-Putnam county line on NY 118 just east of US 6 in Baldwin Place.

OLD CROTON AQUEDUCT

From 1842 to 1955 the Old Croton Aqueduct, a National Historic Landmark, supplied New York City with water. Following the damming of the Croton River, water flowed through the aqueduct to above-ground reservoirs in Central Park and on the present site of the New York Public Library on Fifth Avenue. The northernmost section was reopened in 1988 to furnish water to the Village of Ossining. Although interrupted in places by major highways and urban congestion, the 26-mile surface of the aqueduct provides level, pleasant walks with views of the Hudson River and the Palisades, particularly between North Yonkers and Ossining.

(PALISADES & NYACK ACROSS TO HOOK MOUNTAIN) CROTON RIVER

Along its journey through eleven river communities, the trail offers an opportunity to combine walking with other interests. In

Irvington, it passes through the grounds of Lyndhurst and near to Sunnyside, and in Tarrytown, it passes near Philipsburg Manor and the 300-year-old Dutch Church. There is a small museum with excellent exhibits relating to the construction of the aqueduct adjacent to the Double Arch at Broadway in Ossining. For the naturalist, trail neighbors include Lenoir Nature Preserve on the Yonkers-Hastings border and the Rockefeller State Park Preserve in Sleepy Hollow (North Tarrytown).

Vents, stone towers constructed to keep the water fresh, are located at roughly one-mile intervals. Larger stone buildings, located in Ossining, above the Pocantico River, and in north Yonkers, are waste weirs, which allowed workers to maintain the aqueduct. Access to the "tube" itself can be arranged for groups by contacting the park manager in Dobbs Ferry or the Recreation and Parks Department in the Village of Ossining. The trail, except north of

AQUEDUCT near
DOBBS FERRY

Ossining, is convenient to buses along US 9 and is also served by the Hudson Line of Metro-North. Yellow trail markers appear at road intersections and on telephone poles where walkers must take to the local streets.

For more information, contact the Old Croton Trailway State Park, 15 Walnut Street, Dobbs Ferry, NY 10522; (914) 693-5259.

Yonkers—Tarrytown

Length: 9.2 miles Blaze: yellow
From the Greystone railroad station in Yonkers, a walk uphill and across Warburton Avenue to Odell Avenue leads to the aqueduct. Continuing north, in less than half a mile, a small trail heads east to a gate in the fence surrounding Lenoir Preserve. A similar distance farther north, an old quarry on the east side was served by a railway running from the river under the aqueduct. After passing the original Overseer's House and the

State Park maintenance barns and office in Dobbs Ferry (4.2 miles), the trail continues through the grounds of Mercy College and past Nevis, a colonnaded home built by Alexander Hamilton's son. It passes the Victorian Stiner-Ross octagonal house and eventually enters the grounds of Lyndhurst. Leaving Lyndhurst, the trail goes north along Broadway, crosses the New York State Thruway, and turns right for 100 yards on White Plains Road before returning to the aqueduct again on the left (8.3 miles). From the second road crossing, the Tarrytown railroad station is reached by following US 9 north (the aqueduct runs underneath the sidewalk) and turning left down Franklin Street.

Sleepy Hollow
the Bridge and the Cemetery: Irving's grave on hill in plot with hedge and two tall trees, one a Beech

Tarrytown—Scarborough   *Length: 5.0 miles Blaze: yellow*

From the Tarrytown railroad station, this hike begins on Main Street, going east, turns left on North Broadway, and quickly turns right on Hamilton Place, joining the trail on the left in 100 yards. Where the route is blocked by a breezeway at Sleepy Hollow High School (1.0 mile), hikers can go around the east side of the buildings, and shortly after that they will enter Rockefeller State Park Preserve. After crossing 120 feet above the Pocantico River and passing a waste weir (a square stone building), a wide trail leads off to the east and into the preserve. Crossing NY 117 over a bridge after a sharp left turn, the route continues straight ahead at the next vent (3.0 miles), as the trail narrows. (Hikers should not follow the line of the aqueduct to the left, since it leads to a dangerous part of US 9.) Arriving at a barn by a road, the route heads west across US 9, and at the first bend turns north down a short set of steps and back onto the trail. At the end of this section, a sharp left turn on River Road, right on Creighton Lane, and right on River Road leads to the Scarborough railroad station.

Ossining—New Croton Dam   *Length: 5.5 miles Blaze: yellow*

Going east uphill on Main Street from the Ossining railroad station and turning left on the red-brick-lined path just short of US 9 takes the hiker to the Double Arch, where the aqueduct crosses above Broadway. Broadway, in turn, crosses Sing Sing Kill (the aqueduct museum is in the community center below the bridge on the right), and the trail passes a waste weir (0.7 mile), ascends some steps, and eventually passes through the grounds of the Crane House, now the Mearl Corporation. The white stone marker in the lawn is directly above the center of the "tube." Crossing US 9, the trail leads at 2.1 miles to a small maintenance barn, turns left down the road immediately after the barn, makes the first right, and, on emerging from the underpass, rejoins the trail at the markers above and to the right, around the General Electric Management Center.

From this point, the trail sections are all in woodland, passing above the roaring waters of Croton Gorge and on to the dam. The 19-acre, DEC-owned, Croton Gorge Unique Area, located between the trail and the Croton River near the midpoint of this trail segment, allows hikers to visit the river's edge.

If two cars are available, hikers will not have to retrace their steps and the journey might include the renovated Briarcliff-Peekskill Trailway (green diamond markers), which runs east from the dam to Teatown Reservation (parking lot and exhibits at 1.9 miles).

ROCKEFELLER STATE PARK PRESERVE

The Rockefeller State Park Preserve consists of 859 acres, which were donated to the state beginning in 1983 by the Rockefeller family, along with an endowment for the maintenance and operation of the park. The preserve encompasses rolling hills, woods, fields, streams, and a small lake. The 20 miles of trails, mostly wide carriage roads, are ideal for strolling and cross-country skiing. Permits are available for horseback riding, but bicycles are prohibited.

The preserve represents a portion of the estate of John D. Rockefeller, which stretched from the Hudson River to the Saw Mill River some 3 miles north of where the Tappan Zee Bridge crosses the Hudson. Southeast of the preserve is another large portion of the estate, which is managed by the Greenrock Corporation and is also open to the public.

Access to the preserve is via a right turn from the eastbound lanes of NY 117 about 1.3 miles east of US 9. The Visitor Center and main parking area are to the right. There is a parking fee. Maps are available at the Visitor Center, and are posted there and near Swan Lake to the southeast. For more information, contact Rockefeller Preserve at (914) 631-1470.

A stroll around Swan Lake or up the Overlook Trail is many people's first foray into the park. The many carriage roads are well defined, but they are so winding and interconnected that a trail map or at least a good sense of direction is needed. Because the trails are so clear, many are not marked. Those that are marked are color-coded by regions of the park rather than by the particular trail.

The Greenrock Corporation property is generally hillier than the preserve and less densely honeycombed with trails. Like the preserve, it offers excellent carriage roads. However, no maps are available. This area is accessible from trails on the south side of the preserve. Parking is restricted along adjacent roads. The trails to the northwest side of NY 448 lead back to the preserve; those to the east lead to Buttermilk Hill and the Pocantico Ridge near the Saw Mill River Parkway, which bounds the eastern edge of the property.

TEATOWN LAKE RESERVATION

Teatown Lake Reservation, a 636-acre nature preserve and education center north of Ossining, offers 12 miles of marked trails, including connections to the Briarcliff-Peekskill Trailway and the Croton Aqueduct Trail. From the Taconic State Parkway, take the NY 134 exit and go west 0.2 mile to Spring Valley Road. Turn right and follow the road to the entrance on the right. The reservation is a 5-mile taxi ride from the Croton or Ossining train stations. Admission and parking are free, though fees are charged for programs and Wildflower Island tours. The nature center is wheelchair-accessible and handicapped parking is provided. A public pay telephone is available.

At Teatown, hikers will find a wide variety of natural areas to explore, including the 33-acre Teatown Lake, a scenic gorge, hardwood swamps, mixed forests, meadows, and hemlock and laurel groves. The 1.6-mile Hidden Valley circuit is a particularly rewarding hike. The Lakeside Trail features a 600-foot boardwalk over the lake and access to a bird observation blind. Trail maps are available at the nature center.

Teatown's nature center features numerous natural history and live animal exhibits and a nature gift shop. Outdoor exhibits include a working maple sugar house and live birds of prey. Weekend and after-school educational and outdoor programs for children and families are also offered, as well as children's birthday parties. Tours of Teatown's 6-acre Wildflower Island are available from April to September; advance reservations are recommended.

For more information, contact the reservation at (914) 762-2912.

WARD POUND RIDGE RESERVATION

The largest of Westchester's parks, the Ward Pound Ridge Reservation occupies 4,315 acres in the northeastern part of the county. Over 35 miles of hiking trails wind through hilly terrain, offering a mix of second-growth hardwood forest, hemlock and laurel, bold rock outcroppings, steep ravines, wetlands, and open meadows. The low stone walls that crisscross the forest floor remind the visitor of the more than thirty farms that once existed within the park's boundaries.

The park entrance is off NY 121 at the bridge over the Cross River, about a hundred yards south of NY 35. A basic map showing hiking trails may be obtained at the park entrance; a more detailed map is available at the nature museum. For more information, including parking fees and use of park facilities, contact the park at (914) 763-3493.

Park facilities are concentrated in the northern half of the park along Boutonville Road. Most of the park's picnic areas, a nature museum, and the park office are located along this road, which parallels the course of the Cross River. The southern half of the park offers a more secluded atmosphere. It is reached most easily from the Michigan Road parking and picnic area, which also serves as the center for winter ski touring.

The trail system consists of five major loop trails and numerous minor trails. All the major trails and many minor trails are woods roads with easy grades.

The 4.7-mile white-blazed trail traverses the northernmost section of the park. Accessible from the picnic areas along Boutonville Road, the southern part of the loop offers a pleasant walk along the Cross River. The 4-mile-long blue-blazed trail extends south from the Kimberly Bridge picnic area through the eastern side of the park. One side of this loop rises through open forest to the highest point in the park at 860 feet. Once occupied by a fire tower, the site is marked by an ancient hand pump. The other side of the loop follows the base of the park's rocky eastern escarpment.

From the Michigan Road picnic area, the red trail takes the hiker into the park's more remote southern area. The longest loop, at 5 miles, it offers access to the greatest variety of scenery, from the wetlands of Honey Hollow to open ledges along the park's southern border where the terrain plunges steeply into the Stone Hill River valley. Two shorter loops, the 2-mile yellow and 3-mile green trails, also originate at Michigan Road; both of these use parts of, and are enclosed within, the red-blazed trail.

WARD POUND RIDGE west to BEAR MOUNTAIN

Hikers on the red, yellow, and green trails should note that these trails are marked for ski touring. Ski traffic is one-way counterclockwise, so the hiker walking these trails clockwise must look backward to check trail markers.

Side trails off the red trail lead to some of the park's more interesting features. Most popular is the Leatherman's Cave, named after a homeless nomad clad in scraps of leather who, from 1858 to 1889, followed the same path through the New York and Connecticut countryside, stopping at each of his campsites every thirty-three days. A white-blazed trail leaves the western side of the red trail at a well-marked intersection. After a short distance it forks, becoming a loop of its own. The left fork leads most quickly to the cave. The trail continues over a hill above the cave, where open rocks offer a view to the west over the Cross River Reservoir.

Another side trail, this one off the east side of the red trail loop, leads to Indian Rock Shelter, also called Spy Rock. A sign marks the intersection on the red trail. Purple blazes mark the path to the rock. Native American artifacts found under an overhang suggest that it was used as a shelter. From a small pine grove on top, there is a view of a deep ravine and the cliffs on the opposite side.

Lying to the south of the red loop, an unmarked trail leads to Dancing Rock and Bear Rock. The former is a very broad flat rock surface forming the summit of a hill, which, according to stories, was used for dancing by local settlers. It is reached by leaving the trail at three faded blue blazes on a tree, then proceeding up the slope on a faint path to the highest point in the area. Lying farther to the southwest, Bear Rock is noted for the carving—perhaps prehistoric—

on the rock's west face, which looks like the head of a bear in profile.

Hikers seeking something more challenging than easy walking on woods roads will find opportunities for more strenuous exercise in the many rocky summits, cliffs, and steep ravines in the southern and southeastern sections of the park.

WESTMORELAND SANCTUARY

The 625-acre Westmoreland Sanctuary, with over 9 miles of interconnecting foot trails, has open grassland, stands of hardwood and evergreen trees, a brook valley, modest rocky summits, and Bechtel Lake, named for one of the sanctuary's founders, Edwin Bechtel. The varied habitat produces an abundance of flowers and birds. Established in 1957, this private, not-for-profit sanctuary sponsors wildlife and botanical research as well as educational programs for the public. Activity schedules and trail maps are available near the entrance. The paths are identified by signposts at junctions.

The sanctuary is reached from NY 172 southeast of Mount Kisco. About 0.3 mile west of the interchange with I-684, Chestnut Ridge Road goes south from NY 172. In 1.4 miles, this road leads to the entrance of the sanctuary on the left. There is generous parking in front of the museum. From the south, Westmoreland is reached by taking Exit 4 of I-684 and following the above directions. For more information, contact the sanctuary at (914) 666-8448.

The sanctuary is crossed by thirteen interlocking trails, most less than a mile long. Because all of the trails are blazed yellow, trail junction signposts are prominent. A half-day hike will of necessity use most of these trails. A 5.5-mile hike that visits the perimeter of the sanctuary is described below. It is easy hiking, with elevations varying from 390 to 730 feet.

Trail maps can be picked up at the trailhead kiosk, located at the end of the museum ramp that leads from the parking lot. The hike begins on the Easy Loop Trail, which descends to join the Catbird Trail on the right. This connects to the northern terminus of the Spruce Trail. Turning right (south) onto the Spruce Trail, the hike goes over one of the major hills in the sanctuary and descends toward a marshy area. At the edge of a stream, the Spruce Trail ends where the Brookside and Hemlock trails begin. The hike continues across the stream, where it joins the Hemlock Trail. After 0.4 mile, a side trail to the right leads to Coles Kettle, a remote tract of wetlands at the southern end of the sanctuary. The Coles Kettle Trail is a 1.5-mile closed loop around the wetlands and is itself quite wet in places.

After completing the Coles Kettle loop, the hike resumes following the Hemlock Trail toward the east. The Hemlock Trail ends at the midpoint of the Laurel Trail, and the hike follows its right branch, which passes a pretty patch of sparsely wooded grass field and soon terminates at a T junction. A right (north) turn to join the appropriately named Brookside Trail leads to a descent along the brook to a wooden bridge, beyond which the Brookside Trail ends and the Veery and Fox Run trails begin. The Veery Trail offers a direct route back toward the parking lot.

The Fox Run Trail is the gateway to the hilly northeastern corner of the sanctuary. This trail contours around the base of rocky cliffs, climbs to a col, and meets the Sentry Ridge Trail. The route makes a right (east) turn here and follows this trail for 0.2 mile to the top of a hill with steep slopes and partially obscured views toward the east. The trail turns sharply left (north) to follow the ridge and then descends to a T junction with the Lost Pond Trail. The route turns right (north) and crosses the outlet of the pond on a wooden bridge, after which the small pond comes into view.

Continuing west along the Lost Pond Trail, the route passes a side trail to the even smaller Scout Pond and then begins to climb in earnest. At a level spot, the Lost Pond Trail ends and the Chickadee and Wood Thrush trails begin. The Chickadee Trail is a direct route down toward the parking lot, while the Wood Thrush Trail begins a steep ascent to the highest point in the sanctuary at an elevation of 730 feet. From the broad wooded summit, the Wood Thrush Trail descends to a narrow valley, follows it toward Bechtel Lake, and ends near a small wooden shelter for birders. From the lake, the Easy Loop Trail climbs through a dark forest of evergreen trees and emerges north of the museum.

OTHER WALKS IN WESTCHESTER

The following areas have more limited hiking opportunities than those described above. Nevertheless, they provide a variety of interesting shorter hikes, as well as opportunities to visit a variety of habitats.

Marshlands Conservancy

This 160-acre county-owned sanctuary offers walks of one or two hours on trails that wind through woods, brush, and open fields sloping to salt-marsh areas and tidewater land overlooking Milton Harbor on Long Island Sound. In spring, waterfowl nest along the quiet shore and herons may be seen high in the trees. John Jay, the first chief justice of the Supreme Court of the United States, is buried nearby in a private plot among the evergreens. For information on the conservancy's schedule of guided walks, lectures, and study sessions, call (914) 835-4466. The Marshlands Conservancy is located on US 1, the Boston Post Road, a mile southeast of the Metro-North railroad station in Harrison.

Mountain Lakes

This 1,000-acre camping area, situated in North Salem, contains several ponds and the beginnings of Crook Brook. From I-684 take Exit 6 (Katonah/Cross River), go east on NY 35 to NY 121 in Cross River, follow NY 121 north to Grants Corner, make a right onto Hawley Road, and go 2 miles to the entrance. A trail map is available at the office near the entrance. For more information, call (914) 669-5793.

Muscoot Farm

This 777-acre interpretive farm, owned by the Westchester County Department of Parks, Recreation and Conservation, offers several miles of easy trails through fields and woodlands. A trail map is available at the Visitors Center. The park facilities and programs depict farm life of the 1920s. Muscoot Farm is located in Somers on NY 100 about 1.5 miles south of NY 35. For more information, contact the park at (914) 232-7118.

Saxon Woods Park

Stretching for 2.5 miles through Scarsdale and Mamaroneck along the Mamaroneck River, this county park offers birding in the spring, as well as an interpretive board describing the well-marked trails. Year-round parking is possible at the Saxon Woods Swimming Pool, on the west side of Mamaroneck Avenue just north of the Hutchinson River Parkway. Walk under the parkway, and follow the trail to the picnic parking area (open only from May through October with a parking fee). A park pass is required. For information, call (914) 242-PARK.

Sprain Ridge Park

Grassy Sprain Reservoir, which supplies water to the city of Yonkers, is bounded on the west, beyond the Sprain Brook Parkway, by a ridge and an area of woods about half a mile wide and 3 miles long. This county park may be entered at the north end, on Jackson Avenue, half a mile west of the Sprain Brook Parkway. A park pass is required. For information, call (914) 242-PARK.

Turkey Mountain Nature Preserve

The 124-acre Turkey Mountain Preserve is managed by the Town of Yorktown Department of Parks and Recreation. The entrance is on the east side of NY 118, 0.9 mile north of NY 129 or 1.7 miles south of Underhill Avenue in Yorktown Heights, the latter more convenient for those coming from the Taconic State Parkway. In either case look for the sign for Peter Pratt's Inn across from the intersection. For more information, call (914) 245-4650.

Two trails lead to the summit of Turkey Mountain, one blazed white and the other blazed blue. Together they form a natural loop hike somewhat less than 2 miles long. Going up the blue trail and coming down the white trail is preferable. The blue trail goes north from the parking lot; in a short distance, a wooden map shows the trail system. The blue trail is level for a while, climbs gently, and then rises steeply to the eastern spur of Turkey Mountain, a climb of nearly 370 feet. At 1.3 miles the trail reaches the broad rocky summit (831 feet), which affords a view of the Croton watershed. To the south, just above the curving northbound lanes of the Taconic State Parkway, is the Manhattan skyline. To the west, one end of the Croton Reservoir and the Hudson River just beyond it are visible. To the northwest, the tower on Bear Mountain stands out clearly against the horizon. And to the north, a portion of the Hudson Highlands is recognizable.

The white trail descends from the summit to the southeast. A short distance below the summit, the trail passes by a minor viewpoint to the east. From this viewpoint the trail descends steeply and levels off to cross the marshy lowlands of the preserve, reaching the parking lot half a mile from the summit.

Whippoorwill Ridge Park

Located west of the village of Armonk and east of Whippoorwill Road, this wooded area consists of approximately 70 acres of a ridge typical of those found in north-central Westchester. Outcroppings of schist in a beech-maple forest give it a special attractiveness. Access is from Old Route 22, 0.25 mile south of its intersection with Main Street (NY 128).

EIGHT

FAHNESTOCK STATE PARK

estled in the wooded hills of northern Putnam County on the east side of the Hudson Highlands lie Clarence Fahnestock Memorial State Park and the Hubbard-Perkins Conservation Area. The original core of the park consists of lands acquired by Major Clarence Fahnestock, who began purchasing abandoned farmsteads around 1900. In 1915 he bought the property of the Pennsylvania and Reading Coal and Iron Company, which had discontinued its iron mining operations in the area forty years before. Fahnestock, a Manhattan physician, created a gentleman's farm and shooting preserve, but did not enjoy it for long. He died in France in 1918, leaving his property to his brother, Dr. Ernest Fahnestock. In 1929, Ernest Fahnestock donated 2,400 acres of this property to the State of New York for a park in memory of his brother and 105 acres which would be flooded by the construction of Canopus Lake. By purchase and gift, the park has grown to its present size of 6,732 acres. Fahnestock State Park is administered by the Taconic Region of the New York State Office of Parks, Recreation, and Historic Preservation.

In addition, the state manages the adjacent Hubbard-Perkins Conservation Area. In 1991, the Open Space Institute purchased more than 3,700 acres and then, in 1995, added more than 700 acres from the Perkins estate. Some 2,000 acres of the first purchase were from the estate of Helen F. Hubbard, the sister of Clarence and Ernest Fahnestock. The state purchased the Hubbard portion of the conservation area in 1996 and intends to acquire the Perkins property when funds are available.

The terrain in the park, which is generally not rugged, is dominated by a series of ridges that tend to run from southwest to northeast. One of these ridges culminates in Shenandoah Mountain on the Appalachian Trail just north of the park. The overall elevation in the park is higher than in neighboring districts; thus, snow may remain in the park until the end of March, long after it has disappeared from adjacent areas. Between the ridges lie several lakes and ponds. Just northwest of NY 301 is Canopus Lake, with Pelton Pond opposite it. Stillwater Pond is west of the Taconic State Parkway, and there are several small ponds elsewhere, which in summer mirror Queen Anne's lace and flowering water lilies. Canopus Creek flows through a beautiful ravine.

The park contains a few old hemlock groves, threatened by the woolly adelgid, and large areas of second-growth hardwood forest. Swamps and thick undergrowth of laurel make many sections difficult to penetrate, except where there are trails. Deer are numerous in the park, and a wide variety of birds, including ruffed grouse and wild turkeys, are frequently seen.

The park, which cannot be reached by public transportation, is accessible from NY 301 between the Taconic State Parkway and US 9. Within a mile west of the parkway are a public beach on Canopus Lake, a picnic area at Pelton Pond, and a campground. The park office is located across the road from the picnic area. Free parking is available on NY 301, at several locations near Canopus Lake, at the intersection of Dennytown and Sunk Mine roads, and on the east side of Dennytown Road near an old stone building 1.2 miles south of NY 301. Sunk Mine Road, an unmaintained, unpaved road, has several turnouts where one or two cars may be parked to give access to trails. For more information, contact the park at (914) 225-7207.

History

The Fahnestock area was once known for its thriving iron industry. The Sunk mines to the southwest and the Canada mines near Canopus Lake are part of the Reading Prong, a formation stretching from Pennsylvania to the Berkshires, rich in magnetite, an iron ore. Beginning soon after the American Revolution, these mines were exploited under various owners. At first, the ore was smelted and used locally. Later, it was hauled to the foundry, the furnaces, and the docks in Cold Spring. The West Point Foundry in Cold Spring was best known for its manufacture of the Parrott gun. Robert Parker Parrott, the foundry operator, developed the rifled cannon, which played an important role in the Civil War. Unfortunately, there was never an economical way to transport the ore from these hills to wider markets. Only in boom times could the mines compete. They closed down in 1876 in the midst of a depression, and even Thomas A. Edison's attempt to reopen them in 1890 was a failure. An exhibit at the Nature Center in the Fahnestock campground gives more information about the local iron industry.

Visitors to the park have to imagine this land cleared for farm and pasture, with settlements containing houses, schools, and stores. The schoolhouse foundation in Dennytown (along Dennytown Road near Indian Brook Road) and the Methodist chapel ruins in Odletown (near the junction of Sunk Mine Road and Bell Hollow Road), as well as old stone walls, root cellars, wells, and foundations, attest to a long-gone community life. Miners, charcoal-makers, teamsters, farmers, and their families lived in tiny houses and in boarding houses throughout this part of Fahnestock Park. Dennytown, where the Denny family began iron mining soon after the American Revolution ended, is now a ghost town. So, too, is Odletown, where only a large dam reminds us of the three bloomery forges by Canopus Creek that made bar iron in the early nineteenth century, using ore from the Sunk mines, charcoal from the nearby forest, and the abundant water power from the creek to operate bellows and triphammers.

Old woods roads, often lined with stone fences, are found throughout the park, their contours depressed by the weight of countless heavily loaded wagons. Most roads led to the Hudson at Fishkill or Peekskill. Some connected with the Old Albany Post Road, which was authorized in 1703 to carry the royal mail and in 1785 as a stage line from King's Bridge in the Bronx to the ferry at Albany. Built during the reign of Queen Anne and originally known as one of the Queen's Roads, it has since been mostly obliterated by US 9, though several sections remain unspoiled. One such section, going east from US 9 about a mile south of NY 301, is preserved much as it was in the eighteenth century and is listed in the National Register of Historic Places. Another section is in the Hubbard property, purchased by Open Space Institute.

In 1815 a toll road was constructed from Connecticut to Cold Spring to carry goods, especially iron ore and farm produce, to the Hudson River. Much of the Philipstown (or Cold Spring) Turnpike was obliterated by NY 301, but parts of the original route may be sighted in the park south of the more modern highway.

Canopus Lake, whose waters cover several openings of the Canada iron mines, was created when the Civilian Conservation Corps (CCC) dammed Canopus Creek during the Depression in the 1930s. "Canopus" was the name of an important leader of the Wappingers, one of whose settlements was in a downstream valley of

this creek. The CCC also created Stillwater Pond, enlarged Pelton Pond, and constructed picnic and camping facilities and bridle trails in the park. Hidden Lake and John Allen Pond were created about the same time on land that was still owned by the Fahnestock family.

Trails in Fahnestock and Hubbard-Perkins

There are approximately 50 miles of marked hiking trails in Fahnestock State Park and the Hubbard-Perkins Conservation Area. It is likely that additional trails will be built in the latter area. In addition to the marked hiking trails, many woods roads run through the park. Trails for horses and mountain bikes, some of which are marked, run along many of these woods roads. For example, a horse and mountain-bike trail beginning at the campground and running south past the west side of Stillwater Pond provides foot access to the Clear Lake Scout Reservation. The trail, which begins on a woods road near the end of the campground access road, is blazed white for about the first mile.

Fahnestock's rolling terrain provides opportunities for cross-country skiing along the woods roads when the snow cover is suitable. Another skiing route is Sunk Mine Road, which is not maintained.

Appalachian Trail   *Length 10.4 miles Blaze: white*
This major trail traverses the park. See chapter 19, "Long Distance Trails," for selected sections, or the *Appalachian Trail Guide to New York and New Jersey* for a complete description of the 10.4 miles.

Cabot Trail   *Length: 1.0 mile Blaze: white*
The Cabot Trail begins at the Charcoal Burners Trail (red) 0.6 mile north of NY 301, branches off to the west, and descends along a woods road, passing through open woods. At 0.4 mile it turns left. Straight ahead is private property; please do not enter the posted area. At 0.5 mile, the trail crosses a stream. A short unmarked side trail to Jordan Pond has a bench with a view over the lake. The Cabot Trail crosses a second stream and gradually ascends until, at 1.0 mile, it reaches a clearing and ends at the Perkins Trail (yellow).

Candlewood Hill Trail   *Length: 2.1 miles Blaze: red*
This trail begins where the Appalachian Trail (white) crosses Sunk Mine Road. There are several turnoffs near the trailhead where one or two cars may be parked.

The Candlewood Hill Trail begins with easy walking on an unpaved, fairly level section of Sunk Mine Road. The trail crosses Canopus Creek, passes the end of Bell Hollow Road on the right at 0.7 mile, and turns right into the woods at 1.2 miles. After a moderate ascent of Candlewood Hill, it reaches open rocks and ascends more steeply to the open summit at 1.4 miles, with views in all directions. Continuing south over rocks, the trail turns right onto a woods road at 1.8 miles. At 2.0 miles the trail turns left at a break in a rock wall and descends to Bell Hollow Road, where it ends.

To return to the starting point, hikers can turn right on Bell Hollow Road, follow it 0.7 mile to Sunk Mine Road, and go left 0.7 mile back along the Candlewood Hill Trail to the Appalachian Trail crossing. The section of Bell Hollow Road north of the end of the trail is a woods road and is not suitable for cars.

Catfish Loop   *Length: 3.6 miles Blaze: red*
Beginning at the Appalachian Trail (white) just east of Dennytown Road, the Catfish Loop follows a sinuous path that takes it across the Appalachian Trail, past the end of the Three Lakes Trail (blue), up to a lookout with a view of the Hudson Highlands, and finally back to the Three Lakes Trail. The trailhead can be reached by walking 0.2 mile on the north-bound Appalachian Trail from the parking area on Dennytown Road, 1.2 miles south of NY 301.

The Catfish Loop heads west away from the Appalachian Trail through woods and a barberry thicket, and at 0.2 mile it crosses Dennytown Road about 800 feet south of the parking area. It continues to the southwest through open woods, crossing several stone walls and two small brooks, and ascends to reach a register box at 0.6 mile. The trail crosses a small stream and follows along the park boundary for a short distance. It crosses the Appalachian Trail at 1.1 miles and a horse trail at 1.4 miles, then crosses a brook and reaches one end of the Three Lakes Trail (blue) on the right at 1.5 miles. The Catfish Loop then leads left, departing from a faint yellow-blazed trail, and ascends to reach rock outcroppings at 1.7 miles. From the top of a large rock formation to the right side of the trail there is a view of the Hudson Highlands, including Storm King and Crows Nest.

The trail continues on its undulating course over rocks and through thickets of mountain laurel. It descends and turns right, with a trail to the left heading toward Catfish Pond, which is outside the southern boundary of the park. Having reversed its direction via a 180-degree loop, the trail crosses a brook and ascends over more rocks. At 2.8 miles it starts to follow a stone wall on the left, which is the park boundary. After leaving the stone wall, the trail crosses two clear, unmarked trails and several stone walls before reaching a side trail to the Duck Pond on the left at 3.4 miles. It finally descends and terminates at 3.6 miles at the Three Lakes Trail (blue). To return, hikers should turn left and walk for 1.0 mile on the Three Lakes Trail, which crosses Dennytown Road at the parking area.

Charcoal Burners Trail   *Length: 3.3 miles Blaze: red*
The nineteenth-century iron industry in what is now Fahnestock State Park depended upon charcoal which was a wood product readily available from the forests. The men who felled trees to burn to make charcoal were called wood-choppers or charcoal burners. The Charcoal Burners Trail recognizes those men who spent many lonely hours in the woods.

The trail serves as a connection between Fahnestock State Park and the network of trails in the Hubbard-Perkins Conservation Area. The southern terminus is at the Three Lakes Trail (blue), 0.6 mile north of Sunk Mine Road. The trail crosses the Old Mine Railroad Trail (yellow) at 0.2 mile. Working its way north, up and down over small ridges, the Charcoal Burners Trail passes through open woods and laurel groves until it reaches NY 301 at 1.1 miles. This crossing is 1.5 miles west of where the Appalachian Trail crosses NY 301. In addition to the red blazing, the trail crossing is marked by a white cross painted on a rock outcrop along the north side of the road.

After crossing the road, the Charcoal Burners Trail goes up and over rocks. It turns right at the beginning of the Perkins Trail (yellow) at 1.2 miles and ascends gradually along a woods road through laurel and blueberry bushes. It passes the beginning of the Cabot Trail (white) on the left at 1.7 miles and joins the Fahnestock Trail (blue) at 2.0 miles. Together they reach the dam at Beaver Pond at 2.2 miles and then at 2.3 miles, the Fahnestock Trail goes straight ahead while the Charcoal Burners Trail turns right. Rising up to the ridge, the trail offers limited views at 2.6 miles and a view to the east at 3.2 miles. The Charcoal Burners Trail ends at 3.3 miles at the terminus of the Wiccopee Trail (blue).

East Mountain Loop   *Length: 1.5 miles Blaze: red*
Starting 1.4 miles from the beginning of School Mountain Road (white) on US 9, this loop trail crosses over the top of East Mountain with a view of Fishkill Ridge at 0.7 mile. After reaching a false summit at 0.9 mile, the East Mountain Loop begins its descent on the north slope of the mountain. It makes a sharp

right turn at 1.1 miles. After going through former farm fields and passing stone foundations, the East Mountain Loop ends at School Mountain Road 2.0 miles from US 9.

Fahnestock Trail
Length: 7.3 miles Blaze: blue

The Fahnestock Trail is the main east–west trail in the Hubbard-Perkins Conservation Area. Along its route to the Appalachian Trail in Fahnestock State Park, it is coaligned with three other trails. Hikers need to pay attention as, in all three cases, the Fahnestock Trail is the trail that turns off of the other trails. Parking is on US 9 just north of the intersection with NY 301 and near the Appalachian Trail crossing just west of Canopus Lake on NY 301.

To reach the trailhead, walk 0.2 mile north along US 9 and turn right onto a paved road leading into the Hubbard-Perkins Conservation Area. The Fahnestock Trail and shared-use School Mountain Road (white) begin 0.1 mile from US 9 at a gate where there is a signboard.

At 0.1 mile this broad woods road crosses two steel-decked bridges in quick succession. They pass stone pillars on the left, go over a third steel-decked bridge, and separate at 0.4 mile. The Fahnestock Trail makes a sharp right turn while School Mountain Road continues straight ahead.

As the Fahnestock Trail parallels a stream, hikers have the opportunity to gaze out over the adjacent wetlands. At 0.6 mile the trail leaves the stream and then, at 0.9 mile, makes a sharp left turn. The ascent of Round Hill is steep to the first view to the west at 1.1 miles. The trail climbs gradually up a long ridge dotted with red cedars. Continuing to ascend, the trail crosses a flat area and ascends with steeper switchbacks until at 2.0 miles it reaches a view to the southwest that includes the Bear Mountain Bridge over the Hudson River. Over the next mile, the trail contours along the south slope near the top of Round Hill with occasional views and descends, steeply at times, with several switchbacks to a pass where it follows a woods road over a broad low hill. After crossing a seasonally wet area and making a slightly steeper ascent, the trail reaches a westerly view of the interior of the conservation area at 3.0 miles. Continuing its ascent, the trail reaches a high point with no view and then descends gradually to join the Perkins Trail (yellow) which comes in from the left at 3.9 miles.

The two trails are coaligned along a woods road until the Fahnestock Trail turns left at 4.3 miles while the Perkins Trail (yellow) continues straight ahead. The Fahnestock Trail now runs along the side of a lake, passing a short unmarked trail to a view of the lake at 4.7 miles. The trail gradually turns right, crossing the inlet of the lake on a cement bridge at 4.9 miles. After the bridge, it gradually turns north, still on the woods road, and then, at 5.1 miles, turns right and leaves the woods road. The woods road, if followed, connects with the middle of the Wiccopee Trail (blue), but it has severe problems with water on the trail in wet weather. The Fahnestock Trail reaches the bottom of a gully at 5.3 miles and then ascends through laurel groves to turn right onto a woods road at 5.5 miles.

At the next junction, private property signs are to the right. The Fahnestock Trail bears left and then almost immediately turns right. Take care in this area, as there are unmarked woods roads entering and leaving from the left. As the Fahnestock Trail gradually goes uphill, it passes through wet spots and by a sea of ferns. At 6.0 miles, the Charcoal Burners Trail (red) comes in from the left and together they pass the dam at Beaver Pond at 6.1 miles. The Fahnestock Trail turns left at 6.3 miles, while the Charcoal Burners Trail continues straight ahead.

After leaving the Charcoal Burners Trail, the Fahnestock Trail descends for about 100 yards, joins a woods road, and then crosses two streams. It then

joins another woods road, which it follows to a high point at 6.8 miles. The Fahnestock Trail passes through uneven but moderately open country and descends a short slope. At 7.3 miles, it ends at the Appalachian Trail (white) 0.6 mile north of NY 301, where parking is available.

Old Mine Railroad Trail *Length: 2.2 miles Blaze: yellow*
The Old Mine Railroad Trail is of historical interest and also gives access to many unusual and beautiful areas in the park. During the Civil War, a narrow-gauge railroad was built from the Sunk mines to Dump Hill, located where Dennytown Road meets NY 301. In 1874, another branch was built to the Canada mines. Mule-drawn rail cars carried the ore to Dump Hill, where it was dumped and shoveled into horse-drawn wagons for the final 5-mile trip to Cold Spring. This laborious method of hauling was antiquated the day it was built and could not compete with locomotives shipping ore from the Midwest. Much of this mine railbed was opened as a hiking trail in 1994.

The Old Mine Railroad Trail runs from the Appalachian Trail (white) south of NY 301 along the west side of Hidden Lake and then down to the point where the railbed disappears under the west side of John Allen Pond. A connection is provided out to Sunk Mine Road. The trail offers level walking as railbeds avoid or eliminate the small ups and downs that are a normal part of the terrain. It also affords an unusual opportunity to hike through a marsh without getting wet feet, taking advantage of two causeways that were built up to carry the railbed.

Parking is along NY 301 near the Appalachian Trail crossing or in the western lot at Canopus Lake. The mine railbed is evident almost immediately when hiking south along the Appalachian Trail from the road. Hikers will notice the extensive rock work that was done to bridge several low areas. After 0.7 mile, the Appalachian Trail crosses a small stream and veers left off the railbed. The Old Mine Railroad Trail begins here, following the railbed to the right. It passes through dense laurel growth and, at 0.3 mile, crosses the inlet stream to Hidden Lake. After the trail crosses a causeway, a rock outcrop on the northwest shore of Hidden Lake provides a view of the lake. The trail goes over a second causeway and through the woods, picking up a woods road at 0.6 mile. This road was built in the 1930s and appears to follow the approximate route of the railroad. The Charcoal Burners Trail (red) crosses at 1.1 miles. At 1.5 miles, just before the woods road reaches the park boundary, the trail turns sharply left off the road, passing through laurel to cross the inlet stream to John Allen Pond and reach a point of land at 1.8 miles, where the railbed disappears under the pond.

The trail continues to the right over rocks and follows a woods road, which leads out to Sunk Mine Road, 0.3 mile east of Dennytown Road. The Three Lakes Trail (blue) is 120 yards east (left) along Sunk Mine Road.

Pelton Pond Nature Trail   *Length: 1.5 miles Blaze: yellow*
This easy trail offers a pleasant stroll around Pelton Pond. Parking is available on the south side of NY 301, 0.6 mile west of the Taconic State Parkway. From the sign near the west end of the Pelton Pond parking lot, a short path leads uphill to the trail, which circles the pond. Following the trail to the right, hikers pass through a picnic area and cross the dam at the southwest end of the pond. After a short distance, a woods road goes off to the right, heading toward the campground and a horse trail beyond. Farther on, a red-blazed trail goes uphill to the right to the Nature Center, which is open during the summer. The trail continues around the northeast end of the pond and back to the starting point.

Perkins Trail   *Length: 4.0 miles Blaze: yellow*
Named for the former owners, the Perkins family, this trail starts from the Charcoal Burners Trail (red) less than 100 yards north of NY 301 where the Charcoal Burners Trail takes a sharp right just after crossing an intermittent stream. Heading west over several small ridges, the trail makes a steep descent at 0.3 mile into a field filled with fir trees. The southern terminus of the Cabot Trail is to the right. The Perkins Trail immediately turns left, following the edge of the field, turns right, and heads straight to a gate in the fence. After passing through the gate (please close after using), the trail follows a farm road to reach a dirt road on private property at 0.5 mile. The trail turns left for 200 feet and then turns right through a farm gate (please close). Over the next tenth of a mile, the trail crosses a farm field, parallel to and south of a stone wall. The continuous views to the north over working farm fields and the chance to travel through a different ecosystem make this portion of the trail an unusual opportunity. In the summer, the sun glaring down does not detract from a seemingly endless array of insects, flowers, grasses, and birds.

At the end of the field, the trail goes through another gate at 0.7 mile, makes a 45-degree right turn to cross a rocky field. After going through yet another gate into a third field, the Perkins Trail turns right, follows the fence, and crosses the field on a farm road. The trail descends on the farm road, winding its way through several small fields to enter the woods at 1.2 miles. After passing a high point, it reaches a rocky outcropping with a view to the west and north, before beginning its descent along the ridge.

At the end of the ridge at 1.9 miles, the Perkins Trail makes a sharp right turn, continues its descent, and reaches the eastern bank of Clove Creek at 2.0 miles. Turning, it follows the creek but the distance from the creek varies. At 2.6 miles, the trail crosses Glynwood Road, goes up the hill to a telephone line, and turns right. It reaches a T junction at 3.0 miles and makes a left onto the woods road. In 150 feet, the Fahnestock Trail (blue) comes in from the right.

The trails run jointly until, at 3.5 miles, the Fahnestock Trail continues straight ahead to ascend a ridge and the Perkins Trail turns right and descends. After crossing a series of stone walls, the trail makes a sharp left off a former logging road at 3.8 miles. The Perkins Trail descends along the south bank of a cascading stream, ending at 4.0 miles at School Mountain Road near a bridge. The northern end of East Mountain Loop (red) is to the right on the other side of the bridge.

School Mountain Road   *Length: 4.1 miles Blaze: white*
Shared-use School Mountain Road is the main artery into the conservation area. In winter, even light snow cover offers cross-country skiing opportunities. To reach the trailhead from the parking area just north of the intersection of US 9 and NY 301, walk 0.2 mile north along US 9 and turn right onto the road leading into the Hubbard-Perkins Conservation Area. School Mountain Road and the Fahnestock Trail (blue) begin 0.1 mile from US 9 at a gate where there is a signboard.

At 0.1 mile this woods road crosses two steel-decked bridges in quick succession. The first bridge is over Clove Creek as it flows north. Just before a third bridge, there are stone pillars on a woods road to the left which leads to the site of the former Hubbard mansion. On the other side of that bridge at 0.6 mile, the Fahnestock Trail (blue) turns right. At 1.4 miles, the East Mountain Loop (red) begins at the left to traverse East Mountain. School Mountain Road continues its steady ascent and reaches the terminus of the Perkins Trail (yellow) on the right at 1.9 miles at a bridge. East Mountain Loop rejoins School Mountain Road on the other side of that bridge. The road continues to climb and reaches a Y junction at 2.1 miles, with the trail taking the less distinct left fork. Still climbing, the road reaches a height of land where the Wiccopee Trail (blue) begins to the right at 3.6 miles. Now descending, the road reaches its northern terminus at East Mountain at 4.1 miles, where there is parking for two cars.

Three Lakes Trail   *Length: 5.3 miles Blaze: blue*

The Three Lakes Trail starts from NY 301 near Canopus Lake and travels generally southwest through the park. Various segments of the trail are accessible from NY 301, Sunk Mine Road, and Dennytown Road. Several circular hikes are possible by combining sections of the Three Lakes Trail with sections of the Appalachian Trail. The northern portion of the trail gets fairly heavy use; the section south of Dennytown Road is quiet and very pretty.

To begin at NY 301, cars should be parked at either parking area at Canopus Lake. A walk west on the remnants of the Philipstown Turnpike just south of NY 301 leads, in approximately 250 feet, to the trailhead on the left. The trail follows a woods road to pass old mine pits, and then a swamp on the right. Turning right off the woods road at 0.7 mile, the trail bears southwest. Straight ahead on the woods road is the Green Trail to Clear Lake Scout Reservation. After the turn, the Three Lakes Trail descends gradually, crosses Canopus Creek on a rock bridge, passes a swamp on the right, and ascends moderately to the Appalachian Trail crossing at 1.3 miles.

Some gentle rises offer a view of Hidden Lake before the Three Lakes Trail descends to the southern end of the lake. An unmarked woods road at 1.8 miles leads right and reaches the lakeshore in a short distance, then crosses the outlet of the lake (difficult to cross at times of high water) to intersect the Old Mine Railroad Trail (yellow) 0.1 mile from the Three Lakes Trail.

Approximately 350 feet south of the intersection with the woods road, the Three Lakes Trail passes a trail on the left with faint white blazes, which reaches Sunk Mine Road in about half a mile. The trail continues over fairly level terrain through mountain laurel. After passing the southern terminus of the Charcoal Burners Trail (red) at 2.1 miles, the Three Lakes Trail descends slightly to reach a section of railbed from the mine railroad heading to Sunk Mine toward the left. The foundations of several buildings from John Allen's homestead can be seen to the left of the railbed. The trail goes right along the railbed, but after a short distance goes off to the left. The reason is visible to the right, where hikers will see impressive stone abutments, but the bridge they supported is long gone. The trail continues to the shore of John Allen Pond, follows the lakeshore, and crosses the brook below the lake spillway. The trail then ascends, reaching Sunk Mine Road at 2.7 miles. Sunk Mine Road, to the left, leads to the Appalachian Trail in about 0.6 mile.

The Three Lakes Trail turns right on Sunk Mine Road for 0.2 mile and reenters woods on the left. The trail follows a woods road and then turns left and climbs more steeply, passing the remnants of Denny Mine off the trail to the left. After a steep descent over rocks, the trail passes a swamp on the left, swings right, and reaches Dennytown Road, with a large grassy parking area on the east side, 3.7 miles from the start. The two stone buildings at the north end of the field were built during the 1920s or 1930s by an amateur stonemason. The one that might be mistaken for a chapel reportedly served as a chicken coop. There is water available at a pump.

Joining the Appalachian Trail briefly to cross Dennytown Road, the Three Lakes Trail enters woods to the west. After about 100 feet the Appalachian Trail goes off to the left. The Three Lakes Trail crosses a stone wall and passes a group camping area on the right. The trail ascends moderately through open woods, then levels off and crosses a woods road at 4.1 miles. It passes through a large patch of blueberries to reach a trail register at 4.3 miles. A yellow-blazed trail, which comes in from the Taconic Outdoor Education Center on the right and later goes off to the right, should not be followed, since this area is closed to hikers. The Three Lakes Trail descends through mountain laurel, crosses a stream, and reaches the western end of the Catfish Loop (red) on the right at 4.8 miles. Bearing left (south), the trail emerges above the stream, then descends to follow along its bank through open woods before terminating at the intersection with the Catfish Loop at 5.3 miles. The Appalachian Trail and Dennytown Road are to the left. Either the Catfish Loop or the Appalachian Trail can be used as an alternate return route.

Wiccopee Trail
Length: 1.9 miles Blaze: blue

This interior trail provides a northern link between the Charcoal Burners Trail (red) and School Mountain Road (white). Starting from the northern terminus of the Charcoal Burners Trail, the Wiccopee Trail heads north as it descends the ridge through open oak and blueberries. Turning west and then north again, the trail continues to descend, now though a sparse laurel grove, and reaches a woods road at 0.8 miles where it turns left. Continuing along the woods road for 0.2 mile, it turns right. The Wiccopee Trail winds its way gradually uphill, bypassing wet areas and laurel groves. At 1.9 miles, it reaches School Mountain Road (white), where it ends. Parking for two cars is available on East Mountain Road 0.5 mile to the right.

OTHER AREAS IN PUTNAM COUNTY

There are additional open spaces in Putnam County that provide a range of hiking opportunities. These areas are worthy of exploration although they are not nearly as large as the great state parks such as Harriman and Fahnestock, and generally lack marked trails and detailed hiking maps. Opportunities range from bushwhacking and hiking in DEC multiple use areas to a simple stroll along a cascading brook. For more information on the DEC multiple-use areas, contact the Stony Kill Forestry Office at (914) 831-3109 for the brochure, *Putnam County Multiple Use Areas.*

Clear Lake Scout Reservation

Protruding into the southeastern section of Fahnestock State Park is the Clear Lake Scout Reservation, a camp owned by the Westchester-Putnam Council of the Boy Scouts of America. The scouts obtained the property from a noted authority on glaciers, Dr. William B. Osgood Field, Jr., who had purchased it from the estate of Dr. Ernest Fahnestock in 1935. In 1994 the Open Space Institute acquired permanent conservation easements to preserve the 1,400-acre tract. The Open Space Institute's action prevented the threatened sale and development of the reservation.

Under the terms of the easement, the northern and western parts of the reservation are open to the public for hiking, but hikers must stay away from the area used by the scouts near Clear Lake. Pertinent intersections are clearly marked with signs saying: STOP NO PUBLIC ACCESS. The area is not open to pets or bicycles. Bushwhacking is also prohibited. Most of the major intersections have maps of the area posted on large signs. Hiking in the Clear Lake Scout Reservation is particularly nice in the leaf-off season as the views are more open. Many of the trails are well suited to cross-country skiing.

Hikers can gain access to the reservation by walking south from NY 301 on the Three Lakes Trail (blue) or east from Sunk Mine Road near Candlewood Hill. Warning: Sunk Mine Road is a rough, unmaintained road and is not plowed during the winter. A third access route is via the shared-use trail on the east, which may be reached from NY 301 near Pelton Pond.

Blue Trail   *Length: 2.6 miles Blaze: blue*
The Blue Trail goes to the right from the Candlewood Hill Trail (red) along Sunk Mine Road about 300 yards south of Bell Hollow woods road, where there is limited parking. It proceeds along a woods road for 0.2 mile and it turns sharply left off the road just before a gate. The trail climbs steadily until it reaches the ridgetop at 0.6 mile with a narrow view, seasonally much wider.

At 1.0 mile there is an open view of Clear Lake below. The top end of the Purple Trail is reached at 1.5 miles. The junction with the Green Trail, which leaves the Clear Lake property almost immediately and proceeds left (north) into Fahnestock to connect with the Three Lakes Trail, is at 1.9 miles. From here, the Blue Trail is a woods road heading south. The White Trail branches off to the left at 2.1 miles and the lower end of the Purple Trail is on the right at 2.4 miles. Shortly after crossing a stream, the part of the Blue Trail which is open to the public ends at the junction with the Blue-White Trail at 2.6 miles. The Blue Trail actually forms a complete loop with part of it in the area only open to scouts staying at Clear Lake Scout Reservation.

Blue-White Trail   *Length: 0.3 mile Blaze: blue/white*
The Blue-White Trail connects the Blue and the White trails. It is a woods road whose eastern end was a street of Odletown.

Green Trail   *Length: 0.3 mile Blaze: green*
The Green Trail, connects Fahnestock State Park with Clear Lake Scout Reservation. It begins where the Three Lakes Trail turns right off the woods road 0.7 mile from NY 301 and continues along the woods road ending 0.3 mile later at the Blue Trail.

Purple Trail   *Length: 0.2 mile Blaze: purple*
The Purple Trail is a shortcut across the northern end of the Blue Trail providing a loop back to the top of the ridge. From the lower end it is a gentle climb for the first 300 yards and then climbs steeply with switchbacks to the top of the ridge in the next 100 yards.

White Trail   *Length: 1.4 miles Blaze: white*
From the junction with the Blue Trail, the White trail climbs, steeply at times, to Bushy Ridge where it turns gently to the right along the ridge. At 0.6 mile, there are limited views to the west as the trail follows a stone wall for more than 100 yards. At the end of the stone wall, it starts winding down the ridge to end at Odletown at 1.4 miles. Many stone walls and foundations from the settlement of Odletown may be seen here. If one follows "Main Street" to the left between double stone walls, one reaches the shared-use trail in 0.2 mile. To the left, the shared-use trail leads to Stillwater Pond and eventually to NY 301 near Pelton Pond.

Walter G. Merritt Recreation Area

Nestled against the Connecticut-New York line is a county park with a quiet trail over a mile in length, much of it along a cascading brook. The park entrance is on Haviland Hollow Road 2.4 miles east of NY 22.

Ninham Mountain Multiple Use Area

The 1,023-acre Ninham Mountain Multiple Use Area was established in 1962 on lands purchased from the Rohner farm and the Cornell estate. Bordered on the south by a county park and on the north by private forests, it includes most of the southern end of a long and rugged mountain mass. The focal point of the forest is Ninham Mountain. The highest point for miles around, the mountain was once known as Smalley's Hill after a local family. In the nineteenth century it was renamed in honor of Daniel Ninham, *sachem* (chief) of the Wappingers, who once ruled all the land in Putnam and southern Dutchess counties. After having fought beside the British in the French and Indian wars, Ninham and his followers returned to the Highlands to find their lands occupied by tenants of the Philipse family. Believing that he had been defrauded of his ancestral lands by the Philipses, Ninham appealed to the royal courts in 1765, but without success. He fought on the side of the colonists in the American Revolution. In the end, Ninham and forty of his band, deserted by a company of American soldiers, were killed in 1778 at the Battle of Indian Bridge in the northern Bronx. Surrounded by lakes and reservoirs and commanding a dramatic view of the vast lands once occupied by Ninham and his people, Ninham Mountain is a fitting memorial.

On the lower valley fields, the DEC planted red pine, Norway spruce, and European larch. A fire lookout tower was erected on the mountain and DEC established a field headquarters, an office, and a storehouse for forest fire control operations for Westchester, Putnam, and Dutchess counties. The area is open for hiking, cross-country skiing, mountain biking, camping, hunting, trapping, and fishing; a permit from the ranger is required for camping more than three nights, or for groups of 10 or more.

Ninham Mountain lies some 7 miles east of Fahnestock State Park on NY 301. A shorter southern approach from the Taconic Parkway is via Peekskill Hollow Road to Kent Cliffs. Ninham Mountain is reached by turning east on NY 301 and driving about 3.5 miles to the point where NY 301 crosses West Branch Reservoir on a stone causeway. A sharp left turn onto Gypsy Trail Road (before the causeway crossing) leads to the entrance to the field headquarters, 2 miles beyond on the right. Parking areas have a specified limit on cars to regulate the number of hunters using the forest in season. Another parking area is located off the dirt road running northwest from Gypsy Trail Road to the fire tower. During hunting season (approximately September to February), these limits must be observed. The rules are do not block roads, do not park on the road, do not drive off the road, and confine rambles to state land.

Three well-defined trails or woods roads, all of which run north–south, penetrate portions of the forest. These woods, save for an occasional wetland or pocket of dense laurel and greenbrier, are generally open terrain. With a compass it is possible to fashion a loop of 3 or 4 miles.

One recommended hike is to descend east from the field headquarters via a wide woods road to a beautiful pond created by a small dam across Pine Pond's south inlet. In autumn the massed effect of steepled golden larches rising to the eastern hill line is a magnificent sight. Near the dam, a narrow trail leads back to the east end of the headquarters' road. From here the trail leads south through the red pine plantation to another forest of larches, with views of Ninham Mountain and the valley and hills to the north.

After reaching the county park boundary, the route turns west through the pines and descends, crossing Gypsy Trail Road, into the deep wooded gully of Pine Pond Brook, with its towering tulip trees. Hikers can cross the brook in several places on boulders or fallen trees to follow the clearly marked forest boundary around the south end of an extensive marsh. Here begins the steep climb up the easternmost ridge of Ninham Mountain, a route that keeps always to the west with the blazed boundary in sight. Beyond the crest are several attractive hollows among low hills. Approximately half a mile from the brook the forest boundary turns sharply southeast, but hikers should continue northwest to west to skirt a

Mountain Laurel

marsh and the thickest laurel. At the top of the next hill, the route comes out on the well-defined north–south woods road that descends the south spur of the mountain. Turning north, the route follows old stone walls, passes patches of farmland long returned to woods, and comes out at the locked gate on the gravel road to the tower, where there is parking for about six cars. In another 0.7 mile, the highest point on Ninham Mountain (1,270 feet) is reached, with an 80-foot steel fire tower, which is closed to the public. The view from this point is mostly obscured by trees.

Going down, a traverse southeast through an open young hardwood forest offers a pleasant alternative to the gravel road. A compass bearing of 135 degrees carries the hiker over a lower rocky summit out onto the gravel road at a parking spot for three or four cars. Larches edge this lovely field. From this point, hikers may walk out on the gravel road, which leads to the paved highway and, to the right, the field headquarters. Alternatively, a short trail begins here and leads south to a brook, which may be followed east to its confluence with Pine Pond Brook. The latter is best crossed by turning north and coming out at the bridge on Gypsy Trail Road a short distance beyond. Just up the hill on the left from Pine Pond Brook is an abandoned mine, which was worked in the 1840s by the Hudson River Mining Company in the hope of finding silver, and sporadically as an arsenic mine until 1907. By either route the distance from the small parking area to the headquarters is less than a mile.

NINE

THE HUDSON HIGHLANDS

o other part of the Hudson Valley can match the scenic grandeur of the river's gorge through the Highlands. From Dunderberg north around Anthony's Nose to Storm King and Breakneck, the Hudson is narrow and winding, flanked by hills of a thousand feet or more. Many of the region's most spectacular and popular hikes are found here. Anthony's Nose offers a panoramic view over the Bear Mountain Bridge and the vast expanse of Bear Mountain-Harriman State Parks, while along the rocky spine of Breakneck Ridge, the vistas improve with every step upward.

History

The history of the Highlands is rich and colorful. The naming of Anthony's Nose, the southern gate to the Highlands, is the subject of much conjecture and folklore. On early maps it was called St. Anthony's Nose. Various Dutch Anthonies are also said to have lent it their names, while Washington Irving tells his own tale about the mountain in *A History of New York from the Beginning of the World to the End of the Dutch Dynasty*. About all that can be said for certain is that it was named long before the days of General Anthony Wayne and the American Revolution.

During the Revolution, control of the narrow river passage under Anthony's Nose was critical to Washington's army. Both shores were heavily fortified, lest the British cut off New England from the rest of the rebelling colonies. In 1777 a great iron chain was laid across the river from the foot of Anthony's Nose to

Fort Montgomery. The remains of the fort are still visible on a knob overlooking the river, and just to the south across Popolopen Creek, one wall of Fort Clinton stands below the Trailside Museum at the western end of the Bear Mountain Bridge.

These log and stone ramparts were the scene of a brave defense by Orange County militia on October 4, 1777, against an assault by British troops under Sir John Vaughan. The British finally took the posts and, with the aid of ships, broke the chain. They failed to take advantage of their success, however, and retreated downriver after hearing of the American victory at Saratoga. A second, heavier iron chain laid in 1778 from West Point to Constitution Island, where the river is narrowest, was never breached. Constitution Island, once known as Martelaer's Rock, was fortified in 1775 and renamed in honor of the unwritten British constitution that the Americans claimed to be defending. The island, which has been owned since 1908 by the U.S. Military Academy, may be reached only by special launch from West Point.

Midway between the locations of the two chains, at the foot of Sugarloaf Hill is the site of the Beverly Robinson House, where the most notorious act of treachery in American history took place. Benedict Arnold, commander at West Point, used that house as his headquarters. On September 25, 1780, while at breakfast, he received word of the capture of Major John André, his liaison with the British. Arnold fled immediately, ordering his boatman to row him downriver to the safety of the British ship *Vulture*, anchored near Croton Point. Shortly after his departure, George Washington, Alexander Hamilton and LaFayette arrived at the house, expecting to meet Arnold. Upon reading the dispatch describing the detainment of one "John Anderson" at Tarrytown, then the subsequent confession of Major André regarding his true identity, Wash-

ington realized Arnold's treason. Hamilton, sent to intercept Arnold, returned instead with Arnold's letter of explanation to Washington. The next day André was brought to the house under guard.

On the east end of the ridge of Anthony's Nose are the extensive dumps of the old Manitou Copper Mine. This mine was originally opened about 1767 for iron by Peter Hasenclever, but it was not successful because the ore, smelted in one of his furnaces at Cortlandt south of Peekskill, proved too sulfurous. During the Civil War, the Hudson River Copper Company attempted to mine copper there. When they found iron sulfide instead of copper, they switched their name to the Highland Chemical Company and produced sulfur. The chemical plant, which closed in 1913, was at the foot of the mountain in the hamlet of Manitou.

From Anthony's Nose, one looks down on the Bear Mountain Bridge, the first road bridge over the Hudson constructed south of Albany and the longest suspension bridge in the world at the time it was built. Substantially funded by the Harriman family, who owned an estate on the west side of the river and had donated land there for a state park, the bridge was completed in 1929 for $5 million as a privately owned toll bridge. High tolls (80 cents for car and driver plus 10 cents per passenger in each direction) deterred customers, and the bridge lost money. In 1940, the state took over the bridge for $2.3 million.

The sentinels of the northern gate of the Highlands are Breakneck on the east and Storm King on the west. This area was the scene of one of the most extraordinary engineering feats of the day when the Catskill Aqueduct was tunneled under the river at this point. Most of the time between groundbreaking in 1907 and the opening of the reservoir floodgates in 1912 was taken up by geologic boring of the river bed to find bedrock. Glacial action and erosion had filled in the gorge nearly 800 feet above bedrock. Nearly as impressive an engineering triumph was the construction of the Storm King Highway across the sheer rock wall on the face of Storm King. The highway, completed in 1922, can be seen from Breakneck.

To the northeast is Beacon Mountain, named for the beacon fires kept there by American militia during the Revolution. From 1902 to 1975, the old Mount Beacon Incline Railway climbed the northwest face from the City of Beacon to a casino on the mountaintop. A monument on the summit of North Beacon Mountain erected by the Daughters of the American Revolution was badly damaged by lightning but was reconstructed in 1928.

HUDSON HIGHLANDS STATE PARK

The first efforts to preserve the scenic beauty of the Storm King–Breakneck section of the Hudson River Valley were made by the Hudson River Conservation Society, which worked to persuade landowners to donate property to the State of New York or to include restrictive clauses in their deeds regarding quarrying, mining, and other land uses detrimental to the area's natural beauty. In 1938 the Society succeeded in having 177 acres on the northwest face of Breakneck Ridge deeded to the New York State Conservation Department as gifts of Rosalie Loew Whitney and the Thomas Nelson estate. In 1939, this same group made an appeal to save Anthony's Nose and create a memorial to Raymond Torrey. The donations purchased 200 acres in Putnam County just north of Anthony's Nose, which eventually became part of the Hudson Highlands State Park.

In 1965, as large corporate purchases began to threaten the Highlands with industrial development, the State Council of Parks began planning a program of scenic preservation, which was referred to the temporary Hudson River Valley Study Committee. By citing the Highlands as a high-priority project in its recommendations to the newly formed Hudson River Valley Commission in 1966, and bolstered by continuing enthusiasm for the Highlands among conservation groups, the State Council of Parks and its supporters succeeded in saving Little Stony Point from proposed industrial development in 1967.

In the same year, Jackson Hole Preserve, Inc., a conservation foundation supported primarily by the Rockefeller family, presented a Deed of Trust to New York State for acquisition within the Highlands. Within a year, more than 2,500 acres—including Sugarloaf Mountain, Bull Hill (Mount Taurus), Pollepel

Washington Valley ~ ~ Cross West with three Summits ~ ~ Little Stony Point ~ Constitution Island

Up the Hudson from West Point with snow on the Highland slopes

Island, the south and west faces of Breakneck Ridge, and several riverfront properties—were acquired. These areas form the major part of the northern section of the present Hudson Highlands State Park.

North of the park and the Beacon watershed property lies the 923 acres of the Fishkill Ridge Conservation Area, which is owned by Scenic Hudson Land Trust, Inc., and managed as an extension of the park. The land was purchased in 1992 and 1993 with the assistance of the Lila Acheson and DeWitt Wallace Fund for the Hudson Highlands.

A separate 1,033-acre section of the Hudson Highlands State Park known as the Osborn Preserve lies south of Garrison. The acquisition of this section began when William Henry Osborn II, past president of the Hudson River Conservation Society, donated the Sugarloaf Hill (sometimes called Sugarloaf South) area to the State of New York in 1974. In 1981 and 1982 the National Park Service purchased two additional tracts on the top of Canada Hill for the Appalachian Trail reroute and corridor protection. Just north of the preserve lies the Castle Rock Unique Area, managed by the Department of Environmental Conservation. This area surrounds a privately owned picturesque and romantic castle (closed to the public), which was built in the 1880s as a summer home for the first William H. Osborn, president of the Illinois Central Railroad and grandfather of William Henry Osborn II.

Altogether, Hudson Highlands State Park now comprises of approximately 3,800 acres. The Taconic Region of the Office of Parks, Recreation, and Historic Preservation administers the park, which has the same park manager as Clarence Fahnestock State Park. The Fahnestock park office is located on NY 301 about a

mile west of the Taconic State Parkway. For more information, contact the park at
(914) 225-7207.

Trails in the Northern Highlands

The region north of NY 301 includes the highest peaks in the area and offers
the most strenuous and scenic hiking. Fishkill Ridge to the north, North and
South Beacon mountains, Sugarloaf Mountain, Breakneck Ridge, and Bull Hill
(Mount Taurus) are favorite destinations. While most of the trails are within
the Hudson Highlands State Park and the Fishkill Ridge Conservation Area,
others cross lands owned by the City of Beacon and by private landowners. It
is important for hikers to stay on marked trails in these areas so that trail
access is not endangered.

The trails are accessible from a number of entry points along NY 9D north
of the village of Cold Spring. Local streets near the city of Beacon provide
access to trails in the north, while the eastern trailhead of the Wilkinson Memorial Trail can be reached from US 9. More detailed information is provided
in the trail descriptions below.

Those traveling by train may use the Cold Spring station for access to the
Washburn Trail. On weekends, certain Metro-North trains will stop on request
at Breakneck Ridge; for more information, contact Metro-North at (212) 532-
4900 or from outside of New York City (800) 638-7646.

Breakneck Ridge Trail   *Length: 4.7 miles Blaze: white*
One of the most rugged and scenic of the park trails, the Breakneck Ridge Trail
follows an open ridge from the Hudson River to the top of South Beacon Mountain. Its southern end is just north of the tunnel on NY 9D, 2.1 miles north of
Cold Spring, where Breakneck Point juts into the Hudson River. There is a
small parking area on the west side of the road at the trailhead as well as ample
parking a few hundred yards farther north along the road. The steep climb up
the ridge is dangerous in slippery weather or in high winds.

The trail ascends the western embankment of the highway and crosses
over the tunnel. The first few hundred feet of elevation are gained quickly, as
this is one of the steepest sections of trail in the Highlands. The trail avoids one
long rocky wall by contouring to the left and then crosses right between large
rocks to reach the first of many panoramic viewpoints. Perched high above the
Hudson, this first view is breathtaking and is an ideal place to rest from the

most demanding part of the hike.

Looking back toward the ridge, it is clear that the climb is far from over. The trail now settles into a pattern of descending moderately after reaching a viewpoint, and then climbing steeply to the next viewpoint. In a few places the trail briefly traverses sloping rock slabs near the edge of the south-facing cliffs. Although hikers will need their hands to negotiate some of the rocks, there is no great difficulty and the exposure is minimal. In two places, an easier alternate route is marked with X blazes. At 0.7 mile the Undercliff Trail (yellow) goes off to the right.

At the upper reaches of the ridge, the views are broader though less dramatic. The trail continues its ups and downs through terrain that gradually becomes more wooded. At 1.5 miles the Breakneck Bypass Trail (red) begins on the left. A huge boulder on the left of the trail is an indicator of this easily missed trail junction. Continuing straight, one more 360-degree view is soon reached at one of the ridge's highest points.

At about 2 miles, the Notch Trail (blue) enters on the right and travels with the Breakneck Ridge Trail for the next 0.7 mile. Halfway up to the next knob, a short side trail on the right leads to a view down into the valley between Bull Hill and Breakneck Ridge. At 2.7 miles, the trail joins a well-used woods road for a short distance and comes to a fork where the Notch Trail goes left and soon connects with the Wilkinson Memorial Trail. The Breakneck Ridge Trail goes right, crosses the outlet from a marshy area on the left, and veers left and uphill away from the woods road. The view from Sunset Point is, for northbound hikers, somewhat disappointing compared with the broad vistas along Breakneck Ridge.

From Sunset Point, the trail descends at first gently and then more steeply toward Squirrel Hollow Brook. Immediately after the brook, the Wilkinson Trail (yellow) comes in from the left. The abandoned Casino Trail can still be seen here going to the right. The Wilkinson and Breakneck Ridge trails climb together for a short distance; then the Breakneck Ridge Trail diverges sharply into the woods to the left. This easily missed left turn is normally marked by a small cairn. A steep uphill via the Devil's Ladder reaches a view. The trail continues to the fire tower on South Beacon, about 0.6 mile from the brook crossing.

South Beacon Mountain (1,600 feet), the highest point in the park, towers over the surrounding terrain and offers a commanding view combining urban, rural, and mountain features. Beacon lies below, and Newburgh is to be seen across the widening of the river in Newburgh Bay. In the middle ground are the farms and fields, with interspersed woodlots, of Dutchess and Orange counties; beyond them, across the Wallkill Valley, are the long, level-topped line of the Shawangunk Mountains and, on the far horizon, the sharper outlines of the Catskills. From the top of South Beacon Mountain, the trail descends to the right of the tower, ending at an abandoned trail that can be followed to the right to rejoin the Wilkinson Trail.

Because of its steepness, the Breakneck Ridge Trail takes about three and a half hours to hike in good weather. It is considered the most strenuous hike of the Hudson Highlands. A popular and shorter, but none the easier, circular hike is to climb via the Breakneck Ridge Trail to the top of the ridge, come down via the Breakneck Bypass Trail, and follow the Wilkinson Memorial Trail west back to NY 9D, 0.3 mile north of the starting point. A slightly longer circular hike is to come down the ridge via the Notch Trail to the south and follow the Brook Trail back to NY 9D, 0.4 mile south of the starting point. Energetic hikers with a long day to spare should consider walking the entire length of the Breakneck Ridge Trail and returning via the Wilkinson Memorial Trail, a demanding but rewarding trek.

Breakneck Bypass Trail   *Length: 0.8 mile Blaze: red*
The Breakneck Bypass Trail provides access to Breakneck Ridge, but avoids the difficult rocks at the southern end of the Breakneck Ridge Trail. It begins just over half a mile from the southern end of the Wilkinson Memorial Trail, connecting it to the Breakneck Ridge Trail. At 0.3 mile there is a close view of Sugarloaf Mountain. At 0.5 mile the trail follows a gullied woods road. After reaching a viewpoint at 0.8 mile, the bypass descends from a rock onto the Breakneck Ridge Trail (white) 1.5 miles from its southern end.

Brook Trail   *Length: 0.9 mile Blaze: red*
The Brook Trail follows Breakneck Brook in the valley between Bull Hill (Mount Taurus) and Breakneck Ridge along the numerous old roads that crisscross the valley. The extensive ruins in the valley are from the estate of Edward G. Cornish, chairman of the board of the National Lead Company, who lived here in the 1920s. The mansion, which was destroyed by fire in 1956, and the other major buildings were built by James W. Eaton using rocks from Breakneck Ridge. Farther up the valley are the ruins of a dairy operated by the Cornish family as a gentleman's farm.

The Brook Trail begins immediately south of where Breakneck Brook crosses under NY 9D, 1.7 miles north of Cold Spring. Meager parking is available at the trailhead, with room for a few more cars a bit north or a few tenths of a mile south.

The trail follows a paved surface and quickly ascends to a woods road. After a few switchbacks to rise above the brook, the trail turns left on a hard-surfaced road lined with several dilapidated houses and foundations. A short distance before this road veers left and crosses the brook over a small dam, the trail splits off to the right, going up a short flight of steps and staying on the same side of the valley. A moderate climb within view of the stream brings the trail to another dam. The trail goes right on the woods road coming from the dam, and at 0.5 mile intersects the Catskill Aqueduct, recognized as a road-like clearing through the forest. The trail soon merges with the wide Old Lake Surprise Road, also known as Dairy Road because of the dairy farm that existed in the valley. The road can be followed back to NY 9D, 0.7 mile south of the trailhead. The Brook Trail continues on the heavily eroded road, crosses the Undercliff Trail (yellow) at 0.7 mile, and finally crosses the brook on a wooden bridge. The trail terminates 0.2 mile later at the Notch Trail (blue), which may be followed straight (north) to Breakneck Ridge or right (east) to Bull Hill (Mount Taurus).

Fishkill Ridge Trail   *Length: 4.9 miles Blaze: white*

Fishkill Ridge is the northernmost of the Fishkill mountains, extending 3 miles between the Breakneck-Scofield Ridge and I-84. The abrupt drop at the north edge of the ridge from about 1,400 feet to sea level at the Hudson marks the great fault that bounds the Highlands on the north. The Fishkill Ridge Trail runs from the City of Beacon to the top of the ridge, where it makes a loop with many views.

Access to the western end of the trail is from East Main Street in Beacon. Hikers can follow this road east uphill for about 0.2 mile past the intersection with Howland Street, where a narrow road branches off to the right past private homes until it reaches a metal water tank of the Beacon water supply system. The parking situation is unclear. There is space for a couple of cars on the shady shoulder of the road just before the gate that leads to the water tank. More appropriate may be curb parking on one of the streets near East Main Street. Local police suggest parking at the foot of the old incline railway near the point at which NY 9D makes a sharp left turn as it enters the city, though that adds a walk of several city blocks to the hike. From the Beacon railroad station, hikers should walk up Ferry Street and continue on Main Street for a total of about 1.5 miles. Alternatively, the trail may be reached from a parking area at the end of Sunnyside Road in Beacon Hills, a residential community. From here, a steep woods road goes up to the trail on the ridge.

From Beacon, the trail begins along the continuation of the road that passes in front of the water tank. Following the south side of scenic Dry Brook, the trail ascends steadily, reaching a waterfall at 0.7 mile. From the falls the trail turns north and climbs steeply to Reservoir Road (a dirt road), passing through a hemlock grove. To the left, Reservoir Road is an alternate easy return to Beacon; it is recommended in snowy or icy conditions, as the trail descent to the falls can be quite hazardous.

The trail turns left onto Reservoir Road, but almost immediately abandons it and crosses a woods road. Heading north, the trail ascends, gently at first, then steeply, to a ledge, at 1.1 miles, with views of the Hudson Valley. From here the trail heads east, passes over a series of knobs, and at 1.5 miles reaches the summit of Lambs Hill (1,500 feet), with further panoramic views.

Descending gradually to the south, the trail intersects an eroded woods road at 1.9 miles. This intersection is known as Dozer Junction in honor of the abandoned bulldozer that rests nearby. From here the trail continues northeast along the ridge with viewpoints both north and south. Near the north end of the ridge at 3.2 miles, it reaches the no-longer-bald summit of Bald Hill, the highest point on the ridge, marked by two USGS markers.

From the summit, the trail continues northeast until a switchback to the right brings it down from the ridge crest into the woods. After a gentle descent, the trail turns sharply right to join a rough woods road heading south. The vegetation is lush and varied along these east-facing slopes. The Fishkill Ridge Trail ends at 4.9 miles, where it meets the Wilkinson Memorial Trail (yellow).

The Wilkinson Memorial Trail, which proceeds straight ahead past Hells Hollow, leads back toward the starting point. When the Wilkinson Memorial Trail turns off, the return route continues on the woods road straight downhill, passing a road coming in from the right that leads back to Dozer Junction. After about half a mile, the woods road reaches the Fishkill Ridge Trail, where it intersects Reservoir Road as described above. From here, either the trail going left or Reservoir Road straight ahead may be taken back to the trailhead.

Highlands Trail   *Length: 1.6 miles Blaze: blue*

The Open Space Institute purchased the Lone Star property in 1993, protecting more than 500 acres in the Hudson Highlands. The Highlands Trail, not to be confused with the teal-blazed Highlands Trail on the west side of the Hudson

River, is a portion of a trail that eventually will connect the Hudson Highlands State Park, the Hubbard-Perkins Conservation Area, and Fahnestock State Park. As of 1997, it only provides alternate access to Bull Hill starting 600 feet higher than the Washburn Trail. There is no public transportation to the trailhead. The parking area is on Fishkill Road 0.4 mile from the intersection with NY 301 in Nelsonville.

The Highlands Trail is a woods road that works its way gradually uphill. At 0.3 mile, the trail passes the terminus of the Split Rock Trail (red), which heads off to the left. The Highlands Trail continues to climb gradually, reaching a steeper pitch at 0.7 mile, and then shortly returns to the former grade. At 0.8 mile, the trail goes through a small laurel grove and passes onto state property. At 1.0 mile, the Highlands Trail turns right on a wide, eroded road and heads uphill. To the left, going downhill, is the Split Rock Trail (red), an alternate route back to the trailhead at Fishkill Road. The Highlands Trail continues along the road, and at 1.6 miles it ends at the junction of the Washburn Trail (white) and the Notch Trail (blue).

Notch Trail   *Length: 6.0 miles Blaze: blue*
The Notch Trail begins at the northern end of the Washburn Trail and crosses through notches in the shoulders of Bull Hill (Mount Taurus), Breakneck Ridge, and Sunset Hill. After passing through the valley of Lake Surprise between Bull Hill and Breakneck, it affords a panoramic view from Sunset Hill of the valley and Melzingah Reservoir. The trail then swings around to follow the ridge north of the reservoir and ends south of Dutchess Junction on NY 9D.

The northern end of the trail is on NY 9D, 4 miles north of Cold Spring. There is parking for a few cars in pullouts near the trailhead. Except for the climb up Breakneck Ridge and the walk along the ridge line, the Notch Trail is almost entirely on old farm and woods roads. Because a significant portion of the trail is outside the park, hikers may encounter noisy motorized vehicles, which have caused severe damage, especially near Gordons Brook.

At its southern terminus, the Notch Trail is a continuation of the Washburn Trail north of the summit of Bull Hill. The Notch Trail continues the steep downhill of the Washburn Trail (white), then veers left (west) and descends less steeply for about a mile into the valley of Lake Surprise. After crossing a tributary of Breakneck Brook and then the brook itself on a wooden bridge, the trail comes to the end of the Brook Trail (red). At this junction, the Notch Trail turns sharply right (northeast) on Old Lake Surprise Road, runs past the ruins of an old dairy farm once operated by the Cornish family, and skirts the north side of a pond. Near the end of the pond, the trail leaves the road, turns left, and begins its steep climb to the crest of Breakneck Ridge, with views in several directions.

Joining the Breakneck Ridge Trail (white) in the saddle of the notch, the Notch Trail runs with it to the right for 0.7 mile along the ridge line, with views. Turning left off the Breakneck Ridge Trail, the Notch Trail soon joins the Wilkinson Memorial Trail (yellow), which comes in from the left.

The remaining distance of 2.7 miles is a long, mostly gentle downhill series of curves and loops. After the trail crosses Squirrel Hollow Brook on the hewn timbers of an old wooden bridge, the Wilkinson Memorial Trail branches off to the right. About 0.2 mile farther on, the Notch Trail goes right at a fork, where the left fork is a woods road that descends along Squirrel Hollow Brook to Melzingah Reservoir. The Notch Trail ascends slightly to a shallow notch, and then descends to cross Gordons Brook. It crosses a number of woods roads and unmarked trails where the hiker must take care to stay on the blazed trail until it ends at NY 9D.

Split Rock Trail   *Length: 1.1 miles Blaze: red*
This short trail makes it possible to hike a loop in the Lone Star property purchased by the Open Space Institute in 1993. The Split Rock Trail begins at a massive glacial erratic 0.3 mile from the start of the Highlands Trail, and then goes gradually uphill. Although there are no views, glacial erratics litter the woods off the trail to the right after it turns out of a laurel grove at 0.2 mile. At 0.3 mile the trail reaches an eroded road just past a gate at the edge of the Hudson Highlands State Park. Turning right, the Split Rock Trail heads steeply uphill on the road. After several turns in the road, it ends at 1.1 miles at the Highlands Trail (blue), which continues up the hill on the road.

Undercliff Trail   *Length: 2.3 miles Blaze: yellow*
Built by a volunteer trail crew of the New York-New Jersey Trail Conference, the Undercliff Trail provides a scenic connection between Bull Hill (Mount Taurus) and Breakneck Ridge.

The southern terminus of the Undercliff Trail is on the Washburn Trail, 1.4 miles uphill from its trailhead on NY 9D. The trail begins with an undulating traverse of the western shoulder of Bull Hill. Along the way, stone outcroppings afford views to the south and down at Cold Spring nestled at the foot of the mountain. Hikers should stay on the trail to avoid damaging the low plants that keep the soil from eroding. At the far end of the shoulder (0.4 mile), the trail opens to a view of the ragged profile of nearby Breakneck Ridge, the brooding hulk of Storm King across the river, and the Catskills in the far distance.

From the viewpoint, the trail reverses direction and descends east into a narrow valley. It crosses a seasonal creek, traverses north along the western flank of Bull Hill, and descends using switchbacks to reach a woods road supported by a stone wall. The trail skirts the rubble of what must have been the source of the rocks used to build the wall and descends gently until the road surface vanishes in the undergrowth. The trail turns northwest and continues through what was once a cow pasture on the Cornish estate. At 1.6 miles, it crosses the Brook Trail (red), which follows an eroded woods road. NY 9D is 1.4 miles downhill to the left.

The Undercliff Trail crosses Breakneck Brook and immediately ascends over forested, but rocky slopes. After reaching a cliff, a short traverse along its base leads to a viewpoint over the valley and the Hudson. The trail descends away from the cliff over rocks with boring holes, presumably left from quarrying operations during the construction of the aqueduct. The trail contours right and ascends again, this time to pass over huge boulders that the trail crew dubbed the "Rock Jumble." It ascends more steeply via switchbacks to return to the base of the cliffs. Continuing west, the trail hugs the towering cliff wall, gains some elevation, and turns a corner to penetrate one of the many shallow notches along Breakneck Ridge. Switchbacks ease the final short but steep rise

DOWN THE HUDSON FROM COLD SPRING TO BEAR MOUNTAIN & WEST POINT

to the trail's northern terminus on the Breakneck Ridge Trail (white), 0.7 mile from its trailhead on NY 9D.

Washburn Trail   *Length: 2.3 miles Blaze: white*

Starting from river level, the Washburn Trail climbs 1,400 feet to the top of Bull Hill (Mount Taurus). The trail ends half a mile past the summit, where it links with the Notch Trail (blue). The climb to the summit is one of the most strenuous hikes in the Highlands.

The Washburn Trail starts on NY 9D, 0.8 mile north of NY 301 in Cold Spring and 200 yards north of the intersection with Fair Street. There is parking along the highway. The trail starts up a sparsely wooded area, climbs left through a young forest, and crosses an overgrown field. It turns left on a haul road heading for an abandoned quarry. Before entering the quarry floor, the trail turns sharply right and climbs near the quarry's south rim, with views over the Hudson to Storm King.

From the top of the quarry, the trail climbs steeply at first and at 0.3 mile is joined by an abandoned trail coming from the south. Returning hikers should be careful not to miss this right turn. Continuing north, the trail resumes its steep ascent, with ever-increasing views of the river valley to the west and south. After passing the southern terminus of the Undercliff Trail (yellow) on the left at 1.4 miles and climbing some false summits, the trail finally reaches the wooded summit at 1.8 miles. This point is recognized by the end of an old carriage road that circles the summit. The trail joins the road and soon comes to a lookout with views north and west to Lake Surprise Valley below, then Breakneck Ridge, the Shawangunks, and finally the Catskills in the far distance.

From the viewpoint, the road swings to the east face of the summit with a second similar lookout. After a couple of descending switchbacks, the trail splits off from the carriage road at the end of a tight left curve. (This turn right and downhill is easily missed.) The trail descends straight into Bull Gap, crossing the carriage road twice, and ends at 2.3 miles at the beginning of the Notch Trail (blue), where the footpath crosses the same carriage road that was followed higher up. The road to the right, also blazed blue, is the Highlands Trail, which continues down to the Lone Star property and joins the Split Rock Trail.

A popular circular hike is to combine the Washburn Trail, the Notch Trail, the Brook Trail, and Old Lake Surprise Road (Dairy Road), ending on NY 9D at a stone-pillared gate, 0.2 mile north of the starting point.

Wilkinson Memorial Trail   *Length: 8.0 miles Blaze: yellow*

Named after Samuel N. Wilkinson, a tireless worker for trails, the Wilkinson Memorial Trail begins on NY 9D, 2.4 miles north of Cold Spring and 0.3 mile north of the Breakneck tunnel. There is ample parking on the west side of the road south of the trailhead. The eastern end of the trail may be reached from Old Albany Post Road (Uhl Road on older maps), which goes west from US 9 about 4 miles north of its intersection with NY 301. Roadside parking is available just before a bridge. Do not park close to the houses at the junction beyond the bridge.

From NY 9D, the trail begins by climbing a curving woods road and then crossing a small brook at a large oak at 0.5 mile. A short distance farther on, the Breakneck Bypass Trail (red) begins on the right. Continuing ahead, the Wilkinson Memorial Trail soon crosses a brook and ascends steeply through woods to the base of the rocky summit wall. The short final climb is diagonally across the wall using staircase-like ledges to reach the summit (900 feet) of Sugarloaf Mountain at about one mile. There are views to Bull Hill (Mount Taurus) to the south, Schunemunk to the west, the Shawangunks and Catskills to the northwest across the Hudson, and the ruins of Bannerman's Castle on Pollepel Island in the foreground.

Crossing the top of Sugarloaf Mountain, the trail descends to the east and intersects a woods road. At about 2 miles, the trail crosses a stream and veers left (north) up steep slopes. At the top of this unnamed ridge the trail goes right (east) with an expansive view above Melzingah Reservoir. It then descends to a notch below Sunset Point, where it turns left on a woods road and is joined by the Notch Trail (blue) coming down from Breakneck Ridge. Both trails descend to Squirrel Hollow Brook and cross it on a rickety bridge. Here the two trails part ways, the Notch Trail descending to the left and the Wilkinson Memorial Trail ascending to the right.

The Wilkinson Memorial Trail follows Squirrel Hollow Brook upstream for about half a mile. The Breakneck Ridge Trail (white) merges in from the right and soon goes left, while the Wilkinson continues to follow a woods road up the valley, then leaves the road as it becomes more overgrown. The trail intersects an abandoned wide trail at 4.5 miles, after which a short, steep climb leads to the crest of Scofield Ridge (1,100 feet), with wide views in all directions, including the Manhattan skyline 45 miles away. Other views follow as the trail traverses the ridge. The trail may be difficult to follow here, with cairns frequently marking the way.

At the north end of the ridge, a narrow lookout enables hikers to peer over Hells Hollow. From here the trail goes west in preparation for its descent into the notch between Scofield Ridge and Lambs Hill. The trail makes a sharp right turn at an intersection; the path straight ahead ends a short distance away at a viewpoint over the Hudson River. Leaving the ridge at 6.2 miles, the trail descends on a woods road to the rough Overmountain Road at the notch. Turning right (east) leads to the top of the Hells Hollow cleft, where the eroded road becomes impassable except to pedestrian traffic. The end of the Fishkill Ridge Trail (white) is reached at about 7 miles. The Wilkinson Memorial Trail turns right and starts a long descent, reaching the foot of the Hollow after a couple of long switchbacks. Strewn with boulders that have been falling off the mountain for centuries, this deep valley retains a refreshing layer of cold air through most of the summer. A steep descent of 0.5 mile brings the trail to the valley floor, where it skirts a small pond, then descends gently to a private road at the edge of the forest. The trail turns right toward a junction with Old Albany Post Road, where it terminates.

Trails in the Southern Highlands

The long wooded ridges of Canada Hill (840 feet) and White Rock (885 feet) and the prominent cone of Sugarloaf Hill (765 feet) rise from the eastern shore of the Hudson River north of Anthony's Nose and South Mountain Pass. Cloaked in a forest of oaks, hemlocks, and laurel, and concealing several small ponds, these hills are interlaced with a network of graded trails.

The four primary trails are the Sugarloaf Trail, the Osborn Loop, the Carriage Connector, and the Appalachian Trail. Hikes of nearly any desired length are possible by combining segments of different trails. These trails, which lie mostly within the Hudson Highlands State Park, generally provide relatively easy walking. Unmarked carriage roads extend the number of circular hikes possible even further. These wide woods roads are particularly fine for snowshoeing and cross-country skiing when conditions are favorable.

There are four major access points to the trail network in this area. The Sugarloaf Trail is reached from NY 9D south of NY 403. The Appalachian Trail crosses US 9 at its intersection with NY 403, with parking on a small road running between the two highways just north of the intersection. Very limited parking is available where the Appalachian Trail crosses South Mountain Pass

Road. For those climbing Anthony's Nose on the Appalachian Trail, parking is available on the west side of NY 9D just north of the Bear Mountain Bridge.

Appalachian Trail   *Length: 5.8 miles Blaze: white*
This major trail crosses the southern Highlands. See chapter 19, "Long Distance Trails," for selected sections including access to Anthony's Nose, or see the *Appalachian Trail Guide to New York-New Jersey* for a complete description of the 5.8 miles.

Carriage Connector   *Length: 0.9 mile Blaze: yellow*
The main purpose of the Carriage Connector is to bypass the moderately strenuous climb to White Rock. As the name implies, the trail is entirely on old carriage roads, which makes for easy walking. The trail begins where the southbound Appalachian Trail, coming from the intersection of US 9 and NY 403, leaves the valley and climbs west to White Rock. The Carriage Connector continues north along the valley bottom. At 0.5 mile, a road to the right leads in 0.8 mile to the summit of a hill with an obstructed view. At 0.6 mile, two roads intersect the Carriage Connector; the road to the right leads to NY 403 and the road ahead leads to the park boundary. The Carriage Connector turns left (west) and climbs gently to the saddle between White Rock on the left and Castle Rock on the right. The trail ends where it meets the Osborn Loop (blue). Hikers heading for Sugarloaf Hill should continue straight (west) and those heading for White Rock should turn left (south).

North Redoubt Trail   *Length: 0.3 mile Blaze: red*
North Redoubt is the site of one of the forts built in 1776-1777 to defend the Hudson Highlands. The trailhead is on Philipse Brook Road (known locally as Snake Hill Road and officially as County 11, Bill Brown Road), 0.3 mile east of NY 9D. The nearest parking is along NY 9D, since parking is not available at the trailhead.

The trail begins on the south side of the road directly across from the gate to the Walter Hoving Home. The trail becomes apparent beyond some roadside rocks and goes left (east), paralleling the road. The climb is gentle and contours above a brook. As the trail gradually curves more and more to the right (south), it passes within sight of a private home on the left. At the edge of the property, the trail curves further right (southwest) and becomes steeper. The climb is moderated by a few switchbacks, the last leading toward the summit ridge. The footpath is faint here and disappears entirely as the height of land is reached. Even with the trail blazed, hikers are advised to identify landmarks that can be used to locate the trail on the way back. Continuing in a northerly direction through open woods the trail leads to the summit with a view of the Hudson River framed by the rounded bulk of Storm King and Bull Hill (Mount Taurus). Ruins of stone structures used by the Continental Army can be found near the summit.

Osborn Loop
Length: 3.8 miles Blaze: blue

The Osborn Loop forms most of a loop around the mid-section of the southern part of the Hudson Highlands State Park. A section of the Appalachian Trail completes the loop. The Osborn Loop can be reached from the northwest via the Sugarloaf Trail and from the south or east via the Appalachian Trail. From the west, it can be accessed via the trails of the Manitoga Nature Preserve. A contribution for parking at Manitoga is expected.

One end of the Osborn Loop is at White Rock at a trail junction with the Appalachian Trail. The latter provides the shortest access, in this case from the junction of US 9 and NY 403. The Osborn Loop begins by descending for about a mile into the valley that separates White Rock from Castle Rock to the north. At the bottom it meets the Carriage Connector (yellow) coming in from the right. The Osborn Loop turns left (west) and descends gently to the saddle between Sugarloaf Hill and Castle Rock, where it meets the Sugarloaf Trail (red). The Osborn Loop veers sharply left, now heading in a southerly direction. At 0.2 mile, the trail splits off to the left away from the descending rough and sometimes wet woods road. This road is the other end of the unmarked trail that circles the base of Sugarloaf Hill.

From this point, the Osborn Loop climbs gently at first and then in earnest for a short distance. After a level section, a trail to the Manitoga Nature Preserve goes to the right. A cairn or sign may indicate the spot. After another half-mile of gentle climbing, the Osborn Loop reaches its southern terminus at the Appalachian Trail. One can continue ahead to return to the starting point via the Appalachian Trail or turn right to head south to South Mountain Pass Road.

Sugarloaf Trail
Length: 1.6 miles Blaze: red

Though less than 800 feet high, Sugarloaf Hill is a prominent landmark in the southern Hudson Highlands because of its long summit ridge, conical southwestern shoulder, and proximity to the river. The profile of the mountain is said to resemble a sugarloaf, the solid cone shape in which sugar was imported before the days of granulated sugar.

The shortest hike to the summit begins from NY 9D, 1.0 mile south of its junction with NY 403. Southbound drivers should turn left at the DEC sign for the Castle Rock Unique Area, passing through a gate with two square pillars, one bearing the inscription "Wing & Wing." After turning onto the dirt road, bear left at the fork, pass a red barn on the right, and continue to a gravel parking area. Metro-North Railroad riders can reach the trailhead from the Garrison station by walking half a mile up to the junction of NY 403 and NY 9D and then south on NY 9D.

Hikers can reach the trail from the parking area by walking back to the fork, turning left toward the hills, and turning right at the first unpaved road. Very shortly the trail makes an abrupt turn left across an uncultivated field, climbs straight uphill to a narrow woods road at the edge of the forest, and then goes right. An old wooden gazebo located here is an excellent place from which to enjoy the pastoral setting with West Point and the Highlands in the background.

From the gazebo, the trail is level until it turns sharply left uphill on a wide dirt road. An alternative approach to the Sugarloaf Trail is to continue straight ahead on an unmarked trail that circles the base of the mountain. This 2.3-mile trail connects with the Osborn Loop (blue) on the far side of Sugarloaf Hill. Along this path, in the open field at the foot of Sugarloaf, is a marker indicating the site of the Beverly Robinson house, used as a headquarters by Benedict Arnold.

Continuing on the Sugarloaf Trail, long switchbacks lead up the shady northern slopes. A short distance beyond a small pond on the left is the broad saddle between Castle Rock and Sugarloaf Hill. At a major trail junction, two arms of the Osborn Loop (blue) lead ahead, while the Sugarloaf Trail turns right and begins the final half-mile ascent to the summit. The climb is at first moderately steep, then levels off as it continues to the southern outlook, with its view of the Hudson River, Fort Montgomery, and the distant hills of Harriman Park. One can appreciate the importance of Sugarloaf Hill during the American Revolution as a vantage point for monitoring traffic on the Hudson River. The trail ends here and hikers must double back to the trail junction at the saddle.

OTHER AREAS NEAR THE HUDSON RIVER

Within the Hudson Highlands, there are a potpourri of places to visit ranging from walks along the river to rugged hikes and even a walk across the river on the Bear Mountain Bridge. A few hours are all that are needed to explore some locations, while others require more time. Some sites are so small or ecologically sensitive that they cannot accommodate more than a few visitors per week. Others are managed as sanctuaries, and public access for hiking is not a top priority. These last two groups are best left for people to discover on their own.

Camp Smith

Views abound on this rugged trail from Anthony's Nose through the Camp Smith National Guard Training Site. The trail, opened in 1995, was built by high school dropouts who were part of a federally funded military-style program and by volunteers from the New York-New Jersey Trail Conference. Parking is available along US 6 at the southern terminus of the trail and at its midpoint. Access to the northern terminus is via the Appalachian Trail with parking along NY 9D just north of the Bear Mountain Bridge. This strenuous trail, which is best approached with a car shuttle, has a net elevation gain of 1,100 feet when hiked from south to north. Hikers may see military personnel engaged in tactical maneuvers, and everyone is asked to remain on the trail.

Camp Smith Trail   *Length: 3.7 miles Blaze: blue*
The Camp Smith Trail starts at the old toll house on the road up to the Bear Mountain Bridge (US 6), 0.7 mile north of the Camp Smith entrance. Behind the toll house, the trail turns left and parallels the road, climbing steadily. It drops steeply down through a rock field and turns left before reaching a massive cliff. At 0.3 mile the trail crosses a breached earthen dam. Staying within sight and sound of US 6, it works its way gradually uphill, crossing small ridges. At 0.6 mile, it begins a serious ascent of Manitou Mountain, soon climbing very steeply on a series of rock steps. It turns left, climbs more gradually, and makes a right turn onto the top of the Knife Edge, an open rock face.

The trail drops slightly and resumes its ascent of Manitou Mountain, all the while turning west and toward the river. It passes through a gully as it approaches viewpoints on the brow of the mountain and, at 0.9 mile, turns away from the river and passes through the aftermath of the extensive 1993 fire. The trail turns left toward a rock outcropping with views, and then turns right and away from the views to begin its descent. The rock steps, switchbacks, and sidehill construction make it possible to descend the extremely steep talus slope safely.

At 1.2 miles, the trail reaches the bottom of the slope, crosses a flat area, turns gradually left, and reaches a small rock outcropping with a view. From the viewpoint the trail heads inland and comes to a trail junction at 1.3 miles, where a 440-foot X-blazed trail bypasses the 0.4-mile loop to a view. After the two branches rejoin at 1.6 miles, the Camp Smith Trail continues its descent, crossing intermittent brooks. At 1.9 miles it reaches a parking area on US 6 at a large bend in the road 2.2 miles north of the Camp Smith entrance.

Continuing north to Anthony's Nose, the trail crosses Broccy Creek and heads uphill, paralleling the road. Turning away from US 6, it joins and leaves woods roads and crosses streams. It rises out of a ravine and turns right on a rock outcropping at 2.4 miles with views down to Iona Island. Paralleling the river high over the road, the trail soon begins to climb steeply. Another rock outcropping with a view at 2.7 miles provides a rest spot before the trail turns sharply right. The remaining 0.4 mile is an unrelenting assault on Anthony's Nose. There are seasonal views along the way, with year-round views on open rock slabs and on the top. The trail dips down off the summit to join a woods road. A left turn leads to panoramic views of the Bear Mountain Bridge, Bear Mountain-Harriman State Parks, and the Hudson River. A right turn takes the hiker to the Appalachian Trail where the Camp Smith Trail ends at 3.7 miles. NY 9D is 0.6 mile downhill to the left.

Dennings Point

This 66-acre section of the Hudson Highlands State Park is located in Beacon. Acquired by the state in 1988, the park is open to the public for walking and cross-country skiing. A 1.2-mile trail, which is a woods road, circles the heavily wooded point. The trail is near the water and has vegetation that attracts wildlife, making it a great spot to watch birds.

Though small, Dennings Point is rich in interesting vegetation, wildlife, and local history. In 1785 William Denning, a New York merchant, purchased lands in the area that were forfeited by Beverly Robinson, a Tory who had returned to England. In later years, the Denning family lived in the southern two-thirds of the point. A carpet of myrtle and flowering shrubs are evidence of landscaping long abandoned.

The northern third of the point has been the site of the Dennings Point Brick Works (built in 1925), a lightweight building materials factory, and the Noesting Pin Ticket Company, which made paper clips and other wire products. Clay pits and piles of rejected bricks are scattered throughout the area, and the pin ticket factory building still stands.

Dennings Point can be reached by taking NY 9D to South Avenue in Beacon, turning right onto Dennings Avenue, and following Dennings Avenue Extension to the end. The trail begins 0.3 mile from the end of the road. As of 1997, parking is restricted to the east side of the bridge. From the parking area, hikers can walk south, follow the road over the bridge, and cross the tracks onto the point. Once on the point, the route passes a road to the right, which leads to a park employee's residence. The route to the loop trail turns south and leads to the abandoned Noesting Pin Ticket Company factory building.

The trail starts on the other side of the factory building. Just past the trailhead, at a Y-junction, the trail bears left to follow the eastern shore of the point. Along the way it passes a berm, a cement block house, and a stone foundation. The trail contours some 50 feet from the shore. At 0.6 mile, it passes through a carpet of myrtle. At the end of the point, the trail turns to head north along the western shore with views out over the river. At low tide one can walk along the rocky beach. At 1.1 miles, the trail turns away from the river and arrives back at the pin factory 0.1 mile later.

Little Stony Point

In 1967, this former quarry and gravel shipping site was saved from industrial development. Now a public park, it is managed by the Little Stony Point Citizens Association, a volunteer group, under an agreement with the New York State Office of Parks, Recreation, and Historic Preservation. Parking is near the trailhead on the west side of NY 9D, 0.6 mile north of Cold Spring.

After crossing the railroad tracks on a bridge, an unmarked trail of 0.8 mile circles the point, while a 0.2-mile trail leads to a viewpoint out over the river. The trails offer wide, open views over the Hudson toward Storm King as well as up and down the river. A sandy beach on the north side of Little Stony Point is popular during the summer.

Manitoga

In 1942, designer Russel Wright purchased property which had been damaged by quarrying rock which was used to build the New York Public Library. Calling his property Manitoga, which means "Place of the Great Spirit" in the Algonquin language, Wright began restoring the land. Although the landscape appears natural, it was actually carefully designed with native trees, ferns, mosses and wildflowers as a backdrop. Opened to the public in 1975, the year before his death, Manitoga is now a nature preserve and education center.

Wright is one of the best-known designers of home furnishings. It is estimated that by the 1950s over 125 million pieces of his American Modern Dinnerware were made. Examples of his work are in the Metropolitan Museum of Art and the Museum of Modern Art.

All the trails begin and end together and are laid out in the form of a ladder with each rung crossing over a little higher on the hill. At the top, the trails connect to the Osborn Loop and Appalachian Trail on Canada Hill. The trails at Manitoga are only blazed for clockwise travel and are typically narrower than most hiking trails. The blazes are wooden disks with unique patterns burned into them.

Manitoga is on the east side of NY 9D, 2.5 miles north of the Bear Mountain bridge and 2 miles south of NY 403. It is also accessible from the Manitou whistle stop on Metro-North Hudson Line by walking though Manitou Point Preserve (see below) and north along NY 9D. Parking is available with a suggested contribution. For more information, contact Manitoga, P.O. Box 249, Garrison, NY 10524; (914) 424-3812.

Deer Run Trail *Length: 0.8 mile Blaze: wooden disc*
The Deer Run Trail is the first trail to branch off to the right from the main trail. It shortly crosses a brook on a split log bridge. At Four Corners Room, it rejoins the main trail for the descent back to the trailhead.

Lost Pond Trail *Length: 1.8 miles Blaze: wooden disc*
After the White Pine Trail splits off to the right, the main trail becomes the Lost Pond Trail, named after a small spring-fed pond. The trail starts its descent at the pond and goes through a blueberry field, Boulder Amphitheater and a fern meadow. It rejoins the main trail at Four Corners Room for the final descent.

White Pine Trail *Length: 1.2 miles Blaze: wooden disc*
The White Pine Trail is the second trail to the right from the main trail. It ascends steeply to a hawk's eye-view of the forest below. On the descent to Four Corners Room, it crosses a fern meadow which has New York, Interrupted, Cinnamon, Christmas, and other ferns.

Manitou Point Preserve

Just north of the Bear Mountain Bridge, a 136-acre peninsula juts into the Hudson River. Formerly known as Mystery Point, Manitou Point Preserve offers the enduring natural beauty of the river as well as a sense of the grace of a bygone era. The natural features of the property include a mature wooded upland with numerous rock outcrops, a steep-sided ravine, a portion of Manitou Marsh, and sheer rocky bluffs along the Hudson River.

Manitou Point Preserve was formerly a portion of the estate of Edward Livingston, a descendent of Philip Livingston, a signer of the Declaration of Independence. Edward, a New York City businessman, purchased the property in 1894 as a country home for his family and to establish stables and kennels for his horses and champion Irish wolfhounds. Following the construction in 1894 of a 50 foot arched stone bridge over the railroad tracks and a dam on Copper Mine Brook to create a reservoir, Edward hired the architect George Frederick Pelham to design a home. The brick colonial revival mansion was completed in 1897, with extensive carriage roads, a smaller residence, an ice house, a carriage house and an ox barn added later.

Livingston's daughter, Clarice, maintained the property until 1938 when she sold it. In 1984, Lee Pomeroy, a New York architect, formed the Mystery Point Associates to acquire the property. After extensive renovations, he sold the property in 1990 to Open Space Institute, Inc. and Scenic Hudson, Inc. The mansion is now the national headquarters of Outward Bound, Inc. and is not open to the public.

The property has two distinct trail systems connected by a bridge over the railroad tracks. Some of the trails are old carriage roads, others are narrow trails; several new trails are under development. On the point, there is a loop trail through a mixed forest, a little over a mile long. One third of it is on a narrow ledge with sheer drops into and views over the Hudson River. It may be closed in icy weather. The uplands trails are in a primarily hemlock forest. There will be 2–3 miles of trail on this hillside.

There are two access points to the property, one for cars and the other for pedestrians coming from the Manitou whistle stop on the Metro-North Hudson Line. The upper entrance from NY 9D is 1.8 miles north of the Bear Mountain Bridge. A parking lot is on the left, shortly beyond the entrance through stone pillars with a white gate. The lower entrance, also through stone pillars with a white gate, is a left turn from Manitou Road, 0.1 mile east of the railroad tracks. The dirt road, largely along the edge of Manitou Marsh, leads 0.6 mile to the dirt road coming down from NY 9D. This intersection is just east of the bridge over the railroad tracks. There are several trailheads along the road that lead to the upland trails.

The trails at Manitou Point can be combined with trails at Manitoga (above) and the Appalachian Trail to make a large loop hike of 7 or more miles starting from the whistle stop, or more ambitious hikes that end at Peekskill via the Camp Smith Trail or at Garrison via the Osborn Loop and Sugarloaf Trail.

For current information, contact the New York-New Jersey Trail Conference, (212)685-9699.

DUTCHESS COUNTY

utchess County, one of the origi-
nal counties of New York State, was formed in 1683. The name of the largest
city, Poughkeepsie, is derived from the Wappingers' name for it, which is re-
puted to mean "reed-covered lodge by the little water place." Surprisingly
enough, three centuries later, some quiet places by the water still exist in the
county and some are accessible to the public.

Geology

From a geological viewpoint, the land surface in Dutchess County is the result
of glacial withdrawal, with rolling hills and few rock outcrops. The land rises
fairly steeply, 100 to 150 feet, from the Hudson River's edge. To the east, gently rolling hills give way to the edge of *thrust fault* (a reverse fault characterized
by a small angle between the horizontal and the plane), resulting from the
Taconic Orogeny (mountain building) and leaving hills over 2,000 feet in elevation. The land between the river and the northeast trending mountains is the
result of deposition in inland seas throughout the region's geological history.

Much of the county is farmed, but a considerable area remains in returning forest. Stands of great trees of mixed deciduous and evergreen varieties are
found in a few small areas. Several streams traverse the county, among them
the Fishkill Creek, Wappingers Creek, and Ten Mile River.

Hiking Opportunities

As the mild-natured scenery suggests, most of the hiking opportunities here are not especially rugged. Nonetheless, Dutchess County is far from devoid of hiking pleasures and challenges. Lovely walks can be combined with picnics or with visits to historic mansions along the Hudson River. Hudson Highlands State Park, with trails up Breakneck Ridge and Sugarloaf, lies in the southwest corner of the county. Scenic Hudson's protection of Mount Beacon and Fishkill Ridge ensures that hikers will be able to continue enjoying the open space adjacent to the park (see chapter 9, "The Hudson Highlands"). Brace Mountain is in the extreme northeast part of the county (see chapter 11, "The Southern Taconics"). The Appalachian Trail traverses the county for about 28 miles from the Putnam line to where it enters Connecticut (see chapter 19, "Long Distance Trails").

In addition to the places described here, hikers will find many other enjoyable areas in Dutchess County. The Institute of Ecosystem Studies has over 1,900 acres, while the Innisfree Garden has a few hundred acres. Peggy Turco's book, *Walks & Rambles in Dutchess and Putnam Counties,* describes interesting hikes.

There are six New York State Department of Environmental Conservation Multiple-Use Areas in the county. Most of these areas have only a parking area and a few logging roads. Their primary use is for hunting and logging, but when hunting season is over, they provide many hiking and bushwhacking opportunities. Stissing Mountain and Taconic-Hereford are described in this chapter. For the others, obtain a pamphlet, *Multiple-Use Areas in Dutchess County,* from the DEC at (914) 831-8780.

For information on available facilities, maps, and schedules, contact the Dutchess County Tourism Promotion Agency on US 9 in Hyde Park; (914) 229-0033 or (800) 445-3131. For information on public transportation, contact Metro-North at (800) 638-7646, Amtrak at (800) 872-7245, or the Dutchess County Loop System at (914) 485-4690.

JAMES BAIRD STATE PARK

Located amid working farms, this 590-acre state park was donated to New York State in 1939 by James Baird, an engineer. The following year, a Civilian Conservation Corps camp was established in the park and the golf course and clubhouse were started, to be officially opened in 1948. Other facilities were completed in 1951. In 1997 the park has hiking, cross-country skiing, golf, tennis, picnic facilities, and a restaurant.

Four well-marked, wide trails wind through wooded areas with deciduous trees and some hemlocks. The terrain is generally a series of small ridges with elevation changes of approximately 75 feet. Vertical slaty rock strata form the ridges and are exposed in a few locations. The trails are wide enough for two or three people to walk side by side or for cross-country skiing during the winter. Using the trail map that is available from the park office, hikers can combine the park's trails to make longer hikes.

The park has its own exits north and south from the Taconic Parkway, located 1.2 miles north of the NY 55 exit. For more information, contact the park at (914) 452-1489 and the restaurant at (914) 473-5520.

BOWDOIN PARK

Bowdoin Park is the largest county park. Adjacent to New Hamburg, its 300 acres offer a hiking trail system, cross-country course, baseball and soccer fields, picnic areas, and a nature center with displays of local flora and fauna. The hilly terrain and large, open fields offer views of the Hudson River and the hills on the other side. The well-used park trails are not clearly marked. A trail map is posted at the park office. The longest trail (2.8 miles) is a loop and follows the park's perimeter.

To reach Bowdoin Park, hikers can take the Metro-North train to New Hamburg, walk 0.5 mile from the station up Main Street to Sheafe Road and walk along the road for another 0.5 mile. Automobile access is from NY 9D in the village of Wappingers Falls or from the southbound lane of US 9, 1.5 miles south of Spackenkill Road (County 113). Bowdoin Park has ample parking, but a parking fee is charged on weekends. For more information, contact the park at (914) 297-1224.

HARLEM VALLEY RAIL TRAIL

The Harlem Line of Metro-North extends from New York City north to Dover Plains. Service was discontinued to Copake Falls in Columbia County in 1972. The New York State Office of Parks, Recreation, and Historic Preservation (NYS-

OPRHP) purchased the almost 18 miles between Wassaic and the Columbia County line in 1989 and then leased it to Dutchess County for thirty years, to be used as a shared-use trail. The County Planning Department and the state received an Intermodal Surface Transportation Efficiency Act (ISTEA) grant for the constructing eight miles from Mechanics Street in Amenia to US 44 in Millerton. In 1996, Dutchess County completed a 4.5-mile segment from Mechanics Street to County 58 (Coleman Station). NYS-OPRHP has plans to construct an additional 4-mile section from Ancram to Copake Falls.

When completed, the 10-foot-wide trail will be paved and available for nonmotorized use and the handicapped. Traditionally, in most parts of the country, bikers yield to hikers, but they cannot be relied on to do so; therefore, hikers should keep well to the right when bike traffic is heavy. For more information, contact Dutchess County Planning Office at (914) 486-3600.

HYDE PARK

The Town of Hyde Park boasts a 10.4-mile trail system linking the Franklin D. Roosevelt National Historic Site, Val-Kill National Historic Site, Vanderbilt Mansion National Historic Site, and Mills-Norrie State Park. These trails are the results of cooperative efforts of federal, state, and local governments, not-for-profit organizations, and private individuals. The north–south trail from the Roosevelt home to the Vanderbilt property and the River Trail in Mills-Norrie State Park are designated segments of the Hudson River Greenway Trail.

Roosevelt National Historic Site contains Franklin Delano Roosevelt's home, library, rose garden, grave, and a small museum. Val-Kill, built in 1925, is the former home of Eleanor Roosevelt. Housing her effects and memorabilia, it is the only National Historic Site dedicated to a First Lady. Vanderbilt National Historic Site, the former home of Frederick Vanderbilt, contains a vast collection of antique furnishings obtained in Europe. The landscaping, including a formal Italian garden restored by volunteers, and the views of and across the Hudson River are magnificent. Mills-Norrie State Park has an historic mansion, environmental center, marina, golf course, and camping area.

There are guided tours at the historic buildings, but times are different for each. Admission is charged at the home of Franklin Roosevelt and at the Vanderbilt mansion. This section of the county contains fine examples of large estates that have survived, more or less intact, from the earliest European settlement. Originally they were self-sufficient farm and property holdings comprising thousands of acres, and much of the landscaping is over 100 years old. Since the estates were in the hands of only a few families, their furnishings represent stylistic continuity. The properties were groomed and the vistas developed with a distinct style that, in the case of each family, was allowed to mature.

Aside from the link to Val-Kill, the Hyde Park Trail rolls along beside the Hudson River, sometimes climbing the bordering ridge. Around the mansions the trail meanders through beautiful tailored grounds. In other parts of the estates, the trail passes large specimen trees, small swampy areas, streams, rock outcrops, and wooded areas. Bard Rock, at the north end of the Vanderbilt estate, and Crum Elbow Point, at the Roosevelt home, provide direct access to the river. Three other places in Mills-Norrie also directly touch the river. The trail, in most places, runs along old carriage roads that are suitable for cross-country skiing, given favorable conditions. However, the walker needs to use caution on the portions along roads that connect the sites.

The Hyde Park Trail (green tulip-leaf emblem) is best done as a series of several short walks covering unique sections of the trail: the Vanderbilt Loop (2.4 miles), the Roosevelt home to Riverfront Park and return (5.0 miles), the Roosevelt home to Val-Kill and return (5.0 miles), and the Mills mansion to Norrie Point and return (4.0 miles). In addition, each of the mansion sites has other trails showing other features of its grounds. At Mills-Norrie, the 10-mile trail system allows for a variety of circular hikes and includes carriage roads and horse trails. Cross-country skiing (no snowmobiling) is permitted on carriage roads and the golf course when conditions are favorable.

Automobile and bicycle access to each site is directly from US 9, except Val-Kill, which is accessible from NY 9G. For additional information about the Roosevelt home, Val-Kill, or the Vanderbilt mansion, contact the National Park Service at (914) 229-9115. For information about Mills-Norrie State Park, call the park office at (914) 889-4646. The Town of Hyde Park Recreation Department can provide information about the Hyde Park Trail (914) 229-8086. Maps are usually available at the sites.

LOCUST GROVE

Originally, at the end of the eighteenth century, this privately owned historic site was part of a 350-acre tract, which included a farm, sawmill, store, and a

LOCUST GROVE.

sloop landing, owned by Henry Livingston, Jr. The subsequent owner, John Montgomery, continued to operate it as a farm from 1830 until 1847, when part of the original property was sold to Samuel F. B. Morse, artist and inventor of the commercial electric telegraph. Morse was interested in landscaping the property, with the results still visible. In 1901 the estate was sold to William and Martha Young. He was a lawyer and merchant, heir to a family hardware fortune. She was a collector of Americana: furniture, china, and decorative art. It was their daughter, Annette, who endowed a trust to maintain Locust Grove as an historical site and wildlife sanctuary. The mansion houses the Young collections as well as Morse memorabilia and early telegraph equipment.

The 150-acre sanctuary includes gardens, walking trails, and the historic mansion. A guided tour, for which there is a charge, is conducted through the mansion. In addition, 3.2 miles of interconnected trails run through fields, woods, and gardens. Trail maps are available showing the trails and describing the historic features of the property. The trails have some steep pitches and offer views of the Hudson River.

Access to the property is from the southbound lane of US 9 just south of Poughkeepsie, with parking on the site. Locust Grove is officially open from May 1 to the end of October. Bicycles are not permitted. For more information, contact Locust Grove, 370 South Road, P.O. Box 1649, Poughkeepsie, NY 12601-5234; (914) 454-4500.

PAWLING NATURE RESERVE

The 1,071-acre Pawling Nature Reserve has been owned by The Nature Conservancy since 1958. Managed by a local volunteer committee, the reserve abounds with interesting plants, several of which are rare, and bird species. It is home to a large deer population, reptiles, amphibians, wild turkeys, and occasional coyotes, beavers, and bobcats. Members of a local gun club have permission to hunt during deer season. There are no public facilities in the preserve.

The generally hilly land contained in the preserve was cleared for farming prior to the Revolutionary War, and some of the stone fences built about that time still exist. Hammersly Ridge, trending north–south, is the high point at 1,053 feet above sea level and about 250 feet above the starting elevation. Vegetation is quite lush, and most of the forest is mixed but some large hemlock stands can be found.

About a mile north of the village of Pawling or 2.5 miles north of NY 55 on NY 22 is County 68, North Quaker Hill Road. A right turn and a drive of 1.4 miles leads to Quaker Lake Road on the left. In another mile and a half, past Quaker Lake on the left, the main parking area is reached. Maps are sometimes available at this location and at a register box where the Appalachian Trail enters the reserve from the south. For more information about the Pawling Nature Reserve, contact the Lower Hudson Chapter of The Nature Conservancy, 41 South Moger Avenue, Mt. Kisco, NY 10549; (914) 244-3271.

Appalachian Trail   *Length: 2.7 miles Blaze: white*
From the south, access to the Pawling Nature Reserve property is either from a blue-blazed side trail 0.4 mile from Hurd's Corner Road, or via the Appalachian Trail. See chapter 19, "Long Distance Trails," for more details, or the *Appalachian Trail Guide to New York-New Jersey* for a complete description of the trail.

Blue Trail   *Length: 2 miles Blaze: blue*
From the trailhead, 300 feet south of Quaker Lake, where the Red Trail also begins, the Blue Trail loops though the south end of the reserve. Along its route there are grape vines, striped maples, and dense undergrowth. Traveling through mixed hardwoods, the trail becomes a woods road. A large hemlock grove is at the junction of the Red and Blue trails. A 0.4-mile Blue Trail section is the west access from Hurd's Corner Road, where the Appalachian Trail enters the reserve. Parking is along the road.

Green Trail   *Length: 0.6 mile Blaze: green*
The Green Trail provides access to the reserve from NY 22 on the west, where it runs from the trailhead to the Appalachian Trail. It is reached from NY 22 at

Hutchinson Road, 100 feet along to the corner of Deer Ridge Road. After passing 250 feet along the edge of a neighboring landowner's lawn, the trail meanders upward to a ridge with a view west. It passes through young hardwood forest and occasional hemlock groves. It meets and turns south on the Appalachian Trail, which is joint with the Red Trail at this point, and then heads north to meet the Orange Trail loop before returning to its starting point on Deer Ridge Road. Parking is along the road.

Northern Yellow Trail   *Length: 0.7 mile Blaze: yellow*
This access trail starts at a trailhead and parking area 1.4 miles north of the reserve's main entrance on Quaker Lake Road. The trail goes over a wooden bridge, through deep fern undergrowth, and past several overgrown stone walls. It rises steeply to end at the Appalachian Trail (white).

Orange Trail   *Length: 0.7 mile Blaze: orange*
The Orange Trail starts from the Green Trail soon after its beginning. Shortly, it turns south and then loops back to its starting point, passing through young hardwood forest.

Red Trail   *Length: 2.4 miles Blaze: red*
From the trailhead, which is south of Quaker Lake, the Red Trail climbs through a stand of hemlock and spruce to a junction with the Blue Trail at 0.4 mile. It continues uphill, crossing the Appalachian Trail and climbing north until it temporarily ends at another junction with the Appalachian Trail. There are views down to Quaker Lake along the way. The Red Trail picks up again 0.1 mile to the north (left) along the Appalachian Trail, where it turns left and continues for 0.7 mile back down to Quaker Lake Road, ending at the Yellow Trail trailhead.

Yellow Trail   *Length: 0.6 mile Blaze: yellow*
Access to the Yellow Trail is at the main parking area of the reserve. A registration station with maps and a sign-in book is 150 feet from the parking area. This main access trail almost immediately runs past a deep, cool, hemlock- and fern-filled gorge through which a waterfall flows. At 0.3 mile there is a swamp, which at times hosts many noisy frogs. The trail climbs gradually to the top of the ridge and ends just past the crest at the Appalachian Trail.

POUGHKEEPSIE-HIGHLAND RAILROAD BRIDGE

This 6,767-foot-long railroad bridge crosses the Hudson River 212 feet above the water and offers views up and down the river. First chartered in 1871, the bridge was completed in 1888 at a cost of $10 million. It was the only rail bridge across the Hudson River south of Albany that carried freight. Used extensively until 1969, it was the gateway to southern New England. A fire in 1974 caused major damage and Penn Central ceased operations. At that time engineering studies evaluated the reconstruction possibilities, but nothing was done. Two years later, the bridge was included in the Conrail system who sold it to a private investor in 1984. Ownership again changed in 1990 to another private investor without any work being done on the bridge. In 1990, the efforts of Poughkeepsie resident Bill Sepe, to use the bridge for pedestrians and bicycles, resulted in the formation of a not-for-profit organization, the Poughkeepsie-Highland Railroad Bridge Co., Inc. People with past connections to the bridge have donated memorabilia including the original construction blueprints complete with field notes. This material is displayed at public events and bridge celebrations.

Access to the bridge is only on guided tours at set times on weekends and holidays, otherwise the gate is locked. Children are to be accompanied by an adult. The free tour crosses one-third of the bridge on a metal grating with a handrail. The group has started to build wooden decking across the bridge. Access is from Haviland Road, located about one-eighth of a mile north of the Mid-Hudson Bridge on US 9W. Turn east and proceed about half a mile down Haviland Road to the Central Hudson Gas and Electric Corporation substation on the left side of the road. Parking is along the left side. For information, contact the Poughkeepsie-Highland Railroad Bridge Co., Inc., 65 Gifford Avenue, Poughkeepsie, NY 12601; (914) 454-9649.

REESE NATURE SANCTUARY

From the 1830s, industries and mills developed along Wappingers Creek, a major tributary of the Hudson River. As industry left the area, the surrounding land reverted to its wooded state. In 1982, Francis and Willis Reese donated 98 acres along the creek to the National Audubon Society as a wildlife and nature sanctuary, particularly for migratory birds. Now owned and managed by the

Putnam Highlands Chapter, the Reese Nature Sanctuary provides an unmarked trail on a ridge rising steeply about 60 feet from Wappingers Creek. The trail rolls for 1.25 miles through stands of large deciduous and pine trees. Informal paths lead down to the creek.

Metro-North stops at New Hamburg; from there, Reese Sanctuary is a short walk up Main Street, with access through the southwest corner of New Hamburg Park. Weekday parking is restricted to two hours.

STISSING MOUNTAIN AREA

About midway between the Hudson River and the Housatonic Highlands of Connecticut is 1,400-foot Stissing Mountain. The distinctive dome has striking escarpments at its northern end and slopes gently to join low hills to the south. It contains rock 1.1 billion years old, the oldest in New York State. Stissing's setting is more pastoral than rugged, with forest and pasture land about equal. Yet the mountain and its three lakes do convey a sense of wildness. The fire tower on the summit commands a 360-degree view that includes the Catskills to the west and the Taconics toward the northeast. In clear weather the buildings in Albany can be seen with binoculars.

The American Museum of Natural History, at 79th Street and Central Park West in New York City, has a display highlighting Stissing Mountain and surrounding Dutchess County. The large-scale model, "Bird's Eye View of Stissing Mountain," shows how the dome, composed of Precambrian gneiss, dominates the Pine Plains lowlands, composed of limestone, shale, and slate. This countryside was once covered by glaciers, and the nearby ponds—Twin Island, Stissing, and Thompson—are the remnants of glacial kettles, formed when huge masses of debris-covered ice finally melted some 15,000 years ago.

In 1986, the Friends of Stissing Landmarks (FOSL) formed after the NYS DEC announced plans for the demolition of the 90-foot fire tower. Erected in 1934 by the Civilian Conservation Corps, the tower had been staffed and in service for forty years when aircraft assumed forest fire surveillance. As a local landmark, it appears on the seal of the Town of Pine Plains. Thanks to a citizen petition, the tower was saved. In 1991 The Nature Conservancy gave FOSL one acre of land, which surrounds the tower. FOSL restored the tower and re-opened it to the public in July 1993. Thanks to a gift from the DEC in 1994, FOSL now owns the tower. Trails to the tower are on private land, accessible to the public courtesy of adjacent landowners.

Stissing Mountain

Three trailheads provide access to trails up Stissing Mountain. The first trailhead is from Lake Road, off either NY 199 or NY 82 near Pine Plains. Lake Road is reached by traveling one mile west of the junctions of NY 199 and NY 82. After a left on Lake Road, drivers will find the parking area at 1.7 miles. Hikers can also reach Lake Road by turning at the firehouse one mile south of the intersection of NY 82 and NY 199. The parking area is 1.7 miles from the firehouse.

The trail from the Lake Road parking area is an ideal short hike, with an easygoing, rapid ascent, rewarding views, and a geologically interesting setting. The summit loop can be traversed in two hours or less; however, most hikers will want to allow more time to climb the tower and enjoy the views. From the trailhead on Lake Road, the trail climbs steeply for a short distance until it joins a woods road. The route then turns left, following the woods road up a gentle climb to a trail junction at 0.3 mile with a register box that contains trail brochures. At this point, the yellow-blazed road splits. A rocky, steep trail leads south (left), reaching the tower in 0.3 mile. The woods road continues to the southwest (right), reaching the tower in 0.6 mile. It is more enjoyable to ascend the ridge via the trail and to come down via the road, versus the other way around. Both trails cross private prop-erty, so hikers must stay on the trails.

SEVEN WELLS
DOVER PLAINS

The second trailhead is on Mountain Road, 3.7 miles north of Stanfordville. Five miles south of Pine Plains on NY 82, turn west onto Stissing Lane, and then north at the T junction onto Mountain Road, continuing for 2 miles. There is parking at the cul-de-sac at the end of Mountain Road. The blue-blazed trail is along a woods road through private prop-erty. Along its 2.7-mile route, it passes through young mixed hardwoods and occasional wetland areas. The soil in the area is thin and cannot support dense woodland. The land had been totally cleared by the mid-to-late 1800s, the wood used to provide charcoal for the iron fur-naces at Dover Town and Millerton. At

0.5 mile, it intersects with the trail coming from Hicks Hill Road.

The third trail starts on Hicks Hill Road, off NY 199, 4 miles west of Pine Plains. The trailhead is 3.5 miles south of NY 199. The red-blazed trail, mostly an old logging road, leads through the Stissing Mountain Multiple-Use Area. The trail intersects the Ridge Trail at 2 miles. Turning north at the intersection onto the Ridge Trail leads to the tower in another 2 miles.

There are other trails in the 532-acre Stissing Mountain Multiple-Use Area, where hunting is permitted in season. For more information, contact the New York State DEC office at Stony Kill, NY 9D, Wappingers Falls, NY 12590; (914) 831-3109; or Friends of Stissing Landmarks, Inc., P.O. Box 37, Pine Plains, NY 12567-0037; (518) 398-5673.

Thompson Pond

In 1959, The Nature Conservancy, the Dutchess County Bird Club, and a committee of interested citizens led by the *Register-Herald* of Pine Plains purchased and preserved all of Thompson Pond, at the east base of Stissing Mountain. This 451-acre tract is noted for its great diversity in plant and animal life. In 1973 Thompson Pond became a Registered Natural Landmark.

The shallow pond is a 44-acre bog-pond, with a deep peat deposit, bordered by expanding cattail and bulrush marsh. It is more than a half-mile long and a quarter-mile wide, the most southern of the three glacial ponds. Thompson Pond, Stissing Lake, and Mud (or Twin Island) Pond are the remnants of a glacial kettle, formed when a huge mass of debris-covered glacial ice melted 15,000 years ago, at the end of the Pleistocene Epoch.

The pond, marsh, swamp, and upland forest offer a great diversity of fauna and flora. Over four hundred species of plants have been catalogued, and a vast number of birds recorded, including migratory warblers, marsh birds, and predatory species. The pond teems with fish; the land is home to over two dozen mammal species.

To reach Thompson Pond, drivers should take NY 82 to Pine Plains and turn west at the firehouse onto Lake Road. The parking area is 1.5 miles west and on the left. Cars can be left on Lake Road at the start of the trail, which begins at a small seasonal brook.

From that small parking area on Lake Road, a yellow-blazed trail runs around the pond and through the woods for about 3 miles. Several other minor trails branch off from the main trail. There is a register box with maps 300 yards from the preserve's entrance sign.

The preserve is open all year. Permitted uses include hiking, ski-touring, and studying for education and research. The Thompson Pond Committee oversees the property for The Nature Conservancy. For more information contact the Lower Hudson Chapter of The Nature Conservancy, 41 South Moger Avenue, Mt. Kisco, NY 10549; (914) 244-3271.

STONY KILL FARM

The New York State Department of Environmental Conservation owns this 756-acre site consisting of approximately 3.5 miles of trails, an operating farm with crop fields and pasture, rolling woodlands, and small ponds. Along the Verplanck Ridge Trail there is a rise in elevation of about 70 feet. There are both woodland trails and trails around the active farm area. In the winter, these trails are open for cross-country skiing and snowshoeing. Snow shoes may be rented at the site. Hunting and pets are not permitted on the 756-acre property.

In 1683 Gulian Verplanck and Francis Rombout bought 85,000 acres from the local Native Americans. The land was subdivided and generally farmed. James deLancey Verplanck built the Manor House in 1842 on 1,000 acres, including the present Stony Kill farm area. In 1942, 756 acres were given to the State of New York Department of Education for public use and education. The New York State Agricultural and Technical College at Farmingdale managed the property until 1963, when it became inactive. In 1973 it entered its present phase as an environmental education center.

The wide trails have easy grades. There are interpretive markings along the 0.5-mile unblazed Woodland Trail. The Verplanck Ridge Trail (yellow) is 1.5 miles long. The Sierra Trail (white) runs through flat forest land with a marsh and pond near the trail, offering the choice of a 1.0- or 2.0-mile loop.

Stony Kill is located on NY 9D, 4.5 miles south of Wappingers Falls Village and 2.0 miles north of I-84. A prominent sign is located at the entrance on the west side of NY 9D. Parking is permitted at the Manor House, the farmstead, and the entrance to the Sierra Trail on County 36. For more information, call (914) 831-8780.

TACONIC-HEREFORD MULTIPLE-USE AREA

This 909-acre multiple-use area has a network of trails mostly on logging roads.

Access is from a parking area just south of Tyrell Road on the Taconic State Parkway, a parking area on Tyrell Road, or a smaller parking area near the end of Pond Gut Road off NY 82.

The largest multiple-use area in Dutchess County is actively managed for timber. The easy trails and woods roads meander through dense chestnut oak and hickory forests, interspersed with younger growth full of dappled light. Frequent stone walls attest to the area's farming days. At the northwestern section, there are grassy meadows. A hemlock forest, wetlands, and mixed hardwoods forest appear toward Pond Gut Road.

Hunting in season, mountain biking, and horseback riding are permitted. One woods road (orange) is open to snowmobiles when the conditions are favorable. Permits are required if camping for more three days or for ten or more people in a party. For a map, contact the New York State DEC office at Stony Kill, NY 9D, Wappingers Falls, NY 12590; (914) 831-3109.

TIVOLI BAYS

The Tivoli Bays area is part of the Hudson River National Estuarine Research Reserve. The New York State Department of Environmental Conservation manages the site as a field laboratory for research and education about the Hudson River Estuary and as a wildlife management area.

In 1850, the New York Central Railroad laid tracks on an embankment at the western edge of the bays. Two bridge openings in the North Bay and three in the South Bay allow water to enter and leave with each tidal cycle. Sediments in the bays have been accumulating at an accelerated rate since then, speeding up the evolution of the bays from deep water to wetland.

Tivoli Bays is a large freshwater tidal wetland surrounded by undeveloped land. The average tidal range at the bays is about 4 feet. The 1,640-acre reserve includes 3.1 miles of trails plus woods roads. The 1.0-mile-long North Bay Trail follows the Stony Creek along waterfalls and a tidal creek through a hemlock ravine, mixed deciduous forest, and tidal swamp. The trail to Cruger Island (0.5 mile), through a mature freshwater tidal swamp, floods at high tide and is wet at low tide. The Overlook Trail goes 1.1 miles from NY 9G through rolling fields and woods to a panoramic view of the North Bay, Hudson River, and the Catskills. The Hogback Trail (0.5 mile) climbs through a hardwood forest with many varieties of wildflowers in the spring. It connects the parking area on Cruger Road with the midpoint of the Overlook Trail. Bard College also has trails here that skirt the South Bay.

Additional activities permitted at the site include canoeing and bird watching, as well as hunting, fishing, or trapping in season. Bicycling is permitted on internal roads except during winter and early spring. Swimming and motorized boats are not permitted. Public field programs are offered on weekends.

For additional information, including a brochure with a map, contact the Hudson River National Estuarine Research Reserve, Bard College Field Station, Annandale, NY 12504; (914) 758-5193.

ELEVEN

THE SOUTHERN TACONICS

ast of the Harlem Valley of New York and west of the Housatonic Valley of Connecticut and Massachusetts rise the Taconics. They extend north through western Massachusetts and eastern New York into southwestern Vermont, where they reach their highest elevations. The name "Taconic" is a modern rendering of a Native American name variously spelled Taghkannock and Taghkanic.

Seemingly remote from civilization, much of the highland in the south is protected as a relatively wild area. Streams tumble down forested escarpments, cutting scenic ravines and gorges. The trail system features sweeping views over the adjacent valleys to Mount Greylock to the north, the Catskill Mountains to the west, and the Hudson Highlands to the southwest.

The forest of the southern Taconics is second or third growth, much of it having been cut in the nineteenth century to provide charcoal for the local iron industry on Mount Riga and at Copake Falls. Large dense stands of mountain laurel are a beautiful sight when in bloom in late June and early July, but, along with thickets of scrub oak found on the upper elevations, they encroach on trails and are a barrier to bushwhacking. Several attractive lakes and ponds bedeck the highland. Riga Lake and South Pond in Connecticut and Plantain Pond in Massachusetts have privately owned shorelines where private roads serve camps and cottages. Bingham Pond, highest in Connecticut at 1,894 feet, is a botanically interesting bog.

The area is particularly unusual geologically. In the late Ordovician Period, a

TACONICS
BASH BISH
FALLS
Dickinson
'79

chain of volcanic islands collided with what was then the North American continent, forcing slices of sediment and rock to glide west from the impact. As a result, the Taconics are a *klippe* (displaced terrain sitting on top of rock originally many miles away). This major North American mountain-building episode is appropriately called the Taconic Orogeny.

Mount Everett (2,602 feet) is the highest and most prominent feature in the southern Taconics. The highest point in Connecticut (2,380 feet), also in the South Taconics, is located at the Connecticut–Massachusetts line on the south slope of Mount Frissell, which rises from the tableland to a summit in Massachusetts. This is the only place in the United States where the highest point of a state is not the summit of a land feature. About a mile to the southeast is Bear Mountain (2,320 feet), the highest summit in Connecticut. The highest elevation of the western range is Brace Mountain (2,311) in New York.

The trail system of the southern Taconics features two parallel trails running north–south: the 15.6-mile South Taconic Trail following the western range and escarpment, and a 16.5-mile section of the Appalachian Trail on the eastern range. Other hiking routes consist mostly of side trails ascending to the highland from the valleys on either side. This system provides for circuit hikes, some of which include stretches of unpaved road.

The trail system's real beauty lies in its route through the many gorges of the highland. The best-known is Bashbish Gorge in Massachusetts, with its towering walls and cascading brook ending in Bashbish Falls. Native American legend has it that several people plunged to their deaths over the falls, notably a woman named Bash Bish, whose body was never found and who became the spirit of the falls. The South Taconic Trail and side trails provide access to the gorge. Located on the eastern escarpment at the Connecticut–Massachusetts line, Sages Ravine is another outstanding gorge. Although the Appalachian Trail goes through the ravine, its most scenic and precipitous section is below the trail. Descending the eastern escarpment south of Mount Everett is Race Brook, a notable series of high cascades, paralleled by the Race Brook Trail. South of Copake Falls, on the west side of the highland in New York, the Robert Brook Trail and the Alander Brook Trail lead up deep hemlock-clad ravines to join the South Taconic Trail.

A large part of the New York section of the highland, which lies along the western range and slope, is in Taconic State Park. The park has outdoor recreation and camping facilities at its Copake Falls area south of Hillsdale and at its Rudd Pond area north of Millerton, both at the base of the highland. Cottages and cabins are also available for rent at the Copake Falls area. The season is from mid-May until late October at Rudd Pond and until December at Copake Falls.

The Connecticut part of the highland is loosely called Mount Riga or the Riga plateau, named after a nineteenth-century community of ironworkers at South Pond (Forge Pond) on the highland, where a restored iron furnace can be seen. Most of this section is owned by Mount Riga, Inc., a private conservation-minded body, but the National Park Service has acquired 1,225 acres from this group as a protective corridor for the Appalachian Trail. In addition, the state owns an area of woodland on the eastern slope above Mass. 41, called Mount Riga State Park (undeveloped), while the Appalachian Mountain Club owns 125 acres adjacent to the Massachusetts state line.

The Massachusetts section is larger than that of New York or Connecticut and is occupied by the Town of Mount Washington, which has no post office or commercial establishments and a year-round population of less than a hundred. The hiking trails are mostly in Mount Washington State Forest, including the Mount Everett Reservation, and in the corridor for the Appalachian Trail. Overnight parking at trailheads and trailside camping is prohibited. Deer hunting is permitted in season.

Road access to the highland from New York on the west starts as NY 344, which goes east from NY 22 through the village of Copake Falls, enters the scenic ravine of Bashbish Brook, and becomes Falls Road in Massachusetts. Climbing steeply past Bashbish Falls, it connects with West Street and East Street in Mount Washington. From East Street, a road leading to the top of Mount Everett goes to a picnic area by Guilder Pond, which at 2,042 feet is one of Massachusetts' highest bodies of water. From there, one can walk up to the top of Mount Everett for a panoramic view.

SOUTH TACONIC TRAIL AND ACCESS TRAILS

The highly scenic South Taconic Trail lies mostly in Taconic State Park and Mount Washington State Forest along the western escarpment and range of the southern Taconics. The trail may be divided into two sections that together span 15.6 miles. The longer southern section starts in the Harlem Valley in New York about 5 miles north of Millerton and ends at NY 344 east of Copake Falls, while the northern section continues north to where NY 23 goes over a low point in the Taconic range just east of the New York–Massachusetts line.

Alander Brook Trail   *Length: 1.4 miles Blaze: blue*
Largely a woods road, the Alander Brook Trail ascends to the South Taconic Trail (white) from the Harlem Valley in New York on the west, following a deep ravine. Cars may be parked at the trailhead on Under Mountain Road, 0.8 mile east of its junction with NY 22; this junction is almost 4 miles of the intersection of NY 22 and NY 344 in Copake Falls. The trailhead lies a little north of Boston Corner, famed for having been a lawless "no man's land" in the 1850s when Massachusetts was ceding the area to New York. Just beyond the trailhead, Under Mountain Road turns right and goes to Rudd Pond Road.

The Alander Brook Trail starts in the woods next to a field and heads north; in 150 yards the Robert Brook Trail (red) goes right. The Alander Brook Trail continues north along the base of the highland, and at 0.8 mile crosses Alander Brook and turns right from the woods road. Ascending through mountain laurel, it turns right onto another woods road at 1.0 mile and climbs along the hemlock-clad ravine of Alander Brook. The trail ends at the South Taconic Trail (white), which comes from the opposite direction and turns north here, off the woods road.

A scenic loop hike is possible by turning left here on the South Taconic Trail (white) and ascending to the west summit of Alander Mountain, going right on the Alander Loop Trail (blue), left on the South Taconic Trail, and right on the Robert Brook Trail (red) to descend to the starting point.

Alander Loop Trail
Length: 1.3 miles Blaze: blue

This trail ascends to the top of the east summit (2,250 feet) of Alander Mountain. It starts at the 5.0-mile point of the South Taconic Trail and goes uphill to the northeast. At 1.2 miles, the Alander Mountain Trail (blue) comes in from the right. Continuing uphill, the trail ends at 1.3 miles at the South Taconic Trail. Turning left on the South Taconic Trail (white) takes the hiker south back to the start of the Alander Loop Trail, for a total circuit length of 2.3 miles.

Brace Mountain Trail
Length: 1.6 miles Blaze: none

Providing the easiest access to scenic Brace Mountain, this unmarked woods road on the highland extends from Mount Washington Road in Connecticut northwest to the South Taconic Trail (white) in New York. The trailhead, with space for parking, is on the west side of the road 2 miles north of the dam at South Pond, with a metal gate barring access to the trail by vehicles. The trail follows the woods road through mountain laurel and crosses Monument Brook at 0.5 mile, the low point on the trail (1,850 feet). At 1.3 miles, an overgrown trail forks right and leads to a Connecticut–New York boundary monument and beyond. In a few yards the Brace Mountain Trail enters New York at a stream and climbs steeply west up Brace Mountain on a stony route, with the extension of the Ashley Hill Trail coming in on the right from Massachusetts. After climbing up to the crest, the trail ends at the South Taconic Trail just north of Brace Mountain's peak. Turning left on the South Taconic Trail, hikers can climb 0.2 mile to the open summit of the mountain at 2,311 feet.

Cedar Brook Trail
Length: 1.0 mile Blaze: blue

This trail climbs north across NY 344 from the parking lot below Bashbish Falls at the start of the northern section of the South Taconic Trail (white). It follows a brook, which it crosses several times beginning at 0.6 mile. Some of the crossings are slippery and difficult. At 0.9 mile, the final crossing occurs and the trail ascends steeply to its junction with the South Taconic Trail at 1.0 mile (1.3 miles on the northern section of the South Taconic Trail).

Mount Frissell Trail
Length: 2.2 miles Blaze: red

This trail on the highland in three states goes over two summits, has views, and reaches the highest point in Connecticut, as well as the tri-state boundary point.

It also takes the hiker through dense mountain laurel, scrub oak, and gray birch. The trail starts from Mount Washington Road–East Street at the Connecticut–Massachusetts line (1,830 feet), where there is limited parking. The trail heads northwest in Massachusetts along a woods road, turning left at 0.2 mile onto a footpath that leads into Connecticut. It ascends Round Mountain very steeply, with views from its open crest. Passing over the summit (2,296 feet) at 0.7 mile, it descends northwest into Massachusetts, reaching the saddle between Round Mountain and Mount Frissell. The trail ascends Mount Frissell steeply, and passes its summit (2,453 feet) at 1.2 miles, where there is a trail register off to the right. The trail then descends the south slope of Mount Frissell. Just before the Massachusetts–Connecticut boundary is a view over the highland, after which the trail turns right and in 30 yards reaches the highest point in Connecticut (2,380 feet). It continues west along the state line, descending Mount Frissell with more views. On level terrain the trail reaches the tri-state boundary point at 1.7 miles, where an 1898 granite monument bears the names of New York and Massachusetts but omits Connecticut on the southeast side. The trail continues westward in New York, crossing the extension of the Ashley Hill Trail, a woods road, and ending at the South Taconic Trail (white) by a scenic open section overlooking the Harlem Valley. Turning left on the latter trail, it is 0.3 mile to the summit of Brace Mountain.

Robert Brook Trail   *Length: 1.1 miles Blaze: red*
The Robert Brook Trail begins at the Alander Brook Trail, 150 yards from its western trailhead. The Robert Brook Trail ascends eastward along the ravine of Robert Brook on the rocky route of an eighteenth-century road; it turns north to an 1898 state boundary monument and follows the Massachusetts–New York state line up to a second monument. It continues as a narrow trail in Massachusetts to the South Taconic Trail, making a total ascent of 1,050 feet.

South Taconic Trail, Southern Section   *Length: 9.4 miles Blaze: white*
The southern section of the South Taconic Trail goes from Rudd Pond Farms to NY 344. To reach the southern terminus, drive 5.5 miles north on NY 22 from the traffic light at Millerton, New York. Go right on White House Crossing Road to its end and then left on Rudd Pond Road for 0.2 mile. Turn right on a paved road into Rudd Pond Farms, a residential development, and follow the road around to the east side of the development to a parking area on the left at the end of a field.

From the parking area, the trail goes east along the edge of the field, enters the woods, and starts to ascend the western escarpment of the southern Taconics. A steep, rough section begins at 0.4 mile, the trail passing a high waterfall and ascending cliffs along switchbacks with open views to the west. At 0.7 mile, the trail turns left, crossing a short, red-blazed side trail that passes an attractive pool in a brook before climbing along the escarpment to views over the Harlem Valley. The South Taconic Trail continues north on the escarpment with more views to the west, then climbs South Brace Mountain with views to the south. At 1.4 miles, the trail turns left at a junction, where a trail leads into private property which is closed to the public. Continuing, the South Taconic Trail reaches an open area on South Brace Mountain, which offers a view south over the Riga plateau section of the highland, featuring Riga Lake and South Pond.

Crossing the open area with the summit of South Brace Mountain (2,304 feet) to the right, the trail descends to a saddle and ascends along the open crest of Brace Mountain to its summit (2,311 feet) at 1.9 miles, marked by a large pile of stones. There are views to the east of Bear Mountain in Connecticut and to the northeast of Mount Frissell in Massachusetts.

The trail descends north on a woods road to a junction at 2.2 miles, where the Brace Mountain Trail, also a woods road, leads right 1.6 miles to Mount Washington Road in Connecticut. The Appalachian Trail on the east can be reached by side trails from this road. Continuing north 200 yards to another junction, the South Taconic Trail goes left from the woods road, while the Mount Frissell Trail (red) goes right.

Proceeding along an open crest with views, the trail enters Massachusetts. Regaining the woods road, it continues north on a route previously called the State Line Trail. At 3.0 miles, a blue-blazed side trail goes northeast to the Ashley Hill Trail, which connects with the Mount Washington State Forest Headquarters on the north and with the Mount Frissell Trail on the south. Hikers coming from the north rather than the south should take particular care to bear left at the fork that appears 50 yards south of this junction in order to stay on the South Taconic Trail. At 4.5 miles, the Robert Brook Trail (red) goes left.

The South Taconic Trail, at 5.0 miles, curves left to descend and the Alander Loop Trail (blue) forks right. Descending into New York from Massachusetts, the South Taconic Trail crosses Alander Brook, and 200 feet later meets the end of the Alander Brook Trail at 5.2 miles. Making a sharp right turn off the woods road, the South Taconic Trail climbs gradually and then ascends steeply up the southwest shoulder of Alander Mountain, reaching the open crest at 5.7 miles.

The trail reenters Massachusetts at a boundary marker and goes northeast, featuring views. At 6.0 miles, it reaches the west summit of Alander Mountain (2,240 feet), where there are foundations of a former fire tower. A few yards beyond, the Alander Loop Trail (blue) leads right.

The South Taconic Trail goes northeast a few hundred feet and then swings north along the remainder of Alander's open crest, a scenic section. East is the Town of Mount Washington, with Mount Everett on the eastern escarpment the dominant feature. At 7.9 miles, the trail reaches Bashbish Mountain, the high point of the northern section of the ridge, and descends to a lookout point with Cedar Mountain across Bashbish Gorge to the north. It then descends steeply to the beginning of a level stretch at 8.2 miles, where the South Taconic Trail goes to the left. (Hikers should avoid the blue-blazed trail to the right leading very steeply down to Bashbish Brook, which is not fordable most of the year, even far upstream. The only safe option for hikers who end up at the brook is the grinding walk back up the blue-blazed trail.)

At 8.4 miles, there is a short side trail to the right to a sweeping outlook. The trail soon descends steeply until it reaches a comparatively level area at 8.7 miles. There are old charcoal pits on the right side of the trail beginning at 8.8 miles. The trail reaches a point above a side stream of Bashbish Brook at 9.2 miles and then continues down to NY 344 at 9.4 miles. A campground (reservations should be made in advance) and swimming area in an old mining pit (for which there is a small admission fee) are located here. The village of Copake Falls is located along NY 344 approximately one mile to the west.

South Taconic Trail, Northern Section *Length: 6.2 miles Blaze: white*

The northern section of the South Taconic Trail, which goes from NY 344 to NY 23, begins across NY 344 from the entrance to the lower Bashbish parking area, at an elevation of 725 feet. The Cedar Brook Trail (blue) also starts here, but the South Taconic Trail leaves NY 344 at a point 50 feet west of the Cedar Brook trailhead and then goes northwest into the woods, reaching an old road at 0.1 mile. The trail goes left on the road, leaves the road at 0.3 mile, and heads uphill to the right, passing through a grove of evergreens. At 0.4 mile, the trail reaches another old road, where it joins with an unnamed red-blazed trail coming in from the left. At 0.6 mile, just after the trail makes a sharp left, a white-blazed trail goes off to the right. A few feet after that a yellow-blazed trail comes in from the left, so that the trail is now marked with white, red, and yellow blazes. At 0.9 mile, the yellow-blazed trail goes off to the left and the

South Taconic Trail continues straight ahead. The Cedar Brook Trail (blue) comes in from the right at 1.3 miles, and at 1.6 miles, the South Taconic Trail begins an ascent of almost half a mile, passing a field of ferns at 1.8 miles. At 2.0 miles, the trail becomes level at an open area with a commanding view. The red-blazed trail goes to the left and continues for 100 yards to a viewpoint to the west at an elevation of 1,788 feet, where it ends. The South Taconic Trail continues straight ahead and at 2.1 miles enters a covered arbor. At 2.3 miles, it makes a sharp left, which hikers often miss as their inclination is to continue straight ahead on the woods road. At 2.5 miles, upon reaching North Road (which is paved), the trail turns left, follows the road for about 25 yards, and then turns right into the woods again.

The South Taconic Trail soon crosses a brook near an old springhouse. It climbs Prospect Hill northeastward through dense scrub oak and mountain laurel, and at 2.9 miles reaches the summit (1,919 feet) with open views. Turning left at the Massachusetts–New York boundary monument, the trail reaches an open ledge with panoramic views north, west, and south, including the Harlem Valley and the Town of Hillsdale, New York.

The trail enters Massachusetts, descends Prospect Hill gradually with a viewpoint at 3.2 miles, and follows a lower crest line. It reenters New York and at 3.8 miles, reaches an open section along the edge of the escarpment with views of the valley on the southwest. The trail continues to Mount Fray, parallels its crest, and, at 4.2 miles, turns right and climbs a short distance to the crest, with an open view. It goes north along the broad summit of Mount Fray, reaching the 1,900-foot level. Open areas in scrub growth offer distant views, including Mount Greylock on the northeast. From here on, the trail is on privately owned land, mostly Catamount Ski Area.

At 4.5 miles the trail turns right on Ridge Run, a broad ski trail descending along the ridge line. Just before this right turn, an area with views that includes two chairlift stations is a short distance to the left. While following Ridge Run east for about a mile, the hiker must be careful to avoid being lured onto side trails. Just before the trail reaches a hut at 5.4 miles, a view of Jug End valley and ridge may be seen by climbing a few yards off the trail to the right.

At 5.5 miles the trail turns right into the woods, climbs steeply east for a short stretch, and continues 100 feet along the wooded crest, turning north at 5.6 miles and descending. Entering a driveway at 6.0 miles, the trail meets another dirt road coming in from the left, finally turning left for 65 yards to reach NY 23, where it crosses the height of land. The northern terminus of the

South Taconic Trail is at 6.2 miles. There is a parking area on the south side of NY 23, 150 yards to the left.

MOUNT WASHINGTON STATE FOREST

A trail network on the highland in Massachusetts, connecting with the South Taconic Trail, starts from the Mount Washington State Forest Headquarters on East Street in the Town of Mount Washington. The main components are the Alander Mountain Trail, which ascends to the summit of Alander Mountain, and the Ashley Hill Trail, which goes south to Connecticut. Both trails are woods roads, except for the upper part of the Alander Mountain Trail. There are two side trails, one between the two main trails and one connecting the Ashley Brook Trail with the South Taconic Trail. Attractive hemlock groves are a feature of this area.

The state forest headquarters can be reached from New York on the west by turning off NY 22 and following NY 344 through Copake Falls and its continuation (Falls Road) onto the highland in Massachusetts. At the end of Falls Road (3.8 miles from NY 22), a right turn onto West Street leads in 1.7 miles to its end at East Street, where there is a church. The headquarters is on East Street, 1.1 miles south of this junction. Hikers may park by the trailhead beyond the office.

Alander Mountain Trail   *Length: 2.8 miles Blaze: blue*
For various reasons, it is not easy to keep the Alander Mountain Trail blazed for the first 0.8 mile, so hikers are advised to follow the description carefully. The trail starts at the signboards at the west end of the Mount Washington State Forest headquarters parking area, near a 4-foot boulder. It goes west through a field and enters the woods at 0.1 mile. A few hundred feet later the hemlock cover is reminiscent of the line from Robert Frost's poem, *Stopping by Woods on a Snowy Evening*, "The woods are lovely, dark and deep." At 0.4 mile the trail again enters a field and proceeds in a generally westerly direction to a brook at 0.5 mile. The trail continues to a fork at 0.8 mile, where it goes right; the left fork is the start of the Ashley Hill Trail (blue). The Alander Mountain Trail descends steeply and reaches its lowest elevation of 1,450 feet at a brook, which may be difficult to cross. The trail proceeds northwest, rising high above the brook, and at 1.1 miles swings west. The next 0.9 mile is easy walking over level terrain with only a few mild undulations. At 1.5 miles, a

side trail climbs left to a state forest primitive camping area and goes through the camping area to the Ashley Hill Trail (blue). A brook 500 feet before the Ashley Hill Trail cannot be crossed safely much of the year.

After crossing a small brook at 1.8 miles, the Alander Mountain Trail reaches a confluence of two brooks at 2.0 miles. Crossing over the water at just the point where the two brooks meet, the trail proceeds straight ahead with the upper brook on the left. After 30 feet, the trail turns left to cross the upper brook. From here on the trail climbs ever more steeply to the top of Alander Mountain. At 2.2 miles, the woods road ends and the trail narrows at a cleared area 25 feet in diameter, from which it continues straight ahead to the west. A side trail to the north for cross-country skiers meets up with the main trail 400 feet later. At 2.3 miles, the Alander Mountain Trail becomes a bit difficult to follow for about 400 feet. It first swings left and then uphill to the right through a muddy area, becoming conspicuous again at 2.4 miles. At 2.7 miles, an old, circular stone foundation 10 feet in diameter can be seen 40 feet to the left of the trail. A spring comes out of the ground 100 feet up the trail to the left. On the way back, it is interesting to watch this spring gradually swell to a vigorous brook as it goes down the mountain.

A few hundred feet farther on, there is a small state forest cabin, and two hundred feet beyond that, the trail ends at the Alander Loop Trail (blue). Following the Alander Loop Trail to the right, the hiker reaches the South Taconic Trail (white) after a few hundred feet, the west summit of Alander Mountain (2,240 feet).

Alternatively, the Alander Loop Trail (blue) to the left leads in a few hundred feet to the east summit of Alander Mountain with a view comparable to that of its twin. A little more than a mile later, the Alander Loop Trail leads to the South Taconic Trail (white) a mile south of Alander Mountain.

Ashley Hill Trail   *Length: 3.5 miles Blaze: blue*
From its start at the Alander Mountain Trail, the Ashley Hill Trail climbs southwest along the picturesque, steep ravine of Ashley Hill Brook. At 0.7 mile, the side trail from the Alander Mountain Trail and the primitive camping area comes in acutely from the right; at 1.0 mile, the unblazed Charcoal Pit Trail comes in from the left, where a charcoal pit is visible. The Ashley Hill Trail continues southward on relatively level terrain, crossing a brook at 1.1 miles and another small brook at 2.0 miles. About 100 feet after crossing the second brook, the Ashley Hill Trail makes a sharp left at a junction. The path that

continues straight ahead is a side trail, which proceeds for 1.3 miles to connect with the South Taconic Trail (white). Hikers should take care, as both the Ashley Hill Trail and the side trail are marked with blue blazes. After making the left, the Ashley Hill Trail continues uphill, crosses a brook at 2.5 miles, and reaches the state line at 3.5 miles at a boundary monument. Although this is the official end of the trail, it does continue south without blazes. It connects with the Mount Frissell Trail (red) 100 feet later and in another 0.2 mile with the Brace Mountain Trail (unblazed). However, the trail beyond the state line is not recommended, as it is difficult to follow and impassable at spots in wet weather, and ample alternate routes exist in the area.

THE APPALACHIAN TRAIL AND ACCESS TRAILS

Appalachian Trail *Length: 16.5 miles Blaze: white*
This major trail traverses the South Taconics from Conn. 41 to Mass. 41. See chapter 19, "Long Distance Trails," or the *Appalachian Trail Guide to Massachusetts–Connecticut* for a complete description of the 16.5 miles.

Bald Peak Trail *Length: 1.1 miles Blaze: blue*
The trail starts from a parking area on the west side of Mount Washington Road on the highland in Connecticut, a half-mile north of Mount Riga Road and South Pond dam. The trail climbs east 120 feet in 0.2 mile to the top of 2,010-foot Bald Peak, an open rocky knoll with a wide view over the highland. Continuing another mile eastward over some rough terrain with a net descent of 400 feet, the trail reaches the Appalachian Trail (white) a half-mile northwest of Lions Head.

Elbow Trail *Length: 1.2 miles Blaze: blue*
This trail is reached by driving west from Mass. 41, 3.5 miles south of its junction with Mass. 23 at South Egremont, into the grounds of the Berkshire School at the base of the highland. Hikers may park during the day behind Stanley Hall. Ascending a driveway northwestward and continuing on a woods road that angles up the escarpment with a long switchback (the "Elbow"), the trail follows a route that was an eighteenth-century wagon road. A newer trail parallels the first part of this route. After passing a camping area, the trail reaches the Appalachian Trail (white) 1.2 miles north of the Mount Everett Reservation road and picnic area. Jug End ridge lies to the right.

Lions Head Trail *Length: 0.5 mile Blaze: blue*
This trail provides the shortest access to Lions Head and was the former route of the Appalachian Trail. Parking is near the end of Bunker Hill Road northwest of Salisbury, Connecticut, on the right side below a sign. At the end of the road, the trail turns left through a pasture, descending moderately to cross a brook. Ascending northwest through woods and fields of ferns, the trail reaches the ridge, where the Appalachian Trail (white) comes in from the right. Lions Head is 0.2 mile ahead on the Appalachian Trail, an ascent of 600 feet from Bunker Hill Road.

Paradise Lane Trail *Length: 2.1 miles Blaze: blue*
The Paradise Lane Trail begins on the Under Mountain Trail 1.1 miles from its trailhead on Conn. 41. The Paradise Lane Trail turns left near its start, heading north along the highland. It passes the east side of Bear Mountain in a wetlands, ending at the Appalachian Trail (white) in Massachusetts just north of the state line, where the latter descends to Sages Ravine.

Race Brook Trail *Length: 2.0 miles Blaze: blue*
The Race Brook Trail goes from a parking area on Mass. 41, 3 miles south of Jug End Road, across state land to the Appalachian Trail (white), 0.7 mile south of Mount Everett. The trail has three brook crossings and side trails with views of waterfalls. A designated campsite above the last falls is within a mile of the Appalachian Trail junction.

Under Mountain Trail *Length: 1.9 miles Blaze: blue*
Climbing more than 1,000 feet to the Appalachian Trail (white), this trail provides the shortest access from the Housatonic Valley to Bear Mountain and the adjacent highland. The trail is wet in the spring.

The trailhead is on Conn. 41 (Under Mountain Road), 3.4 miles north of Salisbury, Connecticut, and a short distance south of Beaver Dam Road. From the parking area on the west side of the road, the trail goes west across partly open terrain, enters the woods, and ascends. At 1.1 miles, the Paradise Lane Trail (blue) goes right. The Under Mountain Trail reaches the Appalachian Trail (white) half a mile north of the Bond shelter and 0.9 mile south of the summit of Bear Mountain.

TWELVE

THE CATSKILLS

orth of the more familiar
metropolitan hiking areas are the Catskills, whose high summits and steep climbs
can provide especially rewarding hiking. The paved roads through the mountains are well populated with hotels, bed-and-breakfast establishments, and
private homes, but the higher, more rugged, and remote parts of these mountains are unspoiled. From the summits and other vantage points, the views are
magnificent. To the east, the Hudson Valley is spread out against a backdrop of
New England hills, and in all other directions lie the fir-topped peaks of the
Catskills themselves, with little or no sign of human intrusion.

Thirty-five peaks and ridges in the Catskills have elevations of 3,500 feet
or more, and sixteen of them do not have maintained trails to their summits.
Almost a hundred peaks are over 3,000 feet high. Hundreds of miles of trails of
all degrees of difficulty invite the hiker to this varied and delightful area.

Geology

The Catskills encompass the highest topography in the Appalachian Plateau
Province, with two peaks exceeding 4,000 feet in elevation. The Catskills are
mountainous only in the erosional sense. That is, the region is structurally a
plateau that has undergone a long cycle of stream erosion. Cutting deeply into
the near-horizontal strata, the divides between adjacent valleys are often high
and sharp-crested. The result is mountains with steep sides and flat tops, with
names such as Table, Plateau, and Sugarloaf being good indications of their shape.

The bedrock of the Catskills consists almost entirely of sandstone, shale, and some conglomerate laid down during the Devonian Period in a complex delta-type environment. Elevated in a series of comparatively gentle uplifts to a height thousands of feet above the present levels, this uplifted plateau experienced a long period of erosion that cut down the steep valleys and wore out the broad Hudson Valley, removing still younger Catskill rock formations that once extended east of the river. It also left the highest summits topped by the more resistant late Devonian strata of hard conglomerate, a formation that can be seen on the top of Slide Mountain. The loose pebbles of milky quartz generally distributed there and on other high summits resulted from the physical disintegration of the conglomerate. Variations in resistance of the individual sedimentary layers are responsible for a long series of *cuestas* (asymmetrical ridges, with one slope long and gentle and the other a steeply sloping, near-precipitous scarp). The boldest of these *cuesta* scarps forms the eastern margin of the Catskills and overlooks the Hudson Valley to the east, standing as much as 3,000 feet above the valley.

This geological history of the Catskills can be read in the gentle curves of mountains, curves that are sharper on some slopes, notably on the eastern fronts of Overlook, Kaaterskill High Peak, and the Blackheads, and on Cornell and Balsam Cap. Here are terrace-like cliffs and shelves where level strata have been cut back vertically, probably by ice erosion. But, unlike most mountains, there is relatively little bare rock in the form of flat ledges or high, exposed cliffs. The effects of the glaciation of the Pleistocene Ice Age are not as prominent as in the Adirondacks and the Hudson Highlands. It is probable that the higher Catskills were not covered very deeply by the ice sheets, for foreign material is scarce above 3,500 feet. Even where ice smoothing occurred, the softness of much of the sedimentary rock permitted postglacial weathering to roughen it and break it down into residual soil that has been covered by dense vegetation. The dense forest cover often mantles cliffs 50 to 100 feet high, which are undetectable until they are reached.

Natural History

No area of the Catskills has typical above-timberline alpine flora, such as that found in the Taconics and the Hudson Highlands, which are lower and farther south. Above 3,000 feet the Catskill flora is northern in association but hardly as boreal as might be expected. The heavy residual soil from the soft sandstones has encouraged the invasion of southern or lowland species. Boreal islands of subarctic plants are infrequent. Up to 3,000 feet the vegetation is of the beech-birch-maple-hemlock zone, and above that of the northern spruce-fir. The Hudsonian or subarctic relics are absent except for patches of three-toothed cinquefoil on the ledges of Overlook Mountain at 3,000 feet and on North Mountain east of Haines Falls.

History

The natural beauty of the Catskills is striking—the geology of the mountains, the variety of the forests, and the many wildflowers and birds. But it is also apparent that the land, now tree-covered, has been lived on and worked over. Old stone walls and the remains of a chimney or foundation here and there are evidence that someone tried to farm and perhaps raise a family. A cemetery tells a story of sickness and death in its stones. Barely distinguishable old roads climb to overgrown clearings around vanished lumber camps. Above them there is no path to the fir-clad summits, where timber is so dwarfed and inaccessible that it has never been cut, and where the ledges are covered several feet deep with a humus made by centuries of decaying fir, spruce needles, and moss.

Much has been written about Native Americans, dwarfs, and Rip Van Winkle, making the Catskills a land of mystery and fancy. The Hudson and Mohawk valleys were inhabited and well traveled by Native Americans long before Henry Hudson sailed up the river that is named after him (which he called the North River). The first European settlers were the Dutch, who built trading posts first at Albany, which they called Fort Orange, and then at Kingston, which they called Sopus. Friction soon arose between the Dutch and the local Native Americans, which led to a series of skirmishes known as the Esopus Wars (1655–63). In 1664 the British took New York, including the Catskills, from the Dutch, though fighting between the Dutch and the British continued at various points around the world for another ten years.

In 1708, Queen Anne granted a *patent*, or ownership, for about one-and-a-half million acres of what is now Delaware, Greene, Sullivan, and Ulster counties, including all of what is considered the Catskills, to a group led by Major Johannis Hardenburgh. The circumstances leading up to the granting of the Hardenburgh Patent are unknown, but it had a profound impact on the development of the area. Difficulties in surveying the land and legal battles among the descendants of the original patentees kept most settlers out of the area until well into the nineteenth century.

During the Revolutionary War, the residents of the Catskills were largely on the side of the Revolution. Despite considerable skirmishing in the Catskills between local Tories (and their Iroquois allies) and rebels, no decisive battles were fought. Nonetheless, the fighting that did occur was bloody, especially since the British offered a bounty for white scalps and prisoners.

Industry

The demand for hemlock bark, created by the tanning industry, brought large numbers of settlers to the Catskills. Tanning of hides had been carried out in the United States to a limited extent prior to the Revolution. A tannery was established in Athens, New York, in 1750, but rapid growth came after the War of 1812, when Americans were free to engage in world trade without interference from the British. Oak bark was used to tan shoe-sole leather, hemlock bark to tan leather for uppers and other uses. Because one cord (128 cubic feet) of bark was required to tan ten hides, it was more economical to ship hides to tanneries located near the woods. With their ready supply of hemlock and water, the Catskills soon became a center for the tanning industry. By 1816, there were more than seventy-five tanneries in the mountains, with others being built at a rapid pace. Palenville, Prattsville, and Edwardsville (now Hunter) are existing towns named for the proprietors of these tanneries. The name "Tannersville" remembers the whole industry. By 1825, Greene County was producing more leather than any other county in New York, with Ulster not far behind.

The tanning industry in the Catskills reached its peak during the Civil War and declined rapidly thereafter, as the supply of hemlock was exhausted. By 1867, most tanneries had closed, although the Simpson tannery in Phoenicia operated until 1870. Some idea about the amount of bark consumed may be gained from the report that the Pratt tannery turned out more than two million hides over the course of its existence, which would have required over 200,000 cords of bark.

Cutting down these tremendous trees opened the land to sunlight and conditions more favorable to the growth of birch, maple, oak, and other hardwoods. As these took over, a new industry was born—the making of barrel hoops. This industry began about 1848 and lasted until about 1890, when machine-sawed wooden hoops and steel hoops replaced hand-hewn hoops. Another wood industry that existed for a time was the making of furniture in the *chair factories*, as they were known locally. This industry accounted for some of the large buildings, now vacant, still seen in Catskill towns.

Another Catskill industry was the quarrying of bluestone, a hard, dense, fine-grained, blue-gray sandstone. The industry thrived in the latter part of the nineteenth century, providing curbstone and flagstone for the sidewalks of New

York. The development of Portland cement provided a cheaper alternative and brought large-scale quarrying to an end. Piles of rejected stone may still be found at many places where there were workings or exploratory openings, as in Shandaken or Phoenicia. A few working quarries continue to supply bluestone for walks, patios, and veneer, but the demand is much smaller. Opus 40, near Saugerties, offers a glimpse into the bluestone industry at its Quarryman's Museum. It also has outdoor sculptures and some short hiking trails.

Evidence of farmhouses and cleared fields appears in the Catskills on land that looks impossible to farm. It took many horses to transport bark, lumber, and hides—thousands when the tanning industry was at its peak—and horses require feed. As the land was cleared of hemlock, it was plowed where possible and sown with hay on the steep slopes, with corn or oats on more level areas. Some of the better space was used for potatoes, wheat, and buckwheat for the tannery workers and their families.

After tanning ceased, some farmers attempted general farming, but the soil was poor and the conditions too difficult. All that is left now are fallen chimneys and sometimes an apple tree bearing misshapen, wormy fruit that is enjoyed only by bear and deer. The views from some of these old high-valley farms are beautiful, prompting purchase as summer vacation home sites.

Railroads came to the Catskills in 1866. Four years later, the Ulster & Delaware Railroad began service from Weehawken, New Jersey, to Phoenicia. The line was extended to Stamford, New York, in 1872, and through Stony Clove to Tannersville and the hotels in the North Lake area in 1882. Although regular passenger service has been discontinued on all lines through the Catskills, and most have been abandoned altogether, two short tourist railroads, the Delaware & Ulster Rail Ride in Arkville and the Catskill Mountain Railroad in Phoenicia, still preserve the history of Catskill railroading.

Tourism is now the major industry in the Catskills, and it has a long history. It began in 1824 when the Catskill Mountain House, built on a high ledge near North Lake, opened with ten guest rooms. Patrons were transported by stage from the steamboat docks at Catskill Landing, up through Sleepy Hollow, to the hotel perched high above. So popular was the view from its porch that the Mountain House grew to more than three hundred rooms. Among its frequent guests were Thomas Cole and other painters of the Hudson River School and President Ulysses S. Grant.

Hotel building in the Catskills reached its peak in the late 1800s. In 1878, the Overlook House was built on Overlook Mountain, then the Mount Tremper

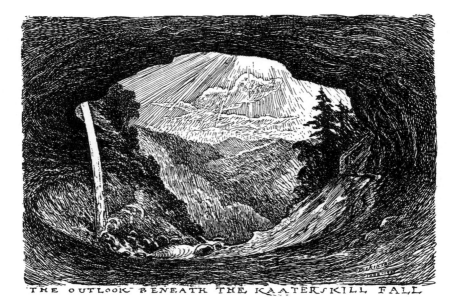

THE OUTLOOK BENEATH THE KAATERSKILL FALL

House in Phoenicia, the Grand Hotel in Highmount, and the Laurel House at Kaaterskill Falls. In 1881, the Hotel Kaaterskill was built on South Mountain. It was said to have 1,200 rooms and to be the largest mountain hotel in the world. None of these structures has survived. The Hotel Kaaterskill burned in 1924, and its property was acquired by the state. The state later acquired the Laurel House and the Catskill Mountain House along with their land holdings. The buildings were burned in 1963. The whole area around North and South lakes, including the network of carriage roads built by the hotels, is managed for public use by the New York State Department of Environmental Conservation. North Lake Campground has become the centerpiece of the area.

The Catskills have played a role in America's art and literature since the early nineteenth century. Washington Irving was not the only author to use the Catskills as a backdrop for his stories. James Fenimore Cooper's Natty Bumpo, or Leatherstockings—the hero of many of his stories—describes Kaaterskill Falls as his favorite place. William Cullen Bryant wrote a lyric poem about the Falls, as did other poets. Thomas Cole and the other artists of the Hudson River School painted Catskill scenes innumerable times. Today, Woodstock continues the Catskill tradition of being an inspiration to the arts by providing a base for artists of all kinds. A walk along the sidewalks of Woodstock provides an opportunity to visit the many galleries and craft shops of the local artisans.

The writer who probably did the most to popularize the Catskills was John Burroughs, whose book, *In the Catskills*, originally published in 1910, introduced many to the beauties of Slide Mountain and the Southern Catskills. By the time Burroughs's book was published, the Catskills had some level of protection for twenty-five years. They received this protection as the result of two very separate concerns: the need to protect the Erie Canal, and Ulster County's tax problems. As early as the 1860s, concerned citizens, who today would be called environmentalists, warned that the massive lumbering operations then taking place in the Adirondacks could lead to soil erosion that would silt up the Erie Canal. Since much of New York City's prosperity depended on goods shipped via the canal, they soon enlisted the support of New York City business leaders. In 1872 this alliance was able to convince the State Legislature to set up a Park Commission to study protecting the Adirondacks. While portions of the Catskills were also being denuded, this was considered to be only a local concern. A year later the Park Commission issued a report favoring an Adirondack forest park, with no mention made of the Catskills. But opposition to the proposed park was also strong, and for over a decade no action was taken.

The Legislature may not have been able to set up a park, but it did know how to raise taxes. Traditionally, when a private landowner defaulted on his taxes, his land became the property of the municipalities. However, in 1879 the Legislature made the counties responsible for such land and the taxes on it. Ulster County soon became the owner of significant areas in the Catskills, and quickly accumulated a tax debt of $40,000.

Both of these problems came together in 1885. Pressure to protect the Adirondacks finally prevailed, and on May 15 a forest preserve was created. As the result of political maneuvering, the act creating the forest preserve also included the Catskill lands for which Ulster County owed taxes. Ulster County's debt was abolished, and in the future the state would pay taxes to the county.

While the law looked good on paper, enforcing it proved almost impossible. Lumbering continued in the Adirondacks. Protection had to be strengthened, which happened in 1894 when the State Constitution was amended, with Article XIV, Section 1 of the Constitution providing:

The lands of the state now owned or hereafter acquired, constituting the forest preserve as now fixed by law, shall be forever kept as wild forest lands. They shall not be leased, sold or exchanged, or be taken by any corporation, public or private, nor shall the timber thereon be sold, removed or destroyed.

This basis for the present-day protection of the Catskills has provided us with vast areas where the only human intrusion is by foot, ski, or snowshoe. Almost pure wilderness and only a few hours from our nation's largest metropolitan area, the Catskill Park covers more than 700,000 acres (1,100 square miles). About 40 percent of it is state land, falling under the "forever wild" clause of the State Constitution.

Climate

A gentle spring day in New York City may be a day of snow flurries or freezing rain in the Catskills. Temperatures are generally lower in the mountains, decreasing as altitude is gained. Snow may accumulate in November and last well into May. Weather conditions can change quickly and one should be prepared with extra clothing and suitable equipment. Although the main roads are plowed, many of the side roads that have no winter residents are not cleared.

The Catskills are beautiful in the winter when covered with snow, and people who hike are likely to enjoy snowshoeing and cross-country skiing. Winter in the woods is exhilarating but exhausting. Hikers and skiers should keep this in mind, along with the fact that daylight ends sooner, when planning winter trips. Recorded weather information can be obtained by calling (914) 331-5555 in Kingston.

Trails and Bushwhacking

Trails in the Catskills are marked with the New York State Department of Environmental Conservation (DEC) plastic markers nailed to trees—blue for trails that run generally north–south, red for trails running east–west, and yellow for connecting trails or trails running diagonally.

Camping is permitted on state land below 3,500 feet and at least 150 feet away from streams, water sources, and marked trails. Camping may be restricted in some areas, and designated sites may be identified to control use in popular areas. Properly built and maintained fires, using only dead and down wood, are also permitted below 3,500 feet. However, most experienced hikers find the safety and efficiency of backpacker stoves a real convenience. The topography above 3,500 feet is subject to harsher weather conditions, where plants and soil do not recover well or rapidly from camping use (and abuse).

Some of the marked trails are described below. The New York-New Jersey Trail Conference publishes a set of hiking maps for Catskill trails. The backs of these maps contain a brief summary of trail information, providing the hiker with an easy reference for both planning and actual walking. More detailed information on hiking trails is available in *Hiking the Catskills*, by Lee McAllister and Myron S. Ochman, also published by the New York-New Jersey Trail Conference, and *Guide to Catskill Trails*, published by the Adirondack Mountain Club.

The Long Path traverses the Catskill Park in a north–south direction for 94 miles. It is overlaid on many of the trails described here. See the *Long Path Guide* for details. In most places the Long Path is designated only by its distinctive plastic marker at the trailheads and junctions.

Although a great deal of the forest land in the Catskills can be explored using marked trails, hikers can find out what the wilderness is really like only by "getting off the beaten path." Trailless travel, or bushwhacking, often leads to interesting discoveries—a little-known waterfall, a balanced rock, or one of the remains of the mountain industries of the last century. Best of all, bushwhacking heightens the hiker's awareness of the environment. Hikers who bushwhack should not blaze or otherwise mark the route. Such independent blazing is illegal, defaces the wilderness, and ruins the experience of hiking in a trailless area for those who follow.

Some trailless Catskill summits, such as Rocky or Balsam Cap, are thickly overgrown with spruce, making bushwhacking a physically demanding endeavor. Others, such as Halcott or Vly, are relatively open. Before leaving the trail, a hiker should have a compass and a topographic map and know how to use both. Most important, all hikers—but especially those who plan to bushwhack—should let someone know where they are going before setting out, and their expected time of return.

To provide an incentive for visiting mountain peaks and areas not usually seen by the average hiker, the Catskill 3500 Club was founded in 1962. Membership in the Catskill 3500 Club is limited to those who have climbed all thirty-five 3,500-foot Catskill peaks—including the trailless peaks—under summer conditions, as well as four specific peaks (Slide, Blackhead, Panther, and Balsam) during the winter. The Club also recognizes as winter members those who have climbed all thirty-five mountains during the winter. Sign-in canisters, maintained by the Catskill 3500 Club, are at the summits of most of the trail-

less peaks. By 1997, over one thousand hikers had qualified for regular membership and more than three hundred hikers had met the requirement for becoming winter members. Club hikes and other functions are open to nonmembers, who are known as "aspirants." Current information on the 3500 Club can be obtained through the New York-New Jersey Trail Conference.

For convenience of description, the Catskill trails covered below are divided into four groups: central (south of NY 28); northern (north of NY 212 and NY 28, east of NY 42, south of NY 23A); northeastern (north of NY 23A); and western (west of Frost Valley and Fleischmanns, northwest of Shandaken.)

Trails in the Central Catskills

Considered by many to be the heart of Catskills hiking, the central area contains the largest known tracts of virgin timber as well as some of the most remote peaks. The vast trailless area around Rocky and Balsam Cap mountains contains some very thick spruce, reminiscent of the Adirondacks.

Wittenberg-Cornell-Slide Trail   *Length: 9.1 miles Blaze: red*
The best-known trails in the Catskills are those that reach the summit of Slide Mountain (4,180 feet), the highest point in this range. Slide Mountain was relatively unknown until the 1870s, when surveyor Arnold Guyot announced that it was the highest Catskills peak. At first this status was denied by the

owners of the large hotels in the northeast Catskills, who for years had claimed that Kaaterskill High Peak, which rises dramatically from the Hudson Valley, was the highest mountain in the area. It, however, is only 3,655 feet high, making it the twenty-third-highest mountain in the Catskills. Slide Mountain was further popularized by writer-naturalist John Burroughs, who wrote about his many treks in the area.

One approach to the Burroughs Range (Wittenberg, Cornell, and Slide mountains) is through Woodland Valley, one of the deepest valleys in the Catskills. The Woodland Valley Road south from Phoenicia at NY 28 follows Woodland Creek. After about 5 miles, near the road's end, is the Woodland Valley State Campground. Cars can be parked in a large hikers' parking lot opposite the campground. In season, there is a small parking fee.

The Wittenberg-Cornell-Slide Trail starts on the side of the road, opposite the parking lot. The trail goes through the campsite and crosses a footbridge over Woodland Valley Creek. In the next 3.8 miles, the trail ascends 2,400 feet to the summit of Wittenberg (3,780 feet). It begins this ascent with an initial steep climb, and then levels off at about 1.2 miles, with limited views down into Woodland Valley. At 2.6 miles, a yellow-blazed trail leads left 0.9 mile to the Terrace Mountain lean-to (no water). The trail soon climbs steeply over a series of rock ledges to the summit of Wittenberg. From the broad rock ledge at Wittenberg's summit, there are views to the east and the south over the Ashokan Reservoir.

From the summit of Wittenberg, the trail goes southwest, following a narrow ridge, and soon begins a brief but steep climb up Cornell Mountain, where a short spur trail leads to the summit (3,860 feet). Cornell is heavily wooded with limited views to the south and east. The trail turns west and, passing open views west and north towards Slide and Panther descends into the notch between Cornell and Slide. It then climbs steeply to the summit of Slide Mountain, passing a fine spring several hundred feet below the top. Just before the open rock top is a tablet with an inscription dedicated to the memory of John Burroughs.

From the top of the ledge there are views to the northeast and east. There is a limited view to the north from a ledge 0.1 mile west of the summit, just to the right of the trail.

From the top of Slide, the red-blazed trail begins a gradual descent westward along the northern front of the mountain on a former bridle path. In less than a mile, the Curtis-Ormsbee Trail (blue) starts to the left. This trail, which descends to the Phoenicia-East Branch Trail (yellow), provides a slightly longer but more scenic route off the mountain.

The Wittenberg-Cornell-Slide Trail continues ahead on the old bridle path for another 1.3 miles before ending at a junction with the Phoenicia-East Branch Trail (yellow). A right turn, following the yellow blazes, leads to the Slide Mountain parking area on Slide Mountain Road (County 47).

The Long Path overlays most of the Wittenberg-Cornell-Slide Trail and continues south along the Curtis-Ormsbee and Phoenicia-East Branch trails.

Pine Hill—West Branch Trail *Length 14.9 miles Blaze: blue*

This trail forms the backbone of a network of trails giving access to five major summits: Belleayre (3,420 feet), Balsam (3,600 feet), Haynes (3,420 feet), Eagle (3,600 feet), and Big Indian (3,700 feet). Hikes can begin at either end or from trailheads in Big Indian (Lost Clove Road), Oliverea (McKenley Hollow Road), Mapledale (Rider Hollow Road), or Seager (Dry Brook Road). Pine Hill, where the trail's northern terminus is located, can be reached by Kingston-Oneonta bus.

This description starts at the southern end on the West Branch Road (County 47), which is also known as Slide Mountain Road. The trailhead is 12.8 miles south of Big Indian Village (NY 28) and 8 miles northeast of Claryville. Cars can be parked opposite the trailhead at the Biscuit Brook parking area.

After a moderate ascent, the trail stays fairly level along the Biscuit Brook Valley, reaching a lean-to at 1.9 miles, then begins a steady climb along Biscuit Brook to a ridge on Big Indian Mountain, where it turns sharply north and climbs to a height of land. The trail passes about 0.25 mile west of the summit, which is considered trailless and marked with a Catskill 3500 Club canister. It then descends moderately into a col, where at 5.8 miles , it reaches a junction with the Seager-Big Indian Trail (yellow). This trail goes downhill southwest 0.9 mile to the Shandaken Brook lean-to, and continues for another 2.2 miles to Dry Brook Road.

Continuing north on the blue markers, the trail reaches the summit of Eagle Mountain at 6.9 miles. This wooded summit, with no views, is considered by many to be the least interesting of all the major peaks. Another easy 1.4 miles brings the hiker to Haynes Mountain (3,420 feet), again with no views. From there it is 0.7 mile gently downhill to a col at 3,000 feet and the Oliverea-Mapledale Trail (red). To the right this trail descends steeply to McKenley Hollow Road and Oliverea; to the left it descends to Rider Hollow and Mapledale. The blue-blazed trail continues moderately uphill 0.7 mile to the summit

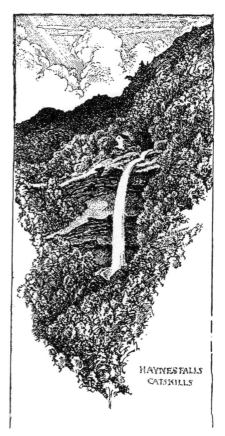

HAYNES FALLS
CATSKILLS

of Balsam Mountain with a view of the Big Indian Valley. Another 1.3 miles of moderate downhill hiking leads to the Mine Hollow Trail (yellow), an alternate way down to Rider Hollow. The Mine Hollow, Pine Hill-West Branch, and Oliverea-Mapledale trails form a 5.2-mile circular route from the parking area on Rider Hollow Road over the top of Balsam Mountain.

The Pine Hill-West Branch Trail continues another 0.9 mile to the site of the former Belleayre Mountain fire tower. Here the Belleayre Ridge Trail (red) branches left to the Cathedral Glen Trail and, in one mile, the summit buildings of the state-run ski area. The blue markers continue, reaching the Belleayre

Mountain lean-to in half a mile, and the junction of Lost Clove Trail (red) in another 0.2 mile. The Lost Clove Trail descends 1.3 miles to a parking area on Lost Clove Road. The Pine Hill-West Branch Trail continues another 2.2 miles to its end in Pine Hill.

Giant Ledge-Panther-Fox Hollow Trail   *Length 7.4 miles Blaze: blue*
This north–south trail over Panther Mountain (3,720 feet) and Giant Ledge

A weathered ledge on top of Slide Mountain
Observe the wave lines and folds of the strata
and the pebbles of the conglomerate
This is the same cave shown
in the capital letter

(3,200 feet) offers a series of lookouts and varied terrain. The complete traverse makes a good day trip if a shuttle can be arranged. Drivers can park at the hairpin turn on Slide Mountain Road (County 47) about half a mile northeast of Winnisook Lake. The hike begins by heading northeast on the Phoenicia-East Branch Trail (yellow) 0.8 mile to the southern end of the Giant Ledge-Panther-Fox Hollow Trail. (The hike can also begin at the northern terminus of the Phoenicia-East Branch Trail at the Woodland Valley State Campground. From the rear of the parking lot at the campground it is 2.6 miles on the Phoenicia-East Branch Trail over Fork Ridge to the junction with the southern terminus of the Giant Ledge-Panther-Fox Hollow Trail.) The parking for the shuttle hike is on Fox Hollow Road, 1.6 miles south of NY 28 in Allaben.

From the junction it is a moderate climb to Giant Ledge. After about half a mile, a spring is located just west of the trail. Beyond the spring, the trail makes a steep, short climb, then follows the east side of Giant Ledge, with a series of views into Woodland Valley and beyond. An easy bushwhack over to the west side reveals views west to the Big Indian Range. After a moderate descent into a col, the trail climbs steeply up Panther Mountain, which is reached at 2.5 miles from the southern terminus and 3.3 miles from the parking area on Slide Mountain Road. From the summit ridge there are several views to the east. The descent from the summit ridge is quite steep at first, in part through virgin spruce. The trail traverses a wide ridge with several viewpoints before descending to the parking area on Fox Hollow Road, 4.9 miles from the summit of Panther. It is 1.6 miles farther on Fox Hollow Road to NY 28 at Allaben, where there is a bus stop.

South of Slide Mountain
Peekamoose and Vicinity

The area south of the Burroughs range is largely trailless—a large bowl drained by the East Branch of the Neversink River. At its eastern rim are Friday and Balsam Cap mountains. Friday (3,694 feet) comes off the shoulder of Cornell and is connected to Balsam Cap (3,623 feet) by a ridge. Swinging around to the southwest from Balsam Cap are Rocky (3,508 feet), Lone (3,721 feet), and Table (3,847 feet) mountains. The summit of Table can be reached by trail, but Lone, Rocky, Balsam Cap, and Friday are all trailless.

Just south of Table Mountain lies Peekamoose (3,843 feet), which together with Table Mountain and Van Wyck Mountain (3,206 feet) closes the bowl of the East Branch. They also form the northern slope of the Rondout Creek watershed. Peekamoose Road—the road from West Shokan southwest to Sundown, Grahamsville, and Liberty—is also

PEAKAMOOSE

called the Gulf Road because of the gulf between the headwaters of the Rondout and the Esopus drainage via Watson Hollow.

Peekamoose and Table mountains may be climbed from either Denning or Peekamoose roads via the Peekamoose-Table Trail (blue), which is part of the Long Path.

The summit of Ashokan High Point (3,060 feet) offers a 360-degree view and is about 2,500 feet above the Ashokan Reservoir. It can be ascended easily by a red-blazed trail that leaves Peekamoose Road 3.9 miles southwest of West Shokan, where there is a parking area on the north side of Peekamoose Road. From the parking area, cross the road and descend to a footbridge over Kanape

Brook. The trail follows along the north side of the brook on a wide woods road for 2.5 miles to a large level area. Just beyond, the road reaches the height of land between Mombaccus Mountain (2,840 feet) and High Point. Shortly beyond that point, the road enters private property and should not be followed. From the height of land, the marked trail leads uphill to High Point, reaching the summit in about a mile. At the summit, a herd path leads to blueberry bushes and a panoramic view of the peaks around Slide Mountain.

Trails in the Northern Catskills

Although more populated and with fewer remote areas than the Southern Catskills, the Northern Catskills have many rewarding climbs, including four trailless peaks and the Devil's Path, a 23-mile backbone trail that touches five major summits and skirts 4,040-foot Hunter Mountain, second-highest in the Catskills. The entrance to this area through Plattekill Clove from West Saugerties is dramatic, with the eastern wall rising half a mile in a horizontal distance of about one mile. The road (closed in winter) requires caution, and the clove itself is extremely deep and steep, with broken and falling rock. Climbing in it is definitely not recommended. Plattekill Clove was the scene of a fatal hiking accident during the winter of 1989. An easier route into this valley is via NY 23A to Tannersville, and then on Platte Clove Road (County 16).

Overlook Mountain

Overlook Mountain is reached via the Overlook Trail and the Overlook Spur Trail. The northern terminus of the Overlook Trail is at a junction with the Devil's Path. The junction is 1.8 miles east of Prediger Road via the Devil's Path (red), or 0.8 mile south of Platte Clove Road via the Old Overlook Road, now a green-blazed trail maintained by the Catskill Center for Conservation and Development. From the junction, the Overlook Trail leads south, passing a lean-to and continuing on a generally level route along the shoulder of Plattekill (3,100 feet) and Overlook (3,140 feet) mountains. At 3.6 miles, the Overlook Trail ends at the Overlook Spur Trail (red), which leads 0.4 mile east to the summit of Overlook. The fire tower is closed, but there are views to the east of the Hudson Valley and the hills of New England. The Catskills occupy the remainder of the horizon, fading range after range into the distance.

Just south of the junction of the Overlook and Overlook Spur Trails is the former site of the Overlook House, one of the great mountain hotels of the nineteenth century. The hotel here burned in the 1920s, and construction of a new concrete building was started soon after, but the Depression ended the dream and the building was never completed. The walls are still standing, with trees growing inside the shell, and stone pillars lie fallen in the weeds. From the trail junction it is possible to continue south on the Overlook Spur Trail (red), a well-maintained woods road, for 2 miles to Meads, where there is parking at the trailhead. Across the road from the parking area is the former Meads Inn, built in 1863 and now a Buddhist center. The distance from Prediger Road to Meads with a side trip to the fire tower is 8.5 miles.

Kaaterskill High Peak

North of Plattekill Clove is Kaaterskill High Peak, the "High Peak" that, as late as 1870, was said to be the highest of the Catskill summits. The top is distinctive, with a cliff on the east side of the summit that is visible from the Hudson Valley. The Long Path traverses the eastern and northern shoulders of the mountain, and a snowmobile trail makes a circuit of both Kaaterskill High Peak (3,655 feet) and its neighbor, Roundtop (3,440 feet).

The easiest way to climb Kaaterskill High Peak is via the unofficial blue trail that starts 3.5 miles north of Platte Clove Road on the snowmobile trail, a short distance from its junction with the Long Path. The sporadically blue-marked trail climbs over the heavily wooded summit to the open Hurricane Ledges on the south side, 4.7 miles from Platte Clove Road. Despite the existence of this trail, Kaaterskill High Peak is considered a trailless peak, but the Catskill 3500 Club does not maintain a canister on its summit.

The Devil's Path   *Length: 25.8 miles Blaze: red*

Named for the rugged country it traverses, the Devil's Path is the backbone of the trail system in the Northern Catskills. The trail starts from Platte Clove Road a mile west of the head of Platte Clove. Its first half goes over the summits of Indian Head (3,573 feet), Twin (3,640), Sugarloaf (3,800), and Plateau (3,840 feet), before emerging at the Devil's Tombstone State Campground in Stony Clove. Since there are trails out from Devil's Kitchen and each of the notches to the north, it is possible to do this portion as a series of day hikes.

The Devil's Path officially starts at the junction of Prediger and Platte Clove Roads. The foot trail begins at the end of Prediger Road, 0.4 mile to the south, where there is limited parking along the road. One-half mile from Prediger

Road, the first junction with the Jimmy Dolan Notch Trail (blue) is reached. To the right, this side trail leads 1.6 miles to Jimmy Dolan Notch, where it reaches another junction with the Devil's Path. Here the Devil's Path turns left and swings east toward the Devil's Kitchen. The Old Overlook Road is reached at 2.2 miles. To the north, the green-blazed road leads in 0.8 mile to Platte Clove Road, passing through the Platte Clove Preserve of the Catskill Center for Conservation and Development.

In another 300 feet, the Devil's Path reaches the northern end of the Overlook Trail, which leads to the Devil's Kitchen lean-to in 0.2 mile and continues to Overlook Mountain. Here the Devil's Path turns west (right) and climbs Indian Head Mountain (3,573 feet), passing several views to the north, east and south, and reaching the summit at 4.6 miles. The trail then descends about 500 feet to Jimmy Dolan Notch at 5.1 miles. At the Notch, the Jimmy Dolan Notch Trail (blue) leads 2.0 miles north to Prediger Road, making possible an enjoyable 7.1-mile loop hike over Indian Head.

From Jimmy Dolan Notch, the Devil's Path climbs steeply, reaching the lower summit of Twin Mountain (3,580 feet) in less than half a mile. Here, hikers are rewarded for their efforts with another view, this one to the south. The main summit of Twin (3,640 feet) is another 0.6 mile farther but the altitude loss between the two summits is less than 200 feet. The trail then drops sharply about 800 feet into Pecoy Notch at 6.8 miles, where the Pecoy Notch Trail (blue) leads north 1.2 miles to Wase Road.

The Devil's Path climbs steeply out of Pecoy Notch, reaching the summit of Sugarloaf Mountain (3,800 feet) at 8.1 miles. There are numerous views on the ascent, and just beyond the summit, a short yellow-blazed trail leads south to another extensive view. The trail descends over 1,000 feet in less than a mile, and at 9.0 miles reaches Mink Hollow, where it crosses the Mink Hollow Trail (blue). A spring is located 0.15 mile north of the trail junction. A left turn (south) leads to the Mink Hollow lean-to in about 250 feet, and to the end of Mink Hollow Road north of Lake Hill in 3 miles. A right turn (north) leads in 0.8 mile to the end of Mink Hollow Road, about 4.5 miles south of Tannersville. From Jimmy Dolan Notch to Mink Hollow, the Devil's Path is also part of the Long Path, which continues to the south on the Mink Hollow Trail.

From Mink Hollow, the Devil's Path again climbs steeply to the summit of Plateau Mountain (3,840 feet) in a little over a mile. It then continues almost level for 2.0 miles along the top of Plateau, passing several views to the north and west before descending 1,500 feet steeply downhill to Stony Clove and NY 214, which

NORTH *and* SOUTH LAKES, NORTH MOUNTAIN   THE CATSKILLS

it reaches at 13.4 miles. Parking is available at the trail crossing of NY 214.

To the west of Stony Clove lies Hunter Mountain (4,040 feet), the second-highest of the Catskill peaks. Although the Devil's Path does not pass over the summit of Hunter Mountain, it does go over a shoulder of the mountain. From Stony Clove it climbs steeply, gaining 1,500 feet in 1.8 miles. It then levels out, slabbing along the 3,500-foot contour line. About 2.2 miles from Stony Clove, it reaches the Hunter Mountain Trail (yellow), which leads north 1.6 miles to the summit of Hunter. About 300 feet farther along the Devil's Path is the Devil's Acre lean-to, which has a spring. From the lean-to, the trail continues on a relatively level grade for another half-mile to a view of Spruceton Valley and Westkill Mountain, then descends steadily into Diamond Notch. Here, at 17.6 miles, there is a junction with the Diamond Notch Trail (blue). To the right it is 1.0 mile to the Spruceton Trail parking area on Spruceton Road. To the left it is 0.5 mile to Diamond Notch lean-to and 2.0 miles to the end of Diamond Notch Road (north of Lanesville) and another parking area.

The Devil's Path continues over West Kill Mountain (3,880 feet) and its western peak. Shortly before the summit (2.3 miles from Diamond Notch) is Buck Ridge Lookout, with a 180-degree view to the south and a short distance to the north, a view toward Evergreen and Rusk mountains. The summit itself, however, is wooded and viewless. The trail continues into a col and over a second summit (3,400 feet), before dropping steeply down into the notch between West Kill and North Dome mountains. The Devil's Path ends at a small parking area on Spruceton Road (County 6).

Other Hunter Mountain Routes

Several additional routes ascend Hunter's lofty peak. From the east, the 2-mile Becker Hollow Trail (blue) starts from NY 214, about 1.8 miles north of Devil's Tombstone State Campground. The Becker family was associated with this mountain for many years. During the 1920s, the oldest son was the fire observer and lived with his family at the fire tower. The father ran the farm, and the daughter served meals to boarders and hikers.

On the west side, the Spruceton Trail (blue) starts at a state parking area 6.7 miles east of the village of West Kill on Spruceton Road (County 6). This trail is the easiest way up Hunter, with the trail following a jeep road formerly used for access to the tower. At 2.2 miles, there is a spring to the right, with the John Robb lean-to just left of the trail a short distance beyond. At 2.4 miles, a yellow-marked spur trail leads in 1.1 miles to the Colonel's Chair and the top of the Hunter Mountain ski lift. The fire tower and summit are reached at 3.4 miles. The trail ends at a junction with the Becker Hollow and Hunter Mountain trails at 3.6 miles. An 8.2-mile circuit of Hunter can be formed using the Spruceton, Hunter Mountain, Devil's Path, and Diamond Notch trails.

Trails in the Northeastern Catskills

This section can be divided into two areas—the historic North Lake area and the majestic Blackhead Range. The 23-mile Escarpment Trail connects the two.

North Lake Area

The focal point of this area is North and South lakes, where there is a state campground with fireplaces, tent sites, picnic areas, and two beaches. To the east is the escarpment with the view that once brought thousands to the Catskill Mountain House. Close by are the remains of the Otis Elevating Railway that once carried patrons up the escarpment to enjoy that famous view. A loop may be made from North Lake passing the many vantage points along the Escarpment Trail (red), and returning via the Mary's Glen Trail (red).

The North Lake area is compact and contains a number of trails. In summer, maps may be available at the gatehouse. Map 40 in the Catskill Trails map set published by the New York-New Jersey Trail Conference shows details of the North Lake area.

Escarpment Trail   *Length: 22.3 miles Blaze: blue*

The Escarpment Trail starts opposite the parking area on Schutt Road, which is on the right just before the North Lake Campground gatehouse. The first highlight occurs at 0.75 mile when the trail passes near the top of Upper Kaaterskill Falls. From near the top of the falls the trail continues southwest to the edge of the Kaaterskill Clove headwall at Layman Monument (in honor of a firefighter who died at this spot in 1900). It reaches Inspiration Point, with its wide views of the Clove and of the Hudson Valley, at 1.9 miles. About half a mile beyond Inspiration Point, the Long Path joins the Escarpment Trail and stays with it to the end. At 4.5 miles, after passing South Mountain and Boulder Rock, the trail reaches the former site of the Catskill Mountain House and the road network around North and South lakes. These roads can be taken to return to the parking area at Schutt Road, a circuit of about 6 miles.

At 5.1 miles, Artist Rock has views of the Hudson Valley, with more views of the valley at 5.8 miles, Newman's Ledge. After passing two trails that lead back to the campground, North Point is reached at 7.2 miles and North Mountain at 7.7 miles. A long ridge walk then leads over Stoppel Point and through Dutcher Notch to Blackhead Mountain (3,940 feet) at 13.6 miles. Acra Point (16.4 miles), Burnt Knob (18.6 miles), and Windham High Peak (19.1 miles) follow in quick succession before the trail descends to NY 23 at 22.3 miles. See the description in the *Guide to the Long Path* for more details.

Blackhead Range

Blackhead Mountain is at the head of a horseshoe of mountains surrounding an area known as Big Hollow or the Black Dome Valley. The north side of the horseshoe consists of Acra Point, Burnt Knob, and Windham High Peak. The south side of the horseshoe is formed by Black Dome (3,940 feet) and Thomas Cole (3,980 feet) mountains, Camel's Hump, and The Caudal. The Blackhead Mountain Trail (yellow) and the Black Dome Range Trail (red) traverse the south leg of the horseshoe. A network of side trails makes trips of varying lengths possible.

A hike of the whole horseshoe is an ambitious trip— 16.9 miles from the end of Elmer Barnum Road to the end of Peck Road. Since these two points are

about 4 road-miles apart, a car shuttle is desirable, but not absolutely necessary. Starting from the end of Elmer Barnum Road, where limited parking is
available, the Black Dome Range Trail (red) climbs steadily, 1,200 feet in 0.9
mile, to The Caudal, a false summit at 3,300 feet. Just before this point is the
first of many views south across the valley to the Devil's Path mountains. The
next half-mile is flat, before a short climb to a second false summit, Camel's
Hump (3,500 feet). A short unmarked trail leads to an overgrown viewpoint.
The trail then descends slightly and passes through an open area before climbing to the summit of Thomas Cole at 2.9 miles. A short side trail leads to a view
to the south. From Thomas Cole it is 0.75 mile of easy down-and-up to Black
Dome and yet another view to the south.

The descent from Black Dome is steep. Midway through the drop, a small
ledge to the left of the trail provides a 270-degree view to the east, north, and
south. At the col between Black Dome and Blackhead (Lockwood Gap), 4.2
miles from the start, the Black Dome Range Trail (red) turns left and downhill,
leading in 1.7 miles to a parking area at the end of Big Hollow Road. To continue on the horseshoe from the col, hikers can take the Blackhead Mountain
Trail (yellow) 0.6 mile to the summit of Blackhead. From Blackhead, the Escarpment Trail traverses 8.4 miles over Acra Point, Burnt Knob, and Windham High
Peak to its junction with the Elm Ridge Trail (yellow). The horseshoe is completed
via the Elm Ridge Trail, which, in 0.9 mile, goes to the end of Peck Road.

While it is possible to walk the horseshoe as a day hike, it is usually done as a
two-day backpack, with an overnight stay at Batavia Kill lean-to. This lean-to is
located on the Batavia Kill Trail (yellow), 0.25 mile west of its junction with the
Escarpment Trail, which is one mile north of the summit of Blackhead.

Two shorter trips are possible from the parking area at the end of Big
Hollow Road. The first is a 4.5-mile circuit over the top of Blackhead, starting
on the Black Dome Range Trail (red), which goes south from the parking area.
At the trail junction in Lockwood Gap, the Blackhead Mountain Trail (yellow)
continues to the summit; then the Escarpment Trail goes north (left) for a mile
to the junction with the Batavia Kill Trail (yellow). The Batavia Kill Trail closes
the circuit to the Black Dome Range Trail, which is followed back to the parking area. The circuit can be done in reverse, but in that direction the climb to
the summit of Blackhead is steeper.

A longer circuit is 6.6 miles over both Blackhead and Acra Point. The
circuit begins in the same manner as described above. However, instead of
descending on the Batavia Kill Trail, the route continues on the Escarpment

Trail over Acra Point to the col between Acra Point and Burnt Knob. At this point an extension of the Black Dome Range Trail enters from the left, and leads downhill (south) to the parking area.

A 7.1-mile traverse of Windham High Peak and Burnt Knob is also possible from the end of Peck Road to the end of Big Hollow Road, with either a car shuttle or a 3.7-mile road walk between them. The hike begins on the Elm Ridge Trail and goes to the Escarpment Trail, over Windham High Peak and Burnt Knob to the Black Dome Range Trail, and then on the Black Dome Range Trail downhill to Big Hollow Road.

Trails in the Western Catskills

The Western Catskills include the northernmost reaches of the lands of the Lenape and the easternmost reaches of the Oneida and Tuscarora nations before they became part of the Hardenburgh Patent. Dutch settlers reached the East Branch of the Delaware River in 1763, but most evacuated during the Revolutionary War. Permanent settlements date from just before 1800, with Delaware County being organized in 1797.

Settlement spread from the valley of the East Branch along its tributaries and hillsides. In many cases, a valley became associated with a particular family. The hillsides provided pasture and the proper climate for cool-weather crops such as cabbage. But the thin, rocky soil wore out quickly, and much once-farmed land has reverted to forest and to state ownership. Foundations, rock walls, and traces of old farm and lumber roads are seen everywhere.

Since the early 1960s, the Pepacton Reservoir has stored water from the East Branch of the Delaware River to supply New York City. Under the reservoir lie the sites of several towns and villages that once served the dairy, lumber, and quarrying industries of the region.

The villages along the East Branch and in the hills west of it were the site of the anti-rent wars of 1844–45, when tenant farmers rebelled against the predominant land ownership of that time in New York. Most of the farmers leased their land from very large landowners, with payment of rent to the land owner every year and payment of one-quarter of the proceeds of the sale of a lease.

More recently the Town of Hardenbergh gained notoriety as the site of a taxpayers' revolt. In the 1970s, all but a handful of its approximately 250 property owners became ministers of a mail-order church in order to receive tax exemptions. They protested the large amount of tax-exempt land owned by religious, charitable, and educational groups, and by the state. By the 1980s, however, New York had placed some five thousand acres of state land back on the tax rolls, and the revolt ended.

Dry Brook Ridge Trail   *Length: 13.5 miles Blaze: blue*

This trail extends from Margaretville, over Patatakan Mountain, the Dry Brook Ridge, and Balsam Lake Mountain to Balsam Lake, where it intersects the Neversink-Hardenburgh Trail. The northern terminus of the trail is reached by turning south off NY 28 at the Agway store in Margaretville and going 0.2 mile to a road paralleling NY 28. The trailhead is 0.1 mile to the left, on the right side of the road. The trail gains elevation rapidly and reaches the top of the ridge known as Patatakan Mountain in 1.8 miles. At 2.7 miles it reaches the German Hollow Trail (yellow), which leads 0.9 mile to German Hollow lean-to, and another 0.6 mile to the end of Chrislong Road in Arkville.

The Dry Brook Ridge Trail continues with moderate ups and downs for the next 3.5 miles, following ledges that offer views southwest across Pepacton Reservoir. At 3.0 miles, the first junction with the Huckleberry Loop Trail is reached, with the second junction being reached at 5.2 miles. There is good blueberry picking here in July and August. Dry Brook spring and lean-to are reached at 8.2 miles. Another 1.2 miles over a slight rise leads to a parking area at Mill Brook Road, which may be followed 2.2 miles to the left (north) to Dry Brook Road, or 0.9 mile right (southwest) to a yellow-blazed trail, which leads 0.2 mile uphill to the Mill Brook lean-to.

The Dry Brook Trail continues south, following a wide woods road along the ridge as it ascends Balsam Lake Mountain. At 1.7 miles from Mill Brook Road, an unmarked woods road leads left about 1.5 miles to the top of Graham Mountain (3,868 feet), with views north and east. A short distance thereafter, the steep Balsam Lake Mountain Trail (red) branches to the right and in 0.8 mile climbs about 400 feet to the top of Balsam Lake Mountain (3,720 feet), where there is a closed fire tower. Less than half a mile farther on the Balsam Lake Mountain Trail are the two Balsam Lake Mountain lean-tos, and half a mile beyond that, after a steep descent, it rejoins the Dry Brook Ridge Trail. From here it is less than a mile downhill to the Balsam Lake parking area at the end of Beaver Kill Road, and the junction with the Neversink-Hardenburgh Trail (yellow). It is about 2 miles farther south on Beaver Kill Road to the northern end of the Mongaup-Hardenburgh Trail (blue).

Long Pond-Beaver Kill Ridge Trail   *Length: 7.5 miles Blaze: red*
This trail connects the Neversink-Hardenburgh Trail (yellow) and the Mongaup-Hardenburgh Trail (blue). From the Black Bear Trailhead parking area at the intersection of Willowemoc and Basily Roads, 0.3 mile north of Round Pond, the trail goes 3.6 miles west along Basily Road to a junction with a short spur trail, which leads south to Long Pond and a lean-to. Turning north, the Long Pond-Beaver Kill Ridge Trail crosses the Willowemoc River on a footbridge, intersects Flugertown Road, briefly joins the Mongaup-Willowemoc Trail (yellow), and then ascends the Beaver Kill Ridge. Climbing sharply at first, the trail follows what appears to be an old lumber road on easy grades. From here it is half a mile to the top of the ridge, where there is a view of Sand Pond below on the left. At the top, the Long Pond-Beaver Kill Ridge Trail ends at an intersection with the Mongaup-Hardenburgh Trail (blue). To the right (north) it is 3.2 miles to Beaver Kill Road. To the left (south) it is 3.2 miles to Mongaup Pond and the state campground.

Mongaup-Hardenburgh Trail   *Length: 6.4 miles Blaze: blue*
The Mongaup-Hardenburgh Trail begins at the north end of the Mongaup Pond State Campground between campsites 144 and 147 on Loop G. It ascends 1.6 miles to the middle peak of Mongaup Mountain (2,989 feet). The trail then follows Beaver Kill Ridge over an unnamed summit at 2.6 miles, and 0.6 mile farther on it intersects the Long Pond-Beaver Kill Ridge Trail (red), which goes 4.0 miles to Long Pond. After passing a spring, the trail reaches the highest point on Beaver Kill Ridge at 4.8 miles (elevation 3,224 feet). It then crosses the Beaver Kill on a footbridge after descending north off the Beaver Kill Ridge to end at the Beaver Kill Road. From here it is about 2 miles north to the Balsam Lake parking area and the Dry Brook Ridge and Neversink-Hardenburgh trailheads.

Starting at the Balsam Lake parking area, the Neversink-Hardenburgh, Long Pond-Beaver Kill Ridge, and Mongaup-Hardenburgh trails make a 20-mile circuit through gentle terrain, with the Long Pond lean-to offering a convenient overnight stop.

Neversink-Hardenburgh Trail   *Length: 10.9 miles Blaze: yellow*
The northern terminus of this trail is at the Balsam Lake parking area at the end of Beaver Kill Road. Except for the first mile and a half, this trail follows an old road along gentle grades ending at Claryville. The southern half of this road can be

driven to Claryville. Many small streams are crossed as the trail passes between the watersheds of the Beaver Kill and the west branch of the Neversink.

After crossing the Beaver Kill at 3.2 miles, the Neversink-Hardenburgh Trail ascends, reaching a height of land. Descending, it reaches Fall Brook lean-to at 4.3 miles. At 5.0 miles the trail enters the first of several clearings. At 5.8 miles there is a small parking area; however, the road is still very rough and parking is recommended at a site on state land at about 6.2 miles. From here the trail continues 2.7 miles by a rough road to a junction with the Long Pond-Beaver Kill Ridge Trail where the DEC maintains trailhead parking, and 2 miles farther to the bridge over the East Branch of the Neversink River in Claryville.

Delaware County

The trails in this gentler area of the Western Catskills center around the towns of Colchester and Andes in Delaware County south of the Pepacton Reservoir. Many hiking trails in this area are also blazed with large yellow snowmobile markers. When these trails are strung together, they form a continuous route of over 22 miles from Little Pond State Campground to Russell Brook Road.

Touch-Me-Not Trail   *Length: 4 miles Blaze: red*

Starting at Little Pond State Campground, the Touch-Me-Not Trail heads northeast over Touch-Me-Not Mountain (2,700 feet). Near the summit of Touch-Me-Not Mountain, another red-blazed trail heads east, crossing Barkaboom Road near Big Pond and ending at Alder Lake Road. From the trail junction of the two red trails, the Touch-Me-Not Trail swings west, passing the junction with the Little Pond Trail (yellow) to the left, which returns to the campground. After ascending Cabot Mountain (2,970 feet), the Touch-Me-Not Trail descends steeply to Beech Hill Road at 4.0 miles, and ends there.

Middle Mountain Trail   *Length: 2 miles Blaze: red*

The Middle Mountain Trail begins 0.25 mile north of the Touch-Me-Not Trail (red) on Beech Hill Road. This route runs about 2 miles west to Mary Smith Hill Road going over Middle Mountain (2,975 feet), with a lookout. It ends at the Mary Smith Trail (red).

Mary Smith Trail   *Length: 4.5 miles Blaze: red*

The Mary Smith Trail continues where the Middle Mountain Trail ends, beginning across Mary Smith Hill Road from the end of the Middle Mountain Trail, and running about 4.5 miles to the west. It crosses Mary Smith Hill (2,767 feet) and Holliday and Berry Brook Road at 3.5 miles (parking) before ending at the junction with Pelnor Hollow Trail (blue). Hikers can follow the Pelnor Hollow Trail northwest for 0.8 mile until it reaches a junction with the Campbell Mountain Trail (blue).

Campbell Mountain Trail   *Length: 5.5 miles Blaze: blue*
The Campbell Mountain Trail starts at the junction with the Little Spring Brook Trail (yellow) and the Pelnor Hollow Trail (blue). The Campbell Mountain Trail continues to Brock Mountain (2,760 feet) at 2.1 miles and across NY 206 at 3.1 miles, where there is room for parking. The Campbell Mountain lean-to is another 1.3 miles farther, and Campbell Mountain Road and a parking area are 1.1 miles beyond the lean-to.

Trout Pond Trail   *Length: 5.4 miles Blaze: blue*
The last link in the network is the Trout Pond Trail. Starting at Campbell Mountain Road across from the end of the Campbell Mountain Trail, it ascends to 2,526 feet and then descends somewhat rapidly to Campbell Brook Road at 2.1 miles. Less than 2 miles farther is Trout Pond and a lean-to, a place for camping and swimming. Though its southern end is busy on summer weekends, few users camp out and get to enjoy the lake during quieter moments. Fishing is popular here but a permit is required, and there are some special regulations. Water is available from the spring just above the northeast inlet of the lake.

At the north end of the lake, there is a trail junction. The Trout Pond Trail continues south along the lake shore and out to a large parking area at Russell Brook Road (1.4 miles). The other trail is the Mud Pond Trail, also with blue markers. This trail heads west and then swings around to the south, ending at an old road near Mud Pond in 1.7 miles. To the right the road leads 0.2 mile to Mud Pond. To the left, it leads one mile to Russell Brook Road and the parking area.

THIRTEEN

THE SHAWANGUNK MOUNTAINS

tanding high above the valleys on either side, the Shawangunk (pronounced SHON gum) Mountain ridge is a continuation of the ridge that is Blue Mountain in Pennsylvania and the Kittatinnies in New Jersey. It reaches from the New York-New Jersey line northeast to Rosendale. Referred to affectionately by hikers and climbers as the "Gunks," the area offers a hiking experience of great variety and beauty. Veteran hikers will find the challenge of rough trails and rock scrambles, while less ambitious hikers may enjoy spectacular views from gentle carriage roads. The dramatic landscape is fashioned of miles of white cliffs and ledges, clear mountaintop sky lakes, deep oak forests, and sparse ridgetop barrens of bonsai-shaped pitch pines.

Geology

At its northeastern end, the ridge rises gradually from the Hudson River Valley near Rosendale as a series of low hills, suddenly dramatized by the "table rocks" near High Falls and by the spectacular Mohonk escarpments of Bonticou Crag, Sky Top, and Eagle Cliff. The first of the five successively higher lakes, Mohonk (1,245 feet), is cradled between the latter two cliffs. From this point southwestward, the ridge grows higher and broader, and at Gertrude's Nose it bends to the west toward Ellenville. The four other lakes, whose shores exhibit striking sculpture of cliff and fallen rock, in order are Minnewaska (1,650 feet), Awosting (1,865 feet), Mud Pond (1,842 feet), and Maratanza (2,242 feet). Near the last is Sam's Point, the highest elevation of the range. The widest point is near Mud Pond. Southwest of Sam's Point, the Shawangunks settle again into a lower and narrower ridge that continues to the New Jersey border at Port Jervis, where it is known as the Kittatinny Mountain.

The narrow Shawangunk Mountain ridge is composed of Shawangunk Conglomerate, a rock so durable that it formed the basis of a substantial quarrying industry during the nineteenth century, providing millstones to grist mills around the country. It forms the slabs, cliffs, *talus* (rock debris), ice caves, and other distinctive features of the Shawangunks. The sharp profile of the ridge is caused by the fact that the resistant conglomerate is sandwiched between bedrock that is much softer and more easily eroded away.

The shale layers that underlie the Shawangunk and Kittatinny mountains also make up the floor of the broad valley, the Great Valley, immediately to the east. Laid down originally as mud deposits in an extensive sea during the Ordovician Period, they were subsequently folded, uplifted, and then eroded during a crustal upheaval near the end of the Ordovician. Near the end of the Silurian Period, the ancestral Taconic Mountains to the east were uplifted. As these mountains eroded, sands and gravels were washed westward in streams, and deposited in braided stream deltas along the margin of a shallow sea that extended far to the west. The successive layers of sands and stream-rounded quartzite gravels that were laid down form the "white stone" of the Shawangunks today.

The earth's crust was folded in a massive deformation that formed the Appalachian Mountains in the early Permian Period. This deformation raised and tilted all these strata into their present position. The shales and limestones that were laid down directly atop the Shawangunk Conglomerate have since eroded to form the floor of the Rondout Valley to the northwest. The massive sandstones and shales that sat atop the Rondout formations have been nibbled back to form the mural front of the Catskills that is so apparent from the Shawangunks today. Glaciers that crossed this region from north to south left their marks as striae or scratches seen most often along the ridgetop.

The northern Shawangunks, from Ellenville north to Rosendale, comprise a 25,000-acre natural area that contains the majority of the Shawangunk trails. The area is divided into four major ownerships, each with its own trails, access points, and fees. At the north end is the Mohonk Preserve, which nearly surrounds the

SHAWANGUNK ESCARPMENT *from* MOHONK
FROM PHOTO BY MARY LOUISE WISE

second area, the Mohonk Mountain House lands. The Minnewaska State Park Preserve occupies the wide mid-section of the ridge, and is the largest single ownership. To the south of Minnewaska is the Sam's Point area. For reasons of clarity, the different sections are treated separately below even though trails do not always respect the boundaries. The Wallkill Valley Rail Trail, although not a mountain trail, is included here because of its proximity and because the Shawangunks are so much a part of its scenery.

Hiking in the southern Shawangunks, from Ellenville south to the New Jersey border, is largely confined to the Shawangunk Ridge Trail. For hiking opportunities in the southern Shawangunks, see chapter 19, "Long Distance Trails."

History

Arrowheads from 6200 B.C.E. testify to the long relationship between humans and the Shawangunks. For centuries, Native American hunting bands undoubtedly roamed the ridge in search of game to bring to their villages below. In 1677 the New Paltz Patent brought French Huguenots to the area. Six of their original stone houses remain on Huguenot Street in New Paltz. They are open for tours seasonally.

As the valleys became settled, and farming inched up the mountainside, the forest along the ridge began a steady decline. First felled for fuel and lumber, trees were used up for a variety of industries that peaked and passed during the nineteenth century. One important industry was charcoal production, which consumed trees voraciously, although the charcoal pits through which trails pass are scarcely recognizable now. Perhaps affecting the area more than any other was the tanning industry, which in the early 1800s began the systematic destruction of the hemlock forests, both here and in the Catskills. All that is left are two notable old-growth stands—the upper Palmaghatt at Minnewaska, and Glen Anna at Mohonk. Using the saplings, which were plentiful in the second growth, the barrel hoop industry followed the demise of the tanning industry, and millions of hoops were manufactured in the Shawangunks.

The thin soil that lies atop the ridge is good for blueberries. Berry-picking flourished as an industry into the 1950s, particularly between Sam's Point and Lake Awosting. The early commercial berry-pickers spent the summer in shacks whose remnants can still be seen near Smiley Road and Lake Maratanza. Remains of a network of trails, marked by cairns and leading to favored picking areas, are still visible as well.

As the West opened to settlers, many farms in this area were abandoned. Coal, and later oil and gas, reduced the demand for wood fuel, allowing the forests to make a gradual comeback. Coinciding with the start of this trend was a romantic fascination with the picturesque and the spiritual in nature, reflected in the painting, literature, and landscape architecture of the time. "Wilderness" vacations became fashionable at luxurious resorts such as the Catskill Mountain House.

Enter the Smiley twins, Albert K. and Alfred H. In 1869 Albert acquired the original 310-acre parcel, comprising Mohonk Lake and the surrounding land, from John Stokes, who had run a tavern on the lake. The brothers, who had been teachers, entered the hotel business, and to maintain the character of the property they added adjoining farms and other private holdings to the estate as they became available. They also began to remodel and expand the small inn until, in 1910, it appeared much as it does today.

In 1879 Alfred H. Smiley opened his own hotel, the Lake Minnewaska House, which originally consisted of two buildings (now removed): Cliff House east of the lake and Wildmere at the north. Both estates expanded until Mohonk reached 7,500 acres, and Minnewaska more than 10,000 acres. Over the years, more than 200 miles of carriage roads and trails were created, all seeking out scenic view spots. As much as any single human factor, the pioneering work of the Smileys and their descendants, in road-building techniques, conservation, and land management practices, has set the direction and the standard for land stewardship and land conservation in the Shawangunks.

Natural History

Fires have had a prominent role in shaping the character of the Shawangunk forests. A complex interplay of species with environmental factors such as droughty soils, drying winds, summer lightning strikes, and millennia of human use has formed the fire-adapted forest communities of the Shawangunk ridgetop. These communities are characterized by pitch pine and oak forests with shrub layers of scrub oak, mountain laurel, and blueberries. Berry-pickers accentuated the trend by periodically setting fires rather than permitting the berries to be shaded out by competing vegetation. The ashes served as fertilizer and the crop flourished. Since the most characteristic species of the Shawangunks are those that have benefitted from the history of fires, we can only wonder at the future of this magnificent landscape now that its popularity for recreation makes fire seem so unwelcome in its traditional role.

A particular legacy of fire ecology is the pitch pine plains atop the ridge in the Sam's Point and High Point areas. This forest community is, to the best of our knowledge, unique in the world. Sometimes described as a pygmy forest, the dense treetops in these pine plains are often no more than 6 to 9 feet high, and frequently smaller—in some places less than 2 feet. Pine barrens and pine plains communities are found elsewhere, but typically they are found in coastal sand plains or glacial outwash plains, not rugged rocky ridgetops.

Once cleared for human uses, the forests returned to the slopes of the Shawangunks, bringing red cedar, birch, white pine, chestnut oak, red oak, striped maple, and red maple. Hemlock has returned to line shady streams and cool north-facing slopes. The second growth has also figured in the resurgence of white-tailed deer, which feed on the low brush not present in a mature forest. Lacking the timber wolf and mountain lion—predators that once roamed the rocky cliffs—deer are more numerous now than ever. Preferring other low bushes to mountain laurel, the increased deer population has indirectly contributed to the flourishing of that beautiful shrub amid the white rocks of the Shawangunks.

Other factors have helped shape the character of today's Shawangunk forests. During the 1910s and 1920s, chestnut blight decimated the American chestnut, previously an extremely important forest tree in many sites. It persists in the form of root sprouts that are sometimes prolific in the Shawangunk forests. Chestnut oak and other oaks have apparently replaced the American chestnut. Chestnut oak is fire-resistant, but vulnerable to gypsy moth defoliation, especially during periods of drought. In some mountainside areas, the gypsy moth infestation may result in nearly complete loss of the forest canopy, releasing a dense regrowth of shrubs and young trees from beneath.

The rugged cliff-and-talus areas are home to several distinctive species of wildlife, including the five-lined skink (a lizard), fisher (a member of the weasel family), and porcupine. After decades of absence, the fisher was reintroduced in the 1970s, and is a natural predator of porcupines. The Eastern woodrat, a dignified cousin to the urban species, disappeared from talus areas in the 1970s. A study in the 1990s found that reintroduced woodrats suffered from a debilitating parasite caught from raccoons.

In the mid-1970s, attempts were made to reintroduce the peregrine falcon to the cliffs of the Shawangunks, one of the last natural nesting places in the eastern United States. Although the peregrine has not become re-established here, the urban cliffs and canyons of New York City's bridges and skyscrapers have attracted a growing population of these majestic birds.

Other species are becoming more common in the area, including the raven, coyote, and black bear, while still others, notably songbirds, appear to be in decline. Researchers at the Mohonk Preserve monitor many species. Detailed records begun by members of the Smiley family extend back to the 1920s. Checklists and additional information on wildlife and plants of the Shawangunk Mountains are available from the Mohonk Preserve, by mail or at their Visitor Center: Mohonk Preserve, Inc., Mohonk Lake, New Paltz, NY 12561; (914) 255-0919.

THE AWOSTING RESERVE

The Awosting Reserve is a private land management and wilderness protection association formed in 1955. It owns more than 4,000 acres in the Shawangunks including much of the south facing slope extending along the escarpment from Gertrude's Nose at the east to the Mud Pond area in the west. The reserve borders Minnewaska State Park Preserve.

The reserve contains a system of footpaths and forest roads. Waterfalls in the property include Las Cascades and the Upper and Lower Palmaghatt Falls. Except for the hikers using the Long Path, all users must have a permit to enter the lands to hike, fish, hunt, canoe, or ski. The area is patrolled by rangers.

For more information, send a self-addressed, stamped envelope to the Minnewaska Trail Club, Box 1234, Pine Bush, NY 12566. For a group day pass, call (914) 895-3315.

Long Path   *Length: 2.3 miles Blaze: turquoise*
See chapter 19, "Long Distance Trails," for a brief description, or the *Guide to the Long Path* for a detailed description of this section.

MINNEWASKA STATE PARK PRESERVE

Minnewaska (11,630 acres) was once the site of two mountaintop hotels. Many miles of scenic trails and historic carriageways wind their way around Lake Minnewaska and Lake Awosting and beyond. The original section of the park, which centered on Lake Awosting, was created in 1971 by the State of New York and The Nature Conservancy. The 1,200-acre section that includes Lake Minnewaska was added in 1987, at the conclusion of a long and spirited legal battle over the proposed development of the site by the Marriott Corporation that might have resulted in the construction of a 450-room hotel and conference center, 300 condominiums, and an 18-hole golf course on the site. A broad coalition of conservation groups led by the local Friends of the Shawangunks, and including the New York-New Jersey Trail Conference, was successful in demonstrating that the site could not support the proposed development, and in establishing the area as a premier state park preserve.

The Shawangunk "sky lakes" of Lake Minnewaska and Lake Awosting are the scenic centerpieces of the park preserve, and the areas from which most other scenic attractions can be reached. These lakes are well known for the exceptional clarity of their water and their aquamarine color. Both lakes are set into white conglomerate cliffs and encircled with carriageways that provide ready access to many views. The numerous scenic overlooks in the park are destinations by themselves, with varied and sweeping views of the lakes, cliffs, expanses of pine barrens, and the valleys below. They include Hamilton Point, Castle Point, Gertrude's Nose, Millbrook Mountain, Murray Hill, Margaret Cliff, Beacon Hill, and the High Peters Kill cliffs. Many are accessible by a choice of trail or carriageway.

In late 1996, Open Space Institute, in conjunction with The Nature Conservancy, purchased the lease held by Ice Caves Mountain, Inc. on the Ellenville-owned lands, which included Sam's Point. Open Space Institute has an option to purchase the entire tract pending finalization of some legal details. This area, which is between the western boundary of Minnewaska and the Village of Ellenville, will be managed by The Nature Conservancy. Old trails, including the Long Path, will be reopened and new trail routes will be established. For current information, contact the New York-New Jersey Trail Conference (212) 685-9699.

Crevice
and
steps

Road

Sams Point

Dickinson

🚶 Trails in Minnewaska State Park Preserve

In addition to providing easy access to scenic areas, the old carriageways that crisscross Minnewaska provide essential linkages. A number of the trails described below begin with a carriageway walk of up to 3 miles. To provide their guests with access to the most scenic spots, the Minnewaska hotels built and maintained over 50 miles of roads on which only horse-drawn vehicles were permitted. In so doing, they left a rich legacy to us all. The carriages are gone, but hiking, horseback riding, ski touring, and bicycling are permitted. In recent years, the carriageways have become the domain of mountain bicyclists in the warmer seasons and of footprint-sensitive cross-country skiers when there is snow. Some abandoned carriageways are partially overgrown, while others are well maintained and sustain heavy use.

Minnewaska contains other trails not described below, including the Long Path (see chapter 19, "Long Distance Trails") and carriageways that are not maintained as trails. The most notable of the latter are the Awosting Falls Carriageway, which offers a brief and popular walk to the waterfall; the Old Smiley Road, a Palisades Interstate Park Commission-owned linkage from Lake Awosting to the base of the ridge at Ellenville; and Stony Kill Path, which links Lake Awosting to Stony Kill Falls.

Beacon Hill Trail   *Length: 0.8 mile Blaze: yellow*

The Beacon Hill Trail is one of the most scenic short hikes in the immediate area of Lake Minnewaska. It begins at the end of the Beacon Hill Carriageway, 0.7 mile from the Lake Minnewaska parking area. From the lot, hikers can reach the path by walking back down the paved entrance road, heading northward for approximately 0.1 mile, and watching on the right for the Beacon Hill Carriageway marker (orange with a black B). A right turn onto the carriageway to its end (0.6 mile) leads to views northward to the High Peters Kill cliffs and Dickie Barre.

The Beacon Hill Trail begins at the end of the orange-blazed carriageway, where it bears right and enters the woods. The trail descends briefly, then climbs gradually, soon reaching an opening atop a rock ledge (0.3 mile) with views to the left, extending across the Coxing Clove. The trail leads generally uphill, winding among low blueberries, pitch pines, woodlands, and rock slabs. Landmarks visible along the way include Dickie Barre, the Sky Top tower, and the backsides of the Trapps and Millbrook Mountain, with the village of New Paltz visible beyond. The trail turns right to re-enter the woods, and soon turns left and drops down to cross a small stream at 0.7 mile. Shortly before reaching its end, the trail winds around a large boulder on the left where sharp eyes will spy the remains of two metal braces that once anchored one of Minnewaska's wooden summerhouses, built to capture the view. Beacon Hill Trail reaches its terminus at an open field that once was the old ball field of Minnewaska. The parking area is reached by crossing the field and turning right on the red-blazed carriageway or turning left for a longer walk around Lake Minnewaska.

Blueberry Run Trail   *Length: 2.2 miles Blaze: blue*
This trail begins at Castle Point, 3.2 miles from the Lake Minnewaska parking lot. (See directions for Castle Point Carriageway, below.) At Castle Point, blue blazes on the right side of the carriageway mark the beginning of the Blueberry Run Trail. The trail begins by climbing a low conglomerate bluff and then making a long and gradual descent, marked by blazes and cairns.

Views of the Catskill Mountains are along the way. The trail crosses a small stream at 1.0 mile, immediately before an intersection with a yellow trail branching left, marked with a sign. It then turns sharply right and traverses dense mountain laurel, beautiful around early June when it is usually in bloom. Sounds from the nearby carriageway may be audible to the left. The trail crosses another small stream and passes beneath a power line at 1.3 miles.

After crossing the Upper Awosting Carriageway at 1.7 miles, the Blueberry Run Trail heads downhill to cross the Peters Kill stream on a footbridge. A short climb up then brings the trail to the Peters Kill or Lower Awosting Carriageway at 2.0 miles. Heading directly across the carriageway, the trail remains level for some time and crosses a small stream before making a brief ascent. The Blueberry Run Trail ends at a junction with the Long Path, between Jenny Lane and Lake Awosting, at 2.2 miles. The hiker may continue in either direction on the Long Path. (See chapter 19, "Long Distance Trails.") To return to Lake Minnewaska, hikers can retrace their steps either to the Lower Awosting Carriageway or to the Upper Awosting Carriageway. A left turn on the Lower Awosting Carriageway leads to the Awosting parking area on US 44-NY 55; turning left on the Upper Awosting Carriageway returns the hiker to Lake Minnewaska.

Castle Point Carriageway   *Length: 4.3 miles Blaze: blue*
The Castle Point Carriageway is the highest within the Minnewaska State Park

Preserve, skirting along the tops of the series of bluffs that define the western rim of the Palmaghatt Ravine, with lofty outward views. It is popular with mountain bicyclists. The Castle Point Carriageway begins at the Lake Shore Drive on the west side of Lake Minnewaska, 0.4 mile from the parking area. It departs westward, soon crossing a grassy hilltop area (a former golf course) with sweeping views northward to the Catskills. The route then enters a sparse oak-and-pine forest that is characteristic of the ridge, and turns generally southward. At 0.7 mile, a carriageway ascends to join from the left, connecting to the Hamilton Point Carriageway, below. Views open to the southeast, across the Palmaghatt Ravine and the Wallkill Valley beyond. The first of the major views, at 1.0 mile, is Kempton Ledge.

The carriageway gradually ascends in a westerly direction, passing beneath a power line at 1.8 miles, then meandering through miniature cliffs known as the Castles, with frequent vistas. At 3.2 miles the carriageway crests the top of the escarpment at Castle Point. Here, at an elevation of 2,200 feet, is a beautiful area for having lunch or just enjoying the panorama. Extensive flat ledges offer nearly 360-degree views of the immediate area. On clear days Schunemunk, Black Rock Forest, and Storm King may be seen to the south, while the Catskills dominate the view to the north. Closer by are views of Lake Awosting, Margaret Cliff, Murray Hill, Sam's Point, and the Wallkill Valley. The Long Path ascends the bluff from the Hamilton Point Carriageway below, and follows the top of the bluff downhill for a short distance.

From Castle Point, the carriageway winds downhill and around a hairpin turn where the Long Path departs to the right, and soon passes beneath the dramatic cliffs of Battlement Terrace that far overhang the carriageway. The Castle Point Carriageway intersects with the Hamilton Point Carriageway (yellow), a prime return route, at 4.3 miles.

Gertrude's Nose Trail   *Length: 3.4 miles Blaze: red*
The Gertrude's Nose Trail begins on the Millbrook Mountain Carriageway, at a point 2.1 miles from the parking area at Lake Minnewaska. From the parking area, the route passes along the right (west) side of the lake, following the red-blazed carriageway until the Millbrook Mountain Carriageway (yellow) forks to the right near the end of the lake, at 0.7 mile. A right turn onto the Millbrook Mountain Carriageway leads to the Gertrude's Nose Trail. At 1.0 mile, the carriageway to Hamilton Point and Castle Point forks off to the right, marking the inconspicuous beginning of the Palmaghatt Ravine. The Millbrook

Mountain Carriageway (yellow) stays left and eventually skirts along the eastern rim of the ravine. A large boulder, known as Patterson's Pellet, is perched on the brink of the cliff on the right side of the carriageway at 1.6 miles. From here, the Palmaghatt is visible as a narrow, cliff-lined gorge that widens and deepens to the southwest. The small stream, the Palmaghatt Kill, flows through the bogs and forests at its bottom. Several hundred yards farther on, at 2.1 miles, a low cairn with red blazes along the right side of the carriageway marks the beginning of the Gertrude's Nose Trail.

Departing the carriageway into pitch pine woods, the trail soon comes to an opening on the right, where an exposed bedrock outcrop affords views across the Palmaghatt Ravine toward the Hamilton Point and Castle Point carriageways on the opposite rim. Continuing through the woods, the trail soon makes an abrupt descent that ends in a shady hemlock stand at the base of the slope. The trail leaves the stand to pass under a power line at 0.5 mile, where it crosses a small stream. A few steps up a low rock ledge brings the trail to a bedrock slab that is open to the top of a low cliff on the right. From here, the trail climbs gradually, following the top of a series of broad, open conglomerate ledges of increasing height that form the rim of the Palmaghatt Ravine. The trail weaves in and out along the edge of the pine barrens forest and the open slabs.

At Gertrude's Nose (1.3 miles), one stands atop the prow-shaped apex of the cliffs, with views across the Palmaghatt to Hamilton Point and Castle Point, and southward

Along the Gertrude's Nose Trail

across the Wallkill Valley. Boulders left by the glaciers are strewn across the open expanses of bedrock. The trail turns left, continuing along the cliff top, with views of the Wallkill Valley. At 2.3 miles, the trail makes a gradual descent and passes beneath the power line once again, at 2.4 miles, then makes a short, steep climb to meander through open slabs and scrubby pitch pines on the southwest shoulder of Millbrook Mountain. Eventually, the Millbrook Mountain Carriageway (yellow) approaches the trail from the left, and runs parallel until both terminate at a viewpoint at the summit of Millbrook Mountain (3.4 miles). The carriageway ends at a small turnaround circle. At the trail junction near the circle, blue blazes mark the terminus of the Mohonk Preserve's Millbrook Ridge Trail to Trapps Bridge, and red blazes heading downslope to the north mark the terminus of the Millbrook Mountain Trail to Lake Minnewaska. The 3.2-mile Millbrook Mountain Carriageway (yellow) or the 1.2-mile Millbrook Mountain Path (red) lead back to Lake Minnewaska.

Hamilton Point Carriageway   *Length: 4 miles Blaze: yellow with black* H
The Hamilton Point Carriageway follows the northern rim of the Palmaghatt Ravine, an immense V-shaped ravine whose side walls consist of a double row of high, vertical cliffs. This is one of the most scenic routes between Lake Minnewaska and Lake Awosting. From the Lake Minnewaska parking area, the Lake Shore Carriageway (red) proceeds for 0.7 mile to the south end of the lake, where a yellow-blazed carriageway forks right and a sign indicates the way to Millbrook Mountain and Hamilton Point. The yellow-blazed carriageway leads to Palmaghatt Junction (at 1.0 mile), where the Millbrook Mountain Carriageway and the route to Hamilton Point fork left, continuing a short distance until the road forks again, at 1.3 miles. The fork ascending to the right joins the Castle Point Carriageway above. This time, hikers take the left fork (yellow-blazed), continuing into a deep hemlock forest. The carriageway soon emerges from deep woods, and views begin to open across the Palmaghatt Ravine. Patterson's Pellet, a large white glacial erratic, can be seen perched on top of the opposite wall. The carriageway begins to skirt the top of the cliffs, with views across the Palmaghatt. The upper section of the ravine visible from here supports a growth of large hemlock trees, which appear to have survived the tanning industry's quest for hemlock bark. The lower, southwestern part of the Palmaghatt is private land and is closed to hikers. The cliffs and ravine northeast of the power line are within the park preserve.

At 2.2 miles, a power line swath is carved across the ravine, and wires, oddly out of place here, pass overhead. After skirting the tops of the cliffs, the carriageway soon swings away from the cliffs and passes through a stand of small trees, until it emerges near Hamilton Point at 3.4 miles. Here, at an elevation of 2,020 feet, hikers get a panoramic view of Gertrude's Nose visible above to the southeast, the Wallkill Valley to the south, and Margaret Cliff and Murray Hill to the west. From there the road makes a sharp bend to the north. A short distance later, the Long Path joins the carriageway for a short distance as it crosses on its way from Margaret Cliff off to the left to Castle Point above on the right. The Castle Point Carriageway (blue) forks right at 3.8 miles; staying left, the carriageway passes beneath the cliffs of the Battlement Terrace a short distance beyond. The carriageway ends at an intersection with the Lower Lake Awosting Carriageway (black).

High Peters Kill Trail   Length: 3.0 miles Blaze: blue

The High Peters Kill Trail starts from the Lower Awosting parking area, at the end nearest the highway. Of the trails described here, it is the only one north of US 44-NY 55, in a part of the park that is notably free of carriageways. From the parking area, the trail immediately crosses US 44-NY 55 and heads into the woods, bearing right. The woods here are mostly oak and maple, with a healthy undergrowth of mountain laurel. The trail soon reaches the ridge line, with views of the highway below on the right. After passing through a split rock, the views open up, revealing the low cliffs of Dickie Barre ahead on the right. From here, the path begins a gradual descent along the tops of the Peters Kill cliffs, amid sustained outward views. The cleared areas visible on the slopes below to the east are the remains of the ski area once operated by the Minnewaska resort. Along the way, the cliffs to the right gradually diminish in stature, giving way to rocky slopes. At 1.6 miles, the trail steepens downhill and bears to the right, to approach the Peters Kill. After crossing a set of two bridges over the Peters Kill at 1.7 miles, the trail starts its ascent up the northwest slope of the rounded section of ridge known as Dickie Barre.

Once on top of Dickie Barre, at 2.1 miles, views of the Catskills open up on the left. The trail then leads left and passes large rocks on the right, soon leveling off for a short time before beginning a steep descent, known in the 1800s as the "Dug Way." It was a road built or dug to transport millstones quarried atop Dickie Barre down into the Coxing Clove, and thence to High Falls or Alligerville, for shipment on the Delaware and Hudson Canal. Millstones were dragged behind oxen or draft horses on a flat wooden sledge called a stone boat.

At the base of the Dug Way, the trail crosses onto the Mohonk Preserve (3.0 miles), where a separate fee is required for day use. Hikers who prefer to remain entirely on state park land may return by the same route with full, open views. Otherwise, hikers can continue downhill to reach the trailhead of the Mohonk Preserve's Coxing Trail (at 3.3 miles), or connecting from there to the Trapps Entry (at 3.8 miles) via the Shongum Path (red). Hikers who choose to use Mohonk Preserve lands should prepare in advance by purchasing a day pass at the Mohonk Preserve Trapps Entry on US 44-NY 55. This day pass also enables hikers to spot a car at the Mohonk end of their hike. (See the Mohonk Preserve section, below.)

Lower Awosting Carriageway   *Length: 3.0 miles Blaze: black*
The most direct route between the park entrance and Lake Awosting is the carriageway that leaves from the rear of the Awosting parking area at the State Park entrance. It is also known as the "Peters Kill Carriageway." The route was originally cleared to a considerable width, and the lack of shade makes for warm walking on hot, sunny days. Even so, its directness and the powerful appeal of Lake Awosting make it well traveled. The carriageway crosses the Fly Brook on a causeway, then immediately climbs a steep hill just before reaching Lake Awosting.

Millbrook Mountain Trail   *Length: 1.2 miles Blaze: red*
This footpath begins at the south end of Lake Minnewaska, 0.9 mile from the Lake Minnewaska parking area. Lake Shore Drive (red) on the right side of Lake Minnewaska, leads to the start of the trail. It continues past the intersections with the Upper Awosting Carriageway (green), Castle Point Carriageway (blue), and the yellow-blazed carriageway (even though it mentions Millbrook Mountain), and descends on a switchback to reach the level of the shoreline at the south end of the lake. On the right side of the carriageway, at 0.9 mile, is the sign for Millbrook Mountain Trail.

The trail departs the carriageway and crosses a rocky, wooded area that is sometimes wet and difficult to traverse because of overflow from the lake. It soon crosses the outlet stream. In dry years, only water gurgling below the rocks may be heard. Shortly after, at 0.1 mile, the trail narrows to run alongside a rock face that is covered with rich lichen. The dropoff to the left may be dangerous in snow and ice, so hikers should exercise extreme caution in winter and early spring. Soon the trail opens to cross a rock slab with an open view on the left, across the Coxing Clove toward the Sky Top tower and New Paltz. Continuing on, the trail descends gradually and enters a shady hemlock stand. After crossing a stream at 0.7 mile, it begins the ascent of Millbrook Mountain. The first section is very rocky and very wet most of the time. The sloping conglomerate slabs, smoothed by glacial action and thinly covered with algae and crustose lichen, can be slippery underfoot. The forest gives way to sparse stands of chestnut oak and pitch pine as exposed bedrock replaces soil underfoot. Nearly halfway up the slope, at 1.0 mile, the Coxing Trail (blue) departs left. The Millbrook Mountain Trail continues uphill, following red blazes until a second, blue-blazed trail departs left at the top of Millbrook Mountain, at 1.2 miles (the Millbrook Ridge Trail). This junction marks the terminus of the Millbrook Mountain Trail; a red-blazed path to the right crosses a sloping conglomerate slab to the summit in about 100 feet, with a 360-degree view.

The return hike to Lake Minnewaska can be via the same route, or along the 3.2-mile Millbrook Mountain Carriageway (yellow), which has its terminus at a turnaround circle at the base of the summit slab.

Upper Awosting Carriageway   *Length: 3.3 miles Blaze: green*
The Upper Awosting Carriageway (Awosting Lake Carriageway) is the most direct route between Lake Minnewaska and Lake Awosting, following an almost-level grade for its entire length. It begins at Lake Shore Drive (red) on the west side of Lake Minnewaska, 0.1 mile from the Lake Minnewaska parking area, at the lake's swimming area. From here, the Upper Awosting Carriageway departs westward, crossing an old orchard area before becoming immersed in sparse oak woodlands. At 1.4 miles, the Blueberry Run Trail crosses, and at 2.0 miles hikers will see a power line swath. The carriageway then trends to the left and begins to enter Huntington Ravine, defined by the overhanging cliffs of Litchfield Ledge on the left and the Overlook cliffs on the opposite side. The Long Path crosses from above Litchfield Ledge on the left, and descends toward Rainbow Falls on the right, at 2.4 miles. The carriageway crosses a stream amid deep forest, then winds around beneath the Overlook cliffs on the left, and at 3.3 miles joins the black-blazed carriageway that encircles Lake Awosting.

MOHONK MOUNTAIN HOUSE

The Mohonk Mountain House, together with the landscape surrounding it, was designated a National Historic Landmark in 1986. Its 2,200-acre grounds, extending from Copes Lookout on the south to the Mountain Rest Golf Course on the north, feature miles of trails and carriageways ideally suited for hiking. Mohonk's hallmark is the rustic gazebo (known locally as a summerhouse) situated atop a cliff or amid boulders to capture an artful setting or view. With the seasons of mountain laurel bloom and autumn foliage seeming to draw the most visitors, other times of the year are the best for quiet contemplation of Mohonk's rugged and varied scenery.

Day visitor passes, parking, maps, and information are available at the gatehouse. A limited number of day visitor passes is sold each day. The day pass entitles the bearer to hike the carriageways, trails, and paths, and to tour the grounds, and is also honored on the adjoining Mohonk Preserve lands. Day visitors are not permitted to enter the Mountain House or to use the lake and its facilities unless purchasing a meal.

In winter, when trails are open for skiing, hiking is not permitted. On busy spring and fall weekends, parking areas may fill up by mid-morning and the gate closes. To find out whether Mountain House trails are open for hiking or skiing or filled to capacity and closed, call (914) 255-1000. An alternate plan is advisable.

Access to the Mohonk Mountain House is reserved for overnight guests

and guests who purchase a meal there. The hiker choosing one of these options may drive up the mountain to the Mountain House, and start the walk there, also earning the opportunity to enjoy the distinctive character of the hotel, as well as certain of its special programs. Reservations for meals are required, and should be made in advance by calling the dining room at (914) 256-2056 or, in the New York metropolitan area, at (212) 233-2244. One overnight program of particular note is the "Hiker's Holiday" package offered each May. Information about reservations for overnight stays may be obtained by calling (800) 772-6646.

To reach the Mohonk Mountain House, leave the New York State Thruway at Exit 18. Turn left onto NY 299 and follow Main Street through New Paltz. Immediately after crossing the bridge over the Wallkill River, turn right at the MOHONK sign. After 0.25 mile, bear left at the fork and continue up Mountain Rest Road to the Mohonk Mountain House gate.

🚶

Trails at Mohonk Mountain House

The center of activity for all day users is the Picnic Lodge Day Visitor Center, where rest rooms, snacks, and additional information are available in season. On busy weekends, a shuttle bus may be available for a fee. The walk to Picnic Lodge begins on the Huguenot Trail, at the back of the parking lot west of the gatehouse. The 1.7-mile route includes both trails and carriage roads, and is marked by signs. Beginning at the parking area, the Huguenot Trail turns right on the Whitney Road carriageway at 0.3 mile, follows this road gradually downhill, and then turns left onto North Lookout Road at 0.5 mile. The route then follows North Lookout Road as it loops around, and turns left onto a trail leading uphill, marked by a sign to Picnic Lodge.

At Mohonk Mountain House, the term "carriageway" that is more familiar to state park visitors is replaced with the historic term "carriage road." They are the same, but hikers should be aware that Mohonk maps and directional signs name carriage roads as "Road" or "Drive." Carriage roads are soft-surfaced, closed to motorized use except for patrol and maintenance, and offer very favorable hiking. *Please note:* The Mountain House area is densely laced with trails and carriage roads, so constant attention to trail signs, landmarks, and a good map is essential.

Additional walks and guidelines for visitors are described in maps and brochures provided with the Mohonk day-use pass. More ambitious hikes extend onto Mohonk Preserve lands and include the Trapps (Undercliff and Overcliff roads), Duck Pond Trail, and Plateau Path. Notable hikes on rough paths that involve rock scrambles, agility, care, and the use of hands as well as feet include Arching Rocks Path and Rock Rift Path

Eagle Cliff Road   *Length: 1.7 miles Signs: directional only*
The Eagle Cliff carriage road is a loop road that offers a great variety of scenery in a relatively short and easy walk. The walk is beautiful in either direction, but the tradition is to walk up the western side, beginning by the tennis courts, and return along the bluff overlooking the Lake.

Humpty Dumpty Road *Length: 1.9 miles Signs: directional only*
This easy carriage road walk traverses the Humpty Dumpty talus, a slide rock area nearly 900 feet in height, extending from Eagle Cliff to Rhododendron Swamp. The sparse trees in the talus are among the oldest in the Shawangunks, dating from pre-colonial times. From the west side of the Mountain House, the route proceeds along Cope's Lookout Road, then turns left on Humpty Dumpty Road. The hike returns to the Mountain House by Short Woodland Drive and Lake Shore Road, making a loop of 1.9 miles.

Labyrinth Path *Length: 0.5 mile Blaze: red*
The route through the talus at the base of the Sky Top cliff is a rough path known as the Labyrinth. Don't let the brief length of this trail fool you! The most rugged way to Sky Top, it winds through narrow defiles, scrambles over boulders, and climbs a rustic ladder, requiring agility and the use of hands as well as feet. From the Mountain House, Lake Shore Road heads south for 0.1 mile to the sign for Labyrinth Path on the left. The hiker is quickly immersed in a tumble of boulders that create a kind of inner sanctum of the Shawangunks. At 0.4 mile, the exhilarated hiker reaches the Crevice formed by a massive block of conglomerate that since glacial times has separated from the main body of Sky Top cliff by several feet. Those electing not to climb the Crevice may quickly descend from the talus on a red-blazed trail to Spring Path and Lake Shore Road, which returns to the Mountain House. A system of rustic ladders climbs through it to join Sky Top Road, which forms a loop at the top. The Crevice is a tight squeeze in places. Travel light, or be prepared to pass your pack separately. Once on Sky Top Road, hikers reach the tower by turning left toward Sky Top Path, reached in 0.1 mile The return trip to the Mountain House vicinity is via Sky Top Path.

Sky Top Path *Length: 0.4 mile Signs: directional only*
One of the most popular objectives for hikers at Mohonk is Sky Top, a prominent cliff whose stone tower, the Albert K. Smiley Memorial Tower, is easily visible from as far as the New York State Thruway. The easiest approach starts near the Mohonk Mountain House heading east past the golf putting green to Sky Top Path, marked by a sign. The path passes the Council House and Conference Center building, climbing and crossing a loop of a carriage road, Sky Top Road, at 0.3 mile. Another loop of the road is reached at the tower.

A winding stairway inside the tower leads to the observation deck. The

Sky Top Ridge seen from the east

views of the nearby valleys and distant mountain ranges from there are well worth the extra effort. On a clear day, parts of six states are visible. Return is the same way, or by the gentler Sky Top Road and Reservoir Path.

Sky Top Road   *Length: 3.0 miles Signs: directional only*
This especially leisurely and indirect carriage road loop to Sky Top is attractive during mountain laurel bloom. From Picnic Lodge, Bruin Path switchbacks briefly uphill to Huguenot Drive atop a low bluff at Garden Overlook. From the Mountain House, hikers can depart directly on the Huguenot Drive carriage road. From Garden Overlook, it's a 0.1-mile walk north on Huguenot Drive to the intersection with Sky Top Road.

The pond along the way often proves productive for watchers of frogs, turtles, birds, and dragonflies. Originally built as a reservoir for the hotel, it is simply home for its many animal tenants. Today's drinking water supply uses a sanitary underground tank nearby. A second reservoir at the base of the Sky Top tower still provides a head of water for the hotel's sprinkler system. These mountaintop reservoirs obviated the need for an unsightly water tower at Mohonk, leaving the stone tower as a solitary landmark. The carriage road forks at the pond to form a loop to the tower from this point; the right fork heads west and is more direct, while the other is more attractive on the return. Sky Top tower is reached at 1.5 miles. The other leg of the Sky Top Road loop leads back to the pond, from which hikers can return to the Mountain House or Picnic Lodge the way they came.

MOHONK PRESERVE

The Mohonk Preserve is New York State's largest non-profit privately owned nature sanctuary. Its 6,250 acres extend for nearly 8 miles along the Shawangunk ridge, from Bonticou Crag to Millbrook Mountain. The original Mohonk estate, assembled by the many purchases of Albert K. Smiley and his descendants during the nineteenth and early twentieth centuries, is divided into two property ownerships, the Mohonk Mountain House and the Mohonk Preserve. The Mohonk Preserve is a nonprofit organization that was formed originally as the Mohonk Trust in 1963. Fees are charged for day-use permits on the preserve, entitling one to hike through the lands of both proprietors, with certain limitations. Permits should be shown to the rangers on request. Day-use passes are available at the Visitor Center or from Mohonk Preserve rangers on patrol.

Hikes on the southern end of the Mohonk Preserve begin at the Trapps Entry on US 44-NY 55 in the town of Gardiner; hikes on the northern preserve depart from the trailhead at the Mohonk Preserve's Bonticou Entry and Visitor Center on Mountain Rest Road, reached by taking Exit 18 of the New York State Thruway to NY 299 west through the village of New Paltz. To visit the Trapps and the southern preserve, continue west on NY 299 to its end, then turn right onto US 44-NY 55 west. The Trapps Entry and parking area are about a half-mile past the Trapps Bridge overpass. Limited parking is also available along the road near Trapps Bridge. Since the Trapps is one of the most popular rock-climbing areas in the northeast, the cliffs and parking areas are often crowded.

To find the Mohonk Preserve's Bonticou Entry and Visitor Center from New Paltz, go west on NY 299. Immediately after crossing the bridge over the Wallkill River, turn right. After 0.25 mile bear left at the fork and continue up Mountain Rest Road to the Mohonk Preserve Visitor Center sign on the right. Park in the lot across the road, on the left, and cross the road (carefully!) to the Visitor Center.

On busy spring and fall weekends, the Mohonk Preserve fills to capacity and closes early in the day, so hikers should plan an alternate destination or activity. Maps and trail guides, as well as yearly memberships and other information, can be obtained by writing to Mohonk Preserve, Inc., Mohonk Lake, New Paltz, NY 12561, or by calling the Visitor Center at (914) 255-0919.

Trails in Mohonk Preserve

Walking ranges from easy, scenic strolls on carriage roads to rough scrambles over boulders, through crevasses and across open ledges. Only a brief indication of the possibilities can be made here; hikers must go, maps in hand, and make their own discoveries.

Bonticou Crag   *Length: 1.6 miles Blazes: red, blue, yellow*
The top of Bonticou (1,194 feet) is a far more rugged and dramatic viewpoint than its modest height would suggest. *Bontecou* is from the Dutch for "spotted cow." The reason for the name is obscure and subject to dispute, but may refer to the mottled appearance of its lichen-covered white conglomerate cliffs. The hike to its summit passes though an interesting variety of terrain that includes upland woods, boulders, rocky ridgetop pine barrens, and a craggy cliff-top summit.

The trail to Bonticou Crag begins from the Mohonk Preserve's Visitor Center on Mountain Rest Road, where hikers can purchase a day-use pass. The hike starts from just outside the Visitor Center entrance, where the beginning of the Bonticou Path is marked by red blazes leading along the edge of the woods, at the top of an open field. The trail heads downhill along an old roadway, entering the woods and passing a small artificial pond on the right. It then proceeds uphill, and comes to an intersection with the Northeast Trail (blue) at 0.5 mile. The route to Bonticou Crag turns right onto the blue trail, following it through hardwood forest and eventually along the base of the crag, crossing a yellow-blazed trail at 0.9 mile. (*Warning:* The yellow trail that ascends the rock face of the crag is a rock scramble that requires agility, confidence, and the use of hands as well as feet.) Continue on the blue-blazed trail along the base of the boulder field, passing the red-blazed trail that branches left at 1.1 miles. The blue trail continues, soon swinging to the right, and leading uphill through rocky woods.

At the top of a short, steep section, the opposite end of the yellow trail branches right, at 1.3 miles, leading to Bonticou Crag. The yellow trail gradually ascends back along the ridge line of Bonticou Crag, amid scrubby forest and increasing northward views toward the Catskills. As hikers proceed along the yellow trail, the route of the blue trail may be visible along the base of the cliffs and boulders below on the right. The yellow trail reaches the dramatic summit of Bonticou Crag at 1.6 miles, with its broad expanses of white conglomerate

Summit of Bonticou Crag

sparsely set with bonsai-shaped pitch pines. The return trip is by the same route.

Millbrook Ridge Trail   *Length: 3.0 miles Blaze: light blue*

The Millbrook Ridge Trail, at the southern end of Mohonk Preserve, is one of the loftiest in the Shawangunks, skirting along the crest atop some of the Shawangunks' tallest cliffs: the Near Trapps, Bayards, and Millbrook Mountain. The trail starts on the Trapps carriage road, 100 yards west of the Trapps Bridge over US 44-NY 55, accessible from the Trapps Entry. Blue blazes on the left side of the road mark the beginning of a trail ascending steep rocky slabs, and framed by twisted pitch pines. Fine examples of glacial scratches, polishing, and chatter marks are evident on the smooth conglomerate slabs as the trail ascends.

The trail quickly crests the ridge at a north-facing viewpoint with a dramatic 270-degree panorama, known locally as the Hawk Watch. During the autumn, this airy spot is often occupied by birders monitoring the southward migration of hawks along the ridge. During the peak of migration, hundreds of hawks of various species may be seen from here in a day, riding the updrafts caused by strong winds deflected over the ridge. The tilted layer-cake structure of the white conglomerate is clearly revealed on the Trapps cliff directly across the highway gap to the northeast. The Dickie Barre cliffs are visible to the west, with the Catskills beyond to the north, and the Wallkill Valley sweeps away below to the east. The trail turns right, and soon emerges not far from the edge of the cliff,

Millbrook Mountain, looking toward the Trapps and Sky Top

which it parallels for much of its way, occasionally offering views across the Wallkill Valley. Hikers should stay on the trail and exercise extreme caution; the many footpaths that trend left toward the cliff edge lead to the tops of the rock climbs. *Do not attempt to follow them.*

At 0.8 mile, a small saddle known as Smedes Cove marks the division between the Near Trapps and the Bayards. At this point, Bayards Path (red) branches right to return to Trapps Road. The blue trail continues, turning left to climb up a short ledge, soon passing a couple of cairns and winding along the edges of conglomerate slabs. Views to the east show the wetlands of the Marakill.

Approaching the south end of the Bayards, glimpses of Millbrook Mountain become more frequent through the treetops ahead, until an opening atop a rounded conglomerate slab suddenly reveals a full view of Millbrook's sheer cliff and wave-shaped profile. The trail turns right to step down from the slab and traverse a second, wider saddle amid dense mountain laurel, soon passing a second red-blazed trail on the right, at 1.8 miles. This is a handy bail-out to the Coxing Trail, which will be the return.

From here, the trail wanders briefly among open slabs and sparse oak woods, until crossing an intermittent stream amid boulders and shady hemlocks. The trail then steps up onto boulders, and soon climbs out of the woods along an airy bedrock ridge, with the bedding planes of the conglomerate turned nearly vertical in places. The Millbrook cliff drops away to the left, with commanding views. From this elevated perspective, the view northeastward along the ridge toward the Sky Top tower clearly shows the structure of the Shawangunks: a wave-shaped serpentine ridge with sheer white cliffs along its southeastern flank.

The trail weaves steadily uphill among rock outcrops and pitch pines to terminate at a junction with red trails at the top of Millbrook Mountain, at 2.9 miles. Within a few steps to the left, following red blazes, the trail crosses onto the Minnewaska State Park Preserve, and gains a dramatic 360-degree view.

The return may be by the same route. An alternative begins along the red-blazed right fork of the junction. This heads downhill to the north, among slabs and pine barrens, reaching a junction with the Coxing Trail (blue) on the right at 0.2 mile. Turn right to follow the blue trail gradually downhill, first among open slabs, then into sparse oak forests, and finally into deep, moist woods. Rock rows indicate earlier agrarian use of this area; after crossing a wet forest area, the trail follows the route of an old farm road. The junction with the red-blazed cutoff trail, branching right, is at 1.3 miles. The Coxing Trail terminates on Trapps Road at 2.0 miles. A right turn along the carriage road leads 3.0 miles back to Trapps Bridge.

Overcliff and Undercliff Roads   *Length: 5.4 miles Signs: directional only*

This easy and level walk on carriage roads loops around the dramatic scarp of the Trapps cliffs, the hub of the southern preserve. Built around 1903, with the aid of few machines, Undercliff Road is especially remarkable, considering that it was built solely to capture the scenic panoramas of the Wallkill Valley and the cliff above. Overcliff Road, which completes the circuit hike, also completes the views toward the remaining compass points, including the Coxing Clove, Rondout Valley, and Catskill Mountains.

The hike begins from the Trapps Entry on US 44-NY 55. The footpath from the upper end of the parking area proceeds uphill to the Trapps Bridge, at 0.1 mile, passes portable outhouses, and continues up rustic stairs to the level of the carriage road. A left onto the carriage road brings the hiker in a few yards to a carriage road intersection with a large, flat-topped boulder in its center. The route turns left again here, onto Overcliff Road. Although the name of Overcliff is misleading (it is not along the top of a cliff), it nonetheless offers sustained panoramic views of the Dickie Barre cliffs, the Rondout Valley, and the Catskill Mountains as it weaves between oak woods, open slabs, and pitch pines. At 2.2 miles, Overcliff Road turns right to meander through a small pass and descend along the face of a low bluff. Overcliff Road continues for 0.1 mile, bearing right to reach a junction of carriage roads at Rhododendron Bridge at 2.5 miles. At this point, the loop turns right onto Undercliff Road. At 3.3 miles,

Trapps Cliffs above Undercliff Carriage Road

Undercliff Road makes an S-turn, revealing the broad face of the Trapps that will loom above on the right until the carriage road again reaches the Trapps Bridge. Along the way, the carriage road traverses open talus with wide views across the Wallkill Valley. Rock climbers become more prevalent on the carriage road as well as on the rocks above, up to the Uberfall, their traditional congregating place on the carriage road, marked by a kiosk, bulletin board, first aid box, and usually a helpful ranger on patrol.

WALLKILL VALLEY

Running through the valley at the base of the Shawangunks and mostly within view of the many southeast-facing cliffs is the Wallkill Valley Rail Trail. Until 1979, the Wallkill Valley Railway brought freight through the Wallkill River Valley between Montgomery and Kingston. With rails and ties now gone, the fine cinder trail surface offers flat and easy walking, in most places for two abreast. It rambles through farms and forests, streams and wetlands, two small towns and the river—almost all within view of the Shawangunks. As of 1997, 12.2 miles of the route were open, in the towns of Gardiner and New Paltz.

The Wallkill Valley Rail Trail is a linear park, a ribbon of public trailway, surrounded on both sides by private land. In many places it passes by homes, backyards, farms, and orchards. Many working-farm roads cross the trail and farm machinery is left nearby. The hiker must be a good neighbor to all of these, staying on the trail at all times and respecting the rights of all property owners. Since the Rail Trail is a shared-use, non-motorized path, mountain bikers, horseback riders, and cross-country skiers also use it, depending on the season. For safety reasons, horses have the right-of-way; hikers should stand quietly to one side of the trail and avoid making sudden movements until equestrians pass. Traditionally, in most parts of the country, bikers yield to both horses and hikers, but they cannot be relied on to do so. Therefore, hikers should keep well to the right when bike traffic is heavy.

The Wallkill Valley Rail Trail first opened in 1991, and is operated as a partnership. In New Paltz, it is owned by the town and village. The section in Gardiner was originally owned by the Wallkill Valley Land Trust, but in 1995 it was conveyed to the Palisades Interstate Park Commission. The entire trail is managed and maintained by volunteers of the Wallkill Valley Rail Trail Association, Inc.

To reach the Wallkill Valley Rail Trail, take Exit 18 from the New York State Thruway and turn west on NY 299 (Main Street) through New Paltz. Turn right on NY 208 South. The southern terminus is on Deniston Road, a small rural road with parking for two or three cars. Limited roadside parking for one or two cars is also available at most other road crossings. More roadside parking is available at the trail crossing at US 44-NY 55 in downtown Gardiner, and municipal parking is available on Plattekill Avenue in New Paltz, three blocks from the trail. Near the north end of the trail, the Springtown Road trailhead can accommodate three or four cars.

Additional information including a brochure with a map is available from the Wallkill Valley Rail Trail Association, P.O. Box 1048, New Paltz, NY 12561-1048. The association has a modest membership fee.

Wallkill Valley Rail Trail   *Length: 12.2 miles Signs: at road crossings*
The southern trailhead is on Deniston Road and marked by a simple sign on the north side of the road. The trail departs northward as a tree-lined corridor between fields. A short distance to the west, Sand Hill Road begins to parallel the trail and

NEW YORK WALK BOOK

the profile of the Shawangunks is visible across fields and through breaks in the trees. Sand Hill Road crosses the trail at 1.4 miles, and continues to run parallel to the east of the trail for another 1.1 miles until the hamlet of Gardiner.

At Gardiner, the trail crosses US 44-NY 55 in the downtown area (at 2.5 miles), with ample parking, refreshments, and other attractions nearby. The old railroad station, dating from 1868, is now an antique shop. North of Gardiner, the trail again traverses open fields with views, crosses a small road at 3.3 miles, and at 3.5 miles meets the intersection of Phillies Bridge Road and Old Ford Road. From Phillies Bridge Road, the trail enters woodlands, crossing a trestle over Forest Glen Road at 4.3 miles, and crosses Bridge Creek Road at 4.5 miles. From Bridge Creek Road it is another 0.8 mile through the woods to Old Ford Road (5.3 miles).

A short distance north of Old Ford Road, the trail enters the town of New Paltz. Traversing orchards and looking out on scenic farmlands that extend to the west toward the Shawangunk Mountains, the Wallkill Valley Rail Trail offers some of the most picturesque views in Ulster County. The trail's elevated bridge over the Plattekill Creek (at 6.3 miles) offers a broad panorama, with Mohonk's Sky Top tower crowning the horizon. A bench about 50 yards south of the bridge provides a place to rest, contemplate the view, or have a picnic lunch.

The trail crosses Cedar Drive at 7.0 miles. A pond and wetland area along the west side of the trail offers occasional views of turtles, birds, and other typical wetland wildlife. The trail crosses Plains Road at 8.2 miles, and a few yards north of here overlooks a small area of rich flood plain forest along the Wallkill River to the west of the trail. This woodland park is accessible via a short footpath, which descends steeply to the riverbank. A short distance downstream (north), a small footbridge crosses a modest-sized stream, and the footpath leads back up to the rail trail.

Caution is advised at the street crossings in the Village of New Paltz, particularly at Main Street (8.5 miles), since it is NY 299, the main route between the Thruway and Mohonk and Minnewaska. A right turn (east) on Main Street leads uphill to good restaurants and shops. Huguenot Street, which roughly parallels the rail trail, proclaims itself the "oldest street in America" (with its original houses), dating from the 1670s.

After the last village street crossing at Huguenot Street (9.5 miles), the trail traverses woodlands and passes a gun club on the east. At 10.5 miles, the trail crosses the Wallkill River bridge. The 413-foot railroad trestle is fully decked and includes benches. It is a quiet destination for picnickers, birders, artists, and musicians. On May 22, 1993, more than one hundred volunteers resurfaced the entire span in a single day. The many hours of preparation included removing nearly one-fifth of the ties because of rot, and rolling all of the remaining ties onto their wider sides to fill the gaps.

A few yards from the end of the bridge, the trail crosses Springtown Road and then passes a horse farm on the east, with the cliffs of Bonticou Crag looming above to the west. The trail intersects a small lane at 10.8 miles and then enters woodlands until it reaches Cragswood Road at 11.9 miles. It continues another 0.3 mile north, where a sign marks the town line between New Paltz and Rosendale. Although the remainder of the route is privately owned, as of 1997, its owner permits trail use as far as Mountain Road in Rosendale.

FOURTEEN

SCHUNEMUNK MOUNTAIN

est of Black Rock Forest in the north-
ern Hudson Highlands, a land formation rises that has several unique and
striking features. Usually pronounced skun-uh-munk, the name means *excellent fireplace* in the Algonquin tongue. This name was given to the Lenni Lenape
village that once existed on the northern spur of the mountain. A peaceful
people, they were variously known as the "Original People," "Chosen people,"
and "People of the Stony Country." The white settlers referred to them as "the
Delaware." Hikers on Schunemunk have much to marvel at, from the continuous views along the ridge to the unforgettable rock beneath their feet.

The northern half of the ridge is a complex comprised of industry, the fine
arts, and open space. This holistic creation involved the Star Expansion Industries, the Ogden Foundation, and the Storm King Art Center with its chief
architect H. Peter Stern, president of Star Expansion Industries and of the Storm
King Art Center. With the complex in danger of being dissolved, the Open
Space Institute, in 1996, with a grant from the Lila Acheson and DeWitt Wallace
Fund for the Hudson Highlands purchased 2,100 acres of Schunemunk Mountain and additional lands. This acquisition ensures access to the mountain and
the preservation of the mountain background for the sculpture of Storm King
Art Center. It will be managed by the Palisades Interstate Park Commission.
The Nature Conservancy owns 163 acres on the northern end of the ridge.

Car access is by NY 17 or the New York State Thruway to Exit 16
(Harriman), then north on NY 32 to Highland Mills, Woodbury, or
Mountainville. Short Line buses, from the Port Authority Bus Terminal in
Manhattan, stop at these same towns.

Geology

An impressive ridge, nearly 1,700 feet high, Schunemunk Mountain is double-crested on its north end. It extends more than 8 miles from Salisbury Mills on its northeastern end to Monroe on the southwest point. On a map it does not seem topographically different from the gneiss and granite Highlands eastward, but geologically it is much younger, composed of sandstone, shale, and conglomerate of Devonian time, with Silurian as well as Ordovician strata at its base. It is part of a long ridge of similar strata extending 40 miles southwest into New Jersey, past Greenwood Lake and Green Pond, and ending near Lake Hopatcong. It was formed as sediments in a shallow sound of the ancient sea that vanished as the Taconic Highlands rose up.

The conglomerate ledges, composed of the highest and youngest of the Schunemunk strata, are conspicuous on the long, level summit, with a hematite stained reddish-purple matrix enclosing white quartz pebbles up to 6 inches in diameter—the remnants of eroded beaches and deltas from the Taconic Highlands to the east. This rock is sometimes called puddingstone. Subsequent lateral pressure from the collision of Africa into North America deformed the formation into a series of folds, with the strata on the east limb of the ridge dipping to the west and those on the west limb dipping to the east. It has also undergone extensive longitudinal and cross-faulting that has further confused the original sedimentary relations. A fault zone led to the cleft in the middle of the northern end, making double crests, with the densely wooded Barton Swamp in the depression between the crests. At the top surface of this rock, the pebbles have been ground flat by the massive layer of slowly moving ice of the last glacier.

On the other side of the valley to the west, and topographically associated with Schunemunk, is a line of wooded knobs of Precambrian gneiss extending from Woodcock Hill (over 1,000 feet), west of the north end of Schunemunk, southwest to Sugarloaf. Their position, bounded on the east by Devonian and Silurian formations and on the west by Ordovician slates and limestones of the Wallkill Valley, has caused much geological speculation. Earlier interpretations held that these knobs were parts of a syncline, or a structural downfold, and were at the original western border of the Highlands, and that the Schunemunk strata had been laid down in this trough. Later studies suggest that these knobs are gigantic overthrust blocks, shoved from the western front of the Highlands during the great push of the Taconic Orogeny. Their relative hardness caused them to stand up as knobs, while softer formations around them wore down into the valleys. Woodcock Hill is made up of both Precambrian gneiss abutting the Oldovician formations on its west foot and Schunemunk strata on its eastern slopes.

Trails on Schunemunk Mountain

The over 25 miles of trails on Schunemunk Mountain offer hikers opportunities to walk along ridges, view cascading streams, and investigate megaliths. Over the years, its trails have had their names changed, been moved, or even been abandoned. In 1997, changes are again underway with trails being extended and a new trailhead established. Since the Sweet Clover and Jessup trails cross an active railroad track, portions of the trails and the trailheads could be moved. For the most current information, contact the New York-New Jersey Trail Conference at (212) 685-9699.

On Schunemunk Mountain, there are different ways of trail blazing—paint on trees and rocks, *cairns* (rock piles), and plastic rectangles nailed to the twisted trunks of the pines. The hiker must be alert to sudden changes in the trail's direction, especially as there are so many distracting views along the ridge.

Barton Swamp Trail   *Length: 3.3 miles Blaze: red dot on white*
Because the Barton Swamp Trail follows the wooded trough that separates the central and western ridges of Schunemunk, it is a sheltered exit to Taylor Hollow at its midpoint where it crosses the Jessup Trail. It provides two access points to the Long Path, and, in 1997, access to the northern trailhead on Otterkill Road.

The trail starts at the Long Path, a short distance west of Barton Swamp. At 0.2 mile, the Western Ridge Trail (blue on white) comes in from the right and leaves from the left after another 0.1 mile. The Barton Swamp Trail continues northeast through the forest, paralleling the headwaters of Baby Brook. At 1.6 miles, the Barton Swamp Trail crosses the Sweet Clover Trail (white), then continues for a distance, crossing the brook occasionally, following one bank for a while, then the other. There are large stands of white birch trees and, at drier spots, mountain laurel. The trail meets the Jessup Trail (yellow) at 1.7 miles and veers west, climbing steeply over rocks to the western ridge where, at 2.0 miles, it makes a right turn onto a woods road. The red dot on white blazes also go straight ahead 100 yards over a viewpoint to connect with the Long Path (turquoise).

Going along the western side of the ridge, the Barton Swamp Trail passes

Schunemunk Mt.
from Deer Hill on Storm King
Sackett Mountain   Continental Road in gully : R.R. in valley : Houghton

through blueberries, scrub oak, and pitch pine. A panoramic view at 2.2 miles is to the north and east with the northern Hudson Highlands in the distance. At 2.8 miles, there is a view to the north over the valley. As the trail descends more steeply, there are almost continuous seasonal views. The Barton Swamp Trail ends at 3.3 miles at the Dark Hollow Trail, 0.1 mile from the parking area on Otterkill Road.

Dark Hollow Trail   *Length: 3.8 miles Blaze: black on white*
In 1997, with the establishment of a parking area on Otterkill Road near the railroad trestle over Moodna Creek, the Dark Hollow Trail became a trail with two distinct parts—a ramble along a woods road and an unrelenting climb to the top of the ridge. Starting from the parking lot, the Dark Hollow Trail follows a woods road steeply uphill, passing the northern terminus of the Barton Swamp Trail (red dot on white) at 0.1 mile. After reaching the level of the trestle, the trail continues climbing less steeply and passes a view over the pastoral valley at 0.2 mile. Over the next 2 miles, the Dark Hollow Trail meanders up and down along a woods road through the open, mixed forest, sometimes closer to the railroad tracks than other times, crossing the Jessup Trail (yellow) at 1.1 miles and the Sweet Clover Trail (white) at 2.2 miles.

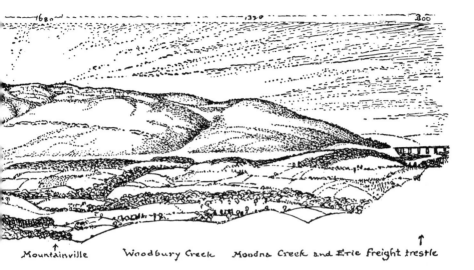

1680   1320   800

Mountainville   Woodbury Creek   Moodna Creek and Erie Freight trestle

About 100 feet south of the Sweet Clover Trail (white), the Deep Hollow Trail turns away from the tracks for the last time and crosses Dark Hollow Brook. The trail passes through a hemlock grove, makes a sharp, right turn, and continues to climb . At 3.1 miles, an unmarked trail goes to Dark Hollow Brook through a thicket of mountain laurel. After passing views of the Hudson River and Storm King at 3.3 miles, the Dark Hollow Trail ends at the Jessup Trail (yellow) at 3.8 miles. The summit of Schunemunk is 0.4 mile south on the Jessup Trail.

Jessup Trail   *Length: 8.6 miles Blaze: yellow*
As the main north–south trail on Schunemunk, the Jessup Trail traverses the full length of the mountain from the parking area on Taylor Road in Mountainville to its terminus on Seven Springs Road. From NY 32 in Mountainville, hikers can walk or drive one-third of a mile west on Taylor Road to the parking area on the right. The trail follows Taylor Road to the north for 0.5 mile where the trail turns left (west) on a faint dirt road through farm fields. The trail enters the woods and joins a clear dirt road in a hemlock grove, where it turns left. On the right side of the road, Baby Brook flows through still pools and cascades, and over a waterfall. The trail, veering right, leaves the dirt road and crosses the railroad tracks at 1.0 mile. It climbs steadily,

about 700 feet in the next 0.8 mile, reaching Taylor Hollow at 1.8 miles. From Taylor Hollow, the Jessup Trail ascends a ridge among pitch pines. The ridge displays the marvelous and unique conglomerate bedrock that makes Schunemunk so fascinating.

For 0.5 mile along the ridge, there is a continuous series of panoramic views of meadows, fields, and Beaver Dam Lake to the north, the Hudson River to the northeast, and Storm King Mountain and the hills of Black Rock Forest toward the east. There are also views of the western ridge of Schunemunk, parallel to the main ridge. The deep fold in the earth between the two ridges, through which the Barton Swamp Trail runs, is the result of intense horizontal pressure on the earth's crust toward the close of the Paleozoic Era. Erosion and additional crustal uplift occurred later. The greater resistance to erosion of the hard conglomerate layer left the ridge standing high above the surrounding valley.

At 2.5 miles the Jessup Trail intersects the Sweet Clover Trail (white), and the two trails turn together to the south. The cracks in the bedrock on the ridge here afford fine blueberry picking in season, usually from middle to late July. The pitch pines exposed on the ridge, stunted into rugged beauty by the winter winds, display their ability to survive the stringent conditions that nature imposes. At 2.7 miles the trail drops into a forested cleft in the ridge, and the Sweet Clover Trail (white) diverges to the left. The Jessup then climbs the ridge again, continuing south. At 3.4 miles the Dark Hollow Trail (black on white) goes off to the left. Both the Sweet Clover and the Dark Hollow trails are convenient for returning to a starting point at the north end of the trail.

The Jessup Trail continues on the ridge, reaching at 3.7 miles, a short spur to the megaliths, a group of huge blocks that have split off from the bedrock. There is a view here toward the western ridge, overlooking Barton Swamp. The highest elevation in the area, which is marked by a cairn, is reached at 3.8 miles. At 1,664 feet, this vantage point provides views of the neighboring summits in Harriman State Park, Black Rock Forest, and the Hudson Highlands from Storm King to the Beacons. There are views of at least four fire towers and the Perkins Memorial Tower atop Bear Mountain to the southeast. On a clear day the higher peaks of the Catskill Mountains are identifiable across the horizon to the north: Slide, Cornell, Wittenberg, Plateau, Sugarloaf, and Indian Head. Toward the west are the Kittatinny Mountains with their monument atop High Point, the highest elevation in New Jersey at 1,803 feet. The Shawangunks, part of the same ridge that forms the Kittatinnies, can be seen toward the northwest, stretching from Sam's Point to Mohonk.

The Jessup Trail continues southward, passing the end of the Western Ridge Trail (blue dot on white) at 3.9 miles, reaching one lookout point after another. Hawks can often be seen circling in the updrafts from the cliffs, occasionally swooping down into the woods below for a meal. At 4.5 miles, another high point, at 1,662 feet, is reached, with more views east and west. The trail continues, occasionally dropping down through gaps in the ridge, before ascending again. At times, the ridge is as smooth as a sidewalk, ground down by the friction of moving glaciers. Occasionally large erratics are found, carried from distant locations by the same glaciers that ground the bedrock smooth. Similarly, a huge boulder of Schunemunk conglomerate can be found on the grounds of Arden House, over 10 miles to the south. At 4.8 miles the Long Path, running northwest and southeast, crosses the Jessup at the widest part of the ridge.

Over the next 1.9 miles, crossing ridges alternating with forested areas, the Jessup Trail now gradually descends over a series of small rises. Views toward the east and west can occasionally be seen through the trees. The trail passes a strange white boulder at 6.7 miles—a glacial erratic of dolomitic limestone originating somewhere to the north and deposited on Schunemunk by the last glacier to grind south across the land. The last good lookout point is at 8.0 miles, where the elevation is 1,320 feet. Farther down, the grade steepens, descending through forests near the end. At 8.6 miles the Jessup Trail terminates at Seven Springs Road. The Highlands Trail (teal diamond) is co-aligned for the southern 5.8 miles.

Long Path   *Length: 7.0 miles Blaze: turquoise*
This major trail traverses approximately 5.2 miles of Schunemunk Mountain, but there is additional mileage to walk to reach or leave the mountain. See chapter 19, "Long Distance Trails," or *Guide to the Long Path* for details.

Sweet Clover Trail   *Length: 2.8 miles Blaze: white*
This trail is a good approach to the east and west ridges of Schunemunk. From the hiker's parking area on Taylor Road, an asphalt road proceeds south past a barn. Turning west into the meadow, the trail becomes a dirt road, turns south, and then turns west into the woods at 0.8 mile. The trail leaves the dirt road to cross the railroad tracks a mile from the start and then shortly crosses the Dark Hollow Trail (black on white).

The Sweet Clover Trail climbs steadily, crossing a slope of flaggy sandstone that plunges down to Dark Hollow Brook far below. This section of the trail is reminiscent of western trails. The trail switchbacks up past the north-ernmost branch of Dark Hollow Brook, crosses a swampy stretch, then heads uphill again. At about 1,450 feet the trail meets the Jessup Trail (yellow) and runs north with it for 0.2 mile on conglomerate rock. It then turns west and drops steeply into Barton Swamp and crosses the headwaters of Baby Brook. After reaching the Barton Swamp Trail (red on white) at 2.7 miles, it climbs steeply to terminate at the Long Path (turquoise) 0.1 mile later. The Highlands Trail (teal diamond) is co-aligned with the Sweet Clover Trail from Taylor Road to the Jessup Trail (yellow) which it then follows south.

Western Ridge Trail *Length: 0.6 mile Blaze:* blue dot on white
This short trail serves as a cross-over for the eastern/western ridges of Schunemunk Mountain. The eastern end begins 0.1 mile south of the 1,664-foot-high summit of Schunemunk Mountain on the Jessup Trail and descends sharply into the Barton Swamp. At 0.4 mile, it joins the Barton Swamp Trail (red on white) for 0.1 mile and ascends the western ridge to end 0.2 mile later at the Long Path (turquoise).

FIFTEEN

STORM KING AND BLACK ROCK FOREST

torm King Mountain looms above the Hudson River like a fortress, dominating the rugged river gorge on the west. Its glowering eastern end rises sheer from the river to more than 1,300 feet and is the dominating feature of Storm King State Park. Just behind it, to the southwest, lies Black Rock Forest, the largest sustained area over 1,200 feet in the Highlands. There, the mountains plunge for more than 1,000 feet to the west, north and south and provide the hiker with sweeping vistas and strongly contrasting habitats.

STORM KING STATE PARK

Much of the terrain in the northern Highlands was preserved for hikers by Dr. Ernest Stillman, a New York physician. In 1922, Stillman gave about 800 acres in Storm King Clove to the Palisades Interstate Park to ensure the preservation of the scenic surroundings of the old Storm King Highway. Subsequent purchases and gifts have added an additional 1,000 acres to the park. This tract forms the foreground for the eastward view from Storm King Highway (US 9W) before it turns west for its descent to Cornwall.

Hikers have long enjoyed the views from Storm King, but few ventured onto the trailless area to the south—Storm King Clove and the North Ridge of Crows Nest. In 1993, volunteers from the New York-New Jersey Trail Conference built a trail in the heart of Storm King State Park, providing hikers with views and points of interest that had been virtually inaccessible. The trail is named after William

Storm King before the highway was cut

Thompson Howell, legendary explorer of the Hudson Highlands.

Born on April 12, 1873, in Newburgh, New York, William Thompson Howell was a man of seemingly boundless energy who would often hike 30 or more miles a day, no matter what the weather. Writer, amateur photographer, and pathfinder, he was best known for his rambles in the Hudson Highlands. Perhaps no man or woman ever loved the Highlands as much as he. With unbridled enthusiasm, he explored their hills and hollows, forests and crags, and abandoned farms and mines. He proposed that the Highlands be protected in a great park that would benefit many. Although in time some of the hills and vistas that he loved became part of the Palisades Interstate Park, Howell never lived to see his dream fulfilled, dying of tuberculosis on April 26, 1916. One of Howell's favorite haunts was a mountain he called "Old Cro' Nest." He explored this rugged area thoroughly, making several camps in its forest. Many narratives describe this exceptionally beautiful Highlands peak.

Storm King is more than just a serene mountain. Its name is associated with a watershed court case that became the basis for environmental law in the United States. In the early 1960s, conservationists became interested in preserving the Hudson Highlands. Since Storm King was part of the Palisades Interstate Park, the mountain was considered "safe," and so conservationists decided to focus their efforts on preserving the eastern Highlands. At the same time, Consolidated Edison announced elaborate plans for Storm King. They wanted to build a powerhouse at the base of the mountain, a 260-acre reservoir within Black Rock Forest, and ten-story transmission towers running across the river to Putnam County. Conservation efforts shifted back to the west side of the Hudson. In 1963 a small group of people met and formed the Scenic Hudson Preservation Conference. The Nature Conservancy, the New York-New Jersey Trail Conference, Natural Resources Defense Council, and the Hudson River Fishermen's Association joined with Scenic Hudson to contest the project. Over the next seventeen years the battle raged, with national and international support. Legal testimony ranged from the esthetical to the practical. Con Edison's efforts to mitigate the negative visual effects were not acceptable as the threat to fisheries remained. A new threat appeared—possible harm to the Catskill Aqueduct and New York City's water supply.

Finally, in December 1980, a negotiated settlement was worked out, calling for Con Ed to drop its plans for the project. The *New York Times* hailed the resolution of this conflict as a "peace treaty for the Hudson." The outcome of the conflict established the right of citizen groups to sue a government agency to protect natural resources and scenic beauty. It set a precedent for national environmental issues dealing with the question of whether commercial developers could carry out development to meet one need at the expense of others.

Trails in Storm King State Park

Aside from the Bobcat Trail, there is nothing easy about the trails in Storm King State Park. Views of the Hudson Highlands and the Hudson River reward hikers far beyond the effort required to arrive at a view point. This small network of trails means that hikers can minimize retracing their steps, especially if a car shuttle is used.

Bobcat Trail   *Length: 0.4 mile Blaze: white*

Hikers wishing to enjoy the views at the North Peak of Crows Nest without a climb should use the Bobcat Trail. It begins on the north side of a small parking lot off US 9W and is south of the large parking lot for the Stillman Trail. Unfortunately, there is no access to or from the southbound lanes of US 9W.

After leaving the parking lot, the trail descends gently, loops to the left, and terminates at the Howell Trail (blue) in 0.4 mile.

By-Pass Trail *Length: 0.4 mile Blaze: white*
The By-Pass Trail connects the Howell Trail (blue) on the southern flank of Storm King to the Stillman Trail (yellow) near the brow of the mountain. Starting 0.4 mile from the northern terminus of the Howell Trail, the By-Pass Trail makes a short descent, ascends rather steeply, and soon reaches a view of Crows Nest, the Hudson River, and Constitution Island. The trail continues northeast, ascending gradually with two more views to the south. Just after the third view, the trail ends at the junction with the Stillman Trail (yellow).

Howell Trail *Length: 3.6 miles Blaze: blue*
The Howell Trail begins just to the left of the Stillman Spring Memorial on NY 218, north of the Lee Gate at West Point. Parking is available on both sides of the road at the spring, with additional parking on the east side of NY 218 both north and south of the trailhead.

Behind the spring the trail turns left and begins a gradual ascent up the north slope of Crows Nest. After several sweeping switchbacks, it turns left on a woods road that comes in from the right and gently descends toward the river. At 0.4 mile, the trail turns sharply right off the road and ascends rock steps. Staying on the road gives a short side trip to the "pitching point," where, at the beginning of the 20th century, logs were tossed down into the Hudson. After a series of switchbacks and rock steps, the trail continues its ascent of the pine- and hemlock-covered spine of Crows Nest's north peak. Along the way it passes several northward views of Storm King, the Hudson River, Breakneck Ridge, and Mount Beacon. On a clear day, the distant Shawangunks and Catskills can be seen. The higher the hiker climbs, the more expansive are the views. At the North Peak (1,000 feet) there is another view just before the trail turns sharply right at 1.4 miles. Occasional cairns mark the trail as it proceeds along the ridge, and more viewpoints open up on both sides, including views to the south of the South Peak of Crows Nest and Constitution Island. The trail begins a gradual descent toward North Point, reaching it at 1.8 miles, with a view of the Hudson River in the distance and the pine and hemlock ridge just traversed.

The Howell Trail continues to descend gradually until, at 2.1 miles, it reaches the terminus of the Bobcat Trail (white) coming in from the left. The trail then follows a woods road and continues its descent into the clove. At 2.5

Newburgh and Beacon from Stormking on the Hudson looking north

miles, it turns left at the junction with the Stillman Spring Trail (white), coming in from the right. After crossing the clove, the trail begins its 700-foot ascent in 0.9 mile in a series of switchbacks and rock steps up to the saddle between Butter Hill and Storm King. At 3.1 miles, it turns right on a woods road coming in from the left. The southern terminus of the By-Pass Trail (white) and views to the south are at 3.2 miles, followed by another view at 3.5 miles. Leaving the woods road, the trail turns left toward the saddle. At 3.6 miles, the Howell Trail terminates at the junction with the Stillman Trail (yellow).

Stillman Spring Trail   *Length: 0.7 mile Blaze: white*
Since many hikers do not wish to reclimb Crows Nest after hiking the Howell Trail, the Stillman Springs Trail offers a quick return to cars parked on NY 218. It begins at the Howell Trail in Storm King Clove and starts its gradual descent to NY 218. Along its way there are seasonal views of Crows Nest, Breakneck, and Bull Hill (Mount Taurus) on the right, and Butter Hill and Storm King on the left. At 0.3 mile, the trail crosses a small stream and continues its descent. At 0.5 mile, it turns sharply right and after a short, but steeper descent, it crosses a stone bridge over a stream, turns, and descends more gradually again. At 0.7 mile, it reaches NY 218, just to the right of the Stillman Memorial Spring.

BLACK ROCK FOREST

Linked to Storm King by the Stillman Trail, the 3,700-acre Black Rock Forest has served as a field station for scientific research and education for more than six decades. The forest was originally set aside in 1928 by Dr. Ernest Stillman for experimentation in forest management and for demonstration of forestry methods. These efforts continued after the forest was donated to Harvard University in 1949, but the focus shifted when it was acquired in 1989 by the not-for-profit Black Rock Forest Preserve. The forest is administered by the Black Rock Forest Consortium, a group of public and private educational and research institutions ranging from the neighboring Storm King School to New York City institutions such as the American Museum of Natural History and Columbia University. The mission of the Black Rock Forest Consortium is to promote scientific research and excellence in education while carefully managing the ecosystem of the forest. Several scientific studies are in progress at any given time and thousands of students visit the forest each year for a variety of educational programs.

Despite this primary emphasis, the consortium is dedicated to keeping Black Rock open to the public for recreational pursuits such as hiking. Visitors are not charged for access, but the consortium is dependent on voluntary contributions to cover a portion of the expense of maintaining the forest.

Natural History

The Black Rock Forest represents a characteristic slice of New York's Hudson Highlands. The area is completely underlain by resistant Precambrian granite and gneiss more than one billion years old.

Botanists have described a number of distinctly different ecological zones in Black Rock Forest. The most widespread plant community is an oak forest, dominated by three species: red, white, and chestnut. Red oak is by far the most common canopy tree in the forest, but at higher elevations and especially on more rocky terrain, chestnut oak dominates due to its greater drought tolerance and fire resistance. Associated hardwood trees include red and sugar maple, pignut and mockernut hickory, and black birch. Common understory trees include the American chestnut, formerly the dominant canopy tree, which was reduced to a nonreproductive status due to the chestnut blight fungus. The most common shrubs are witch hazel and mountain laurel, the latter erupting in a sea of white and pink flowers each June. Low bush blueberry is quite common as well.

A slightly different variant of this community type is found in wetter areas and stream bottoms. Here the canopy is more diverse, with sugar maple more common and a greater component of American beech, basswood, tulip tree, and sweet gum. Common understory trees include ironwood and striped maple, with spicebush in the shrub layer. Yellow birch and sycamore are also found along the stream bottoms. Primarily along north-facing stream drainages, this community gives way to a third type, the dark, dense groves of American hemlock. The year-round shade cast by the hemlocks results in a community with lower species diversity and very little vegetation in the shrub and ground layers. Yet the climatic amelioration provided is a critical factor for much of the forest's wildlife.

As one ascends the ridges toward the summits, the chestnut oak forest gives way to a ridgetop plant community of much smaller stature and different composition. The characteristic trees are scrub oaks and pitch pine, species not able to persist elsewhere in the forest. Soils here are extremely shallow, and these areas are subject to the full impact of wind and weather, as well as the brunt of frequent acid deposition in the form of rain, snow, and fog. Many areas are covered by barren rock or a meadow community of lichens, mosses, and grasses. Hikers are asked to tread delicately in these fragile environments.

Black Rock also possesses several large wetland areas, some open and others covered by trees such as red maple and alder that can tolerate a flooded rooting zone. Shrub cover by species such as leatherleaf is especially dense in many of the wetlands, while other areas are dominated by sphagnum moss. These wetlands fulfill a variety of critical ecosystem functions such as water recharge, flood control, and nutrient recycling, provide breeding grounds for a wide array of species, and are some of the most productive and biologically diverse areas in the Highlands.

Finally, the forest also contains numerous ponds and reservoirs, which supply local communities with water and the hiker with refreshing vistas. Around the perimeters one can often find gray birch, a light-loving species not able to survive in much of the rest of the forest, alder trees, and some spectacular azaleas. Water lilies and spatterdock grow in some of the ponds, providing a beautiful floating floral display in mid-summer. Visitors may be able to see a variety of fish in the ponds, as well as bullfrogs, pickerel frogs, newts, and painted and snapping turtles. Stick lodges and gnawed trees provide evidence of ongoing beaver activity, although the animals themselves are seldom seen. Even rarer are sightings of environmentally sensitive species such as mink and river otter, which have been able to live in this area in small populations.

Deer are the most common large mammal in the forest, most often seen around dawn or dusk. Other common mammals include raccoons, opossums, red and gray foxes, gray, red, and flying squirrels, and longtailed weasels. Coyotes have made a great comeback in this area since about 1985 and their presence can be detected through their tracks, scat, or occasionally the sound of their plaintive calls. Poisonous snakes such as copperheads and timber rattlesnakes have been reported in the forest, but they are seldom encountered. More often seen are black racers, pilot black snakes, garter snakes, and water snakes. In shallow woodland pools and swamps, the calls of a variety of highly vocal frogs may be heard sequentially through the breeding season, from wood frogs and spring peepers, to American toads and gray tree frogs. Beneath moist logs and leaf litter are redbacked and slimy salamanders, while the streams are inhabited by two-lined salamanders and beautiful northern red salamanders.

Finally, the birdlife of the forest is diversified, especially during the spring and fall migratory periods when as many as ninety different species can be seen. Several of the more exposed summits in Black Rock Forest, as well as Storm King Mountain itself, are excellent vantage points from which to observe the autumn migrations of thousands of hawks, including rare peregrine falcons, and of golden and bald eagles. And just as each season features different avian fauna, at the same time each habitat provides different food, cover, and nesting capabilities that support distinctly different birds.

History

Black Rock Forest's cultural history dates from about the time of the American Revolution. The Continental Army used Continental Road, which bisects the forest, as a direct route across the mountains from West Point to New Windsor and Newburgh. From Spy Rock, sentinels from Washington's camp at Newburgh monitored British vessels sailing up the Hudson from Haverstraw Bay. On the west side of Continental Road in the central part of the forest stands a solitary stone house sheltered by tall spruces. Dating from the 1830s, the Chatfield Stone House is the first building shown on early maps of this area and the only building still existing on the property. A fire in 1912 gutted the Chatfield House, but it was reconstructed in 1932 and has been used since that time for storage and, more recently, as a focal point for educational activities.

More than one dozen other residences are known to have existed within the forest boundaries. The inhabitants of these widely scattered farms eked out a subsistence living by pasturing a few acres, cultivating small gardens, and cutting wood as a means of earning cash. Hunting and trapping wild game also added food and revenue sorely needed by these isolated families. An observant hiker can locate these old homesteads by looking for old cellar holes, remnant lilac bushes, stone walls, or dense stands of coniferous trees. Along Continental Road, a number of apple trees remain from the orchards that were planted in the 1800s.

The various stands of trees provide evidence of forest operations in the Stillman era. Most of the conifers represent plantings from the 1930s, including stands of red pine, and Norway and white spruce. Other areas were clearcut in blocks or strips, and today these areas can be detected by looking for stands of trees with nearly uniform diameters. Some of the longest recorded experiments in the entire region can be found marked by blue-staked corner posts and numbered trees. Many of these are long-term forest growth plots under continuous study since the 1930s. Finally, most of the roads and artificial ponds are also legacies from this intensive era of forest management.

Access

Black Rock Forest is open year-round, daylight hours only, for recreational pursuits. However, it may be closed during periods of fire danger, deer hunting, and other times as posted. No motor vehicles of any kind are allowed in the forest without a permit. Bike riding in the forest is restricted to members of the Black Rock Mountain Bike Club; information may be obtained at the Black Rock Forest Headquarters, located north of US 9W at 129 Continental Road in the town of Cornwall. No fires are permitted at any time and camping by the public is not permitted. Anything encountered in the forest, including scientific and educational materials, must be left undisturbed. All organized groups (hiking, birding, and so forth) are required to register with the Black Rock Forest Head-quarters prior to visiting by calling (914) 534-4517. During deer-rifle season, Black Rock Forest is closed.

Bus service to within 2 miles of Black Rock Forest is available from New York City's Port Authority terminal to Mountainville (on the west side of the forest) or to Cornwall-on-Hudson (on the east side). The primary parking area is one mile south of US 9W on the northern side of the forest. Coming from the south, drivers take the first right turn onto Mountain Road, 0.4 mile after the Storm King parking area on US 9W. A sharp right leads through a tunnel under the highway. (The tunnel is passable by small vehicles only; larger vehicles should proceed as below.) The road passes a T intersection at 0.3 mile and continues to the main parking area, large enough for about ten cars. Larger vehicles, or those that miss the Mountain Road turnoff, can proceed north on US 9W to the Angola Road exit to the southbound lanes of US 9W, and proceed as described below.

For visitors coming from the north on US 9W, the entrance to the forest is 1.6 miles south of Angola Road. A right turn on the entrance road and another right turn at the T junction leads to the main parking area. Limited parking is available at other forest entrances, with the largest area immediately adjacent to US 9W, 0.1 mile south of Old West Point Road. Parking on the west side for the major trails is noted in the trails descriptions in this chapter. Formore information, contact the Forest Headquarters at 129 Continental Road, Cornwall, NY 12518; (914) 534-4517.

Trails and Woods Roads in Black Rock Forest

More than 30 miles of forest trails and woods roads crisscross Black Rock Forest. The trails, with steep ups and downs, lead to lookout points, while the roads wind among the reservoirs. Hikers can easily avoid the multi-use roads. When using the roads, keep an eye out for bicycles, forest maintenance trucks, and vehicles driven by scientists and visiting student groups.

The two main forest trails, which run approximately southwest to north-east, are the Stillman Trail (yellow) and the Scenic Trail (white). The Sackett Trail (yellow circle) is also a ridge trail with outlooks to the west and north. Crossing these trails, which are maintained by the New York-New Jersey Trail Conference, are a number of short trails running roughly north to south that can be combined in a variety of long and short walks. To understand the connections, consult map 7.

Along the floor of the forest, meander scenic gravel roads from which hikers can enjoy the reservoirs at closer range. However, to protect the public water supply, swimming, fishing, or other public use of these reservoirs is not allowed. Circular walks in different combinations are possible on these woods roads, which survive from the days when this area was populated by families scattered on small farms.

Arthur Trail   *Length: 0.7 mile Blaze: yellow*
This loop trail is named after the son of Jim Babcock, woodsman, rattlesnake hunter, and first forester and caretaker of Black Rock Forest. It starts and ends at Jim's Pond Road. Going north, the trail coincides with the Scenic Trail (white) for 0.1 mile. It crosses the outlet of Sutherland Pond on unique puncheons—cross-sections of a 2-foot-diameter tree, laid down like pie plates. It ends at the junction of Jim's Pond Road and the Compartment Trail (blue). The Highlands Trail (teal diamond) is co-aligned for 0.1 mile.

Black Rock Hollow Trail   *Length: 1.5 miles Blaze: white*
The Black Rock Hollow Trail provides the quickest access to Black Rock Mountain. The trail starts from a parking area on southbound US 9W less than a mile from the Angola Road entrance and follows a dirt road for 0.6 mile. At the filter plant, it turns right, and goes into the woods. Heading upstream along Black Rock Brook for 0.9 mile, it ends on the Stillman Trail (yellow). A right-hand turn on the Stillman Trail (yellow) leads to the top of Black Rock Mountain in 0.4 mile.

Chatfield Trail   *Length: 0.7 mile Blaze: blue*
This trail, named for a hamlet that is now a part of Cornwall, begins at the Scenic Trail (white), midway from the Arthur and Eagle Cliff trails. Heading northeast, it crosses a brook and ascends steeply through mountain laurel and mixed hardwoods. The grade changes to a gentle ascent while the route goes through a large rock formation, passing a marsh area on the right. After the Chatfield Trail passes the Secor Trail (yellow) at 0.5 mile and the Ledge Trail (yellow) at 0.6 mile, it descends gently to end at Chatfield Road at 0.7 mile near Tamarack Pond.

Compartment Trail   *Length: 1.1 miles Blaze: blue*
From the junction of the Arthur Trail and Jim's Pond Road, this trail travels
north, passing the Split Rock Trail (white) at 0.25 mile. It joins the Stillman
Trail (yellow) for 600 feet, turns right, joining the Highlands Trail (teal diamond) when the Stillman Trail goes left. The Compartment Trail ends on Hall
Road at its junction with the Sackett Trail (yellow circle). The Highlands Trail
(teal diamond) is co-aligned for 0.5 mile.

Eagle Cliff Trail   *Length: 0.1 mile Blaze: blue*
This short trail leads from the Scenic Trail (white), 0.4 mile from the junction
with the Arthur Trail (yellow) to views of the Manhattan skyline at Eagle Cliff.
The Rut Trail (red) leads down the other side of Eagle Cliff to the Stropel Trail
(yellow).

Hill of Pines Trail   *Length: 0.6 mile Blaze: white*
The trail connects Carpenter Road with the Swamp Trail (blue), shortly before
the latter emerges on Old West Point Road.

Ledge Trail   *Length: 0.3 mile Blaze: yellow*
The remains of a fire tower are on this link between the Scenic Trail (white) and
Chatfield Trail (blue). Dr. Stillman had a wooden tower built on the rocky
outcroppings at the highest point of the trail. It was hit by lightning shortly
after it was finished and burned to the ground.

Mine Hill Trail   *Length: 0.2 mile Blaze: yellow diamond*
This trail provides access to Black Rock Forest from the west. Parking is available for two or three cars just above the steep hairpin turn on Mine Hill Road,
0.9 mile from Mineral Springs Road. The beginning of the Mine Hill Trail is
across the road. The Mine Hill Trail starts steeply up a rocky slope reaching
open views to the north and northwest at 0.1 mile. Leaving the viewpoint, the
trail doubles back to the south, ascending on a more moderate grade to end at
0.2 mile at the Sackett Trail (yellow circle).

Reservoir Trail   *Length: 0.7 mile Blaze: blue*
Starting at the Stillman Trail (yellow) just west of the Upper Reservoir, the trail
follows the reservoir outlet brook. It crosses the brook on a small split log
bridge at 0.5 mile and then ends at the filter plant.

Rut Trail   *Length: 0.2 mile Blaze: red*
This short trail leads from the Stropel Trail (yellow) to views of the Manhattan
skyline on Eagle Cliff.

Ryerson Trail   *Length: 0.3 mile Blaze: yellow*
This trail branches right (southeast) from the Scenic Trail (white) 0.2 mile from
Jupiter's Boulder in the southwest part of Black Rock Forest, and short-cuts
over to Jim's Pond Road, where it ends.

Sackett Trail   *Length: 1.6 miles Blaze: yellow circle*
The Sackett Trail offers two viewpoints with wide vistas to the west and northwest as it winds along the crest of Sackett Mountain. It is accessible from the
Mine Hill (yellow diamond) and Stillman (yellow) trails and Continental Road.
Its southern terminus is on the Stillman Trail (yellow), 0.2 mile from Hall Road.
It passes a viewpoint at just over 0.1 mile and then passes the Mine Hill Trail
(yellow diamond) coming in on the left at 0.3 mile. The Sackett Trail continues
north and then east, crossing two brooks. At 1.1 miles the trail arrives at the
crumbling walls and chimney of the old Beattie cabin, built as a family camping retreat before Dr. Stillman owned the forest. Less than a tenth of a mile
later, the Sackett Trail passes the northern terminus of the Compartment Trail
(blue). For about 150 feet, the trail uses Hall Road, named for a family formerly living at the junction of the Continental Road and US 9W. After leaving
Hall Road from the east side, the trail winds around a hill with rocky
outcroppings. It heads east and uphill, ending at Continental Road at 1.6 miles.

Scenic Trail   *Length: 5.9 miles Blaze: white*
This aptly named trail is appealing at any time of year. As the Scenic Trail
meanders across Black Rock Forest, it crosses numerous woods roads and short
trails, thus lending itself to forming interesting loop hikes. The trail is south of
and generally parallel to the Stillman Trail (yellow) until intersecting it and
ending at foot of Mount Misery. The Highlands Trail (teal diamond) is co-
aligned with the Scenic Trail for 1.9 miles as the two trails enter Black Rock
Forest. Access for hikers coming by bus from New York City is via the bus stop
in Mountainville at the junction of NY 32 and Angola Road.
    The Scenic Trail begins at the northern junction of Mineral Springs and
Old Mineral Springs roads. Parking is on the grassy shoulder of the northbound land of Mineral Springs Road. The trail uses Old Mineral Springs Road

for about 100 yards, then turns left onto a stony dirt road diagonally south-east, enters Black Rock Forest, and approaches Mineral Spring Falls (0.3 mile), a triple cascade flowing over a series of ledges through a dark hemlock grove. Continuing straight ahead, the trail climbs up the ravine, paralleling the stream. After making a sharp left near the top of the grade, the trail winds through beautiful hemlock groves and over varied terrain to approach the slopes of Mount Rascal.

After a few short diagonal rises, the Scenic Trail parallels the ridge line and comes to Jupiter's Boulder, (1.4 miles) the first of two outlooks to the north-west, which on a clear day afford distant views to the Shawangunks and the Catskills. The route continues generally northeastward, passing the western terminus of the Ryerson Trail (yellow) at 1.6 miles. After passing through a laurel lane (in full bloom in mid-June), the Scenic Trail turns right onto Jim's Pond Road (1.9 miles) and the Highlands Trail (teal diamond) leaves to the left. The Scenic Trail continues south on the road until turning sharply east, coincides for a short distance with the Arthur Trail (yellow), and then continues on. At 2.2 miles the Scenic Trail passes the southern terminus of the Chatfield Trail (blue), which leads across the forest to Chatfield Road and then passes the Eagle Cliff Trail (blue) at 2.9 miles. The next junction is with the Stropel Trail (yellow) at 3.0 miles, and then a short distance afterwards it passes the Ledge Trail (yellow), leading to the Chatfield Trail. After crossing Continental Road at 3.7 miles, the Scenic Trail continues northeast on Bog Meadow Road, and in less than half a mile it abruptly turns right off the road to meander up Rattlesnake Hill. As the trail continues north over the hill, it crosses Carpenter Road (4.2 miles), then goes up and over Hill of Pines. Shortly after crossing the Swamp Trail (blue), the Scenic Trail ends at 5.9 miles at the Stillman Trail (yellow) on a slope at the southern base of Mount Misery.

Secor Trail
Length: 0.3 mile Blaze: yellow
The Secor Trail is named for a family residing in Cornwall. Starting on Chatfield Road due south of Spagnum Pond, it is a shortcut over to the Chatfield Trail (blue).

Shortcut Trail
Length: 0.4 mile Blaze: yellow triangle
Aptly named, this trail eliminates 0.75 mile along the Stillman Trail (yellow). It begins where the Stillman Trail joins Hall Road, goes south along Hall Road for 0.1 mile before turning west into the woods, and ends at the Stillman Trail at 0.4 mile.

Split Rock Trail   *Length: 0.4 mile Blaze: white*
This short spur trail leads from the Compartment Trail (blue), reaching the lookout at Split (or Echo) Rock at 0.2 mile. It continues past the views of the Manhattan skyline (visible on a clear day), Sutherland Pond, and the hills to the south, and ends at Sutherland Road.

Spy Rock Trail   *Length: 0.2 mile Blaze: blue*
This short spur trail leads from the Scenic Trail (white) 0.1 mile north of the junction with the Ledge Trail (yellow), over rock outcroppings to Spy Rock. One pitch pine marks the summit (1,463 feet), which offers views north toward the Catskills and northwest to the Shawangunks.

Stillman Trail   *Length: 5.3 miles Blaze: yellow*
From the Butter Hill-Storm King parking lot on the northbound side of the road, the Stillman Trail turns left, and follows the road south for 0.2 mile. It is co-aligned with the Highlands Trail (teal diamond) for the next 4.3 miles. Turning right, the trail continues up a steep, rocky ravine. Emerging from the ravine, the grade moderates as the climb continues to a small rocky area at the top of the ridge at 0.5 mile. The trail then winds along the top of the ridge with no well-defined summit. After passing through a dense stand of laurel, it descends steeply, then levels off before beginning a gradual descent to the Upper Reservoir. At 1.0 mile, the trail passes the Black Rock Forest boundary sign. The descent continues over an easy grade with the reservoir visible through the trees to the left. The trail passes close to the north end of the dam and spillway before turning south below the dam.

At 1.3 miles the trail joins Reservoir Road, historically known as Old West Point Road, below Upper Reservoir dam. It then turns right and follows the road to a point opposite the triple blue blaze marking the southeastern end of the Reservoir Trail (blue). Within 500 feet, the Stillman Trail turns left from Reservoir Road, crosses the outlet from the Upper Reservoir, and then diverges left from the Reservoir Trail, which heads north. The Stillman Trail continues southwest up a steep grade over a rocky path and crosses White Oak Road at 1.5 miles. The steep ascent continues and, at 1.6 miles, it reaches the northwest end of the summit ridge. The bare rocks at the summit offer views to the north and west, with Aleck Meadow Dam and part of the reservoir visible.

A tenth of a mile later, the steep descent of the ridge begins. At the bottom of the descent, the trail levels off, turns right, and enters a boulder field. At 1.9

miles, in the middle of the boulder field, the route passes the northern end of the Scenic Trail (white), climbs briefly, and then descends over an easy grade. The trail crosses White Oak Road near Aleck Meadow Reservoir at 2.1 miles. After passing the east end of the dam and the spillway, the trail descends, turns left below the dam, and then crosses the bridge over the outlet of Aleck Meadow Reservoir. Downstream from the bridge, the stream cascades through a narrow ravine in a hemlock grove. The trail continues west along the foot of the dam, and leaves the reservoir at the northwest corner at 2.3 miles. The gradually ascending trail passes the southern end of the Black Rock Hollow Trail (white) on the right at 2.4 miles, and within 300 feet makes a sharp turn to the right within sight of White Oak Road. Hikers should take care, as the terrain is open between the turn and the road, giving the impression that the path is straight ahead. After the turn the trail climbs gradually to the summit of Black Rock at 2.8 miles. There are views to the west, north, and northeast. A blue-blazed trail leads a short distance north over rocks to more open ledges.

The descent on the west side is, at first, steep over rocks and then moderate to a major intersection. The Stillman Trail first joins Hulse Road shortly before the intersection at 3.2 miles, then turns right on Continental Road for a few paces to where the Sackett Trail (yellow circle) begins. The Stillman Trail turns left into the woods while the Sackett Trail goes straight ahead. It is easy to become confused here, as both trails use yellow blazes: the Stillman's are rectangles while the Sackett's are circles. There are small black-and-white signs to help find each trail. Proceeding southwest, the Stillman Trail ascends an easy grade along a ridge and at 3.6 miles reaches the western end of the White Oak Trail (white) on the left.

At 4.3 miles, when Stillman Trail reaches the Compartment Trail (blue) at a large rock with a cairn, the Highlands Trail (teal diamond) turns left on the Compartment Trail (blue) while the Stillman Trail turns right. The Stillman and Compartment trails join together for slightly over 0.1 mile until the Compartment Trail turns sharply off to the right in sight of Hall Road. Less than 100 feet later, the Stillman Trail meets Hall Road at a bend in the road and turns right. The Shortcut Trail (yellow triangle) follows Hall Road to the left. At 4.5 miles, the Stillman Trail turns off to the left and then meets the Sackett Trail (yellow circle) on the right at 4.7 miles. Turning south from this junction and proceeding over easy grades, the Stillman Trail reaches the western end of the Shortcut Trail (yellow triangle) at 5.0 miles.

The Stillman Trail continues south, then turns west, and descends a mod-

WINTER on STORM KING

FIRST FLAG OR WEST ROCK   THE CLOVE   BULL HT

erate grade as it approaches its western terminus. The viewpoint is 5.3 miles from the parking lot on US 9 W. The triple blazes marking the end of the Stillman Trail are visible only from the west.

Stropel Trail   *Length: 0.2 mile Blaze: yellow*
The Stropel Trail begins at Jim's Pond Road. After climbing ledges, it ends at the Scenic (white) a short distance east of the Rut Trail (red), which leads to the Eagle Cliff outlook.

Swamp Trail   *Length: 0.5 mile Blaze: blue*
From Aleck Meadow Road, the Swamp Trail heads east between Mount Misery and Hill of Pines to the Old West Point Road, crossing the Scenic Trail (white) not quite halfway. The trail ends just past the northern terminus of the Hill of Pines Trail (white).

Tower Vue Trail   *Length: 0.7 mile Blaze: yellow*
The Tower Vue Trail lives up to its name and rewards the hiker with views of the old fire tower. Leaving the east end of Arthurs Dam, this trail parallels the eastern shoreline of Arthurs Pond. Going up and down many times before reaching Bog Meadow Road, it is reminiscent of a roller-coaster ride.

White Oak Trail   *Length: 1.2 miles Blaze: white*
The trail extends from the Stillman Trail (yellow) northwest of Sphagnum Pond,

across Continental Road, to White Oak Road south of Aleck Meadow Reservoir. It may serve as a pleasant shortcut by which hikers can avoid the road walk from Continental Road around the north end of Arthurs Pond to White Oak Road.

SIXTEEN

BEAR MOUNTAIN-HARRIMAN STATE PARKS

art of the appeal of Bear Mountain-
Harriman State Parks is the variety of trails looping across the rugged landscape, draped upon the Highlands. This network of infinite combinations is
unmatched in the area surrounding metropolitan New York. The hiker may
choose to scale the steep face of the Timp, savor the views of the Hudson from
high on Dunderberg, or ramble on old woods roads past sleepy swamps and
abandoned mining villages.

The name Harriman Park perpetuates the name of Edward H. Harriman,
the railroad builder who conceived the idea of establishing a park in the Hudson
Highlands, and of his widow, Mary A. Harriman, who carried out his inten-
tion by giving 10,000 acres to the state in 1910. With that nucleus, additional
acquisitions over the years expanded the jointly operated Bear Mountain and
Harriman State Parks to approximately 52,000 acres.

For a history of the park and a complete guide to the marked and unmarked trails, see *Harriman Trails—A Guide and History*, by William Myles
(New York-New Jersey Trail Conference, 1992).

Geology

The Hudson Highlands and their extension southwesterly into the Ramapo
Mountains along the New York-New Jersey border constitute a picturesque
topographic feature of the eastern states. The bedrock is among the oldest of

TORNE: HUDSON RIVER: ANTHONYS NOSE: BEAR MOUNTAIN

1000 feet

1316 feet

No. of East

East

OUR BEST WILD UP
The Vista cleared by Major Welch, on Long Mountain
POP OLOPEN CREEK : HELLHOLE : TURKEY MOUNTAIN in the
VIEW FROM LONG MOUNTAIN : THE MOUNTAIN OF THE

geological record, all Precambrian in age. It includes greatly metamorphosed sandstones, shales, and limestones known as the Greenville Series but is mostly composed of high-grade metamorphic rock, known as the Highlands Complex. Subsequent invasions of granitic magma late in the Precambrian Era have considerably complicated the geology. The banded gneisses display extreme metamorphism of the older sedimentary rocks, and some igneous intrusions. The Highlands probably were once more than 10,000 feet high but most of their mass eroded away before the Cambrian Period. The present hills are the remnants of what was a mountain system comparable to the present-day Rockies, and they constitute one of the oldest landmasses in North America.

Among the striking evidence of continental glaciation in Harriman Park are the abundant glaciated rock surfaces, which are polished, scratched, and grooved, and the many immense erratic boulders transported by ice from the Catskills and elsewhere to the north.

Natural History

Like the rest of the Hudson Highlands, the Bear Mountain-Harriman State Parks harbor a wide range of plant and animal life. The variety of habitats range from the brackish Iona Island marsh at sea level to the mountainous interior. The latter reaches more than 1,300 feet, with thirty-six lakes, numer-

ous swamps, open fields, hemlock forests, and hardwood ridges.

Observers can find roughly forty species of mammals, twenty-five species of reptiles, and more than ninety species of nesting (breeding) birds in this area. Squirrel, deer, raccoon, and woodchuck probably are seen the most often, although beaver, otter, mink, and bobcat are present in limited numbers. While black bear are rare, they have been reported. Hikers may encounter a variety of snakes including garter, water, milk, ring-necked, and hog-nosed. In rocky, open areas, milk snakes and ring-necked snakes can be found, while hog-nosed snakes are occasionally seen sprawled out on sandy roads, trails, and exposures. Copperhead and timber rattlesnakes are less likely to be found as they tend to avoid human contact. Five-lined skinks, which belong to the lizard family, may also scamper across a hiker's path.

With more than 240 species of birds visiting the area, there is plenty of activity to watch in the sky. Among the more exciting birds are wood duck, goshawk, red-tailed hawk, broad-winged hawk, ruffled grouse, woodcock, screech owl, great horned owl, pileated woodpecker, tree swallow, veery, blue-gray gnatcatcher, hooded warbler, black-throated green warbler, prairie warbler, Louisiana water thrush, and scarlet tanager. The two most common and characteristic nesting birds are catbird and towhee, which seem to be everywhere during summer hikes. Iona Island is excellent for birding, with ducks,

IONA ISLAND AND ITS MARSHES AND DUNDERBERG

herons, bitterns, and marsh wrens in summer and its winter ducks and occasional bald eagle in winter. Wild turkeys are becoming more numerous and turkey buzzards are frequently seen.

The mature forests in the park are a blend of evergreen and deciduous varieties. Principal evergreens are red cedar, hemlock, and white pine. The deciduous trees include oak, maple, hickory, ash, tulip, beech, and sour gum. Laurel, rhododendron, witch hazel, spicebush, wild azalea, sweet pepperbush, alder, blueberry, and sumac are among the shrubs found in the park. Iona Island hosts prickly pear cactus. In addition to the well-known flowers of meadow and forest, the hiker can find others less known and even more rare. Ferns, lichens, and mosses abound in the forest, including evergreen species such as polypody, Christmas, and evergreen wood ferns. The lack of understory within the park is due to the mature forest, not to the deer overbrowsing the area.

The Bear Mountain Wildlife Center, right next to the Bear Mountain Bridge, contains a selection of many local plants, birds, animals, and reptiles. A visit here will help the hiker identify much of the flora and fauna within the park.

Iron Mines in the Hudson Highlands

The abandoned shafts, pits, and dumps of old iron mines are among the most fascinating features of the Highlands and the Bear Mountain-Harriman State Parks. At least nineteen known mines were worked at one time or another. The iron is probably of igneous origin, possibly having been a part of an upwelling of molten rock that affected the older rock formations. Mining began in colonial times, about 1730. At its height, during the Civil War, the industry controlled the life of the region and supported a sizable population.

Eventually, smelting with coal replaced smelting with charcoal. The iron deposits of Pennsylvania and the Great Lakes region, so much more easily mined than those in the Highlands, although not so rich in high-quality ore, were exploited. Thus the industry in New York and New Jersey declined and by 1890 had almost completely disappeared. The inhabitants drifted away from the region when there was no more work, leaving houses to fall into the cellar holes still visible along many old roads now overgrown. Apple trees, lilac bushes, and daffodils remain as evidence of these homes.

Refer to William Myles's book, *Harriman Trails*, and Edward Lenik's, *Iron Mine Trails*, for specific characteristics of each of the mines.

Dunderberg Scenic Railway

This uncompleted and abandoned scenic venture is a curiosity of the Highlands. Walkers over Dunderberg Mountain, on the Ramapo-Dunderberg Trail, or on old roads that climb the sides of the mountain, come upon sections of railway grade that can be followed for stretches as long as a mile. For part of its route, the Timp-Torne Trail follows a section of the old railway grade.

Each section ends abruptly and gives little impression of a unified scheme. Complete details and an illustration of the railway layout can be found in *Harriman Trails*, by William Myles. The whole railway can be explored in a day by bushwhacking from one section to the next, once the general plan is understood.

Trails in the Bear Mountain-Harriman State Parks

There are more than 235 miles of marked trails in the parks. This chapter includes most of the marked trails. Parking is noted in specific trail descriptions. Public transportation to Bear Mountain-Harriman is available from the New York Port Authority Bus Terminal. Buses to the Bear Mountain Inn also stop, if requested, along US 9W at Tomkins Cove and Jones Point. Buses and trains to Suffern, Sloatsburg, Tuxedo, Southfields, and Arden give access to trails on the west side of the parks.

Anthony Wayne Trail   *Length: 2.8 miles Blaze: white*

The midpoint of this trail, accessible from the north end of Anthony Wayne parking lot (Exit 17 on the Palisades Interstate Parkway), forms a loop with the Popolopen Gorge Trail (red on white) at Turkey Hill Lake and the Timp-Torne Trail (blue) on the west end of West Mountain. Named for "Mad Anthony" Wayne, a hero of the American Revolution, the trail starts from Turkey Hill Lake and heads south until it crosses US 6 at 0.7 mile. The trail crosses Seven Lakes Drive at 1.0 mile and then continues gently uphill. It crosses the 1779 Trail and shortly thereafter descends to cross the Palisades Interstate Parkway at 1.8 miles. East of the parkway, the trail follows the old Beechy Bottom Road to the left a short distance; then it turns off to the right over the shoulder of West Mountain to end at the Timp-Torne Trail.

Appalachian Trail   *Length: 18.8 miles Blaze: white*

This major trail traverses the park going from NY 17 to the Bear Mountain Bridge. See chapter 19, "Long Distance Trails," for details of selected sections, or the *Appalachian Trail Guide to New York-New Jersey* for a complete description of the 18.8 miles.

Arden-Surebridge Trail   *Length: 6.8 miles Blaze: red triangle on white*

This trail is readily accessible at both ends. Buses from New York City's Port Authority will stop at the park entrance on NY 17 and Arden Valley Road, and car parking is available at the Elk Pen just south of Arden Valley Road, a short distance east of NY 17. The west end of the trail is at a fishermen's parking lot off Seven Lakes Drive at Lake Skannatati.

The trail starts on Arden Valley Road at the entrance to the Elk Pen parking area and soon turns right onto Old Arden Road. At 0.1 mile, the Appalachian Trail (white) turns left over Green Pond Mountain. The Arden-Surebridge Trail continues south, turning left at 0.5 mile and climbing gently onto a plateau. At 1.0 mile it turns left on the route of the former Green Trail and begins a steep ascent of the south end of Green Pond Mountain. Leveling off, it joins Island Pond Road for 0.3 mile and then turns left, looping south for 2.2 miles around a swamp below Island Pond. The Arden-Surebridge Trail meets the Appalachian Trail 3.7 miles from the Elk Pen, just before the Appalachian Trail heads north through the Lemon Squeezer, a curious rock formation. It is worth a quick side trip to climb through the crevices.

After the brief meeting with the Appalachian Trail, the Arden-Surebridge

Trail turns right and in 0.2 mile joins the Long Path (turquoise) coming in from the left. Immediately beyond, the north end of the White Bar Trail will be seen on the right at 3.9 miles. Following the "Lost Road," the Arden-Surebridge Trail passes the southern end of Dismal Swamp and goes up Surebridge Mountain. At 4.2 miles, the Arden-Surebridge Trail goes by the northern end of the Lichen Trail (blue L on white) and then through a hemlock grove to the Surebridge Mine Road. Extensive fire damage in the area will be discernible for years.

The Arden-Surebridge Trail and Long Path reach "Times Square" at 4.8 miles. Hikers must take care in following the red triangles on white, as the Ramapo-Dunderberg Trail (R-D), blazed with a red dot on white, also crosses this multi-trail junction. Just beyond "Times Square," the Long Path leaves the Arden-Surebridge Trail to the right, heading south and east. The Arden Surebridge continues to follow the now descending road to the beginning of the Dunning Trail (yellow) at 5.3 miles.

After crossing a brook, the Arden-Surebridge Trail continues for several hundred feet past water-filled holes of the Pine Swamp Mine on the left and then makes a sharp right turn off the road. It goes on past the northeast corner of Pine Swamp, where the temperature can be 20 degrees cooler than the surrounding areas. Following another old woods road, the trail makes another sharp right turn and climbs gently through a glen to the top of Pine Swamp Mountain. Here are views to the south of Lake Kanawauke, Little Long Pond, Lake Sebago, and the Ramapo ridge. At 6.5 miles, the Red Cross Trail (red cross on white) begins on the left. After descending Pine Swamp Mountain, the Arden-Surebridge Trail ends at Lake Skannatati on Seven Lakes Drive 6.8 miles from the Elk Pen.

Beech Trail   *Length: 3.9 miles Blaze: blue*

The Beech Trail connects the Red Cross Trail with the Long Path east of Seven Lakes Drive. It provides an easy hike without much change in elevation. From the Red Cross Trail (red cross on white), the Beech Trail heads south through deciduous woods, passing over a low shoulder of Flaggy Meadow Mountain, runs along Tiorati Brook for a short distance, crosses the brook on a highway bridge, and briefly turns right to parallel Tiorati Brook Road (closed in winter) at 0.9 mile. When the road is open, parking is permitted here.

The trail gently rises along the eastern slope of Nat House Mountain before crossing Hasenclever Road (a fire road), and continues south through level woods. It comes to an area of stone walls, old fruit trees, lilacs, wisteria, and barberries—all reminders of one-time human presence. Stone foundations and a small family burying ground give a feeling of once-active farm life.

At 2.7 miles the trail joins a woods road and passes under the east flank of Rockhouse Mountain. At 3.3 miles, it crosses County 106 and then passes Green Swamp on the left and an imposing hill of boulders on the right before reaching its end at the Long Path (turquoise).

The Bicentennial Trails

The 1777 and 1779 trails were blazed in 1975 for the bicentennial celebration to commemorate the strategically important military events occurring in the Hudson Highlands during the American Revolution. Under the direction of the Palisades Interstate Park Museum staff, these trails were drawn up following the routes used by the British and American armies in 1777 and 1779, respectively. Where private property restrictions interfered, portions were re-routed, but overall the trails remain faithful to the general routes. The maps consulted were the ones made for General Washington by his official map maker, Major Erskine. The Boy Scouts of America created a special blaze for the trails and marked them with the respective year.

1777 Trail *Length: 10.6 miles Blaze: red 1777 on white circle*
The 1777 Trail comprises three portions: a joint section of 3.0 miles, the 1777E Trail (Fort Clinton branch) of 2.3 miles, and the 1777W Trail (Fort Montgomery branch) of 5.3 miles. The joint portion of the trail begins on US 9W, 0.7 mile south of the intersection with the road leading to Jones Point. There is a small parking area 200 feet south of the trailhead on the east side of US 9W. Starting from the highway, the trail leads to the abandoned hamlet of Doodletown, where it splits into its East (1777E) and West (1777W) sections. The 1777E passes the Bear Mountain Inn, goes through the tunnel under US 9W, and ends at the Trailside Historical Museum. The western portion is an undulating path that ultimately ends at the Popolopen viaduct on US 9W.

1779 Trail *Length: 8.5 miles Blaze: blue 1779 on white circle*
The 1779 Trail begins at the north end of the Popolopen viaduct, with parking available 0.8 mile to the south by following US 9W to the Bear Mountain Inn. The trail is mostly a low-level wooded route that starts by running concurrently with the 1777W (red 1777 on white) and Timp-Torne (blue) trails. At 1.3 miles, the Timp-Torne Trail turns right to ascend the 941-foot Popolopen

Torne with its 360-degree view. At 1.5 miles, the Timp-Torne Trail rejoins the 1779 Trail from the right. Just beyond a fireplace at 1.7 miles, the Popolopen Gorge Trail (red on white) joins from the left. Four trails run concurrently for about a mile when the combined 1779/Popolopen Gorge trails turn right and the combined 1777W/Timp-Torne trails continue straight.

Queensboro Lake appears on the left at 3.1 miles and the 1779 Trail veers left, leaving the Popolopen Gorge Trail at 3.5 miles. Now free of the concurrent trails, the 1779 Trail crosses the Anthony Wayne Trail (white) at 4.5 miles and the combined Appalachian/Ramapo-Dunderberg trails at 6.0 miles. After crossing the Palisades Interstate Parkway at 7.0 miles, the 1779 Trail turns left onto the Red Cross Trail (red cross on white) at 7.6 miles and a tenth of a mile later is joined by the Suffern-Bear Mountain Trail (yellow). Within a tenth of a mile, in quick succession, the Suffern-Bear Mountain Trail leaves to the right and the Red Cross Trail leaves to the left. The 1779 Trail finally emerges at the park boundary on Queensboro Road in the community of Bulsontown. One-quarter mile from the trail's end, paved Queensboro Road intersects Mott Farm Road, with limited parking available on the east side of the latter road.

Blue Disc Trail *Length: 2.8 miles Blaze: blue disc on white*
This trail begins on the gas pipeline right-of-way just west of the parking area in the circle at the end of Johnsontown Road in Sloatsburg. The trail turns left

on a woods road after 0.2 mile and crosses the Kakiat Trail at 0.5 mile. It then proceeds over Almost Perpendicular, which offers views to the south and east. The trail continues north along the ridge and descends gradually to Elbow Brush. It crosses the Tuxedo-Mt. Ivy Trail (red dash on white) at Claudius Smith's Den. Next it continues north over Big Pine Hill, with an all-around view, to its terminus at Tri-Trail Corner at the foot of Black Ash Mountain.

Cornell Mine Trail *Length: 2.5 miles Blaze: blue*
This trail extends from the Bear Mountain Inn to the Ramapo-Dunderberg Trail near the summit of Bald Mountain. The first section of the Cornell Mine Trail is fairly easy walking on woods roads. Beginning at a trail junction about 100 yards behind and west of the Bear Mountain Inn, the trail travels south along the east side of the ice-skating rink, where it is joined by the 1777E Trail. Together they pass through two tunnels under Seven Lakes Drive and the South Entrance Road.

At 0.8 mile, the Cornell Mine Trail diverges left from the 1777E Trail, descends, and intercepts abandoned Doodletown Road. The trail turns left onto the old road, reaching US 9W at 1.0 mile, at Doodletown Brook. Parking is available on the east side of the road. From an elevation of 20 feet, the trail reenters the woods and ascends nearly 1,000 feet in the next 1.4 miles, at first following the top of a deep stream embankment. At about 2.1 miles the final climb becomes steeper. The Cornell Mine Trail ends at the Ramapo-Dunderberg Trail in the col between Dunderberg and Bald mountains. To the west (right), a short climb along the Ramapo-Dunderberg Trail leads to the Cornell Mine and views of Bear Mountain, the Hudson River, and the Bear Mountain Bridge.

Dunning Trail *Length: 3.8 miles Blaze: yellow*
Accessible only via other trails, the Dunning Trail starts at the north end of Stahahe High Peak east of Lake Stahahe on the Nurian Trail (white) after the latter has ascended steeply past the Valley of Boulders. Heading southeast, it threads its way between the north shore of Green Pond and an overhanging wall of stone over a jumble of boulders. It turns east and re-crosses the Nurian Trail before reaching Island Pond Road (a woods road) and follows the road left for a short distance before turning off right. The Dunning Trail soon comes to the Boston Mine, turns right at the mine, then goes up the hill behind it.

In another 0.5 mile, the Dunning Trail turns left and joins the White Bar Trail. It soon leaves the White Bar Trail and turns right onto Crooked Road, a woods road. Several ascents and 0.4 mile farther east, the trail crosses the Ramapo-Dunderberg Trail (red dot on white). It goes southeast passing over slabs of bare rock and then changes to an easterly direction. Soon the Crooked Road goes off to the right, providing a short cut to County 106.

The Dunning Trail turns in a northeasterly direction on a woods road. A large swamp on the right is edged by mounds of tailings from the Hogencamp Mine up the hill to the left. The Long Path (turquoise) soon comes in from the left and coincides with the Dunning Trail briefly before turning downhill to the right toward Lake Skannatati. From here the Dunning Trail becomes straighter and more level and continues in a northeasterly direction. It skirts the west side of Pine Swamp as tall hemlocks form a canopy. Pine Swamp Mine is up on the left but only large piles of tailings from it are visible from the trail. The Dunning Trail continues to follow the woods road until it ends at the Arden-Surebridge Trail (red triangle on white).

Hillburn-Torne-Sebago Trail   *Length: 4.8 miles Blaze: white*
The Hillburn-Torne-Sebago Trail extends from Seven Lakes Drive at the Lake Sebago dam south to the Ramapo Torne, connecting with six other trails along its length. At the north end, parking is available at the Lake Sebago parking area off Seven Lakes Drive, 0.7 mile past the start of the trail and about 4.3 miles from NY 17.

The trail begins on the north side of the brook. It follows Woodtown Road, turns off to the right (south) on a path, crosses the Tuxedo-Mt. Ivy Trail (red on white), and continues on the unmarked Stony Brook Trail for a short distance. Turning off left, it steeply climbs Diamond Mountain, which has a good lookout over Lake Sebago near the top. At the summit, the Seven Hills Trail (blue on white) joins it from the left and both trails continue along the ridge, soon passing at 1.0 mile the Diamond Mountain-Tower Trail (yellow), which descends left to the Pine Meadow Trail (red on white). The Hillburn-Torne-Sebago and Seven Hills trails continue over the summit, then go their separate ways down to Pine Meadow Brook. At the base of the mountain, the Hillburn-Torne-Sebago Trail turns left onto the Kakiat Trail (white). After a few feet, the Hillburn-Torne-Sebago Trail turns off the Kakiat Trail to the right and crosses the brook on a footbridge over the Cascade of Slid. It meets the Pine Meadow Trail (red on white), joins it going left for a short distance, then turns off right up Chipmunk Mountain. At 2.4 miles the Seven Hills Trail joins from the left, coincides briefly, and leaves to the right. The Hillburn-Torne-Sebago Trail crosses the Raccoon Brook Hills Trail (black R on white) at 3.2 miles and, after descending from the view on the Russian Bear cliff, it crosses a brook in a hollow. On the opposite slope, the Seven Hills Trail joins again from the right, then leaves to the right. The Hillburn-Torne-Sebago Trail continues to its terminus on the Ramapo Torne and its scenic overlook at 4.8 miles.

Kakiat Trail *Length: 7.4 miles Blaze: white, or black* K *on white*
Although this trail touches no high or open viewpoints, it offers a considerable variety of terrain. Named after one of the oldest land grants on the east side of the Ramapos, *Kakiat* is a corruption of a Native American word that appears on the land grant patent of 1696. The trail crosses the park, going from the Ramapo-Dunderberg Trail (red dot on white) near Tuxedo to the entrance to Kakiat Park off US 202 in Rockland County.

To reach the Kakiat Trail, hikers follow the Ramapo-Dunderberg Trail from the Tuxedo railroad station, passing under the New York State Thruway, turning left on Grove Drive, and following it until the Ramapo-Dunderberg turns right into the woods. The Kakiat Trail begins at a sharp right turn and follows a woods road and an abandoned utility line around Daters Mountain. At 1.3 miles, at the top of a rise, a path goes left toward Daters Mine. The Kakiat Trail continues on, and the Blue Disc Trail (blue on white) joins briefly at 1.5 miles. In 0.3 mile the Kakiat Trail crosses a gas pipeline, then crosses Spring Brook, and briefly joins the White Bar Trail. Either the Blue Disc or the White Bar trails can be followed to the right for parking at Johnsontown Circle.

At 2.3 miles, the Kakiat Trail crosses Seven Lakes Drive. It reaches a bridge over Stony Brook at 3.0 miles and then crosses over Pine Meadow Brook. The trail then makes a sharp right turn along the north bank of Pine Meadow Brook. It becomes quite rugged as it goes over and around large boulders along the ravine. At 3.4 miles the Kakiat Trail passes the Cascade of Slid, a spectacular sight during the spring runoff. It then briefly joins the Hillburn-Torne-Sebago Trail (white).

Farther on, the Kakiat meets the Seven Hills Trail (blue on white) and both are joined by the Pine Meadow Trail (red on white). All three cross Pine Meadow Brook on a footbridge. The Seven Hills and Pine Meadow trails then head right, while the Kakiat Trail turns left, soon passing the start of the Raccoon Brook Hills Trail (black R on white), which heads left. The Raccoon Brook Hills Trail is crossed again at 4.6 miles, where the two trails join briefly. The Kakiat crosses several ridges and the deep ravine of Torne Brook, as well as the

Suffern-Bear Mountain Trail (yellow) on Cobus Mountain at 6.0 miles. The Kakiat Trail comes down the mountain, mostly on woods roads. Where it passes directly under the power line, the trail makes a sharp left. At the base of the mountain, the Kakiat Trail follows along dirt roads in Rockland County's Kakiat Park, crossing the Mahwah River on a footbridge. The trail ends near the entrance to the park on US 202. Parking is available near the entrance.

Long Path   *Length: 22.8 miles Blaze: turquoise*
This major trail traverses the park, going from Mt. Ivy to Florence Mountain. See chapter 19, "Long Distance Trails," for details of selected sections, or the *Long Path Guide* for a complete description of the 22.8 miles.

Major Welch Trail   *Length: 2.6 miles Blaze: red dot on white*
This trail, which ascends Bear Mountain's north slope, was named in 1944 in honor of Major William A. Welch—an early general manager of the Palisades Interstate Park. Major Welch was basically responsible for launching Harriman's trail network, and it was he who convened the first meeting of the Palisades Interstate Park Trail Conference, which soon became the New York-New Jersey Trail Conference.

The Major Welch Trail starts behind the Bear Mountain Inn and follows the asphalt path along the western shore of Hessian Lake nearly to its north end before making a sharp left (west) into the woods. Climbing gently for a short distance, it then makes another sharp left turn and begins a steep, steady ascent of about 900 feet to the summit at 1,305 feet. There are panoramic vistas to the north along this stretch. Before reaching the summit, the trail crosses Perkins Memorial Drive. Near the top, it goes through a picnic area and turns right onto Perkins Drive, passing Perkins Memorial Tower. The trail descends the south slope of Bear Mountain via a weathered ridge with many viewpoints. At 2.6 miles it ends on a lower section of Perkins Memorial Drive, meeting the Appalachian Trail (white). Parking is available at the Bear Mountain Inn, which is also a destination for a New York City bus.

Menomine Trail   *Length: 2.4 miles Blaze: yellow*
Blazed in 1994, this formerly unmarked trail connects the Long Path (turquoise) to the Appalachian Trail (white) and links up shelters located at both ends. The midpoint is the Silvermine Lake parking lot off Seven Lakes Drive, where rest rooms are available.

(boathouses) Hessian Lake

Starting on the Long Path on Stockbridge Mountain about 0.1 mile south-west of the Stockbridge Shelter, the trail drops gradually on a woods road, which is crossed by other faint old roads, before passing through a picturesque grove of pines on the shore of Lake Nawahunta. Just beyond the grove, the trail crosses the lake inlet and makes a sharp right at the 0.7-mile point onto a fire road leading to Seven Lakes Drive. It crosses the road, passes the Lewis family grave site, and continues through a picnic area to the base of the old Silver Mine downhill ski slope. Going through a section of small boulders, it continues along the west shore of Silvermine Lake. After a short distance, the trail proceeds uphill on an old road to intersect a fire road. It turns left on the fire road and crosses Bockey Swamp Brook, the inlet of the lake. After climbing up to the William Brien Shelter, it ends at an intersection with the joint Appalachian (white) and Ramapo-Dunderberg (red dot on white) trails.

Nurian Trail   *Length: 3.4 miles Blaze: white*
This trail goes from the former Southfields railroad station to the Ramapo-Dunderberg Trail (red dot on white), terminating about 0.4 mile north of the Ramapo-Dunderberg Trail's crossing of County 106, where there is parking.

Parking spaces are available in Southfields at the Red Apple Rest, away from the restaurant. Hikers should follow along the railroad tracks to the north. About 100 yards past the site of the former train station, the trail turns right and descends.

After crossing the Ramapo River, the Nurian Trail crosses the New York State Thruway on a pedestrian bridge. After the bridge, the trail makes a left turn, follows Old Arden Road north for about 0.3 mile, makes a sharp right, and starts the ascent up the west side of Green Pond Mountain. Passing the summit at 1.1 miles, the trail descends to the north end of Lake Stahahe and circles that end of the lake on an asphalt road. In about 200 yards the Nurian Trail goes up the ravine of the Island Pond outlet brook which has numerous falls, proceeding through an area covered with large rocks called Valley of the Boulders. A few spots are difficult to negotiate, especially in winter. The trail turns right (south) near the head of the ravine and goes up along a long sloping rock, passing an outlook point. Shortly beyond, it meets the western terminus of the Dunning Trail (yellow) at 2.0 miles. The Nurian Trail turns left and passes down and through a small valley, crossing the Dunning Trail again before meeting Island Pond Road.

The Nurian Trail goes south briefly on Island Pond Road and then makes a left turn. In another 0.5 mile the White Bar Trail (horizontal white blazes) joins from the left. The trails run jointly for 0.1 mile; the Nurian Trail then turns left and goes downhill. It crosses a brook and climbs steeply up the west slope of Black Rock Mountain to end at the Ramapo-Dunderberg Trail (3.4 miles). The last half of the trail passes through areas with extensive mountain laurel.

Pine Meadow Trail   *Length: 5.5 miles Blaze: red on white*

Those who come by bus to Sloatsburg may walk to the start of the Pine Meadow Trail, 0.7 mile east from NY 17. The trail starts on the south side of Seven Lakes Drive. The most convenient car access is from the parking area at the Reeves Meadow Visitor Center on Seven Lakes Drive, 1.4 miles east of NY 17.

From its western terminus, the trail enters a scrub-filled field on the south side of Seven Lakes Drive at its crossing of Stony Brook, curves left, and follows Stony Brook. It crosses a telephone cable route, and at 0.7 mile passes the terminus of the Seven Hills Trail (blue on white) on the right. In another 0.2 miles, the trail passes the Reeves Meadow Visitor Center. Just beyond, the Reeves Brook Trail (white) begins. The Pine Meadow Trail parallels Stony Brook to a fork, where it swings to the right uphill. Here the Stony Brook Trail (unmarked) continues straight ahead.

more vertical geography

Queensboro trail

Hessian Lake
(Popolopen Creek and its viaduct
Fort Montgomery road past the Torne
Views from Popolopen Torne
down the River and up the
Queensboro Valley

The Hillburn-Torne-Sebago Trail (white) comes in from the left at 2.1 miles, coincides with the Pine Meadow Trail for about 100 yards, and then turns abruptly right. The Pine Meadow Trail levels off and meets the Seven Hills Trail (blue on white) coming in from the right at a fireplace. Both trails run together for a short distance. Soon the Kakiat Trail (white) comes in from the right and all three trails turn left and cross a foot bridge across Pine Meadow Brook. The Kakiat and Seven Hills trails turn left while the Pine Meadow Trail turns sharply right along the brook. At 2.7 miles, the trail reaches the large boulders called *Ga-Nus-Quah* ("stone giants") by the Native Americans.

A short distance later, the Diamond Mountain-Tower Trail (yellow) goes left, climbing Diamond Mountain. Here the Pine Meadow Trail takes a sharp right turn onto a woods road to Pine Meadow Lake. It follows the north shore of the lake and passes the remains of an old pumphouse at 3.7 miles. At the end of the lake the Conklins Crossing Trail (white) starts and goes right. About 0.4 mile farther on, the Pine Meadow Trail crosses Pine Meadow Road East and continues for another mile until it reaches its terminus at 5.5 miles on the Suffern-Bear Mountain Trail (yellow).

Popolopen Gorge Trail   *Length: 4.5 miles Blaze: red on white*
Providing a pleasant walk through the Popolopen Gorge to Turkey Hill Lake,

this trail can be reached from the Bear Mountain Inn parking area by walking north on the paved path along the east shore of Hessian Lake and proceeding north, past a traffic circle, to US 9W. The trail begins on the left, just before the Popolopen Gorge Bridge. The western terminus of the trail can be reached by heading north on the Long Path (turquoise) from the parking area on the north side of Long Mountain Parkway (US 6), located 1.2 miles west of Long Mountain Traffic Circle.

From US 9W, the Popolopen Gorge Trail leads gently down along a woods road 0.2 mile to Roe Pond, where there is an old dam. It continues to follow the steep southern side of the gorge, passing the area called Hell Hole, picturesque in early spring with water dashing over and around the boulders in the brook. The trail then climbs steeply for about 100 feet to the old Bear Mountain Aqueduct, which it follows until joining the Timp-Torne (blue), 1777W, and 1779 trails at 1.4 miles. This area is dominated by a hemlock forest.

The combined trails cross Queensboro Brook on a footbridge at 2.1 miles. After 2.6 miles, the Timp-Torne and 1777W trails continue straight ahead, while the Popolopen Gorge and 1779 trails turn right and skirt the north shore of Queensboro Lake. At 3.2 miles, the 1779 Trail leaves to the left. The

POPOLOPEN CREEK & THE HUDSON FROM BRIDGE

Popolopen Gorge Trail then passes the dam of Turkey Hill Lake. It follows the south shore of the lake until it meets the Anthony Wayne Trail (white) at 4.0 miles. Turning uphill, away from the lake, after a short climb the trail turns right on an old road, continuing through a small ravine to its terminus at the Long Path (turquoise).

Ramapo-Dunderberg Trail *Length: 20.9 miles Blaze: red dot on white*
The Ramapo-Dunderberg Trail (R-D), which goes from Tuxedo to Jones Point, is the oldest of the Bear Mountain-Harriman trails. Built by the walking clubs, it offers diverse terrain and many views. Intersecting twenty-one different trails, it can be combined with them to form interesting circular hikes. Cars can be parked at the Tuxedo railroad station on weekends, and both New Jersey Transit trains from Hoboken and New York City Port Authority buses stop here.

From its start at the Tuxedo railroad station, the R-D crosses the Ramapo River on a footbridge, turns left on the other side, turns right on East Village Road to an underpass of the New York State Thruway, and turns left on Grove Drive. In a few hundred feet, it turns right into the woods, climbing around a ridge and passing, in 75 yards from the road, the terminus of the Triangle Trail (yellow). At 1.2 miles, the Tuxedo-Mt. Ivy Trail (red dash on white) begins, diverging to the right. The R-D continues northeast to the crossing of Black Ash Swamp Brook. Here is a natural rock dam formed by the last glacier. Here also is Tri-Trail Corner, where three trails—the R-D, the Blue Disc (blue dot on white), and the Victory (blue V on white)—meet. The R-D climbs northward to the summit of Black Ash Mountain, with a view near the top over the swamp to the south. The White Bar Trail (horizontal white bar) crosses the R-D in the dip between Black Ash and Parker Cabin mountains. Soon after, the terminus of the White Cross Trail is passed on the right.

The R-D continues north up to the top of Parker Cabin Mountain, which it reaches at 3.4 miles. Here, on the level summit, the Triangle Trail (yellow) comes in from the left, coincides with the R-D for about 150 feet, and then bears right (east). The R-D descends the north side of Parker Cabin Mountain to a gap where it crosses the Victory Trail. From the gap, the trail ascends steeply up Tom Jones Mountain. Near the stone shelter on the summit, there is a view east and south. The trail drops steeply down the northeast slope, where it crosses a brook and then County 106. Parking is available for three or four cars.

North of the paved road, the trail climbs steadily up Black Rock Mountain. Between rock walls the Nurian Trail (white) begins at the left, while the R-D bears right over a rock ledge. Much of the next section of trail traverses open rock. The Bald Rocks Shelter, at mile 6.0, is off the trail to the right about a mile north of the Nurian. To the left of the trail at Bald Rocks is the location reported to be the highest in the park (elevation 1,382 feet). A U.S. Coast and Geodetic Survey marker is anchored in the rock here.

Farther along, the R-D crosses the Dunning Trail (yellow), and then, about

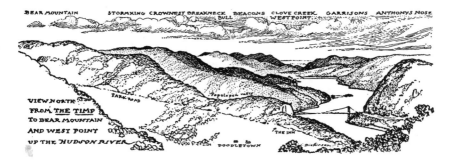

another half-mile northward, the Lichen Trail (blue L on white) meanders north-west over ledges, some with views, and offers a shortcut to the Arden-Surebridge Trail. The R-D winds down from Hogencamp Mountain through woods to "Times Square," where it crosses the Long Path (turquoise) and the Arden-Surebridge (red triangle on white). Hikers should be careful here, as it is easy to go on the wrong trail. After going over several ledges, the R-D begins to climb Fingerboard Mountain. As it levels off at the top, the Appalachian Trail (white) comes in from the left at 8.8 miles. Shortly thereafter the trail passes the west end of the Hurst Trail (blue), which leads in a few hundred feet to the Finger-board Shelter and then goes down to Seven Lakes Drive.

At Arden Valley Road the Appalachian Trail continues straight (north) while the R-D turns right (east), following the paved road past the Tiorati traffic circle. About 0.3 mile east of the circle, the trail turns left into the woods and proceeds east over Goshen Mountain. It descends and then joins the Appalachian Trail again at a plank bridge 1.3 miles from the circle. Another 0.8 mile later the R-D comes to the William Brien Memorial Shelter and the southern termi-nus of the Menomine Trail (yellow). At 0.9 mile, farther northeast, the R-D crosses the Silvermine Ski Road, which can be followed left to Silvermine Lake.

The trail crosses a streambed and heads steeply up Black Mountain, with views to the west. The trail then levels and winds along the top. Another climb to a rock ledge at 13.7 miles provides views to the south, including the Man-hattan skyline when weather permits. A descent, fairly steep at first, leads down the mountain's east slope, crossing the 1779 Trail, then a woods road, and finally the Palisades Interstate Parkway. East of the parkway, the combined R-D/Appalachian Trail goes through woods to Beechy Bottom Brook. Past the brook, the trail turns left and briefly follows a woods road. Just shy of 15 miles, the R-D turns right and ascends to Beechy Bottom East Road while the Appalachian Trail continues straight ahead.

The R-D then ascends steeply to the southern end of West Mountain. On an open area near the top, the trail meets the Suffern-Bear Mountain Trail (yellow) just above the ledge called Cats Elbow, with views to the south into the interior of the park.

After coinciding briefly, the Suffern-Bear Mountain Trail turns north (left) while the R-D swings east across the summit. It descends into Timp Pass where, at 16.6 miles, it meets the Timp-Torne Trail (blue) and the eastern terminus of the Red Cross Trail (red cross on white). Here also, the unmarked Timp Pass Road heads north to Doodletown. Rising above is the Timp, a striking cliff with a pronounced overhang, one of the most picturesque rock faces in the park. From Timp Pass, the R-D and Timp-Torne ascend over a rough talus slope, up under the overhanging cliff. The R-D turns right at the top, but the best overlook is from the open summit a few steps to the left, with its sweeping views south and the Manhattan skyline in the distance.

After 0.2 mile, the Timp-Torne exits right, while the R-D Trail continues east, enters the saddle between the Timp and Bald Mountain, where it crosses the 1777 Trail, then climbs steeply up Bald Mountain to the summit, with views west and north. Just off the summit to the left of the trail is the Cornell Mine, from which iron ore was taken. Continuing east, the trail soon passes the terminus of the Cornell Mine Trail (blue), which comes up from the left. At 19.3 miles, the R-D passes the unmarked Bockberg Trail on the right. As the R-D descends steeply in places, it crosses the graded embankment of the uncompleted Dunderberg Scenic Railway bed several times. After crossing US 9W, the R-D ends at Jones Point.

Ample parking is available at the trail's end on the Hudson River. Buses from the Port Authority Bus Terminal in Manhattan, go to Bear Mountain and will stop to discharge or pick up passengers on US 9W where the road to Jones Point turns off (2 miles north of the village of

Tomkins Cove). From there, it is a brief walk to the trailhead.

Red Cross Trail   *Length: 7.9 miles Blaze: red cross on white*
The Red Cross Trail goes through the middle of the park, generally southwest, from the intersection of the Ramapo-Dunderberg (red triangle on white) Trail and Timp-Torne Trail (blue) at Timp Pass to the Arden-Surebridge Trail, 0.25 mile north of the Lake Skannatati parking area on Seven Lakes Drive.

From its eastern terminus, the Red Cross Trail descends steeply along a woods road and at 0.5 mile briefly joins the North "Ski" Trail. At 0.9 mile, a trail leads off to the left toward the Addisone Boyce Girl Scout Camp. Shortly thereafter the trail goes right, away from the woods road, and crosses Beechy Bottom Road at 1.4 miles. It turns right at 1.9 miles, joining the 1779 Trail. Within the next 0.2 mile the Suffern-Bear Mountain Trail (yellow) joins and leaves, and the 1779 Trail leaves.

At the Palisades Interstate Parkway (2.2 miles) the trail jogs left along the northbound lane before crossing it, the center median, and the southbound lane. It turns left down the southbound lane before entering the woods to the right. The trail goes through a wet section, where Owl Swamp Brook comes down from the right and skirts a marsh to the left. About 1.2 miles from the parkway, an unmarked woods road, leads right (north) toward the William Brien Memorial Shelter at the north end of Letterrock Mountain. At 4.7 miles, the trail passes the northern end of the Beech Trail (blue). It encounters another swampy area before crossing Tiorati Brook on rocks. Depending on water flow, hikers may have to seek an alternative crossing up- or downstream.

From the brook (5.4 miles) the trail ascends to a grassy ball field and crosses it and paved Tiorati Brook Road. Some parking is available off the north side of the road just left (east) of the trail. The Red Cross Trail continues south on a prominent woods road until it passes the Hasenclever Mine at 6.0 miles on the left. The trail turns right on a cross road and then right again off the road before ascending Hasenclever Mountain. Shortly after crossing a telephone line, it goes south, then briefly north, before passing the north end of Lake Askoti, where a beautiful point of rock juts into the water. Crossing Seven Lakes Drive at 7.5 miles, the Red Cross climbs Pine Swamp Mountain to terminate at the Arden-Surebridge Trail (red triangle on white).

Reeves Brook Trail   *Length: 1.6 miles Blaze: white*
This trail begins at the Pine Meadow Trail (red on white) about 100 yards from

JACKIE JONES (FIRE TOWER) 1140   CRANBERRY CONKLING   BRUNDIGE
(E.of S. (LADENTOWN)   HASSENCLEVER   ROCKHOUSE   HIGH HILL 1240   S. of E)
(SUFFERN)

FINGERBOARD 1360

1030

ENGINEERS POLICE

1430

FROM IORATI TOWER 1350'

Dilkinson

Lake Tiorati formerly Cedar Pond

the Reeves Meadow Visitors Center (parking available), 1.4 miles east of NY 17 on Seven Lakes Drive.

The trail makes a gradual ascent, approaching Reeves Brook at 0.2 mile, with the brook on the left for some distance. After a woods road leaves to the right at 0.5 mile, the trail ascends fairly steeply. At 1.4 miles, it crosses the Seven Hills Trail (blue on white). It terminates at its junction with the Raccoon Brook Hills Trail (black R on white) 0.3 mile later.

Seven Hills Trail   *Length: 6.6 miles Blaze: blue dot on white*
The trail starts on the east side of Seven Lakes Drive, 4.0 miles from NY 17, opposite the entrance to the Lake Sebago parking area. It ascends Conklin Mountain, joins Woodtown Road, and crosses Diamond Creek. The Seven Hills Trail then turns right, off Woodtown Road, and starts its traverse of Diamond Mountain. It soon crosses the Tuxedo-Mt. Ivy Trail (red dash on white). The trail briefly follows a fire road and passes views of Lake Sebago. The Diamond Mountain Tower Trail (yellow) begins at the left at 1.4 miles. In another 0.1 mile, the Hillburn-Torne-Sebago Trail (white) comes in from the right and joins the Seven Hills Trail. At 1.7 miles, the other end of the Diamond Mountain-Tower Trail leaves to the left. The Hillburn-Torne-Sebago and Seven Hills trails continue together and go over the summit of Diamond Mountain.

Past the summit, the Hillburn-Torne-Sebago Trail diverges sharply right. The Seven Hills Trail continues ahead, making a steep descent to Pine Meadow Brook, where it turns left onto the Kakiat Trail (white). The joint trails meet the Pine Meadow Trail (red on white) coming in from the left, and all three trails cross Pine Meadow Brook on a footbridge. The Kakiat Trail turns off to the left while the joint Seven Hills and Pine Meadow trails turn right. Shortly, at a fireplace, the Seven Hills Trail turns off left and goes up hill; the Pine Meadow Trail continues straight ahead. At 3.0 miles, coming from the right, the Hillburn-Torne-Sebago Trail rejoins and soon leaves to the left.

After a steep descent, the Seven Hills Trail briefly follows a gas pipeline. It then crosses the Reeves Brook Trail (white) and passes the start of the Raccoon Brook Hills Trail (black R on white) on the left at about 4.0 miles. Soon afterwards it reaches Torne View. After another 0.4 mile, the Hillburn-Torne-Sebago Trail joins once more, coming in from the left. The trails run together for 0.2 mile, before the Seven Hills Trail turns right to go down the mountain while the Hillburn-Torne-Sebago Trail continues ahead. The Seven Hills Trail turns north, crosses Beaver Brook, skirts a large swamp, and finally reaches its terminus on the Pine Meadow Trail. To the right, a short hike on the Pine Meadow Trail leads to parking at Reeves Meadow.

Suffern-Bear Mountain Trail   *Length: 23.5 miles Blaze: yellow*
This trail from Suffern to Bear Mountain is quite rugged in many places. The southern terminus is just north of the commuter parking lot off NY 59 and US 202, just south of the New York State Thruway overpass (hiker parking permitted on weekends only). Access to the southern portion of the Suffern-Bear Mountain Trail is also possible from the parking lot off US 202 at the southern terminus of the Kakiat Trail.

About 500 feet north of the Thruway overpass on NY 59, the trail turns sharply right from the sidewalk and goes steeply up to a viewpoint on the slope of Nordkop Mountain. Joining a woods road for a time, it follows north along the ridge of the Ramapo Rampart. After leaving the woods road, the trail continues over the fairly level mountaintop, crossing a gas line.

About 1.5 miles from Suffern, the trail climbs out of a hollow, goes up a rock formation known as the Kitchen Stairs, and soon crosses another gas line and then a power line. At 3.2 miles the Suffern-Bear Mountain Trail reaches the Valley of Dry Bones, an area of giant boulders. Continuing on, the trail crosses yet another gas line, and passes two big boulders called Grandpa and Grandma Rocks. Shortly beyond is the intersection of the Kakiat Trail (white), at 4.5 miles. The Suffern-Bear Mountain Trail proceeds north over Cobus Mountain, then descends to the Conklins Crossing Trail (white). It continues up a steep slope to the Stone Memorial Shelter. A mile after the shelter, the Suffern-Bear Mountain Trail passes the terminus of the Pine Meadow Trail (red on white) on the left.

The Suffern-Bear Mountain Trail reaches the summit of Panther Mountain at 7.7 miles with a view toward the Hudson River and surrounding villages. After a descent, the trail crosses the Tuxedo-Mt. Ivy Trail (red dash on white) at a stone fireplace almost a mile farther on. At 9.4 miles, the Red Arrow Trail comes in from the right. The Suffern-Bear Mountain Trail, going northwest, crosses Woodtown Road and reaches Third Reservoir at 10.1 miles. Climbing Breakneck Mountain, the trail meets the beginning of the Breakneck Mountain Trail (white), where it turns right (northeast). There are views to the east as the trail follows the crest to Big Hill Shelter at 11.2 miles. The trail then encounters the Long Path (turquoise) briefly, drops along some ledges, and crosses a woods road and the Old Turnpike, which is now a buried telephone cable right-of-way. The Suffern-Bear Mountain Trail reenters the woods, climbing gradually up the south side of Jackie Jones Mountain (1,276 feet) to the microwave relay tower and old fire tower. The trail then leaves the road and goes northeast over Panorama, a viewpoint over High Tor and the Hudson River. The Suffern-Bear Mountain Trail descends northward past the large glacial erratics known as the Three Witches. It enters the ruined Buchanan estate, ORAK (KARO spelled backwards—the estate was built by an executive of the company that made the syrup), before rejoining the blacktop road just before County 106 (Gate Hill Road). This point is 13.2 miles from Suffern. Parking is on the south side of the road.

The Suffern-Bear Mountain Trail turns right to cross a brook on the highway bridge, and then turns left onto a woods road. Soon it veers right, climbs a ridge, and passes a large boulder on the left known as the Irish Potato at 13.8 miles. The trail descends, with Upper Pound Swamp visible to the right, and then goes down to Lake Welch Drive. Parking is possible a half-mile west on Tiorati Brook Road, which is closed in winter. At 15.6 miles, the Suffern-Bear Mountain Trail turns right, parallels the road, and then goes over and across the Palisades Interstate Parkway.

After crossing the parkway and paralleling it a short distance to the left, the Suffern-Bear Mountain Trail makes a sharp right turn and starts an extremely steep ascent of the south side of Pyngyp Mountain. At 16.0 miles, halfway up the mountain, is a memorial tablet to Harold Scutt, who first scouted the trail in 1925.

At and near the summit (1,016 feet), there are panoramic views to the southeast. Descending to a woods road in the notch beyond, the trail turns right for 100 yards, then goes left across a brook, past a fireplace, and up to the summit of the Pines, with viewpoints to the north.

Beyond the Pines, the Suffern-Bear Mountain Trail turns left onto a woods road, the route of the Red Cross (red cross on white) and 1779 trails. After 400 feet, the trail turns right, leaving the road, and in another 0.5 mile crosses Beechy Bottom Road. It then climbs Horn Hill (930 feet) and, after a gradual descent, crosses another woods road (North Ski Trail) at 18.8 miles and then climbs up the southern spur of West Mountain.

After climbing steeply and making a turn called the Cats Elbow, the Suffern-Bear Mountain Trail meets the Ramapo-Dunderberg Trail (red dot on white) at an open ledge. The two trails join for a short distance, and then at 19.2 miles the Ramapo-Dunderberg swings east, while the Suffern-Bear Mountain Trail goes left, northward into the hollow between the two summits of West Mountain. After the Suffern-Bear Mountain Trail climbs again to the crest of West Mountain, the Timp-Torne Trail (blue) enters from the left at 19.8 miles and departs right 0.3 mile later. (On the latter trail, a little way to the east, is the West Mountain Shelter and views of the Manhattan skyline.)

The Suffern-Bear Mountain Trail then climbs to another high point. It curves left down a steep talus slope to a gully where, after crossing a brook, it follows its left bank to the Doodletown Bridle Path, a woods road. It briefly goes left on the bridle path, then swings right to cross the 1777W Trail. The Suffern-Bear Mountain Trail then rejoins the bridle path for about 0.5 mile until it reaches a bend in the path, where it goes left uphill to Seven Lakes Drive. As it continues up and over the shoulder of Bear Mountain, it is joined by the Appalachian Trail (white) from the left at 23.0 miles. Both trails pass the ski jump and continue to the terminus of the Suffern-Bear Mountain Trail at the signpost 100 yards behind the Bear Mountain Inn. Parking is available at the Inn, where buses also stop.

Timp-Torne Trail   *Length: 10.9 miles Blaze: blue*
The trail begins on the west side US 9W just south of its intersection with Jones Point Road. Buses from New York City will stop to discharge or pick up passengers here. Parking is available on the west side of US 9W, just north of the trailhead.

Soon after entering the woods, the trail passes the lower tunnel of the Dunderberg Scenic Railway and begins its initial steep ascent up the southeastern slope of Dunderberg Mountain. The trail meanders past massive rock outcroppings and occasional views of the Hudson River before it turns left on a completed grade of railway bed at 0.7 mile. It briefly turns right, then left on another grade, to approach the huge but never completed upper tunnel. After looping around the tunnel and past a small seasonal water course, it crosses the unmarked Jones Trail at 1.2 miles. It then begins to ascend again with more views of the Hudson River. At 2.7 miles the Timp-Torne Trail crosses the 1777 Trail and passes an overlook on the left atop a large rock outcropping. The trail drops a bit until it is joined from the right by the Ramapo-Dunderberg Trail (red dot on white). The two trails, sharing the same route, pass the Timp, with its views to the right at 3.3 miles. Descending steeply, the two trails reach the intersection of the Red Cross Trail (red cross on white) and the unmarked Timp Pass Road at 3.6 miles. The Timp-Torne Trail then branches right and climbs first moderately and then steeply to the West Mountain Shelter at 4.3 miles. Weather permitting, the Manhattan skyline can be seen on the southern horizon from this point.

Continuing along the ridge of West Mountain, the trail is joined from the right by the Suffern-Bear Mountain Trail (yellow) at 4.4 miles, which coincides for 0.3 mile and then departs left. The Timp-Torne Trail joins the Appalachian Trail (white) after another 0.1 mile and, following the west ridge of West Mountain, offers vistas of the park and the Hudson River. At 5.6 miles it diverges left from the Appalachian Trail and gradually descends West Mountain, crossing the Fawn Trail (dark F on pink) and reaching the terminus of the Anthony Wayne Trail (white) on the left at 6.6 miles. At Seven Lakes Drive the Timp-Torne joins the 1777W Trail, crosses the Drive and the Palisades Interstate Parkway, and turns right onto the old Fort Montgomery Road. The Popolopen Gorge (red on white) and 1779 trails join from the left at 7.2 miles. All four trails gradually descend into the Popolopen Gorge. At 8.4 miles, the Timp-Torne, 1777W, and 1779 trails turn left and cross Popolopen Brook via a small bridge while the Popolopen Gorge Trail continues straight ahead. At 0.1 mile beyond the bridge, the Timp-Torne Trail, leaves the 1777W and 1779 trails, turns left into the woods, crosses Mine Road, and climbs very steeply to the summit of

Popolopen Torne (941 feet), which offers a 360-degree view.

The trail then drops 500 feet, recrosses Mine Road, and rejoins the 1777W and 1779 trails on the route of an old aqueduct. The three trails eventually terminate on US 9W just north of the Popolopen Gorge Bridge. Parking for these trails is at the Bear Mountain Inn, 0.8 mile south, which also serves as a bus stop.

Triangle Trail   *Length: 5.2 miles Blaze: yellow triangle*
The Triangle Trail makes an easy loop from the Ramapo-Dunderberg Trail (red dot on white) near Tuxedo to the Tuxedo-Mt. Ivy Trail (red dash on white) near the Dutch Doctor Shelter. Parking is available on weekends at the Tuxedo railroad station, which is accessible by bus or train from New York City.

From the station, the Ramapo-Dunderberg Trail (red dot on white) leads to the start of the Triangle Trail on the left in 0.5 mile. After 2.6 miles, the White Bar Trail (horizontal white bar) joins the trail from the left on the side of Parker Cabin Mountain. The trails coincide for a short distance, until the Triangle diverges left. The Triangle Trail then climbs steadily to the top of Parker Cabin Mountain, where it joins the Ramapo-Dunderberg at the summit. After about 100 feet, the Triangle Trail diverges right to the sharp eastern edge of the mountain, where there is an outstanding lookout over Lakes Skenonto and Sebago. The trail starts down steeply and then continues more easily over low ridges and level areas, crossing the Victory Trail (blue V on white) at 4.1 miles.

The Triangle Trail skirts Lake Skenonto and, farther on, Lake Sebago, and ends at its junction with the White Bar Trail at 5.25 miles. To the left, the White Bar leads in about 0.1 mile to the Dutch Doctor Shelter and, just beyond, meets the Tuxedo-Mt. Ivy Trail (red dash on white). The triangle is completed by following the Tuxedo-Mt. Ivy Trail sharply right and hiking 2.7 miles back toward Tuxedo.

Tuxedo-Mt. Ivy Trail   *Length: 8.2 miles Blaze: red dash on white*
The Ramapo-Dunderberg Trail (red dot on white) leads to the start of the Tuxedo-Mt. Ivy Trail (red dash on white) on the right in 1.2 miles. In 0.3 mile the Tuxedo-Mt. Ivy Trail reaches Claudius Smith's Den, an overhanging rock formation used as a hideout during the Revolutionary War. The trail climbs alongside the caves, crossing the Blue Disc Trail (blue on white). At the top of the hill the White Cross Trail (white cross) starts, heading left. The Tuxedo-Mt. Ivy Trail then goes over the shoulder of Blauvelt Mountain and down into the valley to cross Spring Brook. Shortly after, the White Bar Trail (horizontal

white bar) joins from the left. Dutch Doctor Shelter is 0.1 mile to the left on the White Bar Trail.

The Tuxedo-Mt. Ivy and White Bar trails continue together on a woods road for 500 feet. The Tuxedo-Mt. Ivy Trail then turns off to the left and goes over the ridge, crosses a camp service road, and skirts the south shore of Lake Sebago, arriving at Seven Lakes Drive. The trail crosses the drive, turns left over the dam at 2.4 miles, and drops down the embankment on the right. Here is the start of the Hillburn-Torne-Sebago Trail (white). The Tuxedo-Mt. Ivy Trail veers right on a wide path and shortly crosses the Hillburn-Torne-Sebago Trail again, which makes a broader loop to reach this point. The Tuxedo-Mt. Ivy Trail heads uphill on the north side of Diamond Mountain, crossing the Seven Hills Trail (blue on white) at 3.3 miles.

The Tuxedo-Mt. Ivy Trail descends and crosses Woodtown Road (3.5 miles), Pine Meadow Road West (4.3 miles), and Pine Meadow Road East (5.1 miles). A few hundred feet farther on, the Breakneck Mountain Trail (white) begins, branching to the left. The Tuxedo-Mt. Ivy Trail continues east and then follows a woods road to Woodtown Road, on which it turns right briefly. It diverges left, goes through a swampy area, and, at a fireplace, crosses the Suffern-Bear Mountain Trail (yellow) at 6.65 miles.

Descending gradually, the trail passes the start of the Red Arrow Trail (red) on the left, continuing down over some rocky footing. The trail leaves the woods at a power line, turns left on a service road, crosses under the power line, and heads back right on another service road, finally turning left down a dirt road to a paved road where parking is available.

The parking area is reached from US 202 (heading north) by turning left at the light at the junction of Routes 202 and 306. A short right and a left turn onto Mountain Road at the church, and then left again on the private road to the power station (marked Dead End), leads to the parking area, in a field to the right.

White Bar Trail   *Length: 7.7 miles Blaze: horizontal white bar*
One of the oldest trails in the park, the White Bar connects the Arden-Surebridge Trail (red triangle on white), approximately 0.2 mile east of the Lemon Squeezer, with the Johnsontown Road Circle parking area in a fairly direct north–south line.

After leaving the Arden-Surebridge Trail, the White Bar Trail goes south on a woods road, then meets and for a short distance coincides first with the Dunning Trail (yellow) and then with the Nurian Trail (white). After crossing County 106 at 2.1 miles and 0.1 mile west of a parking area, the trail goes over the top of Carr

Pond Mountain at 2.7 miles. It drops steeply down into Parker Cabin Hollow at 3.1 miles. It again follows a woods road and then starts a long, steady climb up the shoulder of Parker Cabin Mountain. At 3.5 miles, the Triangle Trail (yellow) joins it from the right.

Claudius Smith
hideen
near
Tuxedo

In the saddle between Parker Cabin and Black Ash mountains, the Triangle Trail turns left at 3.7 miles while the White Bar Trail continues south and in another 0.2 mile crosses the Ramapo-Dunderberg Trail (red on white). After crossing the White Cross Trail, the White Bar Trail crosses the shoulder of Blauvelt Mountain. The White Bar Trail passes the terminus of the Triangle Trail (yellow) at 5.7 miles and then the Dutch Doctor Shelter. The Tuxedo-Mt. Ivy Trail (red dash on white) briefly joins from the right at 5.9 miles. The White Bar Trail turns right off the Tuxedo-Mt. Ivy Trail and continues south on a woods road. At 6.8 miles, the trail approaches Seven Lakes Drive at a vehicular gate, turns right into the woods, and joins unpaved Old Johnsontown Road to end at the Johnsontown Road Circle parking area.

SEVENTEEN

THE PALISADES

ome unknown early voyager up the Hudson named the cliffs of the lower river the Palisades, probably because the giant pillars of traprock bore a likeness to the palisaded villages of the Native Americans. This unique geological formation begins at the Rahway River in New Jersey, crosses the western edge of Staten Island, continues north along the river into Rockland County, New York, turns inland at Haverstraw Bay, and then ends abruptly at Mount Ivy. The cliffs are most prominent from Edgewater, New Jersey, to Haverstraw, New York, with a brief detour inland at Nyack. The Long Path traverses most of the ridgetop. When combined with the numerous intersecting or nearby trails and byways, it offers many opportunities for circular routes encompassing not only woods and meadows but history and interesting architecture.

Well-documented Palisades events began on September 13, 1609, when Henry Hudson, sailing on the *Half Moon,* made his second anchorage of the day opposite the present location of Fort Lee, New Jersey. Hudson sailed north on the river as far as the present site of Albany in search of the Northwest Passage, and returned on finding no outlet up the river.

History of Palisades Interstate Park

The beginning of the Palisades Interstate Park dates from the time when New York City was slowly aroused to the devastations of the quarrymen blasting along the cliffs for traprock. About the middle of the nineteenth century much of the loose and easily accessible talus was pushed down to be used as ships' ballast. The real menace to the Palisades came with the demand for more concrete to build skyscrapers and roads. Quarries were opened from Weehawken to Verdrietige Hook above Nyack. To check this activity, New York and New Jersey jointly created the Palisades Interstate Park Commission (PIPC) in 1900. Enabling legislation was pushed in New Jersey by the New Jersey Federation of Women's Clubs. In New York, Andrew H. Green, founder of the American Scenic and Historic Preservation Society, worked for the necessary legislation with the support of Governor Theodore Roosevelt and other conservation-minded officials. Land was acquired and developed as parks with all needed facilities.

In the early days most of this development was accomplished with gifts of money donated by the commissioners and interested individuals, but funds for development projects have been provided by the two states. Of the many individuals who contributed generously of time, talents, and money in creating the system of parks, special recognition must be given to George W. Perkins, Sr., who was the Commission's first president and the organizing genius of its development. With the story of his leadership should be coupled the generosity of J. Pierpont Morgan at a critical time, and other notable gifts of land and funds, both private and public. As a result, quarrying of the river faces of many mountains in Rockland and Bergen counties was stopped. Later the Park Commission was also charged with preserving the natural beauty of the lands lying in New York State on the west side of the Hudson, including the Ramapo Mountains as well as state park lands in Rockland and Orange counties and those in Sullivan and Ulster counties outside the Catskill Forest Preserve.

In 1933, John D. Rockefeller, Jr. offered to PIPC certain parcels of land on top of the Palisades that he had been assembling for some time. He wanted to preserve the land lying along the top of the Palisades from uses that were inconsistent with PIPC's ownership and to protect the Palisades themselves. He also hoped that an adequately wide strip of the land might ultimately be developed as a parkway. In that year there seemed little likelihood of finding funds for a parkway, but various lines were explored. In 1935, legislation was passed that enabled the Commission to accept the deeds to the land offered. Additional properties were donated by the Twombleys and by the trustees of the estate of W. O. Allison. The parkway, completed to Bear Mountain in 1958, is a tree-lined, limited-access drive for noncommercial traffic only. Since 1937 both the New York and New Jersey sections of the Palisades Interstate Parkway have been administered by the Palisades Interstate Park Commission under a compact that legally cemented a uniquely successful tradition of cooperation between two states.

Geology

The contrast between the red sandstone, in horizontal strata at the bottom of the cliffs, and the gray vertical columns above it, may intrigue the hiker in the Palisades. The bedrock of the Palisades section of the Palisades Park is of two

pulpit of rock

kinds: sedimentary sandstones and shales, and igneous intrusive basalt. Both were formed during the late Triassic and early Jurassic periods. At that time, as dinosaurs began to dominate the land mass, the Atlantic Ocean basin started to open. Down-dropped fault blocks formed. For some millions of years, sand and mud washed down from surrounding highlands and spread out over wide areas in sedimentary layers thousands of feet thick. Consolidated by pressure and by the deposition of mineral matter that penetrated the porous mass and cemented particles together, these deposits are the reddish-brown horizontal strata known to geologists as the Newark Series.

After these sedimentary strata were laid down, molten rock was forced upward through rifts and then between sedimentary layers to form a single, prominent sill, the Palisades, about 1,000 feet thick for some 40 miles along the Hudson. As the molten mass cooled underground, contraction fissures broke the sheet into crude vertical columns, often hexagonal or pentagonal in outline. The gradual erosion of the sandstone exposed these contraction joints to the elements. Repeated freezing and thawing caused huge blocks to peal off, thus creating the talus slopes at the base.

Newark sandstone forms the walls of most of the old Dutch farmhouses in northern New Jersey and Rockland County, as well as the brownstone fronts of many older private homes in Manhattan. The reddish ledges of Newark sandstone are exposed in many places along the shore path. The rock occurs near the river level but is often hidden behind the talus.

TALLMAN MOUNTAIN STATE PARK

As the southernmost components of the Palisades Interstate Park in New York, 687-acre Tallman Mountain State Park stretches along the Hudson River from the hamlet of Palisades to the Village of Piermont. Access to this park is via the main entrance off US 9W or at the bike path entrance and parking lot located one mile south and just north of the intersection of US 9W and Oak Tree Road. The old-time charm of the hamlet of Palisades makes it seem hardly credible that it should still exist so close to New York City. Old Dutch houses with greenswards and gardens, and former artists' cottages, are scattered up and down the park-like hillsides.

Oak Tree Road (Washington Spring Road) leads east to Snedens Landing, the western end of the Dobbs Ferry route established in 1719. In 1775, Mollie Sneden, whose house still stands under the cliff, piloted the ferryboat carrying Martha Washington across the river on her way to join her husband in Cambridge. Also on this road is the site where the American flag received, by order of Parliament, its first salute from the British in May 1783. Oak Tree Road leads west, to the village of Tappan, with its DeWint House (Washington really did sleep there), the 1776 House, and the execution site of John André, the British major and spy during the American Revolution.

Long Path   *Length: 3.4 miles Blaze: turquoise*
This trail crosses the Tallman Bike Path four times. See the *Guide to the Long Path* for complete descriptions of the 3.4 miles.

Tallman Bike Path   *Length: 2.1 miles Blaze: directional signs*
To reach this bike path, hikers and cyclists enter Tallman Park from the southern entrance, where there is a parking lot, and follow the bike path markers along a woods road, also the Long Path at this point. The Long Path soon departs left, but intersects the bike path four times before reaching the Sparkill. At any of these crossings, the Long Path can be used to return to the starting point. On the left of the bike path are elongated, elevated mounds of earth at right angles to each other. Originally built as berms to retain oil seepage from an oil tank farm that was to be established here, some are now filled with rainwater and, although shallow, make good birding sites. This entire area is a haven for frogs and salamanders, which breed in the pools each spring, as well

as a veritable wildflower paradise in April and May with Spring Beauties, Anemones, Dutchman's Breeches, Mayflowers, and many others. After paralleling the river for a while, the road becomes paved, goes down an incline, and enters a small picnic area with a comfort station. The bike path markers continue northward through the park on paved roads. A detour up the road from the traffic circle, to the North Hill picnic area along the escarpment, leads to views of the river, Hook Mountain, and the Tappan Zee Bridge. The bike path descends to river level, where it leaves the pavement and runs alongside the tall reeds and marsh of the Piermont Marsh. The bike path joins the Long Path for the last time and a road just before crossing a bridge over the Sparkill. The Village of Piermont, originally called Tappan Slote, is just over the bridge.

PIERMONT

Piermont was once the bustling terminus of the Erie Railroad, whose original charter stipulated that it had to be built entirely within New York State. A mile-long pier was built in the shallow part of the river in 1840 so that passengers could transfer directly from trains to boats for New York. Eleazar Lord,

the railroad's founder, renamed the village in honor of his pier. His mansion, The Cedars, known as Lord's Castle, still stands on the hillside almost directly west of the pier. The village-owned pier and its extensive development make an interesting diversion with views up and down the river. The oblique right turn off of the bike path at the beginning of the business district leads to the pier. On the way to the end of the pier, hikers can see a variety of bird life, including herons, ducks, rails, swallows, and wrens, and a variety of trees including white mulberries, cottonwoods, and willows. The Piermont Marsh is preserved as an estuarine sanctuary.

Piermont has many interesting arts and crafts shops. A stop at a restaurant or coffeehouse makes a delightful pause. The hourly Red & Tan Lines 9A bus to New York stops at the small park near the bridge across the Sparkill.

Old Erie Railroad Bed   *Length: 3.0 miles Blaze: unmarked*
In 1870, the Nyack spur of the Northern Railroad of New Jersey was inaugurated with great fanfare and much real estate speculation. This spur was active until 1965. The Tappan Zee Bridge, which opened in December 1955, siphoned off its ridership. The right-of-way, which is now owned by the villages through which it passes, just below the level of US 9W, extends into the Nyacks.

To reach this byway with its seasonal views of the river and adjacent Westchester, hikers must follow the Long Path (turquoise) up the hill to the old Piermont station, now a private residence. The Old Erie Railroad Bed is entered alongside the chain-link fence. It proceeds north, crosses a trestle, passes the Grandview station site, and finally emerges onto the southern end of Broadway in South Nyack. There is space for parking here. The right of way continues on across the New York State Thruway into Nyack.

To return to Piermont, hikers can take the Long Path south at the intersection of NY 59 (Main Street) and Mountainview Avenue in Central Nyack, or catch the hourly Red & Tan Lines 9A bus along Broadway. Nyack and Upper Nyack offer a collection of antiques and crafts shops, restaurants, and preserved Victorian and other architectural buildings.

BLAUVELT STATE PARK

On the ridge above Piermont and Grandview, known as Clausland Mountain, several trails intersect the Long Path in 590-acre Blauvelt State Park, a component of the Palisades Interstate Park system. (*Blauvelt* is Dutch for "blue field.")

The park began in 1910 as a rifle range for the New York National Guard. Designed to replace a facility at Creedmor, Long Island, it was abandoned within three years after many complaints about – and equally many attempts to remedy the problems of – bullets landing on the east side of the ridge. The camp was turned over to the Palisades Interstate Park Commission and since then has been used as a YWCA summer camp, an ROTC training center during World War I, and again as a military training ground for the soldiers from nearby Camp Shanks, a troop staging center during World War II. In 1997 there is no evidence of these intervening uses. Only the shadowy tunnels, decaying target support walls, and a few small buildings remain. Patricia Edwards Clyne, a Hudson Valley author, used Camp Bluefields as the setting for her children's book, *The Curse of Camp Gray Owl*.

Access to Blauvelt State Park is from the south or west. From the south, parking is available in the Tackamac Park lot off Clausland Mountain Road. From there hikers can follow the Long Path as it crosses a stream above a small dam pool, heads uphill, emerges through the gap in a stone wall, and reaches an embankment, the former firing line for the 1,000-yard range. Here an orange blaze appears, which marks, often poorly, a roughly one-mile-long trail that circumnavigates the western portion of the old range. Part of this trail consists of the original paved access road running east–west, which ends just west of where the Long Path intersects the orange trail for a second time in the midst of a white pine forest. This road can be followed westward to Greenbush Road just off NY 303, where there is parking for several cars.

Farther north along the Long Path and beyond the last remnants of the firing range, a white-blazed trail departs left. It leads to a series of red-, white-, and red-and-white-blazed trails, mostly on woods roads, in the northeast corner of the park, and often poorly blazed. However, Tweed Boulevard runs along the eastern edge of the park and the Long Path is found just east of Tweed.

Long Path   *Length: 1.5 miles Blaze: turquoise*
See the *Guide to the Long Path* for a complete description of the 1.5 miles.

HOOK MOUNTAIN & ROCKLAND LAKE STATE PARKS

Hook Mountain State Park (676 acres) and Rockland Lake State Park (1,079 acres) are the next hiking areas in the Palisades Interstate Park system. Just north of the Nyacks, the Palisades ridge, which had moved inland to form a shallow bowl, returns to the river's edge. The familiar columnar formations reappear as Hook Mountain, jutting its massive curved and quarried face into the river and demarcating the Tappan Zee from Haverstraw Bay. The name is derived from the Dutch *Verdrietige Hoogte* (tedious or troublesome point) because of the contrary winds that sailors encountered while trying to round it. Hook Mountain's southernmost summit rises to 728 feet, the second highest (after High Tor) along the Palisades ridge.

In the last quarter of the nineteenth century, the quarrying, which started on the Jersey Palisades, spread upriver, threatening to deface Hook Mountain on the Tappan Zee and the entire riverfront. There was a bustle of new activity at some of the landings, such as Snedens, Tappan Slote (Piermont), Rockland Landing, and Waldberg (Snedekers), where ferries plied across the river or where steamers docked en route to New York. In 1872, the erection of a stone crusher at Hook Mountain signaled the beginning of large-scale operations. By the turn of the century, this and thirty-one smaller quarries between Piermont and Nyack were in vigorous operation. Sentiment was growing to stop this defacement, as had been done on the Jersey Palisades. George W. Perkins, president of the Park Commission, had the greatest part in stimulating this opinion among philanthropic men and women of wealth. He believed the forested hills of the Highlands of the Hudson, famous for their scenery and as Revolutionary strongholds, would be an outlet for the people of the metropolitan district. Besides various bond issues, the Commission was aided in its plans by generous contributors, including members of the Harriman, Perkins, and Rockefeller families, who have been adding to park holdings even up to the present time.

The first of the purchases at Hook Mountain was in 1911, with the acquisition of the large quarry at the south end of the mountain. By 1920 the last of the quarries ceased operations, and the public had a 6-mile-long park along the river where once such a park seemed only a dream.

Rockland Lake was the hub of another great industry that broke the serenity of the riverfront—the harvesting of Rockland Lake ice from 1831 to 1924. The discoverer of the superiority of ice from spring-fed Rockland Lake is unknown, but its renown spread to New York City, where the better restaurants would accept no other. In 1711, John Slaughter purchased land at Rockland Landing, including Trough Hollow. A dock was built and gradually some commercial traffic appeared, but Nyack and Haverstraw had better natural facilities. As ice was harvested, it was conveyed to Rockland Landing by a sort of "escalator" and loaded onto river boats. Later, the giant Knickerbocker Ice Company was formed, at one time employing four thousand men. Icehouses measuring more than 350 feet long, 100 feet wide and 50 feet high, each with up to a 100,000-ton capacity, were situated at the northeast corner of the lake. In 1860, a cog railway was built through Trough Hollow, connecting lake and dock. A spur line of the West Shore Railroad also ran to the icehouses. Nevertheless, the growth of mechanical refrigeration permanently halted ice harvesting operations in 1924. After that Rockland Lake became a popular, privately owned recreation center for summer swimming and picnicking and winter ice-skating. In 1958, the Commission acquired 256-acre Rockland Lake and the surrounding upland areas. Later, additional acreage was purchased to include the entire "bowl."

The Long Path runs along the escarpment above, while a bike path follows the river's edge from the ruins of Haverstraw Beach State Park in "Dutchtown," a quaint section of Haverstraw, to Nyack Beach State Park in Upper Nyack. The three connecting paths to the Long Path, one each at the north, south, and middle points of the magnificent facade of the Hook, allow for circular hikes of varying lengths. The full loop of the Long Path and bike path is 12 miles.

Long Path   *Length: 6.1 miles Blaze: turquoise*
The Long Path takes the high route. See the *Guide to the Long Path* for a complete description of the 6.1 miles.

Hook Mountain Bike Path   *Length: 4.9 miles Blaze: unmarked*
The northern terminus of the Hook Mountain Bike Path has two access points for those traveling by car. The first is to park off US 9W, just north of NY 304, on Scratchup Road in the Tilcon parking lot. Hikers should follow the Long Path (turquoise) south as it crosses US 9W to the white-blazed connector trail. This trail descends steeply alongside a quarry to a paved road and an abandoned and vandalized stone ranger cabin. Fifty yards to the right the unpaved bike path leads south along the cliffs and 60 feet above the river.

The other automobile access is from Dutchtown. The parking area is reached by continuing north on US 9W, going past the NY 304 intersection, and turning right on Short Clove Road over the railroad tracks. Make a hairpin right onto Riverside Avenue and proceed south, passing through the quarrying operations into Dutchtown. Continue south to a barricade and a small parking area. Hikers should proceed on foot along the same paved road marked as a bike path.

The bike path is at first level and then descends gradually. Where it begins to ascend again, a little-used trail diverges left. This trail leads to Haverstraw Beach State Park, where there once was a thriving settlement known, at various times, as Waldberg Landing, Snedekers Landing, or Red Sandstone Dock. At low tide (about two-and-a-half-hours later than at Sandy Hook), hikers can walk north about 200 yards along the river's edge toward the next jutting point to a large granite boulder just below the high water mark. Inscribed on this rock are the words ANDRÉ THE SPY LANDED HERE SEPTEMBER 21, 1780. The low land projecting from the opposite shore almost to the middle of the Hudson is Croton Point, with Tellers Point at its southern tip. This was the delta of the old Croton River, formerly at river level but now elevated to a height of 80 feet. The crust of the earth gradually rose with the disappearance of the last glacier and the removal of the tremendous weight of ice. Beyond are the Westchester hills of a more ancient metamorphic terrain.

The paved bike path continues south and up a mild incline to reach the abandoned ranger cabin across from the connector trail with the Long Path, mentioned above. Shortly after leaving the paved section, the bike path comes to the first of the abandoned quarries in Hook Mountain State Park. It continues along the level of the division between the red sandstone and the overlaying traprock. The princess tree grows here on the diabase talus slopes resulting from old rockslides. The common tree of the upper level is the box elder, and along the path are many hundred-year-old hemlocks and striped maple or moosewood trees, rare this far south. The slopes are covered with a lush growth of evergreen ferns, and wildflowers in the spring.

A small stone cabin on the right was perhaps used by a quarry watchman or for storing explosives. On the river side, huge concrete abutments are just discernible under their natural camouflage netting of vines and ivy. These were used to support the conveyor slides that moved the traprock from the quarry to the barges below. At the end of the second quarry, a path bears left to Rockland Landing North (2 miles from the ranger cabin at the end of the paved road). Descending to the river, the overgrown path leads past stone comfort stations and picnic tables, all in various stages of decay. This area was developed in the early 1930s by the Work Projects Administration (WPA) and the Civilian Conservation Corps (CCC). They were abandoned after the war when the water quality became so bad that the beaches had to be closed to swimming. Immediately beyond, another abandoned stone building sits on the cliff side of the path, and just beyond that an old, almost undetectable woods road bends up the ridge to Trough Hollow. This narrow and precipitous road was the original route between the river and Rockland Lake on the west side of the ridge.

Back on the bike path, and just beyond the Trough Hollow intersection, is the third quarry, somewhat larger than the others, and once landscaped as part of the park development. Upon close inspection, a baseball backstop is hidden within the vegetation, and a little farther south at a jog in the path, another trail descends left into the abandoned picnic/beach area. Above, the columns of the cliff face reveal Triassic intrusive diabase (traprock). The path descends sharply on a paved section to the remains of Rockland Landing South. Here, pier pilings are visible in the river, as well as the automatic navigation beacon on a reef in the river, known to mariners as Rockland Light. It was at this location that the ice blocks from Rockland Lake reached the river's edge via the "escalator." It was also here that the Day Liners would dock to disgorge their passengers to enjoy the recreational facilities at both Rockland Lake and Rockland Landing North.

The now-paved path turns upward and reaches a woods road 3.5 miles from the northern connector trail. The route to the right leads past an occupied stone ranger cabin and sharply up a paved road to the top of the ridge, crossing the Long Path, into the hamlet of Rockland Lake with its quaint Knickerbocker Fire House. Beyond lies Rockland Lake State Park, which has facilities for strolling, cycling, boating, fishing, golf, tennis, swimming, and picnicking, with plenty of parking (for a fee) and access to the Red and Tan Lines 9A bus to New York City at the south entrance. This paved road to the ridgetop is the middle of the three connector paths. To return to the parking area on US 9W near NY 304, hikers should follow the Long Path north from the top of the ridge. A foreshortened Hook circular hike is possible by leaving the Long Path at this point and returning to Upper Nyack along the bike path.

To the left, after ascending from Rockland Landing South, the woods road runs along the riverside edge of the largest of the quarries. The cliffs here rise 400 feet or more, with columnar fluting noticeable at the south end. However, the path quickly drops down to the river's edge at a small point, with several picnic tables. It continues south close to the sandstone cliffs, where a park lean-to was built of plentiful talus. This part of the bike path is heavily used by strollers, joggers, and cyclers, as well as by hikers. South of the last of the quarries is Nyack Beach State Park, now only a picnic area (4.9 miles from the northern terminus) with parking (seasonal fee). The WPA built a red sandstone

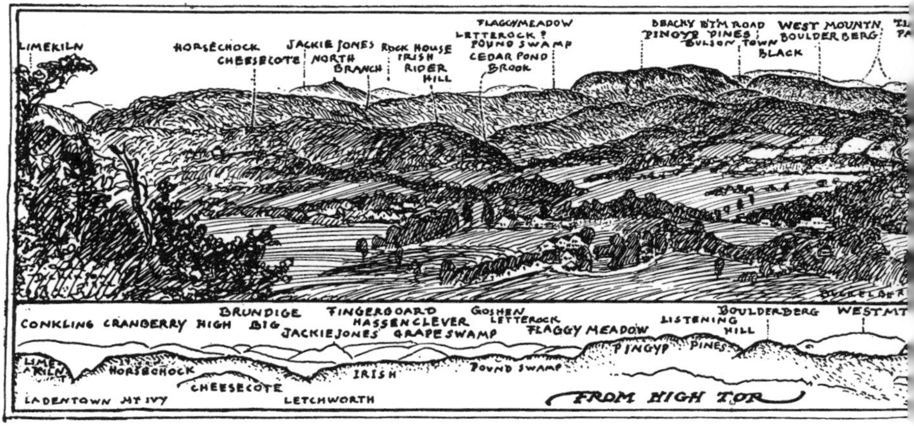
LIMEKILN
HORSECHOCK
CHEESECOTE
JACKIE JONES
NORTH
BRANCH
ROCK HOUSE
IRISH
RIDER
HILL
FLAGGYMEADOW
LETTEROCK ?
POUND SWAMP
CEDAR POND
BROOK
BEACHY B'T'M ROAD
PINGYP PINES
BULSON TOWN
BLACK
WEST MOUNTN
BOULDERBERG
CONKLING
CRANBERRY
HIGH
BRUNDIGE
BIG
JACKIEJONES
FINGERBOARD
HASSENCLEVER
GRAPESWAMP
GOSHEN
LETTEROCK
FLAGGY MEADOW
LISTENING
HILL
BOULDERBERG
WESTMT
LIME
KILN
HORSECHOCK
CHEESECOTE
IRISH
POUND SWAMP
PINGYP
PINES
LADENTOWN
MT IVY
LETCHWORTH
FROM HIGH TOR

building, now only open for special events, underneath the concrete conveyor bunkers left over from the quarrying operations.

From the entrance kiosk of the park, the south connector trail (white) travels briefly south on Broadway before turning right onto Larchmont, alongside Marydell Camp to Midland Avenue. It turns south on Midland Avenue and, within 100 yards, turns right into the woods. Continuing through the woods, it gradually ascends to join the Long Path, 100 yards from where it leaves US 9W.

Alternately, hikers can walk south on North Broadway which has unusual houses, both old and new. At Old Mountain Road, a detour right uphill for about 200 yards leads to Rockland's oldest cemetery on the right. Continuing south on Broadway to Castle Heights Avenue (one mile from Nyack Beach Park) brings the hiker to a Red and Tan Lines 9A bus stop and a delicatessen. Farther south along Broadway is the Village of Nyack.

HIGH TOR STATE PARK

High Tor, one of Rockland County's most striking landmarks, was once used as a signal point by colonists during the Revolution. Long cherished as part of the Van Order farm on its south side, High Tor was threatened by quarrying for its traprock, as Elder Van Order grew older without descendants. Maxwell Anderson's picturesque play, *High Tor*, and local attachment to the little peak

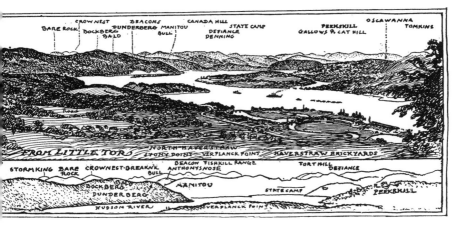

roused the Rockland County Conservation Association, the Hudson River Conservation Society, and the New York-New Jersey Trail Conference to action. Their campaign resulted in the purchase of the ridge and its presentation in 1943 to the Palisades Interstate Park Commission.

High Tor State Park (564 acres), the most northern component of the Palisades Interstate Park system on the Palisades proper, is located off South Mountain Road. Although the park is primarily a summer swimming facility, a woods road leads north from the parking lot to cross the Long Path along the ridgetop and continue north to the top of the promontory known as Little Tor.

In 1995, Scenic Hudson, Inc., purchased the former vineyard property south of High Tor, which will be managed as part of the park and will have a trail making a loop with the Long Path. The Deer Path (unmaintained) begins on the west side of US 9W just south of the Riverside Nursing Home (parking is limited). It follows a woods road and then switchbacks steeply up the escarpment, intersecting the Long Path just south of High Tor.

Long Path   *Length: 3.5 miles Blaze: turquoise*
The Long Path is the only hiking trail on the Palisades between Long Clove and Mt. Ivy. See the *Guide to the Long Path* for a complete description of the 3.5 miles.

EIGHTEEN

THE GREENWOOD LAKE AREA

he long sliver of water that re-
sulted when Peter Hasenclever built a dam at Long Pond to provide power for
his ironworks downstream is now known as Greenwood Lake. The ironworks
site is still in evidence, and hikers on the Sterling Ridge Trail can see the old
furnace and giant waterwheels—one of them rebuilt—just south of a
hemlock-laced section of the Wanaque River. The Monksville Reservoir in West
Milford and Ringwood, created by damming the Wanaque River north of the
Wanaque Reservoir, was completed in 1987. The ironworks site, now Long
Pond Ironworks State Park, was protected, though much beautiful land was
submerged. Most of the area east of the lake that does not lie within New Jersey
state parks is within the formerly privately owned Sterling Forest. In 1997, the
fight to save Sterling Forest from development continues. See chapter 1, "Trails
and Trail Development," for more details.

Bearfort Ridge, consisting of Paleozoic sandstone and quartz conglomerate, is the southern continuation of Schunemunk Mountain in New York.
Greenwood Lake is a shale and limestone valley. This down-faulted wedge is
sandwiched between the Wawayanda and Wyanokie plateaus.

BOUNDARY WALKS

For someone highly skilled in the use of compass and topographic map, tracing
the New York-New Jersey boundary can be an excellent exercise and a true
challenge. The southern boundary of Rockland and Orange counties runs for
many miles through the deep woods of the Highlands. At the end of every mile,

measured from the Hudson River, there is a small and inconspicuous stone marker. All the other boundaries of New Jersey are natural shorelines or river courses.

The northeastern boundary was first defined in 1664, when James, Duke of York, sold the province of New Jersey to Berkeley and Carteret. The terminal points were defined as the mouth of "the northernmost branch of the said bay or river Delaware, which is 41° 40' of latitude [there is no such point], and the intersection of latitude 41° with Hudson's River." The actual positions of the terminal points were not agreed on until 1769. In 1770, a joint Colonial boundary commission tried to locate the line, but was discomfited by a show of weapons and other evidence of unfriendliness on the part of residents of the coastal plain section. Consequently they took to the woods to do what they could toward defining the boundary there. The cause of all this hostility, one may surmise, was local satisfaction with a state of affairs that made it difficult for either colony to collect taxes. The job was finally completed, however, and mile markers were set in 1774. Many of them can still be found down among the leaves and bushes, with their antiquated and amateurishly carved lettering.

A more precise survey was made just one hundred years later, in 1874, and was followed by a joint state resurvey in 1882, when new markers were set alongside the old stones. The new ones are of granite, with dressed tops 6 inches square projecting 6 inches out of the ground. Even these are difficult to find, particularly under a heavy snow.

The 1874 and 1882 surveys, made with reference to astronomically fixed positions, revealed that the boundary of 1774 had the general shape of a dog's hind leg, for a reason unsuspected by the pioneers. The 1774 survey was done with the magnetic compass and, since the Highlands are full of magnetic iron ore, the compass line rambles accordingly. At Greenwood Lake the marker was 2,415 feet, or nearly half a mile, southwest of the straight line between the termini. Since the land in the Highlands was of little value, the commissioners, being practical men, left well enough alone and did not disturb the mileposts of 1774. New York State thus retained, through magnetic attraction, a good many acres that the Duke of York intended to convey to the proprietors of New Jersey.

The most interesting walk begins with Stone Number 15 in Suffern and continues approximately northwest for 33.5 miles to Stone Number 49, near Port Jervis. Number 21 is about a tenth of a mile east of the old road leading north from Ringwood Manor and the White Trail, which starts there. Number 23 is about a tenth of a mile northwest of the woods road that leads southwest from the vicinity of the former Sterling Furnace, and it can be reached by a

GREENWOOD LAKE *seen from near* TERRACE POND

woods road leaving the Sterling Ridge Trail (blue on white) about a mile north of Hewitt. Number 26 is on the northwest shore of Greenwood Lake, and the State Line Trail (blue dot on white square) has its start there. The distance between Numbers 22 and 23 is just under 0.9 mile; evidently, someone accidentally dropped ten chains (660 feet) from his count in 1774. In some sections the boundary is hazily indicated by dim dark-red blazes on the trees, deviating from the true course as if marking surveyors' gores.

The best time to follow the boundary is in the beginning of winter after the lakes and swamps are frozen, but before the snow has become too deep to permit finding the markers.

ABRAM S. HEWITT STATE FOREST

Immediately west of Greenwood Lake lies the Bearfort Mountain area, almost wholly within the Abram S. Hewitt State Forest, which is administered by Wawayanda State Park. It includes Surprise Lake and offers many viewpoints. Access to the trails is chiefly from a point on the Warwick Turnpike not far from the southern end of Greenwood Lake. The trails are also accessible from the Appalachian Trail.

Greenwood Lake extends across the state line with portions of its shoreline densely settled, particularly on the west side of the lake. The hiking trails are along the ridge and offer views over the lake. For more information, contact

Wawayanda State Park, P.O. Box 198, Highland Lakes, NJ 07422; (201) 553-4462.

Appalachian Trail   *Length: 0.8 mile Blaze: white*
This long-distance trail provides a 0.3-mile connection between the State Line Trail (blue dot on white square), reached as the Appalachian Trail enters the Forest, and the Ernest Walter Trail (yellow). The southbound trail continues west of that trail junction for half a mile before leaving the park. See the *Appalachian Trail Guide to New York-New Jersey* for a complete description of the trail.

Bearfort Ridge Trail   *Length: 2.4 miles Blaze: white*
This trail, accessible via NJ Transit buses 196 and 197, starts near a concrete bridge, where parking is available, on the north side of Warwick Turnpike, about a mile west of the intersection with Lakeside Road (County 511). From the eastern end of the bridge, the trail ascends through a hemlock grove to a woods road, but soon turns left as the Quail Trail (orange) continues straight ahead. The Bearfort Ridge Trail passes two small streams, and then climbs steeply to the top of the ridge, where there are open views to the south and west. It continues at basically the same elevation, about 1,300 feet, except for short descents into stream channels. For over a mile, the trail follows conglomerate rock ridges in a summit forest of pitch pine and scrub oak. Just before its northern end at the Ernest Walter Trail (yellow), there are several viewpoints, including a view of Surprise Lake to the north. The Highlands Trail (teal diamond) is co-aligned for the entire length.

Ernest Walter Trail   *Length: 2.1 miles Blaze: yellow*
This interior trail, accessible from other trails, is named for a dedicated hiker and trail worker. It encircles Surprise Lake and West Pond. Its eastern terminus is 0.6 mile from the trailhead for the State Line Trail. At 0.2 mile from the beginning of the trail, a large, glacially-smoothed projection of conglomerate provides views to the east of Greenwood Lake and Sterling Ridge. Crossing west, the trail passes Surprise Lake and a rhododendron grove, ascending to the Bearfort Ridge Trail (white). The trail continues cross-ridge, with many abrupt and rocky ups and downs. Turning north, with continued rocky footing, the trail eventually emerges at the Appalachian Trail. The Highlands Trail (teal diamond) is co-aligned from the Bearfort Ridge Trail to the Appalachian Trail.

Quail Trail   *Length: 2.2 miles Blaze: orange*
This trail leaves the Bearfort Ridge Trail (white) 0.1 mile from the Warwick Turnpike and follows woods roads uphill most of the way to its end at the junction with the Ernest Walter Trail (yellow) at Surprise Lake. It provides a more gradual ascent than the Bearfort Ridge Trail (white) but is somewhat wetter, particularly in spring. Several swampy sections must be negotiated after crossing Cooley Brook at 1.4 miles.

State Line Trail   *Length: 1.2 miles Blaze: blue dot on white square*
The trail begins about seventy feet south of the New York-New Jersey state line on County 511, on the north side of a stream that passes under the road. Unfortunately, parking is difficult near the trailhead. Public transportation via NJ Transit buses 196 and 197 is available. From the trailhead, the trail soon crosses a brook and, after about a quarter of a mile, begins a climb through an oak forest following a rocky streambed. Near the top of the ridge, at 0.6 mile, the Ernest Walter Trail (yellow) veers off to the left while the State Line Trail continues over a series of rocky ridges until it terminates at its junction with the Appalachian Trail (white) on the main ridge.

STERLING FOREST

Sterling Forest played an important role in the history of early mining and the smelting industry and contains remains of over twenty old mines and several furnaces. Several of the mine shafts have been filled in and closed. Sterling Mine, one of those that no longer can be seen, opened in 1750. Its shaft sloped nearly 1,000 feet under Sterling Lake. It was the principal iron producer from 1900 to 1921, when it closed down along with the other Sterling workings. Southwest ridges are faced on the west by steep rugged cliffs, hidden in dense forest and invisible from any outside point, but striking to encounter in this little-visited region.

As this book was going to press in Spring 1998, it is not known what the use restrictions will be on the former Sterling Forest Corporation lands in New York. For more information, contact the Palisades Interstate Park, Administration Building, Bear Mountain, NY 10911; (914) 786-2701.

Allis Trail   *Length: 2.5 miles Blaze: blue*
The Allis Trail, which serves as an access point to the Appalachian Trail (white),
was named for J. Ashton Allis, a pioneer hiker and trail builder in the metropolitan area. Parking is on NY 17A. If coming from the east, it is 1.4 miles west
of the traffic light at the Sterling Forest Ski Area. If coming from the west, the
parking is on the north side of the road just after a sharp right turn, 1.5 miles
from the Sterling Ridge Trail parking and 3.3 miles from the junction of NY
210 and NY 17A in Greenwood Lake village. The trailhead is on NY 17A, 80
yards east of the parking, but it is safer to follow the pipeline east from the
back of the parking area to the top of a rise.

Almost immediately after leaving its southern terminus on NY 17A, the
trail crosses a pipeline and a power line before reaching Sterling Mountain,
where there is a view of Schunemunk Mountain. From here, it descends to the
Appalachian Trail west of Mombasha High Point. The Highlands Trail (teal
diamond) is co-aligned for the entire length.

Jennings Hollow Trail   *Length: 3 miles Blaze: yellow*
Starting less than a mile from the southern terminus of the Sterling Ridge Trail
(blue on white), this old road follows a brook for the first 1.5 miles, passing the
stone walls and foundations of former farms. It crosses the brook at the base of
a mountain, where the brook tumbles down over rocks through a hemlock
ravine near the New Jersey-New York state line. Here the trail turns west and
south on another woods road, and ends on the East Shore Road at a wooden
bridge. About a quarter mile before the southern terminus, an alternate route
recrosses the brook and returns to the Jennings Hollow Trail about one mile
from its start at the Sterling Ridge Trail.

Sterling Ridge Trail   *Length: 8.6 miles Blaze: blue on white*
The Sterling Ridge Trail traverses the Tuxedo Mountains between Hewitt and
NY 17A in Sterling Forest. One of the highlights of a walk on the Sterling
Ridge Trail is the ruins of Peter Hasenclever's Long Pond Ironworks near its
southern end. Founded in 1766 and in operation until 1882, the ironworks
once supported a thriving community.

The New Jersey portions are protected as parts of Long Pond Ironworks
and Passaic County parks. The New York section is now owned by the Palisades
Interstate Park Commission. As this book is going to press in Spring of 1998, it is
not known what the use restrictions will be on the former Sterling Forest Corpora-

tion lands. For more information, contact the Palisades Interstate Park (see above). Parking is available at the junction of East Shore Road and Passaic County 511. Public transportation is via New Jersey Transit buses 196, 197 and 196/197.

The trail begins in New Jersey at the guard rail blocking the old main street of what was the village of Hewitt. It is lined with remnants of the sawmill and other village buildings in the form of foundations and crumbling walls. The road intersects with another old road at the site of what was the company store. The trail proceeds to the furnace site as it angles across the road.

The ironworks site is officially closed to the public, and hikers are requested to remain on the trail. The complex contains the remains of the old furnace, which dates back to the eighteenth century, and in the past has been the object of vandalism. The ruins of the Hasenclever furnace were discovered in a mound covered with leaves in 1956 and were excavated in 1967. Two original 25-foot waterwheels were burned in 1957. One has been stabilized in its ruined condition; the other was reconstructed on its original hub in 1994 with a grant from the New Jersey Historic Trust and Green Acres funds. The Friends of the Long Pond Ironworks are spearheading restoration efforts and offer public tours and programs. For more information, contact them at (973) 839-0128.

Waterwheels of the Long Pond Ironworks

From the furnace site, the Sterling Ridge Trail, at 0.4 mile, crosses the river on a suspension bridge to follow an old road, which veers away from the river and follows a tributary. At 1.1 miles, the trail passes the beginning of the Jennings Hollow Trail (yellow). The Sterling Ridge Trail ascends Big Beech Mountain, levels off, and ascends more steeply. The false summit has views to the southwest (2.0 miles) and the summit has views of Bearfort Mountain and the Wyanokies (2.2 miles). The Sterling Ridge Trail begins a steep descent and reaches the New York-New Jersey state line at 2.6 miles.

After crossing several woods roads, the trail ascends to reach, at 3.1 miles, a high point with views to the south and then, at 3.4 miles, descends to a view to the west. At 3.9 miles, the trail makes a right turn followed by a steep ascent and then level ridge walking. At 5.0 miles, the trail makes a sharp left turn and ascends to reach the fire tower with 360-degree views of Sterling Forest. Over the next 2.1 miles, the Sterling Ridge Trail has many ups and downs, with viewpoints along the way including views of Sterling Lake at 5.9 miles and 6.4 miles. The trail crosses a power line at 7.5 miles and enters the woods. At 8.6 miles, it reaches NY 17A where it ends. The trailhead is 1.8 miles east of the junction of NY 210 and NY 17A in Greenwood Lake village. A wide spot on the south side of the road accommodates parking for a few cars. During the non-hunting season, the Highlands Trail (teal diamond) is co-aligned for the entire length.

NINETEEN

LONG DISTANCE TRAILS

ost trails that cannot be walked comfortably from end to end in one day are considered long distance trails. These trails, typically spanning multiple chapters within this book, can be completed by hiking one section at a time or by backpacking. Hikers need to plan for transportation at the end point. Alternately, hikers can cover a segment of the trail out to a point and then hike back to the starting point the same way they came or on a different trail, if one is available.

The New York area boasts two premier long distance trails—the Appalachian Trail and the Long Path. Both trails have separate guidebooks, so only selected sections are described here. The Long Path Trail System includes the Shawangunk Ridge Trail, which connects the Appalachian Trail at High Point State Park in New Jersey with the Long Path.

As of winter 1997, two other long distance trails are growing. Ninety-five miles of the Highlands Trail are open and blazed. Eventually, it will go from Storm King Mountain on the Hudson River to the Delaware River. The Hudson River Greenway Trail will run from New York City to Albany on both sides of the Hudson River. Long distance trails that are contained within a single region are described in the relevant chapter of this book. The Long Island Greenbelt, Long Island Pine Barrens, and Nassau-Suffolk trails are examples of this type of long distance trail.

APPALACHIAN NATIONAL SCENIC TRAIL

The Appalachian Trail, known by hikers as the AT, runs from Springer Mountain in Georgia to Mount Katahdin in Maine, a distance of about 2,150 miles. In the New York area it runs from the Delaware Water Gap to Connecticut. In general it follows the spine of the Appalachian Mountains and seemingly goes over every mountain along the way.

Benton MacKaye, a regional planner, first proposed the trail in the *Journal of the American Institute of Architects* in 1921, in an article entitled "An Appalachian Trail, a Project in Regional Planning." He foresaw the large concentration of an urban population along the east coast and their need to retreat to nature for spiritual renewal.

The first section of the Appalachian Trail was built by volunteers from the New York-New Jersey Trail Conference in 1922-23, from the Bear Mountain Bridge to the Ramapo River south of Arden in Bear Mountain-Harriman State Parks. The following year they completed the section from Arden to Greenwood Lake. The entire trail from Georgia to Maine was completed in 1937; however, much of it was on private land and subject to interruptions as landowners changed. In 1968 Congress passed the National Trails System Act, which designated the Appalachian Trail and the Pacific Crest Trail, as the first official National Scenic Trails. As of 1997, there are twenty National Scenic and Historic Trails. Additional provisions of the Act included assigning responsibility for the National Scenic Trails to the National Park Service and the U.S. Forest Service, acquiring rights-of-way for the trail where it is outside federal or state lands, and protecting the trails from incompatible uses—specifically, limiting the Appalachian Trail to primarily foot traffic. Funding for land purchases first became available in amendments to the Act in 1978. In 1982, New Jersey became the first state to acquire a complete corridor on protected lands.

In 1984, the U.S. Department of the Interior signed an agreement with the Appalachian Trail Conference (formed in 1925) to manage the trail and the newly purchased corridor. The Appalachian Trail Conference delegates its responsibilities to trail clubs along the length of the trail. In this area, the New York-New Jersey Trail Conference has responsibility for the 162 miles in New York and New Jersey. This cooperative agreement among national, state, and local governments and volunteers serves as a model for efficient use of resources in an era of declining budgets. In 1996, only 45 miles of trail remain unprotected, with the year 2000 the target date for protecting the whole trail.

Every year, several hundred people *thru-hike* the Appalachian Trail, that is, they hike it continuously from end to end, generally taking from five to seven months to complete it. Many other people complete the trail over several years or decades, doing it a section at a time.

The *Appalachian Trail Guide to New York-New Jersey* and similar guides for other states describe the trail in great detail, with comments about trail features every few tenths of a mile. These guides are revised every three to five years. The *Appalachian Trail Data Book*, published by the Appalachian Trail Conference, is revised yearly and covers the whole trail in less than a hundred pages. It lists only major features along the trail, such as road crossings, shelters, rivers, and mountain tops. The trail is uniformly marked with a 2"x 6" painted white, vertical blaze. Most major road crossings are well marked, and the basic trail route appears even on most commercial road maps, although not always accurately.

Orange and Rockland Counties

From the New Jersey state line to the Bear Mountain Bridge, the Appalachian Trail crosses a series of ridges in 36.7 miles. The result is a trail that rewards its hikers with sights ranging from sweeping vistas to more contained pockets of beauty. Along the way hikers pass unique geologic features and historic sites, many from the Revolutionary era.

The first section of the entire Appalachian Trail was constructed from Bear Mountain to the Ramapo River in 1922–23. The exact route on Bear Mountain is lost in history, but pieces of many older routes can be found by adventurous off-trail hikers. The lowest point on the trail, 124 feet above sea level, is marked by a sign in the middle of the Trailside Museums, through which the trail passes. The museums specialize in native plants, animals, reptiles, and birds. *Hikers should take care to follow the white blazes*: as the AT crosses Harriman State Park, it intersects, or briefly shares the path with ten other trails.

Greenwood Lake Loop
Length: 14 miles Blazes: various

This ridgetop hike begins in New York state, but extends into New Jersey. The starting point is where the AT crosses NY 17A, where parking is available. The hike begins by heading south through thick woods. After about 2 easy miles, the AT opens out onto the magnificent "sidewalks" of Mount Peter/Bearfort Mountain. These long, upturned ledges are made of Devonian pudding-stone, a conglomerate mix of vividly colored red sandstones and red-and-white quartz pebbles and chips. The trail follows these ledges 5.9 miles south from the starting point and into New Jersey. The ledges give views of Greenwood Lake far below and Sterling Ridge across the valley. On a clear day, the skyscrapers of Manhattan can be seen glinting in the late afternoon sun. An interesting loop can be created by turning left onto the State Line Trail (blue). After 0.2 mile, the trail intersects with the Ernest Walter Trail (yellow). The loop turns right on the Ernest Walter Trail and follows it past Surprise Lake, a glacial pond. The trail then loops back and intersects with the AT again. A right turn to follow the AT back along the cliffs leads to the starting point on NY 17A. The Highlands Trail is co-aligned for portions of the Appalachian and Ernest Walter trails.

NY 17 to Lakes Road
Length: 8.7 miles Blaze: white

Parking for this hike is available at the Elk Pen parking area on Arden Valley Road, about 0.1 mile east of the New York State Thruway. From here, hikers can walk west 0.3 mile and cross NY 17. From this point, the trail makes a very steep ascent up Agony Grind to the first shoulder of Arden Mountain, which offers views back over Harriman Park and to the south. The grade becomes more moderate, with views to the southwest and north to the Catskills. At 2.1 miles the trail crosses paved Orange Turnpike, bearing to the left for a short distance, then continuing into the woods. The trail passes Little Dam Lake and then crosses East Mombasha Road at 3.5 miles. From here the trail traverses Buchanan Mountain, with several sweeping views. After crossing West Mombasha Road, at 5.2 miles, the trail enters an open field, which is a designated butterfly refuge. The next reward is the view from Mombasha High Point. From here it is 2 miles to Fitzgerald Falls, a pleasant 25-foot cascade though a rocky cleft. It is 0.3 mile from the base of the falls to Lakes Road, where parking is available. The Highlands Trail is co-aligned with the Appalachian Trail for 1.5 miles north of Lakes Road.

Tiorati Circle to Elk Pen
Length: 5.5 miles Blaze: white

This hike begins at the parking lot at Tiorati Circle on Seven Lakes Drive. From here, a 0.3-mile walk uphill on Arden Valley Road leads to a left (south) turn onto the AT. The trail proceeds generally though open woods and crosses four ridges. The first mile provides several views back over Lake Tiorati. After passing the Hurst Trail to Fingerboard Shelter, the AT turns sharply to the right, passing through a mixed forest of hardwoods and hemlocks broken by several laurel thickets. In about half a mile, the trail descends to a small brook and the impressive remains of the Greenwood Mine, one of the major sources of iron ore during and after the Civil War. The AT crosses the Long Path at 2.9 miles and continues to pass through open woods until reaching the top of Island Pond Mountain. From here a steep path leads down through a unique rock formation known as the Lemon Squeezer. The trail passes north of Island Pond and up to the crest of Green Pond Mountain in 1.0 mile. It is another mile of gradual descent to Arden Valley Road and the parking at the Elk Pen, where a herd of sixty elk imported from Yellowstone Park roamed from 1919 to 1942.

Bear Mountain Inn to Silvermine Lake
Length: 9.5 miles Blazes: various

Parking for this hike is at the Bear Mountain Inn, where there is a fee, in season. Behind the Inn, near the playground area, several trails converge. This hike begins on the combined AT and the Suffern-Bear Mountain Trail (yellow), heading south until the AT splits off to the right at 0.6 mile. The AT now begins to climb Bear Mountain in earnest, gaining 700 feet of elevation in the next 1.2 miles. During the ascent, switchbacks offer views of the Hudson Valley to the north and south. The views continue as the trail proceeds to the west. On the descent, it reaches and follows along Perkins Drive for 0.5 mile. At the bottom it crosses Seven Lakes Drive before entering open woods and making a gradual ascent to the ridge of West Mountain. There are almost continuous views to the west for a mile along the ridge. The trail descends steeply to Beechy Bottom Road which it crosses and parallels below, while descending gradually. Shortly the Ramapo-Dunderberg Trail (red dot on white) joins from the left and the two trails descend less steeply to cross the Palisades Interstate Parkway at 6.2 miles. Great care should be taken when crossing this heavily traveled, high-speed road.

After crossing the road, the trail crosses the 1779 Trail (blue 1779 on white circle) and climbs, steeply at times, to Black Mountain at 6.9 miles, where there are open views of the Hudson River to the east and the Manhattan skyline to the south. In 0.4 mile, a viewpoint of Silvermine Lake to the west is reached. The trail descends very steeply to cross an unmarked fire road (cross-country ski trail in winter) at 7.4 miles and reach the William Brien Memorial Shelter at 8.3 miles. To complete the hike, hikers should turn right at the Menomine Trail (yellow) which leads 1.2 miles to the Silvermine Lake parking lot on Seven Lakes Drive.

Putnam and Dutchess Counties

The Appalachian Trail extends 52 miles from the Bear Mountain Bridge (over the Hudson River) to the Connecticut line. After crossing the line near Hoyt Road, it continues in Connecticut for a while before looping briefly back into New York on the top of Schaghticoke Mountain.

Anthonys Nose *Length: 1.2 miles Blazes: white, blue*
From the east end of the Bear Mountain Bridge, where there is parking along NY 9D, this hike heads north on the AT, leaving NY 9D at the county line and proceeding steeply uphill until the trail intersects a gravel road. The AT turns left onto the road, but this hike turns right on the Camp Smith Trail (blue) and leads in approximately 0.6 mile to the cliffs at the top of the formation known as Anthonys Nose, which rises directly above the Bear Mountain Bridge's east abutment. The open rocks afford views up and down the Hudson River, as well as Bear Mountain State Park across the river. Return is via the same route (2.4 miles total).

Canada Hill *Length: 1.1 miles Blaze: white*
From the junction of US 9 and NY 403, the southbound AT crosses a field and follows two carriage roads until, at the terminus of the Carriage Connector Trail (yellow), it turns left and goes steeply uphill. On top of the ridge the AT turns left on a wide woods road. The destination of the hike is a viewpoint at the end of a short blue-blazed side trail less than 0.1 mile from the turn on the right (1.1 miles from the road). An alternate return is following the Osborn Loop (blue), which continues along the woods road when the AT makes a sharp right turn off it. After a long downhill on the Osborn Loop, the trail turns right at the other terminus of the Carriage Connector Trail (yellow). The Carriage Connector Trail is followed until it ends at its junction with the AT, which is then followed back to the trailhead (for a total round-trip distance of 3.5 miles). Longer hikes can be planned by using more of the Osborn Loop, which parallels the AT to the west and below along the entire ridge.

Canopus Lake Overlook *Length: 2.3 miles Blaze: white*
From NY 301 in Fahnestock State Park, the AT heads north 2.3 miles to an overlook at the north end of the lake. En route there are several small views of the lake. This hike is particularly nice at the end of June when the mountain laurel is out. Return is via the same route (4.6 miles total). Roadside parking is available on NY 301 near the trailhead.

Depot Hill *Length: 2.5 miles Blaze: white*
This northbound hike starts at the intersection of Stormville Mountain Road and Grape Hollow Road near the bridge over I-84. Parking is available along Grape Hollow Road. A pleasant walk of 2.2 miles rewards the hiker with views over the surrounding hills and west over the Hudson Valley to the distant Catskills. The remaining 0.3 mile leads to the Morgan Stewart Shelter. The return hike is by the same route (5.0 miles total).

Cat Rocks *Length: 3.2 miles Blaze: white*
Starting at the Appalachian Trail railroad station (Harlem Line of Metro-North, weekends only, 1-800-METRO-INFO), where the trail crosses NY 22 (parking available), the southbound trail heads west over the tracks. It then climbs Corbin Hill, going through almost a mile of open fields on the western slope (caution is advised, as the fence is electrified). At 2.3 miles, the trail crosses West Dover Road at a large oak tree, thought to be the largest tree on the entire AT. The trail climbs West Mountain steeply for half a mile up to Cat Rocks, with views to the east and south. The return hike is via the same route (6.4 miles total).

Pawling Nature Reserve *Length: 5.9 miles Blaze: white*
This hike also starts at the Appalachian Trail railroad station, mentioned in the Cat Rocks description above, but this time follows the northbound AT east, crossing NY 22 and, shortly thereafter, Hurds Corners Road (Old Route 22). The route passes an historic water tower that was formerly part of the water system for the farms and homes along the road as well as the former Sheffield Farms Dairy, visible across Hurds Corners Road. Crossing fields actively used for grazing and farming, the hiker enters the Pawling Nature Reserve at a register box, where a map of the reserve is posted; copies of the map may be available to allow exploration of the trail system in the reserve. Remaining on the AT, the hike finally leaves the reserve's property, passing the Gates of Heaven Cemetery on property formerly part of the Harlem Valley State Hospital. The trail

crosses unpaved Leather Hill Road and shortly arrives at the Wiley Shelter, more than fifty years old. The return walk is by the same route (a total round trip of 11.8 miles), or hikers can continue on across paved Duell Hollow Road, crossing Duell Hollow Brook and finally emerging on paved Hoyt Road at the New York-Connecticut state line, with parking available just off the AT (a total of 7.1 miles).

Schaghticoke Mountain   *Length: 3.7 miles Blaze: white*
From the Bulls Bridge parking lot on Bulls Bridge Road, just west of the village of Bulls Bridge on US 7 in Connecticut, the AT goes west 0.2 mile on the road and turns north on Schaghticoke Road. In 0.3 mile, the trail leaves the road and switchbacks up the slope of Schaghticoke Mountain, still in Connecticut, and levels out as it enters New York. At 3.7 miles from the start, a viewpoint is reached on rocks, with views to the southwest of the Housatonic River Valley. Return is by the same route (7.4 miles total).

Connecticut and Massachusetts

The South Taconic section of the Appalachian Trail extends along the eastern range of the highland in Connecticut and Massachusetts. It has rough sections, especially in Massachusetts, but has views from Lions Head and Bear Mountain in Connecticut and from Race Mountain, Mount Everett, and Jug End Ridge in Massachusetts. The northern part of the New York section goes in and out of Connecticut. From Bulls Bridge to the beginning of the South Taconics in the town of Salisbury, a distance of about 38 miles, the AT largely follows the Housatonic River—sometimes on the ridge above it and sometimes for long stretches right along the bank.

The trail is divided into the Connecticut and Massachusetts sections, managed, respectively, by the Connecticut and Berkshire chapters of the Appalachian Mountain Club. Backpackers hiking the Connecticut section should camp within the designated camping zones, two of which have shelters (Bond and Riga). In the Massachusetts section, hikers may camp at designated campsites, in dispersed camping zones, or at the Glen Brook shelter.

See also the South Taconics section for numerous side trails that provide access to many intermediate points on the trail. Consult the *Appalachian Trail Guide to Massachusetts-Connecticut* for more details about the Appalachian Trail.

Connecticut South Taconics   *Length: 7 miles Blaze: white*
The trail starts on the west side of Conn. 41 (Under Mountain Road), 0.8 mile

north of its junction with Conn. 44 in Salisbury. Parking for hikers is available at the trailhead. The trail goes west in woods and then ascends a woods road on a switchback, passing a camping zone on the left at 0.2 mile. The trail climbs northwest along the wooded slope, turning southwest before climbing steeply up the ridge of Lions Head. At 2.0 miles, the trail goes right at a junction.

At 2.2 miles, the Lions Head Bypass Trail (blue) goes straight ahead while the AT turns right and climbs a steep pitch to the south lookout of Lions Head at 2.3 miles. This lookout offers a view south and east over the Housatonic Valley. The trail continues north along the Lions Head summit (1,738 feet, an ascent of 1,000 feet from Conn. 41), passing the Bypass Trail on the left before reaching the north lookout at 2.4 miles, where the view features Bear Mountain and Mount Everett on the north. The trail descends, and at 2.7 miles, the Bald Peak Trail (blue) goes left 1.1 miles over Bald Peak to Mount Washington Road.

The AT continues north on relatively level terrain, crossing Ball Brook at 3.6 miles, where there is a designated camping zone. The Bond Shelter is reached at 4.2 miles, nicely situated to the right of the trail above the south branch of Brassie Brook. At 4.7 miles, at Riga Junction, the Under Mountain Trail (blue) goes right and descends 1.9 miles to Conn. 41. In another 0.2 mile, the AT turns right from a woods road. This road, called Bear Mountain Road, goes 0.9 mile northwest from here on level terrain to Mount Washington Road at a point 0.3 mile south of the Connecticut-Massachusetts line.

The trail makes a steady 430-foot ascent of Bear Mountain through stunted growth, with views southward from ledges. At 5.6 miles there is a stone monument near the summit. Erected in 1885, it was vandalized in the 1970s and has been stabilized as a permanent relic, but only to half of its original height. From here there is a view east over the Housatonic Valley, including Connecticut's Twin Lakes. A short distance west of the trail is the open summit of Bear Mountain at 2,320 feet, the highest summit in Connecticut, with broad views over the highland.

The trail descends the north slope of the mountain very steeply. At 6.2 miles, it goes right from a woods road, the Northwest Road, which goes 0.75 mile west from here to Mount Washington Road just south of the Connecticut-Massachusetts line. The trail enters Massachusetts, where the Paradise Lane Trail comes in from the right from the Under Mountain Trail, and descends through hemlocks to Sages Ravine Brook. It follows the cascading brook eastward downstream for two-thirds of a mile through the upper part of Sages Ravine, an attractive area that is a designated camping zone. The brook crossing at 7.0 miles marks the end of the Connecticut section.

Massachusetts South Taconics
Length: 9.5 miles Blaze: white

From the Sages Ravine Brook crossing, the AT ascends eastward, levels off, and turns north from Sages Ravine. The trail ascends an eroded stretch and crosses Bear Rock Brook at 1.3 miles. To the right of the trail the brook goes through an attractive area with hemlocks, where hikers have camped, and then drops down the escarpment as Bear Rock Falls, with a view from the top.

The trail ascends along the edge of the escarpment with occasional lookouts on the right. At 2.0 miles, it emerges onto the open cliffs of Mount Race, which it follows for 0.25 mile, with sweeping views eastward over the Housatonic Valley. The trail then ascends to the summit of Mount Race (2,365 feet) at 2.5 miles, a bare rock with a 360-degree panoramic view. The trail descends Mount Race steadily to the notch between it and Mount Everett where, at 3.7 miles, the Race Brook Trail (blue) goes right. The latter passes a camping area by the headwaters of Race Brook before descending 1.5 miles to Conn. 41 and passing a series of waterfalls and cascades of Race Brook.

The AT ascends steeply 700 feet, with views southward, to the summit of Mount Everett at 4.6 miles. An open area with scrub growth, it has a fire tower that is closed to the public, and broad, distant views, including New York's Catskill Mountains on the western horizon. The trail turns right here and goes along the eastern slope of Mount Everett with views eastward, descending past the upper parking area of the Mount Everett Reservation road, which has a view and a stone shelter that is not authorized for camping. The trail descends to cross the road at an angle and reaches the reservation's picnic area at 5.2 miles. Beyond, a red-blazed trail goes left, following a beautiful route around Guilder Pond.

The trail proceeds northeast and north, descending on a rough route through dense mountain laurel. At 6.4 miles, the Elbow Trail (blue) goes right and descends 1.2 miles to the Berkshire School, west of Conn. 41. The AT reaches the beginning of Jug End Ridge and follows its narrow crest with peaks or knolls of descending elevation, starting with Mount Bushnell at 7.0 miles. At the north end of the ridge crest, at 8.7 miles, a prominent rock outcropping, Jug End, offers a view of Jug End Valley to the west.

The trail swings abruptly right, passes another open view from a cliff, and descends roughly and steeply southeastward over rock ledges, moderating somewhat to reach unpaved Jug End Road in the Housatonic Valley at 9.5 miles. From this north end of the Southern Taconic section of the trail, it is 0.8 mile left on Jug End Road and Avenue Road to Mount Washington Road (1.3 miles west of South Egremont), and 1.6 miles right on Jug End Road to Conn. 41.

LONG PATH

When Vincent and Paul Schaefer originally conceived the idea of the Long Path in the 1930s as New York's version of the Long Trail in Vermont, they had a unique vision. The trail would consist of an unmarked route through backcountry and wilderness corridors loosely linking points of interest. Today's Long Path System—with town walks and wilderness, interconnections and co-alignments with other trails, and an extension into new territory to the north and west—is a tribute to those who have added their own vision to that of the founders.

The Long Path (LP) obtained its name from Raymond Torrey's weekly column, "The Long Brown Path," in the *New York Post*. Torrey was one of the founders of the New York-New Jersey Trail Conference in 1920. The Schaefers' idea, nurtured by Torrey, gained momentum, and in the 1930s construction of the trail in the area of the Palisades was begun. With the death of Torrey in 1938, the initial burst of energy faded, and it was not until the 1960s that Robert Jessen and Michael Warren took up the challenge and began laying out the Long Path that currently exists.

The Long Path System comprises about 300 miles of trail, making it longer than Vermont's Long Trail—and more mileage is under way. While the business of building trails has not changed appreciably since the Long Path's beginnings, contemporary legal hurdles make bridging streams and moving boulders seem like child's play. Nonetheless, many dedicated members of the hiking community are willing to work at not only protecting what is already there, but also proposing improvements and additions. Thus, the Long Path represents a living trail system, one whose size and shape are ever changing, one that responds to environmental challenges and takes advantage of emerging opportunities. Since the fifth edition of the *New York Walk Book* was published, more than 100 miles of new trail have been added to the Long Path, and countless relocations have improved the hiking experience in established areas.

While problem areas remain along the way—mostly on private lands, but even parklands are not immune from trouble—the trail affords a rich variety of hiking experiences: partial day hikes to isolated spots, full day hikes across ridges and mountaintops, and backpacking adventures in wilderness areas. Thus, the Long Path is emblematic of all that the Trail Conference stands for—the building, maintaining, and preserving of hiking trails in New Jersey and New York—and provides access to the pleasures and rewards of hiking to an enormous and diverse population in the metropolitan area and beyond.

The *Guide to the Long Path* covers the Long Path from the George Washington Bridge to Thacher State Park outside of Albany. The trail is blazed in a shade of turquoise called parakeet aqua. However, the trail overlays other trails in many places, especially the Catskills. In these areas it is usually only marked with a plastic Long Path marker at the trailheads. A sample of hikes is given below. See the guidebook for other sections and more details.

New Jersey State Line to Schunemunk Mountain

The Long Path wends its way along the Palisades and though Bear Mountain-Harriman State Parks before heading west to cross Schunemunk Mountain 64 miles from the state line. Bear Mountain-Harriman State Parks contain 20 miles of the Long Path. It intersects, and sometimes coincides with, many trails within the park, making good loop hikes. William Myles's *Harriman Trails* should be used for more detailed information. One crossing is with the Appalachian Trail, 4.8 miles north of Seven Lakes Drive. Taking the Appalachian Trail 52 miles south to High Point State Park in New Jersey leads to the beginning of the Shawangunk Ridge Trail, an alternate route to the Long Path in Minnewaska State Park.

High Tor to Little Tor   *Length: 2.5 miles Blaze: turquoise*
The trail leaves from South Mountain Road (County 90) off of US 9W south of Haverstraw and climbs steeply up to High Tor in 1.1 miles. High Tor has 360-degree views, with the peaks of Harriman Park to the north readily visible. Continue on to Little Tor 2.5 miles from the start. From Little Tor, there is a view of Garnerville, West Haverstraw, and clay banks once used in brick making—a most profitable local industry of the 1800s. The advent of quick-drying cement, the Panic of 1893, which caused many facilities to close, and a disastrous mud slide in the early 1900s sealed the demise of the industry.

Long Mountain   *Length: 0.6 mile Blaze: turquoise*
Starting at the parking lot on US 6 (the Long Mountain Parkway), the LP crosses the Popolopen Gorge Trail (red dot on white) and climbs to the Torrey Memorial at the top of Long Mountain. Raymond Torrey was one of the greatest advocates of hiking known to this area. The 360-degree views from the summit are best to the east and south. Return by retracing the approach route or by continuing on the LP down a series of switchbacks until reaching a woods road in Deep Hollow (0.4 mile), turning left (south), and following the unmarked woods

road back to the southbound LP.

Schunemunk Mountain   *Length: 6.9 miles Blaze: turquoise*
The LP leaves NY 32 at the railroad trestle about 1.6 miles north of the Highland Mills bus station. Parking is available at the west side of NY 32 about 0.1
mile south of the trestle. The route follows the trestle to the top and heads
north along the railroad tracks about 0.4 mile. It turns left through a gravel pit
and turns right crossing a small stream as it enters the woods. The trail climbs
steadily for over half a mile, then turns up a rocky defile to Little Knob. It ascends
a wooded incline, a talus slope, and edge of a cliff bordered with twisted pitch
pines to reach High Knob at 1.4 miles with views to the east, north, and south.

From High Knob, the LP descends north along the top edge of the high,
pine-bordered cliff above an impressive ravine. At the saddle of this ravine, the
trail climbs steeply to the top of another rock wall. High Knob and its cliffs are
visible from here. The trail then goes northwest, ascending gradually in 0.5
mile to a view to the north. It then descends slightly and crosses the headwaters
of Dark Hollow Brook. From here it climbs steadily northwest, where, at 2.6
miles, it joins the Jessup Trail (yellow) with views east and west.

The LP continues northwest down a gentle slope, enters the woods, and
descends a series of ledges overlooking Barton Swamp and the western ridge;
the last ledge is steep. The trail plunges down a talus slope into Barton Swamp,
crosses a brook, jogs left onto a woods road and then to the right. The trail
then gently ascends the ridge only to descend into a saddle, passing the southern end of the Barton Swamp Trail (red on white) at 4.1 miles.

Continuing on the western ridge, the LP darts back and forth across the
exposed conglomerate, passes over some deep crevasses, and ducks behind scrag-
gly growths, into forested areas and across treeless surfaces. At 5.1 miles, it
intersects the Sweet Clover Trail (white). At the end of the western ridge, the LP
enters land belonging to The Nature Conservancy, set aside to protect rare
species of moths and timber rattlers. At 5.6 miles, the LP meets the 100-yard
spur of the Barton Swamp Trail (red on white) which connects to the main
portion of the Barton Swamp Trail.

Turning left, the LP begins its descent. Within minutes the geology and
ecology change. No longer is the ground covered with the pinkish-white conglomerate. The stunted and gnarled vegetation of the windswept ridgetop gives
way to a forest of taller trees. After some switchbacks, at times utilizing woods

roads, the trail ends at Hil-Mar, a summer retreat, where parking is available.

Schunemunk Mountain to the Shawangunks

In 1995, this section of the Long Path replaced the former route through Orange County. It still has some road-walks and crosses some private lands which may cause further changes to the route. A complete description is in the *Guide to the Long Path,* but seek current information from the New York-New Jersey Trail Conference before attempting this section.

The Shawangunks to the Catskills

The Long Path wiggles its way through the "Gunks," providing hikers with panoramic vistas. Since it crosses other trails in Minnewaska State Park Preserve, there are ample opportunities for loop hikes. With the Open Space Institute's purchase of the lease on the Ellenville watershed lands, a portion of the Long Path, which had been closed, will be reopened. For current information on this segment south and west of Vankeeder Kill Falls, contact the New York-New Jersey Trail Conference.

Jenny Lane to Mud Pond   *Length: 9.3 miles Blaze: turquoise*
Jenny Lane is an obscure dirt road 1.2 miles west of the Minnewaska State Park entrance on US 44-NY 55. An unpaved parking area is reached by turning right on Jenny Lane and then right again. The LP turns west just before the parking area and crosses US 44-NY 55. Entering the woods again, it soon crosses the Sanders Kill, which may be flooded or completely dry depending on the season.

The trail ascends gradually, shaded for the most part by rather stunted hardwoods whose roots encounter only a thin layer of soil, with solid rock ledges just beneath. In June the seemingly limitless clusters of mountain laurel provide a spectacular display. On hot days, this shady route should be the preferred approach to Lake Awosting. Several bare ledges provide views to the south of Litchfield Ledge, the Huntington Ravine, the Peters Kill, and the Lower Awosting Carriageway.

At 2.6 miles, the trail comes to a power line, makes a jog to the right, and reenters the woods. At 3.3 miles from Jenny Lane, the trail turns onto the Lower Awosting Carriageway, crossing an earthen causeway over Fly Brook. A side trip to Lake Awosting is possible by continuing for half a mile on Lower Awosting Carriageway.

After entering the woods to the left, the LP ascends ledges and crosses the

The Long Path just below Castle Point

outlet of Lake Awosting, before arriving at a view of the Peters Kill. A little farther to the north there is a view to the east of Litchfield Ledge and Huntington Ravine. Descending through hemlock and mountain laurel, at 0.6 mile from the earthen causeway, it reaches Rainbow Falls, with its cool mist. Ascending to a carriageway, the trail turns right, going approximately 0.4 mile before re-entering the woods on the left. A steep climb over rocks to the top of Litchfield Ledge at 5.3 miles reveals views to the west and north of the Catskill Mountains and later of Lake Awosting to the south.

The trail bears left on a carriageway to begin a gradual ascent to Castle Point at 5.8 miles, the high point on the trail at 2,200 feet, and views of the Hudson Valley. Descending steeply to a carriageway, the trail bears right on the roadway for about 200 yards before re-entering the woods on the left. On the descent, the trail passes a small cave and tunnel through the rocks. After crossing a brook and a woods road, the trail ascends steeply to Margaret Cliff at 7.2 miles. Descending gradually over ledges with views to the south, the trail makes a sharp left turn from the ledges and reaches an old carriageway, which it follows for a short distance before turning off to the left. The trail then ascends to the summit of Murray Hill with a 360-degree view. After traveling briefly on Lake Shore Drive, the LP turns left into the brush and continues southwest.

The trail enters a region of mostly open ledges, stunted pine trees, and frequent clumps of blueberry bushes mixed with laurel. The ledges are not continuous—in places breaking up into jumbled rocks, or splitting to form deep crevices. The ledges terminate on the south as vertical cliffs.

Three-quarters of a mile from Lake Awosting, the LP reaches Mud Pond. The property owners have specifically asked that hikers *not* follow the old trail around the south side of the lake. The LP then passes through an area of blueberry bushes and reaches a series of open, flat ledges that come down to the water's edge, affording a view. Bearing left through hemlock trees, the trail crosses the outlet of Mud Pond, where an old beaver dam may be observed on the left.

The Catskills

As the Long Path winds its way 94 miles through the Catskill Park, it goes over many mountains. It follows many existing trails and endless combinations of circular hikes are possible. See chapter 12, "The Catskills," *Hiking the Catskills*, or the *Guide to the Long Path* for more details.

North of the Catskills

The Long Path continues north of Catskill Park from East Windham to John Boyd Thacher State Park for 84.8 miles, temporarily stopping within 15 miles of Albany. This portion of the Long Path features parklands with views of the Schoharie Valley and reforestation areas. See the *Guide to the Long Path* for a complete description of the 84.8 miles.

Vroman's Nose   *Length: 2.0 miles Blazes: various*

As evidenced by the initials in the rocks, people have been coming to the top of Vroman's Nose for over a hundred years. Once on top, hikers will see why—a sweeping view across the Schoharie Valley and Vroomansland to the Catskills. The Vroman's Nose Preservation Corp. owns the mountain and preserves it, forever wild.

From a parking area on West Middleburgh Road, a green-blazed trail ascends 600 feet to meet a red-blazed trail and the Long Path (turquoise), which comes in from the right. The red trail ends and hikers use the Long Path and the green trail. The view to the right on the way to the summit is across the Schoharie Valley towards the Catskills. The joint trails reach the summit at 1.0 mile and then follow the escarpment with views along the edge. The trails reach an overhanging promontory with views up and down the valley. The green-blazed trail ends, the Long Path joins a blue-blazed trail to descend, sometimes

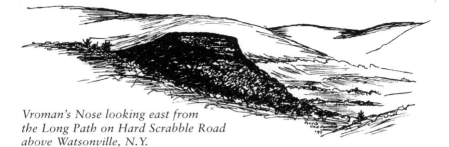

Vroman's Nose looking east from the Long Path on Hard Scrabble Road above Watsonville, N.Y.

steeply, through the woods. The return to the parking area on West Middleburgh Road is via the yellow-blazed trail on the left at 1.7 miles.

NY 443 to Thacher State Park *Length: 7.4 miles Blazes: turquoise*
This section of the Long Path affords the hiker an opportunity to view working farms and travel along hedgerows; it ends with spectacular views and dramatic cliffs. To reach this section of the Long Path, take the NY State Thruway to Exit 22 (Selkirk). Turn right on NY 144 and continue south to NY 396. Turn right on NY 396 for 6 miles to South Bethlehem, where NY 396 ends and becomes Albany County 301. Stay on County 301 for another 6 miles to its end at NY 443 in Clarksville. Turn left to follow NY 443 west for about 5.6 miles to its second intersection with Stage Road, where there is parking. This intersection is 1.7 miles after where NY 443 and NY 85 split.

From the intersection of Stage Road and NY 443, the Long Path heads uphill along Stage Road, passing several local farms, one of which has an expansive view across the field to the west. At 0.6 mile, the trail turns left by a beaver pond and crosses the edge of a field before climbing a small steep ridge. At the top of the hill, the trail makes a sharp left to go through a hemlock forest and then begins its descent at 1.6 miles. The Long Path crosses Elm Drive at 1.9 miles, where there is limited parking, and then follows a hedgerow. After crossing a pipeline, the trail reenters the woods and descends to a stream. At 2.3 miles, the trail reaches a larger stream and then turns left to follow the stream through the woods. After reaching a small spruce plantation, it emerges into a larger spruce plantation and leaves the stream at 2.7 miles. The trail begins to ascend Roemer's High Point at 3.0 miles with its 270-degree views of the Catskills to the south and the Adirondacks to the north. It follows the ridge, descends first gradually, ascends a small hill (3.5 miles), and finally descends steeply.

Entering Thacher State Park, the Long Path descends along a series of switchbacks into a ravine. Here the Long Path marking changes from the turquoise paint blazes to blue round plastic LP tags. At 4.2 miles, the trail emerges on a ski slope and heads downhill.

After crossing Beaver Dam Road at 4.7 miles, the Long Path turns left on a trail that parallels the road and then turns right to follow a gravel park road. At 5.3 miles, the trail joins a nature trail which comes in from the right and continues its gradual descent into the ravine. After turning right and crossing the ravine, the Long Path turns left and, at 5.7 miles, leaves the nature trail. At the request of park officials, all blazing ends at NY 157. At 6.0 miles, the trail follows a woods road along the edge of a picnic area. It descends right along a gravel path to reach a paved access road which it follows to NY 157. After crossing NY 157, the Long Path reaches the overlook parking area, turns left and follows the escarpment. It reaches the viewpoint over Mine Lot Falls at 6.8 miles. The trail follows the unblazed Indian Ladder Trail (when it is open) to the bottom of the falls where Long Path continues along the Indian Ladder Trail to its terminus. Other times, the Long Path continues along the escarpment. In 1997, the northern terminus of the Long Path is at the northern end of the Indian Ladder Trail.

THE SHAWANGUNK RIDGE TRAIL

The Shawangunk Ridge Trail (SRT), part of the Long Path system, begins at the junction of the Appalachian and Monument trails in High Point State Park. When the northbound Appalachian Trail turns east, the SRT continues 28 miles northeast to join the Long Path.

When the Long Path was relocated in Orange County, it utilized part of the SRT as it heads northward. Thus a portion of the SRT is formally described as the Long Path and the rest retains its singular identity and is part of the Long Path system. The two trails meet on the ridge one mile north of Old NY 17. Southwest of this point is the SRT; to the north and southeast is the Long Path.

Hikers are rewarded with a rich variety of geological formations and diversity of the ecosystems along the route. In a twenty mile section, dramatically exposed ridgetop rises 900 feet above an expansive thriving 17,500-acre wetland. The following segment is representative of the trail, but see the *Guide to the Long Path* for a complete description.

Otisville Road to Old NY 17 (County 171)   *Length: 10.0 miles Blaze: turquoise*
This section of the Shawangunk Ridge Trail is appealing for hikers who are rail buffs or birders. The trail follows a converted railbed along the Basha Kill, a lake or wetlands depending on the season. To reach the trailhead, take NY 17 to Exit 114 (NY 211) west through Middletown and Otisville. Parking is available where the trail crosses in a pull-out 0.3 mile from the corner of NY 211 and Otisville Road, 11 miles from Otisville. To reach the six parking areas within the Bashakill Wildlife Management Area, take NY 17 to US 209. Go south on US 209, turning left onto Haven Road, to reach South Road. The parking areas are north and south along South Road. To reach parking at the north end of this section, take NY 17 to Exit 114 (Highview). Turn left on Old NY 17, and proceed downhill 1.0 mile. When the road makes a hairpin turn to the left, take a right turn onto a gravel road to the VFW post.

Following Otisville Road north for 0.3 mile, the Shawangunk Ridge Trail passes steep cliffs, turns up to the right, and ascends to the top of the ridge, where there is a view west. It continues up and down through these woods with signs of logging evident for 2 miles and the final descent brings the trail to the south end of the Basha Kill.

Over the next 5.5 miles, the trail follows an abandoned railbed that, when last active as a railroad, was part of the New York, Ontario & Western (O & W) Railroad system, but originally was allied with the competition, the Erie Railroad. Because the O&W initially refused to blast its way through to Monticello, the town financed another line to connect with the Erie at Port Jervis. This line was eventually expanded to include a branch to Ellenville and then all the way to Kingston. It dealt a severe blow to the Delaware & Hudson Canal, which could not compete with the greater flexibility and all-weather capabilities of the railroads.

The trail hugs the shore of the Basha Kill—a 6-mile-long shallow lake in the springtime and a thriving wetland in the summer and fall. The Basha Kill is home to a wide range of birds including many migratory species. There are numerous bird-feeding stations along the way. The parking areas along this route make it readily accessible to the public. Hunters in their season and birders also make use of the area. Nonetheless, it offers an unusual perspective, since hiking trails most often are located on the highest lands.

After passing through the main parking area for the New York State Department of Environmental Conservation's Bashakill Wildlife Management Area, a short nature trail leads to an elevated platform that allows a view of several bird-feeding stations. Along the way, signs identify species of trees. The railbed is regained north for another 1.5 miles until it reaches a paved road on the outskirts of Wurtsboro. The trail goes to the left and continues on town streets, turning right onto Old Route 17. A railroad station on the right has been converted into a private residence which houses O&W railroad memorabilia, including a caboose. Continuing, the road begins to climb to yet another section of the abandoned O&W railroad. The bridge abutments where the tracks would have crossed the road are still visible. This portion was known as the High Line because of the tunnel that was blasted halfway up the Shawangunk Mountains. This railroad line ran from Weehawken, New Jersey, through the West Shore railroad junction in Cornwall to the western Catskills. This section of the trail ends at the old train station that has been converted to a VFW post. For a side trip, hikers can follow the railbed eastward, which leads to the Highview Tunnel. Though the tunnel is impassable, the brickwork of the tunnel portal is still in evidence.

Old NY 17 (County 171) to NY 52   *Length: 9.6 miles Blazes: various*

As one of the more dramatic stretches along the Shawangunk Ridge, this section has frequent views in all directions, and is dotted with pitch pine, scrub oak, and blueberry bushes. Outcroppings and boulders of the white conglomerate that is characteristic of the northern Shawangunks add bright color and open vistas to the hiking experience.

To reach this section, take NY 17 to Exit 114 (Highview). Turn left onto Old NY 17, and proceed downhill 1.0 mile. When the road makes a hairpin turn to the left, make a right turn onto a gravel road to the VFW post, where parking is available. The parking is at the north end of the this section at the overlook where NY 52 crosses the Shawangunk Ridge, near Cragsmoor.

After leaving the O&W rail bed by the VFW post, the trail ascends through the forest. At 1.0 mile, the Shawangunk Ridge Trail reaches the top of the ridge where the Long Path comes in from the right and continues north along the ridge. The forest thins out, and different vegetation begins to predominate. The gnarled, dwarfed scrub oak and the windswept pitch pine are a testament to the harsh conditions on this exposed ridgetop. Views from here include the Catskills and the northern reaches of the Shawangunks. The Neversink Valley provides a contrast to the rolling hills, and the Basha Kill spreads out to the south.

The Long Path crosses seasonally spreading streams and woods roads, some of which lead to abandoned mines. After crossing Summitville-Roosa

Gap Road at 4.1 miles, the trail regains the ridgetop, passing more scrub oak and reaching additional viewpoints. From here the monument at High Point State Park can be seen. The trail continues north along the ridgetop, and more blueberry and mountain laurel can be seen among the brush. A knoll just off the trail at 6.4 miles offers a 360-degree view. To the north are the white rock outcroppings of Gertrudes Nose and Sams Point. In the more distant north are the jagged profiles of the Catskill Mountains. To the east, the gap of the Hudson River formed by Breakneck Ridge and Storm King Mountain can be seen.

Continuing north, the trail makes a general descent and heads into the deeper woods below the ridgetop. The distinctive scrub oak and pitch pine cover are left behind for the next half mile. When the trail enters DEC property at 6.7 miles, the blazes change to blue discs. After crossing a dirt road that leads to Cox Road, and passing through an area crisscrossed with stone walls, the LP begins a gentle ascent. It leaves the DEC property and climbs to the open ridgetop, weaving in and out of the dense growth for well over a mile.

At first, the trail skirts the eastern cliffs, running parallel to some deep crevices. There are seasonal views to the east before the trail crosses to the western slopes of the ridge. The large open slabs of the distinctive white rock of the Shawangunks allow prolonged glimpses of the grandeur to the north and west, including the rounded peaks in the Catskills and the stark cliffs of Bear Hill Preserve. At 8.3 miles, the Long Path begins a long descent with a brief view before it drops steeply into the woods. After crossing a woods road and a significant stream, it begins to climb steadily, and reaches, at 9.4 miles, a view of the Rondout Valley below and the Delaware & Hudson Canal and the Ontario & Western Railroad to the west. The trail descends to reach NY 52 at 9.6 miles, where parking is available at a pullout 0.1 mile from the trailhead.

HIGHLANDS TRAIL

The Highlands Trail highlights the natural beauty of the New York and the New Jersey Highlands region, and draws the public's attention to this endangered resource. It is a cooperative effort of the New York-New Jersey Trail Conference, conservation organizations, state and local governments, and local businesses. When completed, it will extend over 150 miles from Storm King Mountain on the Hudson River in New York south to Phillipsburg, New Jersey, on the Delaware River. The route will connect major scenic attractions in both states. Ultimately, a network of trails including alternate routes and shared-use paths is envisioned.

The Highlands Trail is a combination of co-alignment on established trails, new trails, and road walking. The co-aligned route bears both blazes, except for the Appalachian, Sterling Ridge, and Allis trails, which have plastic Highlands Trail logos at critical points. Hikers must pay attention at intersections and turns, as the Highlands Trail often leaves one trail to join another. See individual trail descriptions for more details of the co-aligned trails.

Black Rock Forest requires all organized groups (hiking, birding, and so forth) to register prior to visiting by calling (914) 534-4517.

During deer rifle season, there is no entry to either Black Rock Forest or Black Rock Fish and Game Lands.

Permits are required to hike in the Pequannock Watershed. Contact the Watershed at (973) 697-2850. The Watershed also has restrictions on hiking during hunting season.

Camping will not be permitted along the Highlands Trail. Thru-hiking opportunities will depend on the establishment of bed-and-breakfast facilities along the route that will be willing to cater to hikers. A guide to the Highlands Trail will be available at a future date.

Storm King to Bellvale Mountain   *Length: 29.2 miles Blaze: teal diamond*
From Mountain Road in Cornwall, the Highlands Trail heads along the Stillman Trail (yellow) over the top of Storm King Mountain. It continues to US 9W, where there is parking, crosses US 9W, and enters Black Rock Forest. At 7.6 miles, the Highlands Trail goes straight on the Compartment Trail (blue) while the Stillman Trail turns right on the Compartment Trail in the opposite direction. Over the next 0.7 mile, hikers need to watch for blazes indicating turns as the Highlands Trail leaves and joins three trails. The Highlands Trail follows the Compartment Trail for 0.6 mile until the latter ends at the junction with the Arthur Trail (yellow) on Jim's Pond Road. The Arthur and Highland trails are joint on the woods road for the next 0.1 mile with the Highlands Trail staying on the road when the yellow blazes leave to left. The Highlands Trail follows Jim's Pond Road for another 0.1 mile until it reaches the Scenic Trail (white) at 8.1 miles. Turning right off the road on to the westbound Scenic Trail, the Highlands Trail goes mostly downhill, crossing Black Rock Fish and Game lands to reach NY 32 at 11.6 miles.

The teal blazes follow NY 32 for 1.0 mile and then make a left onto Taylor Road. After crossing the New York State Thruway, the trail reaches the parking area for the Schunemunk trails at 12.9 miles from the start. From the parking area, the trail joins the Sweet Clover Trail (white) up to the Jessup Trail (yellow) which the Highlands Trail now follows to the left, running south for 5.8 miles to Seven Springs Road (21.5 miles), where it turns right.

For the next 7.7 miles, until it reaches the Appalachian Trail (white), the teal diamonds are the only blazes. After following Seven Springs Road for 0.5 miles, the Highlands Trail turns off the road, through the woods and up and over a ridge to cross NY 208 at 22.5 miles. After following the shore of Orange-Rockland Lake, it reaches Museum Village Road, which it follows, crosses NY 17, and reaches a commuter parking lot at 23.1 miles. The Highlands Trail utilizes an abandoned railbed for a mile as it heads west, crossing back over NY 17. Just before a bridge, the Highlands Trail turns right and heads down an embankment. Making a left under the bridge onto Oxford Road (County 51), the Highlands Trail follows the road and reaches NY 17M at 24.8 miles. After a quick jog across NY 17M, the trail turns right on to Lazy Hill Road. The trail follows an abandoned paved road through undeveloped Goose Pond Mountain State Park. At 26.4 miles, it goes left at Laroe Road (County 45), where there is parking.

The Highlands Trail follows Laroe Road for 0.5 mile until it turns right on Sugarloaf Mountain Road. The trail turns left after 0.2 mile, and follows the power line for 1.1 miles. The Highlands Trail turns right off the power line and goes 1.0 mile up Bellvale Mountain, where it joins the Appalachian Trail (white).

NY-NJ Line, Nonhunting season   *Length: 16.8 miles Blaze: teal diamond*
In this section, the Highlands Trail has either plastic logos or teal diamonds at turns or intersections. The Highlands Trails turns left to follow the northbound Appalachian Trail (white) 0.4 mile to Lakes Road, where parking is available. The co-aligned trails continue to Fitzgerald Falls at 0.7 mile and then separate at 1.9 miles at the northern terminus of the Allis Trail (blue), which the Highlands Trail then follows, reaching NY 17A at 4.4 miles. The teal diamonds indicate a right turn and follow the road to the north end of the Sterling Ridge Trail (blue on white) at 5.9 miles.

As this book was going to press in Spring 1998, it is not known what the use restrictions will be on the former Sterling Forest Corporation lands in New York. For more information, contact the Palisades Interstate Park, Administration Building, Bear Mountain, NY 10911; (914) 786-2701.

Parking is available on NY 17A at both trailheads. The Highlands Trail turns left and travels 10.9 miles on the Sterling Ridge Trail, ending at 16.8

miles at the junction of East Shore Road and County 511, where there is parking.

NY-NJ Line, Hunting season   *Length: 16.0 miles Blaze: teal diamond*
In this section, the Highlands Trail has either plastic logos or teal diamonds at
turns or intersections. The trail goes straight on the southbound Appalachian
Trail (white), for 3.2 miles to NY 17A, where parking is available. After cross-
ing the road, the co-aligned trails pass the terminus of the State Line Trail
(blue) at 9.1 miles and reach the Ernest Walter Trail (yellow) 0.2 mile later. The
Appalachian Trail makes a sharp right while the Highlands Trail continues
straight ahead, now aligned with the Ernest Walter Trail. At 10.3 miles, the
Highlands Trail makes a sharp right turn onto the Bearfort Ridge Trail (white).
The trails go 2.5 miles to the terminus of the Bearfort Ridge Trail on Warwick
Turnpike, where parking is available.

Turning left, the Highlands Trail follows Warwick Turnpike, which be-
comes Greenwood Lake Turnpike (County 511) as it approaches Greenwood
Lake. The trail continues 3.2 miles along the road south and east, reaching
East Shore Road at 16.0 miles, with parking available.

For the continuation of the Highlands Trail though the rest of New Jersey,
see "Long Distance Trails," in the *New Jersey Walk Book*, a companion to this
book.

HUDSON RIVER GREENWAY TRAIL

The Hudson River Greenway Trail is a trail system envisioned for both sides of
the river from the mouth of the Mohawk River to the New Jersey border on the
west side and from the Troy Dam to the New York City line on the east side. It
will cross both urban and rural areas to connect the valley's historic, cultural,
and recreational resources. Industries, public works, railroad tracks, and private homes at the river's edge prevent the trail from following the shoreline for
its entire length. The exact location of the trail will depend on the voluntary
participation of public and private landowners.

As of 1996, just over 100 miles of trail have been designated. These designated sections are almost entirely on public lands and utilize existing trails,
some of which are described in this book, or are along village or city streets.
For more information, contact the Greenway Conservancy for the Hudson River
Valley, Capitol Building Room 254, Albany, NY 12224; (518) 473-3835.

FURTHER READING

This list of books is meant to be a starting point for those people wishing more information. Many of these books, particularly the trail guides, have frequent revisions, so be sure you use the latest versions. For historical information, consult a local history room in a public library, a local museum, or an historical society.

Backcountry Ethics

Hampton, Bruce and David Cole. *Soft Paths: How to Enjoy the Wilderness Without Harming It.* Harrisburg, PA: Stackpole Books, 1988.

Hodgson, Michael. *The Basic Essentials of Minimizing Impact on the Wilderness.* Merrillville, IN: ICS Books, 1991.

Waterman, Laura and Guy Waterman. *Backwoods Ethics: Environmental Issues for Hikers and Campers.* Woodstock, VT: The Countryman Press, Inc., 1993. 2nd rev.

———. *Wilderness Ethics: Preserving the Spirit of Wilderness.* Woodstock, VT: The Countryman Press, Inc., 1993.

Flora and Fauna

Barbour, Spider and Anita Barbour. *Wild Flora of the Northeast.* Woodstock, NY: Overlook Press, 1995.

Boyle, Robert H. *The Hudson River: A Natural and Unnatural History.* New York: W. W. Norton and Company, 1979.

Cobb, Boughton. *A Field Guide to Ferns and Their Related Families: Northeastern and Central North America.* Boston, MA: Houghton Mifflin Company, 1975.

Conant, Roger. *A Field Guide to Reptiles and Amphibians of Eastern and Central North America.* Boston, MA: Houghton Mifflin Company, 1991. 3rd ed.

Fadala, Sam. *Basic Projects in Wildlife Watching: Learn More about Wild Birds and Animals through Your Own First-hand Experience.* Harrisburg, PA: Stackpole Books, 1989.

Forrest, Louise R. *Field Guide to Tracking Animals in Snow.* Harrisburg, PA: Stackpole Books, 1988.

Kieran, John. *A Natural History of New York City.* Bronx, NY: Fordham, 1982. 2nd ed.

Kiviat, Erik. *The Northern Shawangunk Mountains: An Ecological Survey.* New Paltz, NY: Mohonk Preserve, 1988.

Krieger, Louis C. *The Mushroom Handbook.* Mineola, NY: Dover Publications, 1967.

Miller, Dorcas S. *Berry Finder: A Guide to Native Plants with Fleshy Fruits.* Berkeley, CA: Nature Study Guild, 1986.

Murie, Olaus J. *Field Guide to Animal Tracks.* Boston, MA: Houghton Mifflin Company, 1975.

Niering, William A. *Wetlands.* Audubon Society Nature Guides. New York: Alfred A. Knopf, 1985.

Peterson, Roger Tory. *A Completely New Guide to all the Birds of Eastern and Central North America.* Boston, MA: Houghton Mifflin Company, 1980. 4th rev/en ed.

Petrides, George A. *A Field Guide to Eastern Trees.* Boston, MA: Houghton Mifflin Company, 1988.

Robbins, Chandler S., Bertel Brunn, and Herbert S. Zim. *Birds of North America.* New York: Golden Press, 1983.

Stalter, R. *Barrier Island Botany for the United States.* Dubuque, IA: William C. Brown, 1993.

Stanne, Stephen P., Roger G. Panetta and Brian E. Forist. *The Hudson: An Illustrated Guide to the Living River.* New Brunswick, New Jersey: Rutgers University Press, 1996.

Stokes, Donald W. and Lillian Q. Stokes. *A Guide to Animal Tracking and Behavior.* Boston, MA: Little, Brown and Company, 1987.

Sutton, Ann and Myron Sutton. *Eastern Forests.* Audubon Society Nature Guides. New York: Alfred A. Knopf, 1985.

Food

Angier, Bradford. *Field Guide to Edible Wild Plants.* Magnolia, MA: Peter Smith, 1992.

Jacobson, Cliff. *Cooking in the Outdoors: The Basic Essentials.* Merrillville,

IN: ICS Books, 1989.

Prater, Yvonne and Ruth Dyar Mendenhall. *Gorp, Glop and Glue Stew: Favorite Foods from 165 Outdoor Experts*. Seattle, WA: The Mountaineers, 1981.

Richard, Sukey, Donna Orr, and Claudia Lindholm (ed.). *NOLS Cookery*. Harrisburg, PA.: Stackpole Books, 1991. 3rd ed.

Viehman, John (ed.). *Trailside's Trail Food*. Emmaus, PA: Rodale Press, 1993.

Weiss, John. *The Outdoor Chef's Bible*. New York: Doubleday, 1995.

Geology

The American Geological Institute Staff. *Dictionary of Geological Terms*. New York: Anchor Press/Doubleday, 1984. 3rd rev. ed.

Chew, V. Collins. *Underfoot: A Geologic Guide to the Appalachian Trail*. Harpers Ferry, WV: Appalachian Trail Conference, 1988.

Geological Highway Map of Northeastern Region (Map No. 10, United States Geological Highway Map Series, National Bicentennial Edition). The American Association of Petroleum Geologists, P.O. Box 979, Tulsa, OK 74101. 1976.

Isachsen, Yngvar W. et al. *Geology of New York: A Simplified Account*. New York State Museum Education Leaflet Series No. 28. New York State Museum Science Center, Cultural Education Center, Albany, NY 12230. 1991.

Wyckoff, Jerome. *Rock Scenery of the Hudson Highlands and Palisades*. Lake George, NY: Adirondack Mountain Club, 1971.

Health

Auerbach, M.D., Paul S. *Medicine For The Outdoors: A Guide to Emergency Medical Procedures and First Aid for Wilderness Travelers*. Boston, MA: Little, Brown and Company, 1986.

Forgey, William W. *First-Aid for the Outdoors: The Basic Essentials*. Merrillville, IN: ICS Books, 1988.

———. *Wilderness Medicine*. Merrillville, IN: ICS Books, 1987. 3rd ed.

Rosen, Albert P. *Health Hints for Hikers*. New York: New York-New Jersey Trail Conference, 1994.

Wilkerson, James (ed.) *Medicine for Mountaineering and Other Wilderness Activities*. Seattle, WA: The Mountaineers, 1992. 4th ed.

355

Hiking and Camping

Angier, Bradford. *How To Stay Alive in the Woods*. Magnolia, MA: Peter Smith, 1983.

Churchill, James E. *The Basic Essentials of Survival*. Merrillville, IN: ICS Books, 1989.

Evans, Jeremy. *Camping and Survival*. New York: Crestwood/MacMillan, 1992.

Fletcher, Colin. *The Complete Walker III*. New York: Alfred A. Knopf, Inc., 1984. Rev/en 3rd. ed.

Frazine, Richard. *The Barefoot Hiker*. Berkeley, CA: Ten Speed Press, 1993.

Getchell, Annie. *The Essential Outdoor Gear Manual*. New York: McGraw-Hill, 1995.

Goll, John. *The Camper's Pocket Handbook. A Backcountry Traveler's Companion*. Merrillville, IN: ICS Books, 1992.

Jacobson, Cliff. *The Basic Essentials of Camping*. Merrillville, IN: ICS Books, 1988.

———. *The Basic Essentials of Trailside Shelters and Emergency Shelters*. Merrillville, IN: ICS Books, 1992.

Kuntzleman, Charles T. *Complete Book of Walking*. New York: Pocket Books, 1992.

Logue, Victoria. *Backpacking in the Nineties. Tips, Techniques and Secrets*. Birmingham, AL: Menasha Ridge Press, 1993.

Meyer, Kathleen. *How to Shit in the Woods*. Berkeley, CA: Ten Speed Press, 1989.

Roberts, Harry. *Backpacking: The Basic Essentials*. Merrillville, IN: ICS Books, 1989.

Ross, Cindy and Todd Gladfelter. *A Hiker's Companion: Twelve Thousand Miles of Trail-tested Wisdom*. Seattle, WA: The Mountaineers, 1993.

Seaborg, Eric and Ellen Dudley. *Hiking and Backpacking*. Champaign, IL: Human Kinetics, 1994.

Sierra Club, San Diego Chapter Staff. *Wilderness Basics: The Complete Handbook for Hikers and Backpackers*. Seattle, WA: The Mountaineers, 1992.

Sumner, Louise Lindgren. *Sew and Repair Your Outdoor Gear*. Seattle, WA: The Mountaineers, 1988.

The Ten Essentials for Travel in the Outdoors. Seattle, WA: The Mountaineers, 1993.

Townsend, Chris. *The Backpacker's Handbook*. New York: McGraw-Hill, Inc., 1992.

Viehman, John (ed.) *Trailside's Hints and Tips for Outdoor Adventure*. Emmaus, PA: Rodale Press, 1993.

Hiking and Camping - Children

Euser, Barbara J. *Take 'em Along: Sharing the Wilderness with Your Children*. Boulder, CO: Cordillera Press. Inc., 1987.

Foster, Lynne. *Take a Hike! The Sierra Club Kid's Guide to Hiking and Backpacking*. Boston, MA: Little, Brown and Company, 1991.

Lewis, Cynthia C. and Thomas J. Lewis. *Best Hikes with Children in the Catskills and Hudson River Valley*. Seattle, WA: The Mountaineers, 1992.

Michaels, Joanne and Mary Barile. *Let's Take the Kids! Great Places to Go with Children in New York's Hudson Valley*. New York: St. Martin's Press 1990.

Silverman, Goldie. *Backpacking with Babies and Small Children*. Berkeley, CA: Wilderness Press, 1986.

Sisson, Edith A. *Nature with Children of all Ages: Adventures for Exploring, Learning and Enjoying the World around Us*. New York: Prentice Hall Press, 1982.

Hiking and Camping - Map and Compass

Baynes, John. *How Maps are Made*. New York: Facts on File, Inc., 1987.

Fleming, June. *Staying Found: The Complete Map and Compass Handbook*. Seattle, WA: The Mountaineers, 1994. 2nd ed.

Jacobson, Cliff. *Map and Compass: The Basic Essentials*. Merrillville, IN: ICS Books, 1988.

Kjellstrom, Bjorn. *Be Expert with Map and Compass*. Greenwich, CT: Macmillan, Inc., 1976, new rev. ed.

Randall, Glenn. *The Outward Bound Map and Compass Book*. New York: Lyons and Burford Publishers, 1989.

Hiking and Camping - Winter

Conover, Garrett and Alexandra Conover. *Snow Walker's Companion: Winter Trail Skills from the Far North*. Camden, ME: Ragged Mountain Press/ International Marine Publishing Company, 1994.

Dunn, John M. *Winterwise: A Backpacker's Guide.* Lake George, NY: Adirondack Mountain Club, 1989.

Gorman, Stephen. *Winter Camping.* Boston, MA: Appalachian Mountain Club Books, 1991.

Prater, Gene. *Snow-shoeing.* Seattle, WA: The Mountaineers, 1988.

Randall, Glenn. *Cold Comfort: Keeping Warm in the Outdoors.* New York: Lyons and Burford, 1987.

Weiss, Hal. *Secrets of Warmth.* Seattle, WA: Cloudcap, 1992. 2nd ed.

History

Adams, Arthur G. *The Catskills: An Illustrated Historical Guide with Gazetteer.* Bronx, NY: Fordham, 1994. 2nd rev.

Bedell, Cornelia F. (comp.) *Now and Then and Long Ago in Rockland County.* The Historical Society of Rockland County, 20 Zukor Road, New City, NY. 1992. 3rd ed.

Burgess, Larry E. *Mohonk: Its People and Spirit.* New Paltz, NY: Mohonk Mountain House, 1993.

Carmer, Carl. *The Hudson.* Bronx, NY: Fordham, 1989.

Clyne, Patricia Edwards. *Hudson Valley Tales and Trails.* Woodstock, NY: The Overlook Press, 1990.

Cohen, David S. *The Ramapo Mountain People.* New Brunswick, NJ: Rutgers University Press, 1986.

De Lisser, Richard Lionel. *Picturesque Catskills. Greene County.* Saugerties, NY: Hope Farm Press, 1988.

Diamant, Lincoln. *Chaining the Hudson.* New York: Citadel Press, 1994.

Dunwell, Frances F. *The Hudson River Highlands.* New York: Columbia University Press, 1991.

Evers, Alf. *The Catskills: From Wilderness to Woodstock.* Woodstock, NY: Overlook Press, 1984.

Flexner, James. *Hudson River and the Highlands: Photographs by Robert Glenn Ketchum.* New York: Aperture, 1985.

Fried, Marc B. *Tales from the Shawangunk Mountains.* Lake George, NY: Adirondack Mountain Club, 1981.

Garvey, Edward B. *Appalachian Hiker.* Oakton, VA: Appalachian Books, 1978.

Haagensen, Alice M. *Palisades and Snedens Landing from the Beginning of History to the Turn of the Twentieth Century.* Irvington, NY: Pilgrimage Publishing, 1986.

Haring, Harry A. *Our Catskill Mountains*. Reprint Services Corporation, P.O. Box 890820, Temecula, CA 92589-0820. 1993.

Howat, John K. *The Hudson River and Its Painters*. Avenel, NJ: Random House Value Publishing, 1991.

Howell, William. *The Hudson Highlands*, New York: Walking News, Inc., 1982.

Mack, Arthur C. *The Palisades of the Hudson*. New York: Walking News, Inc., 1982.

Murphy, Robert Cushman. *Fish-Shape Paumanok—Nature and Man on Long Island*. Great Falls, VA: Waterline Books, 1991.

O'Brien, Raymond J. *American Sublime: Landscape and Scenery of the Lower Hudson Valley*. New York: Columbia University Press, 1981.

Ransom, James M. *Vanishing Ironworks of the Ramapos*. New Brunswick, NJ: Rutgers University Press, 1966.

Schaefer, Vincent. *Vroman's Nose. Sky Island of the Schoharie Valley*. Fleischmanns, NY: Purple Mountain Press, Ltd., 1992.

Serraro, John. *The Wild Palisades of the Hudson*. Upper Saddle River, NJ: Lind Publications, 1986.

Smeltzer-Stevenot, Marjorie. *Footprints in the Ramapos: Life in the Mountains before the State Parks*. Sloatsburg, NY: M. R. Smeltzer, 1993.

Smiley, Ruth H. *The Land of the Sky Lakes: A Photographic Essay by Ruth H. Smiley*. New Paltz, NY: The Mohonk Mountain House, 1994.

Smith, Philip H. *Legends of the Shawangunk and its Environs*. Syracuse, NY: Syracuse University Press, 1965.

Snyder, Bradley and Karl Beard. *The Shawangunk Mountains: A History of Nature and Man*. Mohonk Lake, New Paltz, NY: Mohonk Preserve, Inc., 1981.

Waterman, Laura and Guy Waterman. *Forest and Crag: A History of Hiking, Trail Blazing and Adventure in the Northeast Mountains*. Boston, MA: Appalachian Mountain Club Books, 1989.

Trail Guides

Albright, Rodney and Priscilla. *Short Nature Walks on Long Island*. Old Saybrook, CT: Globe Pequot Press, 1993. 4th ed.

Anderson, Katherine S., revised and expanded by Peggy Turco, *Walks and Rambles in Westchester and Fairfield Counties*, Woodstock, VT: Backcountry Publications, 1993, 2nd ed.

Brown, Michael P. *New Jersey Parks, Forests and Natural Areas. A Guide*.

New Brunswick, NJ: Rutgers University Press, 1992.

Chazin, Daniel D. (ed.) *Appalachian Trail Data Book*. Harpers Ferry, WV: Appalachian Trail Conference, Issued annually.

Connecticut Walk Book. Connecticut Forest and Park Association, 16 Meridan Road, Rockfall, CT 06481. 1993. 17th ed.

Dann, Kevin and Gordon Miller. *Thirty Walks in New Jersey*. New Brunswick, NJ: Rutgers University Press, 1992.

Drotar, David Lee. *Hiking the U.S.A.: A Sourcebook for Maps, Guidebooks, Inspiration*. Washington, DC: Stone Wall Press, 1991.

Gourse, Leslie. *The Best Guided Walking Tours of New York City for Residents and Tourists*. Old Saybrook, CT: Globe Pequot Press, 1989.

Guide to the Long Path. New York: New York-New Jersey Trail Conference, 1996. 4th ed.

Hardy, David, Sue Hardy and Gerry Hardy. *Fifty Hikes in Connecticut*. Woodstock, VT: Backcountry Publications, 1996. 4th ed.

Harrison, Marina and Lucy D. Rosenfeld. *A Walker's Guidebook: Serendipitous Outings near New York City including a Section for Birders*. New York: Kesend Publishing, 1988.

Lenik, Edward. *Iron Mine Trails*. New York: New York-New Jersey Trail Conference, 1996.

Mack, Arthur C. *Enjoying the Catskills*. Ithaca, NY: Outdoor Publications, 1972.

McAllister, Lee and Myron Steven Ochman. *Hiking the Catskills: A Guide for Exploring the Natural Beauty of America's Romantic and Magical Mountains on the Trail and "Off the Beaten Path"*. New York: New York-New Jersey Trail Conference, 1989.

McMartin, Barbara and Peter Kick. *Fifty Hikes in the Hudson Valley from the Catskills to the Taconics and from the Ramapos to the Helderbergs*. Woodstock, VT: Backcountry Publications, 1994. 2nd ed.

Miskowski, Nick. *Hiking Guide to Delaware Water Gap National Recreation Area*. New York: New York-New Jersey Trail Conference, 1994. 2nd ed.

Myles, William J. *Harriman Trails. A Guide and History*. New York: New York-New Jersey Trail Conference, 1992.

New York-New Jersey Trail Conference. *Appalachian Trail Guide to New York-New Jersey*. Harpers Ferry, WV: The Appalachian Trail Conference, 1994. 13th ed.

————. *Day Walker*. New York: New York, NY: New York-New Jersey Trail

Conference 2nd ed forth-coming.

———. *New Jersey Walk Book*. New York: York: New York-New Jersey Trail Conference, 1998.

Ryan, Christopher J. *Guide to the Taconic Trail System in Berkshire County*. Amherst, MA: New England Cartographics, 1989.

Scheller, William G. *Country Walks Near New York*. Boston, MA: Appalachain Mountain Club Books, 1986. 2nd ed.

Scofield, Bruce. *Circuit Hikes in Northern New Jersey*. New York: New York-New Jersey Trail Conference, 1995. 4th ed.

Scofield, Bruce, Stella J. Green, and H. Neil Zimmerman. *Fifty Hikes in New Jersey: Walks, Hikes and Backpacking Trips from Kittatinnies to Cape May*. Woodstock, VT: Backcountry Publications, 2nd ed. forthcoming.

Turco, Peggy. *Walks and Rambles in Dutchess and Putnam Counties*. Woodstock, VT: Backcountry Publications, 1990.

———. *Walks and Rambles in Orange and Ulster Counties*. Woodstock, VT: Backcountry Publications, 1996.

Wadsworth, Bruce. *Guide to Catskill Trails*. Lake George, NY: Adirondack Mountain Club, 1994. 2nd ed.

Weinman, Steve. *A Rock with a View: Trails of the Shawangunk Mountains*. Rosendale, NY: Canal Press, 1995.

Wood, Robert S. *Dayhiker*. Berkeley, CA: Ten Speed Press, 1991.

Zatz, Arline. *New Jersey's Special Places: Scenic, Historic and Cultural Treasures in the Garden State*. Woodstock, VT: The Countryman Press, 1994. 2nd rev. ed.

INDEX

Page numbers in **bold** refer to trail descriptions.
Page numbers in *italics* refer to illustrations.

Abram S. Hewitt State Forest, 323-25
Acra Point, 213, 214-15
Adirondacks, lumbering, 199
Agony Grind, 332
Alander Brook Trail, **182-83**, 184-85
Alander Loop Trail, **183**, 185-86, 189
Alander Mountain, 182-83, 185-86, 189
Alander Mountain Trail, **188-89**
Albert K. Smiley Memorial Tower, 239
Aleck Meadow Reservoir, 274
Allen, John, homestead of, 129
Alley Pond Park, 55-57
Allis, J. Ashton, 4, 326
Allison, W. O., 308
Allis Trail, **326**
Almost Perpendicular, 286
American Museum of Natural History, 152
American Revolution. *See* Revolutionary War
Anderson, Maxwell, *High Tor*, 318
André, John, 138-39, 155
Anthony's Nose, 137-38, *138-39*, 139, 140, 153, 157, *278-79*, 334
geology of, 37
Anthony Wayne Trail, **282**, 293, 302
Anti-rent wars, 215
Appalachian Mountain Club, 181, 336
Appalachian Mountains, 222
Appalachian Plateau, 35, 41-42, 193
Appalachian Trail (AT), 10, 329-31, **332-38**
Bear Mountain-Harriman State Parks, 282, 289, 295-96, 301-2, **332-33**
Dutchess County, 164, 169-70, **335-36**
Fahnestock State Park, 121, 122, 126, 129-30, **335**
first section, 4, 331
Greenwood Lake area, 8-9, 324-26, 332
and Highlands Trail, 351-52
Hudson Highlands, 141, 152-54, *154*, 156-57, 159, **334**
and Long Path, 340, 346

Southern Taconics, 185, 190-91, **336-38**
Appalachian Trail Conference, 330-31
Arching Rocks Path, 238
Arden Mountain, 332
Arden-Surebridge Trail, **282-83**, 287, 295, 297, 304
Arkville, N.Y., 197
Arnold, Benedict, 138-39, 155
Arthur Kunz County Park, 73
Arthurs Pond, 275
Arthur Trail, **269**, 270, 272, 350
Arthur W. Butler Memorial Sanctuary, 100-1
Artist Rock, 213
Ashley Hill Brook, 189
Ashley Hill Trail, 183-5, 188, **189-90**
Ashokan High Point, 207
Ashokan Reservoir, 203, 207
Atlantic Barrier Beaches, 85-89, *86*
Atlantic Coastal Plain, 43-44
Audubon Society, 6
Reese Nature Sanctuary, 171-72
Awosting Falls Carriageway, 229
Awosting Lake, 222
Awosting Reserve, 226

Baby Brook, 253, 255, 258
Babylon, Long Island, 87
Backpacking, 26-27
Baird, James, 164
Bald Hill, 146
Bald Mountain, 286, 296
Bald Peak Trail, **190**, 337
Bald Rocks Shelter, 294
Ball Brook, 337
Balsam Cap Mountain, 194, 202, 207
Balsam Lake Mountain Trail, 216
Balsam Mountain, 204, 205
Bannerman's Castle, 151
Bard Rock, 167
Barrel hoop industry, 196, 224
Barrier beaches, 67
Barrier islands, 85-89

Mianus River Gorge, 103-4
Middle Mountain Trail, **218**
Mill Brook lean-to, 216
Millbrook Mountain, 227, 229, 233, 236, 241, 243, **244**, 244-45
Millbrook Mountain Carriageway, 231-32, 233, 236
Millbrook Mountain Path, 233
Millbrook Mountain Trail, 233, **235-36**
Millbrook Ridge Trail, 233, 236, **243-45**
Miller Pond, 71
Mill Neck, wildlife sanctuary, 90
Mills-Norrie State Park, 166-67
Millstones, transport of, 234
Millwood railroad station, 104
Milton Harbor, 113
Mine Hill Trail, **270**, 271
Mine Hollow Trail, 205
Mine Lot Falls, 346
Mineral Spring Falls, 272
Mining, 32
   of clay, 65
   Fahnestock State Park, 118-19, 126
   Hudson Highlands, 281
   Manitou Copper Mine, 139
   Ninham Mountain, 135
   Sterling Forest, 325
   See also Quarrying
Mink Hollow, 210
Minnewaska, 227
Minnewaska Lake, 6-8, 222, 223, 227-36, 245, 342
   Castle Point Carriageway, 230-31
Mishow (conference rock), 47
Mohawk River, 352
Mohonk escarpments, 221
Mohonk Lake, 221, 224
Mohonk Mountain House, 223, 236-38, 241
   trails, 238-40
Mohonk Preserve, 222-23, 235, 241
   trails, 242-46
Mombaccus Mountain, 208
Mombasha High Point, 326, 332
Monarch butterflies, 64
Mongaup-Hardenburgh Trail, 216, **217**
Mongaup Mountain, 217
Mongaup Pond, 217
Mongaup-Willowemoc Trail, 217

Monksville Reservoir, 321
Monroe, Will, 4
Montauk Point, 43, 84-85, **85**
   Ronkonkoma Moraine, 68
Montaukett Indians, 83
Montgomery, John, 168
Monument Brook, 183
Monument Trail, 346
Moravian Cemetery, 60, 62
Morgan, J. Pierpont, 308
Morgan Stewart Shelter, 335
Moriches Inlet, 86, 88-89
Morse, Samuel F. B., 168
Moses, Robert, 52
Motorized vehicles, 11-12, 25, 147
Mountain biking, 75
   Black Rock Forest, 267
   Blue Mountain Reservation, 96
   Dutchess County, 176
   Fahnestock State Park, 121
   Minnewaska State Park Preserve, 229, 231
   Ninham Mountain Multiple Use Area, 133
   Wallkill Valley Rail Trail, 247
   See also Bicycle paths
Mountain ecology, 29-34
Mountain Lakes, camping area, 114
Mountain Laurel, *134*, 225
Mountainville, N.Y., 268
Mount Beacon, 164
Mount Bushnell, 338
Mount Everett, 180, 182, 186, 336, 338
Mount Fray, 187
Mount Frissell, 180, 184
Mount Frissell Trail, **183-84**, 185, 190
Mount Ivy, 307, 289
Mount Misery, 271, 272, 275
Mount Peter, 332
Mount Race, 338
Mount Rascal, 272
Mount Riga State Park, 181
Mount Spitzenberg, 97
Mount Taurus. *See* Bull Hill
Mount Washington, 181-82, 186, 188
Mount Washington State Forest 181-82, 188-90
Mud Pond, 219, 222, 344
Mud Pond Trail, 219

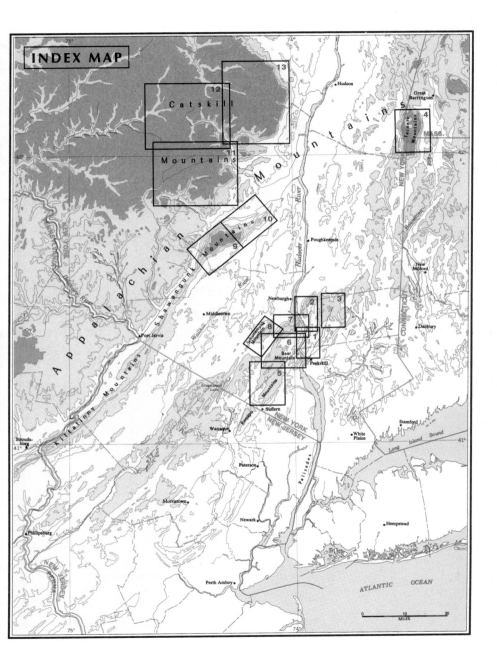

LEGEND

——————— Marked Trail

    (B) Blue   (BL) Black   (BR) Brown   (G) Green

    (W) White   (Y) Yellow   (R) Red   (O) Orange

– – – – – – – Unmarked Trail or Woods Road

    —— – – —— State Boundary

    —— – – —— County Boundary

    ========= Highway

    ——————— Main Road

    ——————— Secondary Road

    P   Parking

    KO   Keep Out

    ★   Viewpoint

    S   Shelter

    ◉   Tower

    ⚒   Mine

    ✕   Quarry or Pit

    •   Spring or Well

    ⚊⚊   Marsh

    •*1423*   Spot Height in Feet
                 (contours every 100 feet, except in the Catskills)

    + + + + + Railroad

    + + + + + Abandoned Railroad

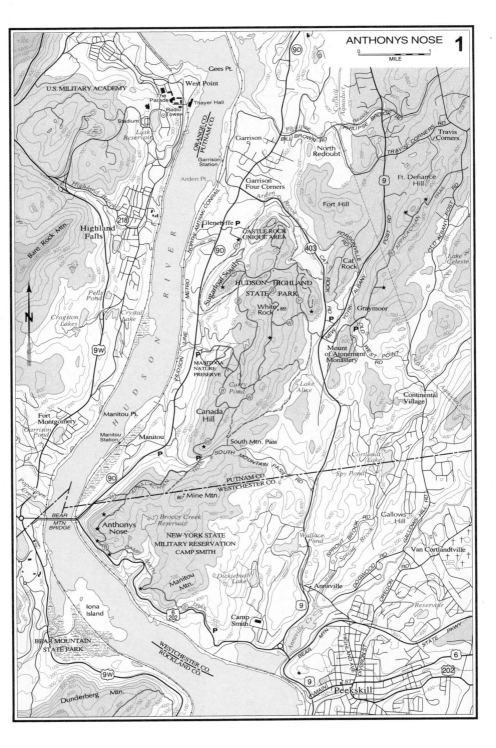

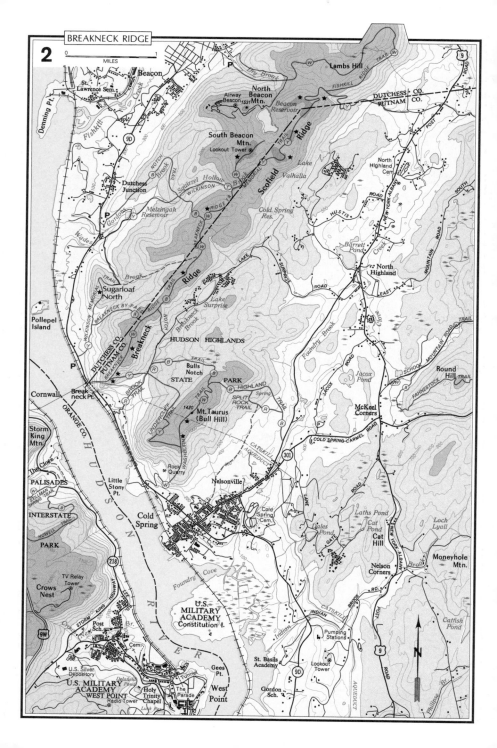

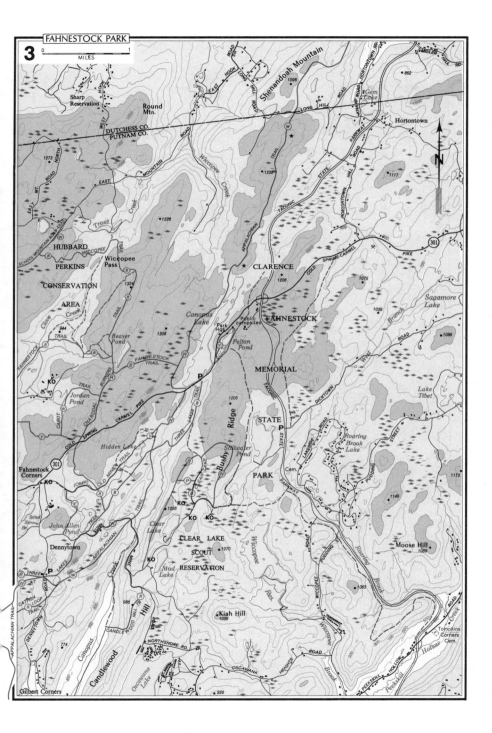

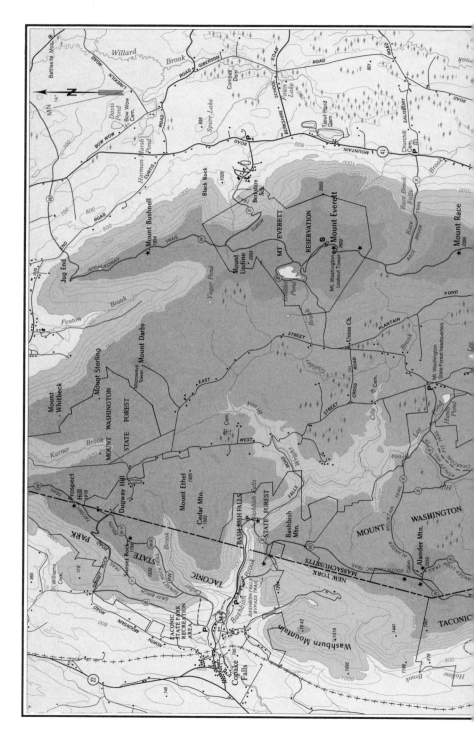

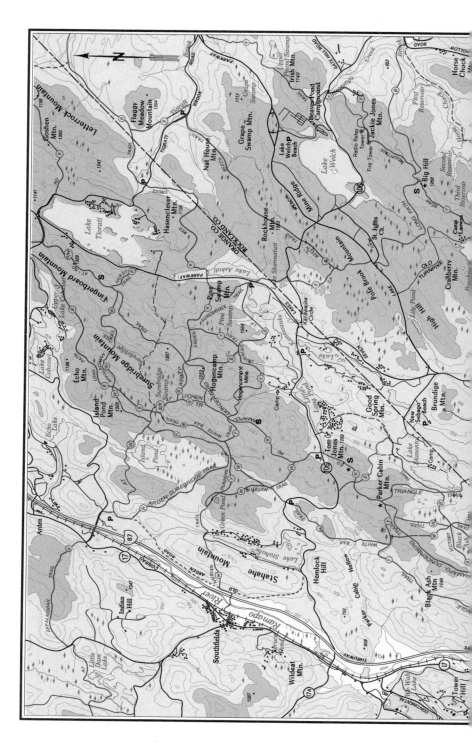

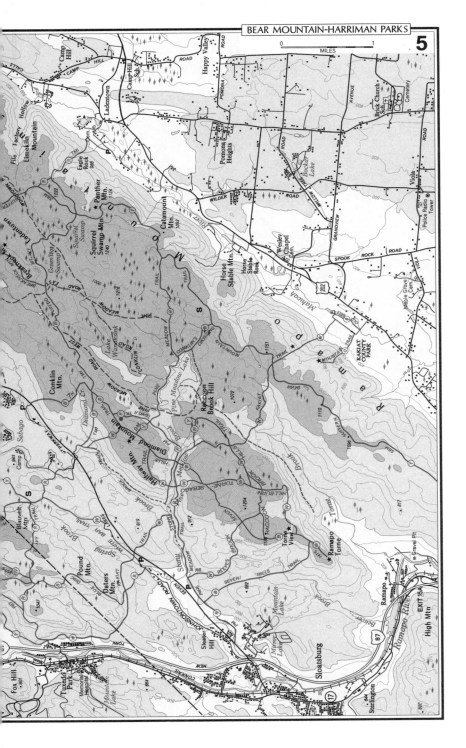

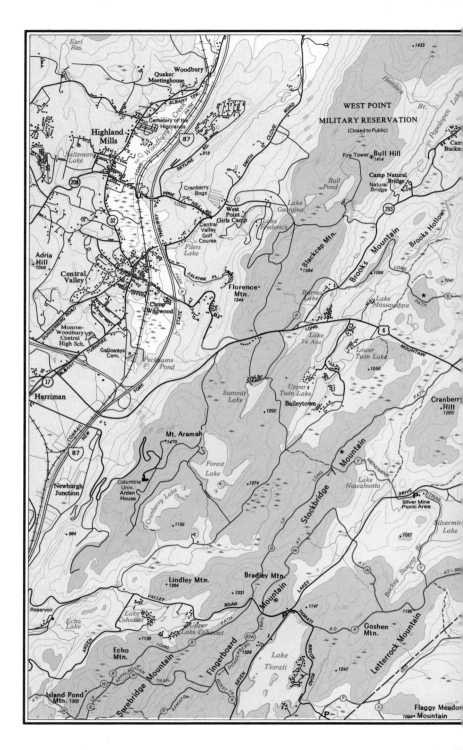

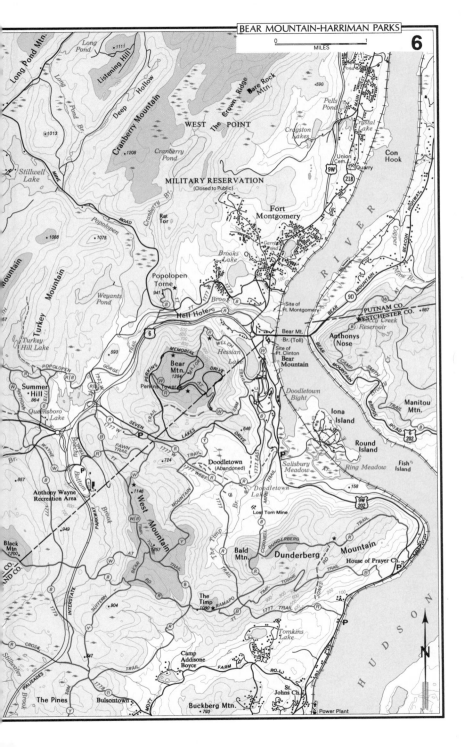

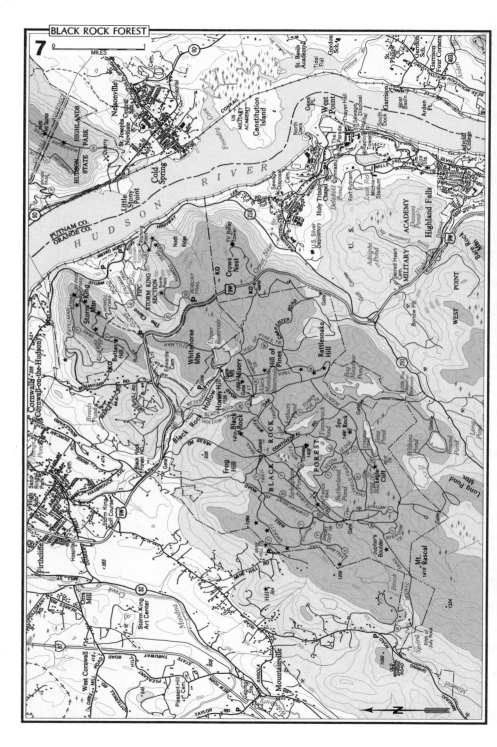

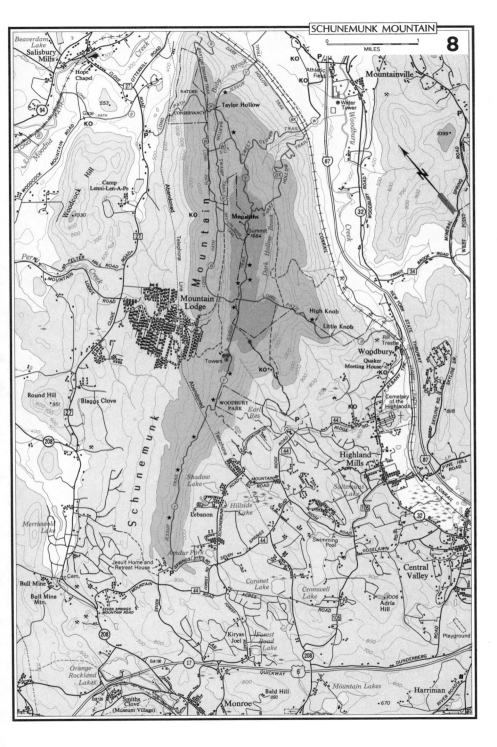

0   1
MILES

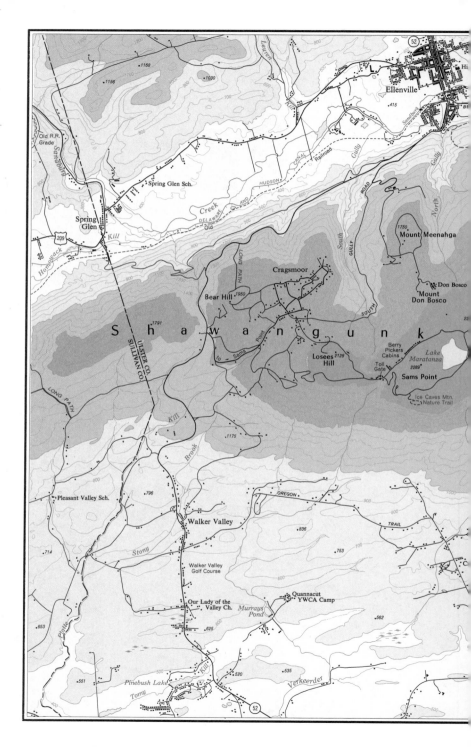

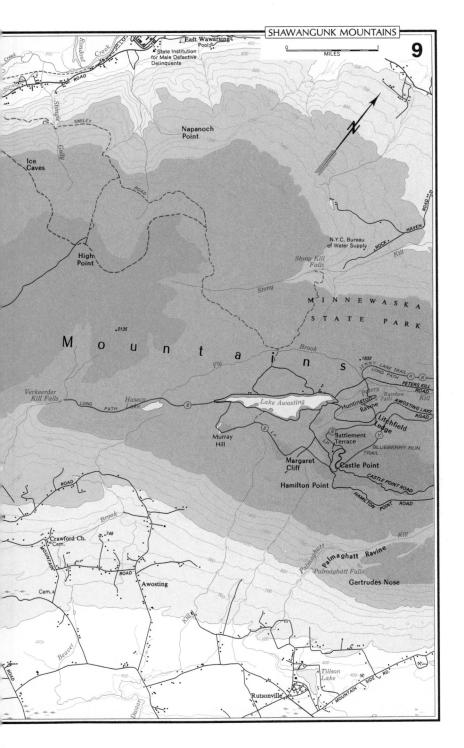

MILES

Rondout Creek

East Wawarsing
Pool

State Institution
for Male Defective
Delinquents

Shingle Gully

SMILEY

Napanoch
Point

Ice
Caves

ROAD

High
Point

N.Y.C. Bureau
of Water Supply

ROCK

HAVEN

ROAD

Kill

Stony Kill
Falls

Stony

M I N N E W A S K A

S T A T E   P A R K

.2135

Brook

M o u n t a i n s

Fly

.1832

JENNY LANE TRAIL

LONG PATH

PETERS KILL
ROAD

Verkeerder
Kill Falls

LONG   PATH

Haseco
Lake

Lake Awosting

Peters

Rainbow
Falls

AWOSTING LAKE

Kill

ROAD

Huntington
Ravine

Litchfield
Ledge

Murray
Hill

L.P.

Battlement
Terrace

BLUEBERRY RUN

TRAIL

Margaret
Cliff

Castle Point

CASTLE POINT ROAD

Hamilton Point

HAMILTON   POINT   ROAD

ROAD

Brook

Kill

Crawford Ch.
Cem.

.748

Palmaghatt Ravine

MOUNTAIN

ROAD

Palmaghatt Falls

Awosting

Gertrudes Nose

Cem.

KILL

Beaver

Brook

Tillson
Lake

MOUNTAIN   SIDE   RD.

Rutsonville

Duaut

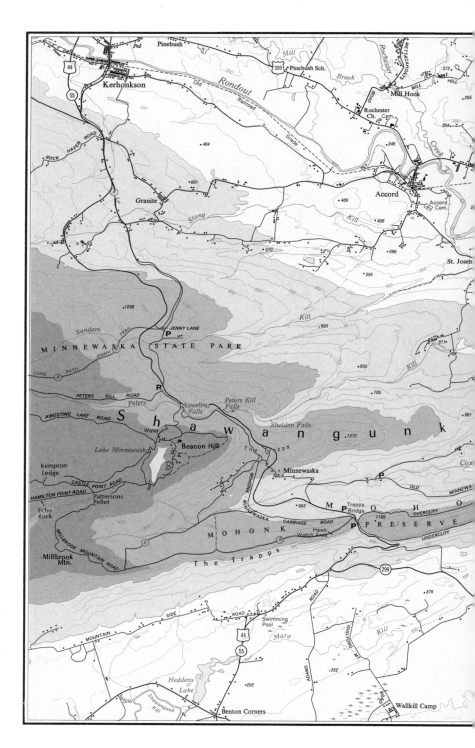

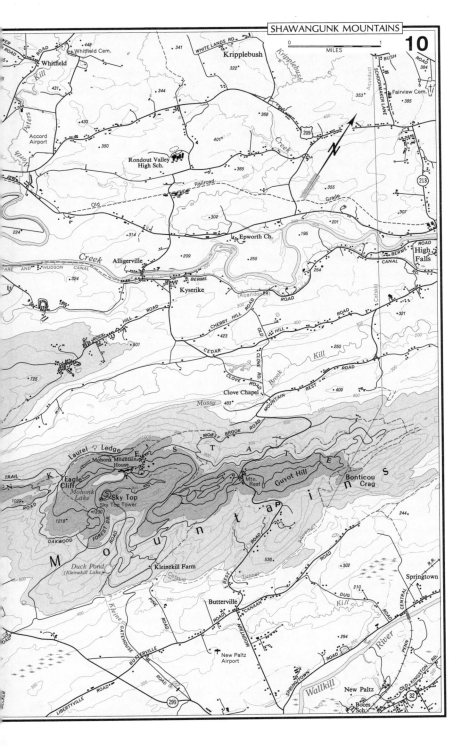

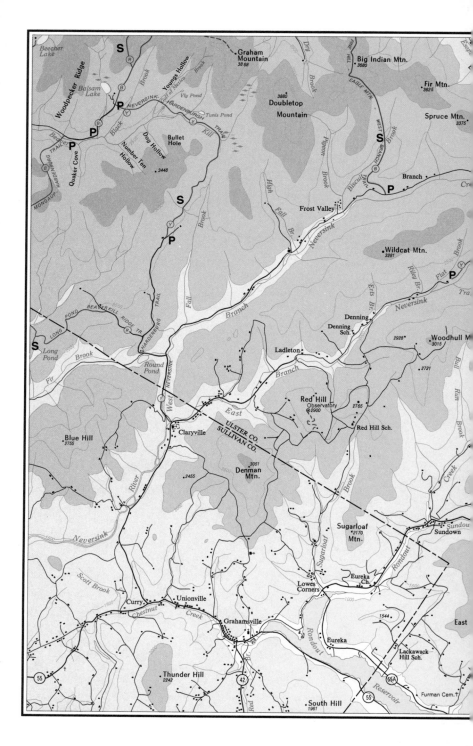

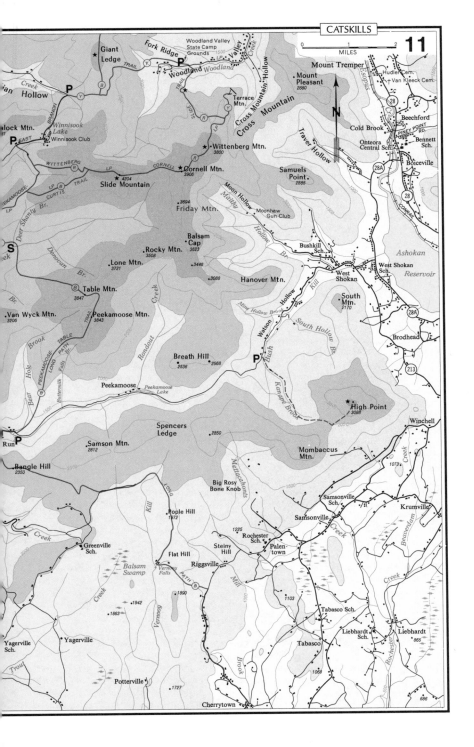

0 1 2
MILES

Giant
Ledge

Fork Ridge

Woodland Valley
State Camp
Grounds

Woodland
Woodland Valley

Cross Mountain Hollow

Cross Mountain

Mount Tremper

Mount
Pleasant
2880

Hudler Cem.
Van Kleeck Cem.

N

Beechford

Cold Brook

PINEY POINT RD.

Bennett
Sch.

Onteora
Central Sch.

Boiceville

Creek
Hollow

P

P

Y

B

TRAIL

SOUTH

Terrace
Mtn.

Winnisook
Lake

Winnisook Club

P EAST

lock Mtn.

WITTENBERG

LP

B

CURTIS

TRAIL

R

Wittenberg Mtn.
3800

Cornell Mtn.
3906

Cornell

Slide Mountain
4204

Samuels
Point
2885

Traver Hollow

28

Beechford

28A

1600

CONRAIL

Ashokan

Reservoir

West Shokan
Sch.

West
Shokan

West Shokan

Friday Mtn.
3694

Moon Hollow

Maltby Hollow

Moonhaw
Gun Club

Bushkill
Sch.

Balsam
Cap
3623

Rocky Mtn.
3508

Lone Mtn.
3721

3446

3088

Hanover Mtn.

South
Mtn.
2170

Watson Hollow

Kill

South Hollow

South Hollow Br.

28A

Brodhead

Table Mtn.
3847

Van Wyck Mtn.
3206

Peekamoose Mtn.
3843

Donovan Br.

Deer Shanty Br.

PEEKAMOOSE

LONG PATH

TABLE

TRAIL

Breath Hill
2536

2568

Rondout Creek

Peekamoose

Peekamoose
Lake

P

Bush

Kanape Brook

Mine Hollow Brook

213

High Point
3098

Winchell

S

PEEKAMOOSE

Bear Hole Brook

Buttermilk Falls Br.

B

Spencers
Ledge

2850

Mombaccus
Mtn.

Creek

1073

Run

P

Samson Mtn.
2612

Bangle Hill
2350

LONG

Kill

Pople Hill
1972

Big Rosy
Bone Knob

Mettacahonts

Samsonville
Sch.

Samsonville

Krumville

Beaverdam Creek

Greenville
Sch.

Balsam
Swamp

Flat Hill

Vernooy
Falls

Riggsville

VERNOOY PATH

B

Steiny
Hill

1225

Rochester
Sch.

Palentown

Creek

Winchell

Creek

1890

1942

1863

Mill Brook

1103

Tabasco Sch.

Liebhardt
Sch.

Liebhardt
865

Yagerville
Sch.

Yagerville

Creek

Trout Creek

Potterville

1727

Cherrytown

1068

Tabasco

Rochester Creek

686

Vernooy Kill

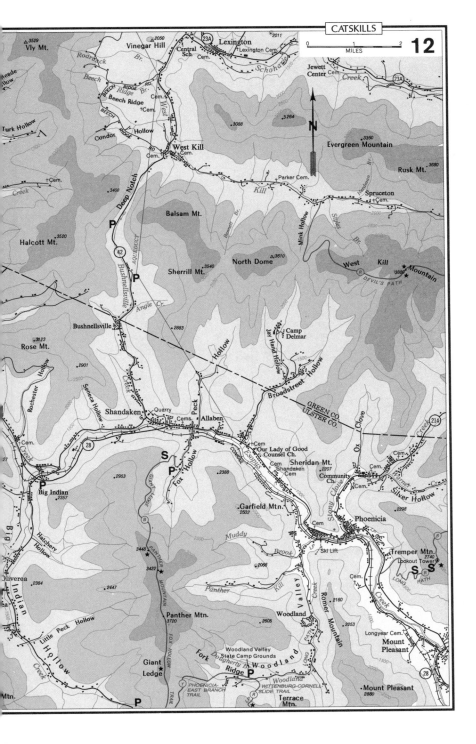

0   1   2
MILES

△3529
Vly Mt.

Roaróxck

△2050
Vinegar Hill

Central
Sch.

23A
Lexington

Lexington Cem.

•2011

Schohole

Jewett
Center

Cem.

Creek

23A

Beech

RIDGE

Beech Ridge

BEECH Ridge
RD.
Br.
Cem.

†Cem.

Turk Hollow

Condor

BEECH

RIDGE

Hollow

WEST

West Kill
Cem.

Cem.

•3088

•3264

Evergreen Mountain

•3350

N

Rusk Mt.
•3680

Creek

†Cem.

•3408

Deep Notch

Parker Cem.

Kill

Spruceton

†Cem.

Bennett Br.

Balsam Mt.

North Dome
△3610

•3540

Mink Hollow

West   Kill   ★Mountain

Stiles Br.

R

DEVIL'S PATH

•3880 ★

Halcott Mt.
•3520

P

42

AQUEDUCT

Bushnellsville

P

Sherrill Mt.
•3540

Angle Cr.

Rose Mt.
•3123

•2901

Bushnellsville

•2883

Peck

Hollow

Jay Hand Hollow

Camp
Delmar

•1500

Broadstreet Hollow

GREEN CO.
ULSTER CO.

Rochester Hollow

Seneca Hollow

Creek

Shandaken

Quarry

Cems.

Allaben

Esopus

Clove

Ox

214

Creek

Cem.

•28

Cem.

Cem.

SP
P

Fox Hollow

GIANT LEDGE

•2953

•2388

Townsend

Our Lady of Good
Counsel Ch.

Cem
Sheridan Mt.
•2207
Shandaken
Cem

Community
Ch.

Cem.

Cem.

Silver Hollow

Warner

Cem.

•2298

Big Indian
•2357

P

Indian

Big

Hatchery
Hollow

•2384

Oliverea

•2447

B

Garfield Mtn.
•2532

3448 ★

PANTHER

Muddy

•1500

Brook

Ski Lift

LF

Panther

•2066

Romer

Phoenicia

Stony Clove

Mountain

•2160

Cem.

Tremper Mtn.
Lookout Tower
•2740

S S ★

LONG

PATH

SS ★

Little Peck Hollow

•2447

MOUNTAIN

Panther Mtn.
•3720

Woodland

•2605

•2253

Longyear Cem.

Mount
Pleasant

Hollow

Creek

Mtn.

Giant
Ledge ★

FOX HOLLOW TRAIL

Fork

Dougherty

Ridge

Woodland

Valley

Woodland Valley
State Camp Grounds

LONG PATH

P

WITTENBURG-CORNELL-
SLIDE TRAIL

•1500

28

P

T

PHOENICIA-
EAST BRANCH
TRAIL

Woodland

★

Terrace
Mtn.

Mount Pleasant
•2880

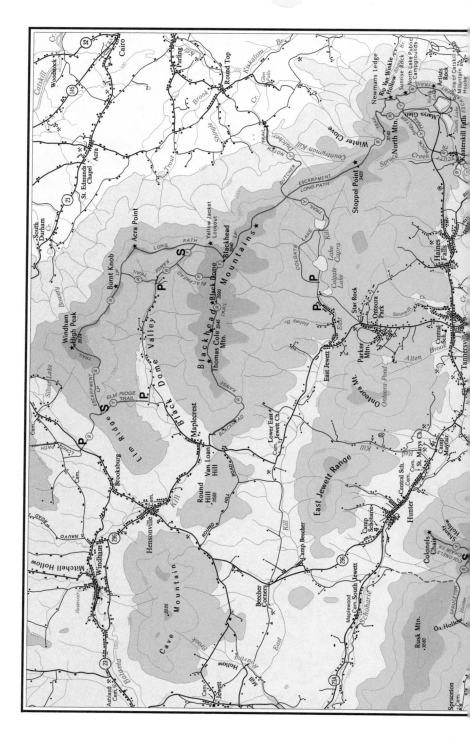

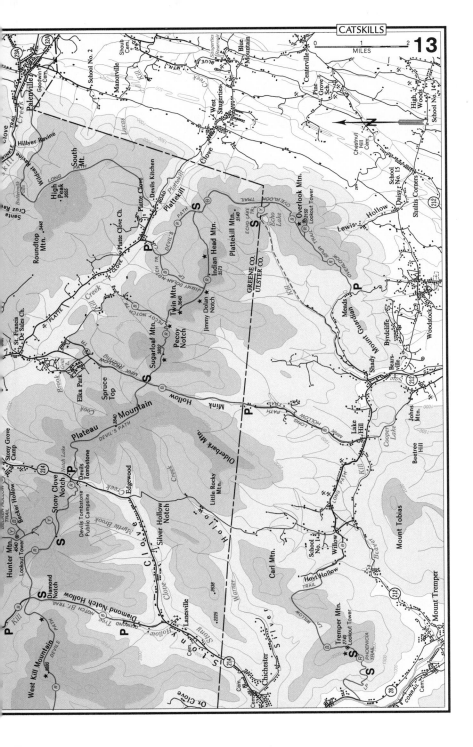

0　　　　1　　　　2
MILES